POLITICS & THE STRUGGLE FOR DEMOCRACY IN GHANA

POLITICS & THE STRUGGLE FOR DEMOCRACY IN GHANA

AN INTRODUCTION TO POLITICAL SCIENCE

DR. JOSEPH K. MANBOAH-ROCKSON

PARTRIDGE

Copyright © 2016 by Dr. Joseph K. Manboah-Rockson.

ISBN: Hardcover   978-1-4828-6322-2
         Softcover   978-1-4828-6323-9
         eBook   978-1-4828-6324-6

All rights reserved. No part of this book may be used or reproduced by any means, graphic, electronic, or mechanical, including photocopying, recording, taping or by any information storage retrieval system without the written permission of the author except in the case of brief quotations embodied in critical articles and reviews.

Because of the dynamic nature of the Internet, any web addresses or links contained in this book may have changed since publication and may no longer be valid. The views expressed in this work are solely those of the author and do not necessarily reflect the views of the publisher, and the publisher hereby disclaims any responsibility for them.

Print information available on the last page.

To order additional copies of this book, contact
Toll Free 0800 990 914 (South Africa)
+44 20 3014 3997 (outside South Africa)
orders.africa@partridgepublishing.com

www.partridgepublishing.com/africa

Contents

Prefaces vii
Chapter Outline xi
Chapter 1   The Ghanaian Heritage 1
Chapter 2   Constitutional Democracy 27
Chapter 3   The Political Process 57
Chapter 4   Political Parties 74
Chapter 5   The Parliament (Legislature) 105
Chapter 6   The Presidency (Executive) 122
Chapter 7   The Courts (Judiciary) 144
Chapter 8   Civil Service System 165
Chapter 9   Interest Groups 186
Chapter 10 Civil Society Organizations (CSOs) 201
Chapter 11 Civil Rights 216
Chapter 12 Civil Liberties 230
Chapter 13 The Media 240
Chapter 14 Local Government 257
Chapter 15 The Politics of National Policy 279
Chapter 16 Making Economic Policies 289
Chapter 17 Making Social Policy 325
Chapter 18 Making Foreign and Defence Policy 345
Chapter 19 Regionalism and Regionalization in Africa 354
Chapter 20 The African Union (AU) 417

Prefaces

Democracy is hard to massage or manage as a model of government; perhaps it is the most complex and difficult of all forms of government. It is filled with tensions and contradictions, and requires that its members labour diligently to make it work. *Democracy* is not designed for efficiency, but for probity and accountability. A democratic government may not be able to act as quickly as a dictatorship, but once committed to a course of action, it can draw upon deep wellsprings of popular support. *Democracy*, even in its American and United Kingdom (Britain) form, is never a finished product, but is always evolving. The outer forms of government in the United States have altered little in two centuries, but once we look past the surface, we discover great changes. No one claims that the American or the British models, as successful as they have been for the United States and Great Britain, are the model that all democracies should follow. Ghana does not have to follow the unitary system of government because it is one, analysts might say, which is riddled with inadequacies of development, which is explained in this book regarding decentralization (district/metropolitan/municipal concept) in this country. Each nation must fashion a government out of its own culture, value system, conscience, and history. In this view, democracy, as inherited from the United Kingdom by Ghana's first president, Dr Kwame Nkrumah, has been diluted over time with that of the American republican system and seems to be posing a problem. This book is a description of this kind of blend and the required institutional framework necessary to foster a multiparty democracy that will stand the test of time and bring unity and understanding amongst Ghanaians.

Meaning of Democracy

The world *democracy* is coined from Greek words: *demos* (people) and *kratos* (rule). It is one of the concepts in political science where there is no agreement on its definition. Democracy is defined by Joseph Schumpeter as a system 'for arriving at political decisions in which individuals acquire the power to decide by means of a competitive struggle for the people's vote' (Diamond, 1999). Dahl defines democracy as a conception of polyarchy, which has two other dimensions: *opposition* (organized contestation through regular, free, and fair elections) and *participation* (the right of virtually all adults to vote and contest for office). The third dimension embedded is that of *civil liberty*. Polyarchy comprises freedom to vote and contest for office and also freedom to speak and publish dissenting views, as well as freedom to form and join organizations and alternative sources of information. Indeed, democracy is regarded as a government system that involves the widest spectrum of participation, either through elections or through the administration of the accepted or adopted policies of a state, known most times as the constitution of that country. Democracy is therefore a government founded on the principle of *rule of law*; a principle that is against arbitrariness, highhandedness and dictatorship and autocracy. Etymologically, democracy means *government by the people* and that is where the problem lies. In the world today, there is hardly any country that can make a public statement that it is not *governing by the will of its people*. But the big question is: what do we mean by 'the will of the people'? People are not a homogeneous category. Logically there has never been a state or city where 'the people' means every individual in the state or city participated in the election of the president of the country or the parliamentarian. Even in the Athenian city where democracy is said to have started, direct democracy did not mean that every person in the city had the right to participate in decision-making, for Athenian democracy excluded slaves, children, women, and resident aliens. Another factor that is said to influence democracy is society; socially, race, religion, ethnicity, and even gender may play a role in determining participation. And economically, the access to resources may influence participation as well; thus, certain groups, on the basis of social or economic factors, may be deprived of participation. Some influence voters by giving them money to vote for them. Others, on the basis of their economic status, may be excluded from participation in the political process of the country, and this is true not just of the case of developing countries but can be seen even in the developed world.

Explaining Democratic Sustenance

Scholars have argued that a country's movement toward *democracy* depends on the existence within society of certain preconditions that may be economic, social, or political in nature. In making these determinations, many scholars have cited economic factors as essential to democratization. The development paradigm proposed by one such scholar was in 1959 and again in 1960, when S. M. Lipset connected democratization with economic growth of a country. This was also followed in 1968 by Daniel Lerner, who also connected democracy with the modernization of a country, in terms of that country's economic growth. The analogy drawn by these scholars confirms the association between stable democracy as an indication of national wealth, communication, industrialization, education, and urbanization. In trying to explain how a country can sustain its democracy, S. M. Lipset explained that democracy strives in a country in which 'the level of a country's economic development independently affects the orientations conducive to democracy of its citizens.' A conclusion drawn from Lipset's analysis is that, for a country to achieve and maintain a successful democracy, its economic progress must be in tune or *at par* with its democratic pursuits so that there are no agitations from citizens pressured by harsh economic conditions for frequent changes. Despite the emphasis on economic development for a country's democratic endurance, significant factors such as political culture (devoid of ethnic violence), legitimacy (free and fair elections), and suitable institutions (legislature, judiciary, and executive) are also important. Democracy is an antithesis of military governance or militarism and associated with accountability and transparency, consensus-building, free and fair elections initiated to determine the winner at acceptable and agreed intervals by the people. Within a democracy, there must be a credible opposition capable of replacing an incumbent government by offering an alternative outline of politics and strategies that is likely to appeal to the electorate.

In conclusion, *democracy* and how to sustain it requires the existence of certain conditions, which may be social, economic, or political in nature. Of these variations, the focus on politics is most important in terms of institutional development as being essential for the sustenance of democracy. In this book the focus is that the development of economic and social conditions in Ghana may have helped in the gradual growth of democracy like most advanced countries, and it is also the growth of democratic ingredients that has contributed to the transformation going on in the country. Most developing countries, including Ghana, are following the path of democracy because they see democracy as being linked to development and a source where values like freedom, liberty, and equality can be realized. But democracy has been adopted in most cases without taking into consideration these contextual differences. Whereas some countries have succeeded where favourable social, economic, and political conditions exist, others are struggling where the same conditions exist. Ghana has all the conditions needed to sustain and perfect its democracy, but since 1992 there have been numerous challenges confronting the country, which indicates an evidence of a struggle for the achievement and the consolidation of democracy. With these experiences, this book is about the politics therein of Ghana, as well as the challenges inherent in every transition since 1992, and the processes required to consolidate democracy.

Chapter Outline

Chapter 1. **The Ghanaian Heritage.** Human beings live in societies and each person has his/her own values, which can conflict with the values of others in the society. Therefore, rules must be established to allow all persons to coexist within the society without conflicts escalating to violence. This is the role of politics—to establish laws, rules, and ways of interacting that benefit the entire society. Who participates in politics, how governments are formed and run, and the unique case of democratic government are reviewed, with a focus on the politics impacting the emerging democratic country of Ghana.

Chapter 2. **Constitutional Democracy.** Ghanaians have long been sceptical of politics and politicians because of the history of government in their country. Several attempts have been made at democracy, but it took a revolution in 1979 to begin the journey to a constitutional democracy where power is shared by three branches, the executive, the legislature, and the judiciary, with a president who is both head of the government and head of state. Ghana's constitution was ratified in 1992, recognizing basic rights of all citizens.

Chapter 3. **The Political Process.** Governments play roles in the day-to-day lives of all citizens; indeed, most societies are run like mini governments. This chapter explores the concept of government and how it differs from social organizations through involuntary membership and comprehensive authority, where government rules apply to every Ghanaian citizen and government has the legitimate right to punish rule breakers. In return, the government assures the nation's survival. The form of government will dictate the level of control exerted upon the citizenry.

Chapter 4. **Political Parties.** Political parties perform key tasks in a democratic society, such as aggregating and articulating needs and problems as identified by members and supporters; socializing and educating voters and citizens in the functioning of the political and electoral system and the generation of general political values; balancing opposing demands and converting them into general policies; activating and mobilizing citizens into participating in political decisions and transforming their opinions into viable policy options; channelling public opinion from citizens to government; and recruiting and training of candidates as well as selecting them for public office. This chapter explores how Ghanaian political parties enable their members' and supporters' demands to be represented in parliament and in government, and compare Ghana's multiparty system to other party systems existing elsewhere on the globe.

Chapter 5. **Parliament (Legislature).** This chapter describes Ghana's parliamentary system, the functions and duties of its Members of Parliament and various committees within the legislature.

Chapter 6. **The President (Executive).** The power of the Executive Branch rests with the president of the Republic of Ghana, who also acts as the head of state and the commander-in-chief of the armed forces. The powers of the position are discussed, as are the many roles carried out by the president.

Chapter 7. **The Courts (Judiciary).** The courts system of Ghana is compared with that of the UK and Australia, which it closely resembles. From Ghana's independence in 1957, the courts system, headed by the chief justice, has demonstrated extraordinary independence and resilience.

Chapter 8. **National Bureaucracy (Civil Service System).** A national bureaucracy is the name given to a large organization that is structured hierarchically to carry out specific functions within a government. This chapter describes the nature of bureaucracies (e.g. Weberian, acquisitive, monopolistic models)

Chapter 9. **Interest Groups.** The actions of some groups in any country reveal whether they are influential in the political process. This chapter explores which groups in Ghana are most influential or those considered wielding power, such as business-oriented trade associations (representing oil, gas, women's groups, the insurance and legal professions, etc.). Other groups having considerable influence include automobile spare parts dealers, bankers, and to an extent, the Ghana Private Road Transport Union, schoolteacher associations, civil and local government staff associations, and other associated groups.

Chapter 10. **Civil Society Groups.** This chapter explores the features that make one a good citizen. Liberal-pluralist and Marxist-Leninist routes are examined for establishment of political socialization. Ghana has not had a history of strong civil society groups; these have tended to be corporatist and authoritarian. The development of a civil society is still an ongoing process in Ghana.

Chapter 11. **Civil Rights in Ghana.** Ghana's constitution guarantees civil rights such as freedom of expression, religion, peaceful assembly, travel, etc. Nevertheless, societal discrimination is still prevalent, and tribal and domestic violence remain issues that continue to infringe on citizens' civil rights. This chapter examines civil rights issues in Ghana from a historical perspective based on the civil rights battles of other countries.

Chapter 12. **Civil Liberties.** Civil liberties are freedoms that are guaranteed to people to protect them from an over-powerful government. This chapter explores the rights and freedoms enjoyed by the citizens of Ghana.

Chapter 13. **The Media and Ghanaian Politics.** Mass media have had a profound effect on Ghanaian politics, bringing political issues directly to the average citizen. The Internet is expected to increase the awareness of politics in the general Ghanaian populace. However, at present, mass media is used more for entertainment than for political news: the rise of the information society has yet to give rise to an informed society in Ghana.

Chapter 14. **Local Governments.** Ghana has relied heavily on local governments since its independence in 1957. This chapter looks at the decentralization plans currently in place to provide regional legislation that fits well with local and tribal interests. Ghana presently has a total of 13 sub-metropolitan district councils, 1,300 urban, zonal, town, and area councils, and 16,000 unit committees.

Chapter 15. **The Politics of National Policy.** This chapter explores the changing role of the Ghanaian government, which is now placing increasing emphasis on setting overall direction through policy and planning, on engaging stakeholders and citizens, and sometimes on empowering stakeholders or partners to deliver programs and services. The environment for policy and planning has increased in complexity in Ghana. The ownership of issues is often unclear, especially when more than one department and often more than one level of government are involved. The general community is also increasingly claiming ownership of policy issues and process. Globalization and fiscal resource limitations contribute to the confusion. This chapter shows how this complex environment steadily increases the demand for good public policy and places increasing demands on managers, policy analysts, planners, and others involved in the design and delivery of policies and programs.

Chapter 16. **Making Economic Policies.** This chapter explores the various efforts taken by the government to restore Ghana's economy, mostly by boosting the country's exports. A previous reliance on cocoa and mineral exports now no longer supports the economy because of devastating drought and falling commodity prices, so economic policies are aimed at broadening the range of exports and trading partners. Under the sway of free-market forces, production has increased in Ghana's traditionally strong sectors, cocoa and gold, thereby reverting to the pre-independence economic structure; still, a more broadly based economy has not developed. Ghana's economy remains in a state of arrested development.

Chapter 17. **Making Social Policies.** Social policy in Ghana concerns primarily the laws, programs, and rules that address issues such as welfare, healthcare, crime, environmental problems, abortion, and education. This chapter explores the complexity of social policy debates, which tend to be contentious because people often hold sharply contrasting views about the best course of action that benefits the people and because they perceive so much to be at stake. Social policy is, to a large extent, dominated by economic policy, because economic policy determines the amount that government is prepared to spend.

Chapter 18. **Making Foreign and Defence Policy.** In broad terms, Ghana's foreign policies are aimed at maintaining and promoting the favourable position and security of the Republic of Ghana in the international arena. This chapter examines Ghana as it faces the new millennium; it is challenged to become more isolated from the rest of the world, while others argue that the nation must remain an active participant in the world community, even as the world becomes a more uncertain and dangerous place.

Chapter 19. **Economic Communities of West African States (ECOWAS).** There is a concerted effort to integrate the economies of several West African nations, to bolster and strengthen the finances and trade capabilities of developing nations on the continent. This chapter explores the rationale and anticipated outcome for ECOWAS and its expected impact on Ghana's economy and independence.

Chapter 20. **The African Union.** The African Union is an African formation and one of the world's most important intergovernmental organizations. It is composed of fifty-three countries in Africa, including Ghana, and is loosely based on the European Union concept. The aim is to improve the economic, political, and social situations for the billion people that live on the continent.

Chapter 1

THE GHANAIAN HERITAGE

One basic fact of human life is that people live together and not in isolation. *Social scientists* generally define the largest group in which people live as a *society*. *The Ghanaian society therefore can be described as a group of people living in a common environment and having common traditions, institutions, activities, and interests.* When we reflect, as Ghanaians, upon our lives and try to understand what has happened to us, we realize that our stories must be told in terms of our relationships with other people: parents and teachers, boyfriends and girlfriends, supporters and opponents, or bosses and dependents. To be human is to interact with, to affect and be affected by other human beings, every day of our lives, but to interact with others is to be in conflict with them, to some extent. *Why is this?*

In the world, human beings are alike in certain respects, but no person is exactly like any other in every respect. One of the most significant differences between each person is their personal values. A *value,* as the term is used here, *is an object or situation deemed to be of intrinsic worth, or something to be esteemed and sought.* People place *value* on things they consider important and desirable, whether it is a Mercedes-Benz car, passing grades, social prestige, peace of mind, or a brave new world. Social scientists agree that different people have different values and that every person acts in some way to realize his or her value. Whenever people come in contact with each other, their values will conflict to some degree. In a world of limited resources, some values are satisfied, while others go unsatisfied. Consider the yearly budget reading of Ghana: the finance minister will always remind Members of Parliament that there are many competing areas of government, but the presented budget is what the government can currently afford. If taxes are increased to support higher welfare payments, then some taxpayers will be unhappy.

As we live our daily lives, continue our education, and study what interests us in order to find a good job, we discover that others also want these same things. Not everyone is equally successful in achieving his or her goals and obtaining what they value. This is true of even our most lofty aims; we all want a better, more just world, but we do not all agree on the best way to achieve this. In order to achieve our goals, we work and rest, study and practice, speak and demonstrate, vote and not vote, tell the truth and lie, or obey the rules and break them. All the while, we strive, in competition with others who pursue different goals in different ways. Conflict, then, is an essential and inescapable consequence of living in a society rather than in isolation.

Political Conflict in Society

Wherever people live together in a society, most members of that society will believe that certain values can only be satisfied by rules that bind everyone within that society. Most people regard government action as the best way to obtain authoritative and binding rules. We define conflict over what societal rules should be as political conflict. In Ghana, most political conflict is also ethnic, which results in many ethnic groups taking up arms against each other in territorial wars; I call them uncivil territorial wars. These conflicts stem from economic hardship due to lack of jobs and opportunities for young people to grievances over ethnic relationships. Many conflicts, in any society, are fought outside the political arena, such as economics, academics, sports, and marriage. The point that is being made here is that no society—traditional or modern, more advanced or less advanced, democratic or authoritarian—is entirely without political conflict. In modern societies—Ghana not the exception—most conflicts over *values* become political conflicts.

What Is Politics?

Politics is deciding who gets *what*, *when*, and *how*. It is the method by which people try to take more of whatever there is to take—whether it is money, prestige, jobs, respect, sex, or even power itself. Politics occurs in many different settings. We talk about office politics, student politics, union politics, and church politics, but political science limits its usage to *politics in government*. So what is the science of politics?

Political science is the study of politics, or the study of who gets *what*, *when*, and *how*. The *who* are the political participants, who include voters, interest groups, political parties, the media, corporations, labour unions, lawyers, lobbyists, and elected government officials. The *what* of politics are public policies—the decisions made by the government concerning issues such as social welfare, healthcare, national defence, law enforcement, and thousands of other policies important to a society. The *when* and *how* are the political processes, including campaigns and elections, political news reporting, television debates, fundraising, lobbying, and decision-making in the Flagstaff House, the halls of Parliament, the ministries, and the law courts. Political science is generally concerned with three questions: *Who governs? To what end? And by what means?* Throughout this book, we will be concerned with who participates in politics, who benefits most from government decisions, who bears the greatest costs, and how these decisions are made.

Different Areas in Political Science

Political science is commonly divided into five distinct sub-disciplines that include:

- Political theory
- Comparative politics
- Public administration
- International relations
- Public law

Political theory is concerned with the contributions of various classical thinkers such as Aristotle, Cicero, Plato, Niccolo Machiavelli, and many others. *Comparative politics* is the science of comparison and teaches different types of constitutions, political actors, legislatures, and associated fields from an intrastate (country-to-country) perspective. *Public administration* is the implementation of government policies. Putting it another way, public administration is often regarded as including also some reasonability for determining the policies and programs of governments. Specifically, it is the planning, organizing, directing, coordinating, and controlling of government operations. The pursuit of the public good by enhancing civil society, ensuring a well-run, fair, and effective public service are some of the goals of the field. Therefore, public administration can be described as the development, implementation, and study of branches of government policy. *Public law* is that area of constitutional, administrative, criminal, and international law that focuses on the organization of the government, the relations between the state and its citizens, the responsibilities of government officials, and the relations between sister states. It is concerned with political matters, including the powers, rights, capacities, and duties of various levels of government and government officials. *International relations* refer to the interaction between nation-states and intergovernmental or transnational organizations. Political science is methodologically diverse and appropriates many methods originating in social research. These approaches include *interpretivism, positivism, behaviourism, structuralism, post-structuralism, realism, institutionalism, rational choice theory,* and *pluralism*. Political science, as one of the social sciences, employs methods and techniques related to the type of inquiry sought: *primary sources* such as *historical documents* and *official records*, and *secondary sources* such as *scholarly journal articles, survey research, statistical analysis, case studies, experimental research,* and *model building*.

Subfields in Political Science

Most political scientists work in one or more of the following five areas:

- Comparative politics, including area studies
- International relations
- Political philosophy
- Public administration
- Public law

Some political science departments classify methodology and scholarship on the domestic politics of particular countries as distinct subfields. In the United States, American politics is often treated as a separate subfield. Instead of the traditional classification, some academic departments organize scholarship into thematic categories that include political behaviour, political philosophy (public opinion, collective action, and identity), and political institutions (legislatures and international organizations). Political science conferences and journals often emphasize scholarship in categories even more specific. For example, the American Political Science Association has forty-two organized sections that address various methods and topics of political inquiry.

Politics in Everyday Conversation

Many people in Ghana engage in politics unknowingly in their daily conversations with others. The word *politics* and its derivatives come up repeatedly in day-to-day conversation in schools, government offices, and even in churches and homes. Most of us think we know what such statements mean when a classmate accuses, say, Master Nakoja of being undeservedly chosen as the editor of the school paper because of *politics* when the National Democratic Congress (NDC) or the New Patriotic Party (NPP) is accused of assisting Master Nmukanjo Konja to be elected as the Students' Representative Council (SRC) president ahead of the students' favourite, Ms Augustina Mensah; or when a university vice-chancellor charges that politicians are interfering with higher education, or when a newspaper columnist declares that a tax levied on cellular talk time to balance the budget is *politically impossible*. We are likely to nod sagely and perhaps add a sigh for the imperfections of human nature, but all that said is *politics* or political conversation.

These statements offer hints as to what *politics* means to most people. It has to do with *distributing desirable things in scarce supply* and deciding *who gets what*, probably, as people often say, the lion's share of whatever is to be shared. It operates not only within the government but also in private groups like a school competition for a newspaper editor and other competitive elections in colleges, social clubs, and institutions. The word *politics* often suggests selfish squabbling for private gain, rather than enlightened cooperation for the common good of all. There is no doubt that *politicians* have a poor reputation in public *opinion polls* across the world. Statistics have shown that the only professions thought to have even lower ethical standards than politicians are insurance salespeople, labour union leaders, advertisers, and car salespeople.

On the other hand, while most people look down on politicians, they admire statesmen, who are past politicians. The only trouble is that many can never agree on which public figures deserve which label. To some, for example, the first president of the republic, Dr Kwame Nkrumah, was a great president—he has even been named the 'man of the century' and continental citizen of Africa. But to others he was a lying and selfish politician. Similar disagreements have existed about almost every other president, from Dr Kofi Busia, Dr Hilla Liman, and Flight Lt. Jerry John Rawlings to President John Agyekum Kufuor. Some observers suspect that, for most people, a statesman is simply a government leader they like and a politician is one they dislike. This suspicion has led some commentators to say that a statesman is a dead politician; others declare that a statesman is a politician held upright by pressures from all sides. It has also inclined most politician scientists to use the terms *politics* and *politicians* in the more neutral senses, an adoption we will be using throughout this book.

Politics and Government

What distinguishes government politics from politics in other institutions in society? After all, parents, teachers, unions, banks, corporations, and many other organizations make decisions about *who gets what* in society. The answer is that only government decisions can extend to the whole society, and only government decisions can legitimately use force. Other institutions encompass only a part of society, for example, students and faculty in a college, members of a church or union, employees or customers of a corporation. Individuals have a legal right to voluntarily withdraw from non-governmental organizations. By contrast, governments make decisions affecting everyone, and no one can voluntarily withdraw from the government's authority (without leaving the country and thus becoming subject to some other government's authority). Some individuals and organizations—gangs, crime families—occasionally use physical force to get what they want. In fact, the history of Ghana is not without violence or force used for political ends.

Government thus enjoys legitimacy, or rightfulness, in its use of force. A democratic government has a special claim to legitimacy because it is based on the consent of its people, who participate in the selection of its leaders and the making of its laws. Those who disagree with a law have the option of working for its change by speaking out, petitioning, demonstrating against the law (protests), forming interest groups or parties, voting against unpopular leaders, or running for office themselves. Since people living in a democracy can effect change by working within the system, they have a greater moral obligation to obey the law than do people living under regimes in which they have no voice. However, there may be some occasions when civil disobedience, even in a democracy, may be morally justified.

The Purposes of Government

All governments in the world, including that of Ghana, tax, penalize, punish, restrict, and regulate their people. The government of Ghana—a unitary system of government modelled along the British parliamentary system—has 10 regions and roughly 262 local or metropolitan, municipal, or district governments (MMDs). Each year, the Parliament of Ghana enacts about thirty new laws, and makes about seventy-eight rules and regulations. The regions have no parliaments, but instead have regional coordinating councils (RCC). The districts are also divided into area or zonal councils, districts' assemblies (DAs), and zonal security councils. *Why do people put up with governments?* An answer to this question can be found in the words of the preamble to the Constitution of Ghana: 'That *we the people* . . .' In other words, '*the Sovereignty of Ghana resides in the people of Ghana in whose name and for whose welfare the powers of government are to be exercised in the manner and within the limits laid down in this [1992] Constitution*; for reasons best known to us, [we Ghanaians] have come out with this Constitution to guide us in governing ourselves.' Therefore, people put up with governments in terms of paying taxes and obeying laws for many reasons; among many other reasons are the following:

To Establish Justice and Insure Domestic Tranquillity—First, the purpose of any government is to manage conflict and maintain order. We might think of government as a social contract among people who agree to allow themselves to be regulated and taxed in exchange for protection of their lives and property.

No society can allow individuals or groups to settle their conflicts by street fighting, murder, kidnapping, rioting, bombing, or terrorism. Whenever government fails to control such violence, we say that there has been a breakdown in law and order. Indeed, when government loses control consistently, the government itself often breaks down. Without the protection of government, human lives and property are endangered, and only those skilled with fists and weapons have much of a chance of survival. The seventeenth-century English political philosopher Thomas Hobbes described life without government as 'a war where every man is enemy to every man' and 'where people live in continual fear and danger of violent death'.

To Promote the General Welfare—Government promotes the general welfare in a number of ways. It provides public goods—goods and services that private markets cannot readily furnish either because they are too expensive for individuals to buy for themselves (for example, the children's park near the National Theatre in Accra, the Tema Highway, or the Accra Sports Stadium and other stadia in the country) or because if one person bought them, everyone else would 'free-ride' or use them without paying (for example, clean air, police protection, or national defence). Nevertheless, Ghanaians acquire most of their goods and services on the free market, through voluntary exchange among individuals, firms, and corporations. Government also regulates society. Free markets cannot function effectively if individuals and firms engage in fraud, deception, or unfair competition, or if contracts cannot be enforced. Moreover, many economic activities impose costs on persons who are not direct participants in these activities. Economists refer to such costs as *externalities*. A factory that generates air pollutants or waste water imposes external costs on community residents who would otherwise enjoy cleaner air or water.

To Secure the Blessings of Liberty—All governments must maintain order, protect national security, provide public goods, regulate society, and care for those unable to fend for themselves. Democratic governments, however, have a special added responsibility—to protect individual liberty by ensuring that all people are treated equally before the law. In a true democratic dispensation, no one is above the law. The president of Ghana must obey the Constitution and laws of Ghana, and so must Members of Parliament, ministers, judges, justices, the military, and the police. A democratic government must protect people's freedom to speak and write (freedom of the press) what they please, to practice their religion, to petition, to form groups (freedom of assembly) or parties (but not based on tribal or ethnic lines), to enjoy personal privacy, and to exercise their rights if accused of a crime. The concentration of government power can be a threat to freedom. If a democratic government acquires great power in order to maintain order, protect national security, or provide many collective goods and services, it runs the risk of becoming too powerful for the preservation of freedom. The worry therefore is how to keep government from becoming so big and powerful that it threatens the individual liberty it was established to protect.

The Meaning of Democracy

Over the centuries, various thinkers in many different cultures have contributed in various ways to the development of democratic governments. Early Greek philosophers have contributed to the true meaning of the word *democracy*, which means *rule of the many*. Nevertheless, there is no single definition of democracy, nor is there a tightly organized system of democratic thought. It is better, perhaps, to speak of democratic tradition than of a single democratic ideology. Unfortunately, the looseness of the term *democracy* allows it to be perverted by anti-democratic governments. There is hardly a nation in the world that does not claim to be democratic. Governments that outlaw political opposition, suppress dissent, discourage religion, and deny fundamental freedoms of speech and press still claim to be democracies, democratic republics, or people's republics. There are a number of such 'democratic republics' in the world, such as the Democratic Republic of Korea (being the official name of Communist North Korea), the Democratic Republic of Saudi Arabia, Iran, and many around the world. These governments defend their use of the term *democracy* by claiming that their policies reflect the true interests of their people, but they are unwilling to allow political freedoms or to hold free elections in order to find out whether their people really agree with their policies. In effect, they use the term as a political slogan rather than a true description of their government. Democracy was born and even invented in the Western world by the ancient Greeks and it has long been closely associated with the development and institutional arrangements of the West, including both Western Europe and its extension in North America.

Democracy, as a new mechanism for Ghanaians since 1992, has been a good fit in the West for several decades, and tied to the Western culture and institutions. Implied therefore in the above is the notion that democracy is more than a mere set of institutional arrangements that we have in Ghana, such as regular elections, the notion of checks and balances, separation of powers, and so on, which any country can imitate with minimal constitutional engineering. It is, however, not sufficient to conceive of democracy in this world without first mentioning what brought about democracy.

Democracy was consolidated by events such as the Renaissance, the Enlightenment, and the sense of individualism, pragmatism, tolerance, and rationality to which these movements gave rise. At the social level, it is difficult to conceive of democracy without first mentioning a degree of equality or egalitarianism among the citizens. But for countries in Africa, Asia, and many that are rooted and driven by class, racial, and ethnic divisions, the same formula of institutional tinkering does not work. That is, creating political parties or parliaments does not magically transform these countries into democracies. In summation, democracy is usually correlated to some degree and sense of egalitarianism and the rise of a strong middle class.

Direct versus Representative Democracy

Direct democracy is where everyone actively participates in every decision. It is also called pure or participatory democracy. Such a democratic process is rare. The closest approximation to direct democracy may be a small village meeting, where everybody comes together face to face to decide about the village affairs. This type of village meeting is rapidly vanishing because citizens cannot spend so much of their time and energy in community decision-making.

Representative democracy is the expectation that millions of people cannot come together and decide every issue. Instead, representatives of the people are elected by the people to decide issues on their behalf. Elections must be open to competition so that the people can choose representatives who reflect their own views. Elections also must take place in an environment of free speech and press so that both candidates and voters can freely express their views. Finally, elections must be held periodically so that representatives can be thrown out of office if they no longer reflect the views of the majority of the people. Therefore, no government can claim to be a representative democracy unless:

- Representatives are selected by vote of all the people;
- Elections are open to competition;

- Candidates and voters can freely express themselves;
- Representatives are selected periodically.

So, when we hear of 'elections' in which only one party is permitted to run candidates, candidates are not free to express their views, or leaders are elected for life, then we know that these governments are not really democracies, regardless of what they may call themselves.

Liberal Democracy

Liberal democracy is used to describe the type of democracy practiced in Western countries, such as the United States of America. Democratic governments allow their people to choose their leaders freely at intervals. Other features of liberal democracy include the enjoyment of human rights, the existence of opposition parties, and the reliance on majority rule. Features of liberal democracy include:

a. Free and fair elections—the ability to organize free and fair elections to elect the representatives
b. Universal adult suffrage—the right to be included to vote when the person attains a certain age—18 years in Ghana
c. Observance of rule of law—the observance of equality, liberty, and legality and the absence of the arbitrary use of power by the ruling government
d. Freedom of the media—the existence of a vibrant and free press in the country
e. The existence of opposition parties—the existence of alternative forms of government and the ability of such parties to vote against a law.

Throughout this book, as we examine how well representative democracy works in Ghana, we will consider such questions as participation in elections and why some people do not vote, whether parties and candidates offer the voters real alternatives, whether modern political campaigning informs voters or only confuses them, and whether elected representatives are responsive to the wishes of voters—the kinds of questions that concern political science.

Who Really Governs?

Democracy is an inspiring ideal. But is democratic government really possible? Is it possible for millions of people to govern themselves, with every voice having equal influence? Or will a small number of people inevitably acquire more power than others? To what extent is democracy attainable in any society, and how democratic is the Ghanaian political system? *That is, who really governs?*

Other features that need to be emphasized to have a full understanding of democracy and its meaning, as well as its possibilities, are the diversities within that country. For example, can you have democracy in countries when the levels of literacy or of socio-economic development are so low that people have no sense of national politics or are so preoccupied with scratching out a daily subsistence that they have no time, energy, or interest in politics? Can democracy be practiced in a situation where the gaps between rich and poor are so vast that the notions of egalitarianism or 'one person, one vote' are a joke or a farce? Can democracy be present where votes are sold (vote buying) to the highest bidder? Or can democracy be sustained in a so-called democracy where the armed forces or religious authorities intervene in the political process to nullify the popular vote?

In order words, democracy is more than a narrow and particular arrangement of political institutions to serve the people. Democracy is embedded in the history, culture, sociology, economics, philosophy, and even in the religion of the West, and we cannot describe democracy without these realities of life and history. The question therefore is: if democracy is tied up closely with all these ingredients above to the West, how can the non-West, which lacks this same history and traditions, be expected to develop Western-style democracy? In short, how can societies like Ghana, Nigeria, Cameroon, Libya, and others—who never experienced the Renaissance, the Enlightenment, the Protestant Reformation, the Industrial Revolution, and the rise of capitalism, the British (1689) or French (1789) revolutions, or the scientific revolution ushered with Galileo and Newton—develop the same kind of democracy as that of the West? Can an analysis be quickly reached here that if all these ingredients and more were necessary for the growth of Western-style democracy, then surely countries that lacked these ingredients will have to enact their own systems of democracy, with their own institutional forms, and their own ingredients and priorities?

What Then Is Democracy?

Democracy, therefore, is not an export commödity for the consuming public; it cannot be transplanted like a rose bush from one cultural flower bed to another in one's garden. Rather, it requires a careful nurturing and adjustment to local conditions of that particular country. As such, a country can proffer specific institutional suggestions about the electoral systems of either parliamentarianism or presidentialism. But without similar historical, cultural, social, economic, or even religious conditions and philosophical traditions, the nature of a democracy—and even the possibility of establishing democracy—is going to vary considerably from country to country.

In practice therefore, democracy may take many different forms in many different societies, as in Libya, South Africa, Britain, Nigeria, Togo, the United States of America, or Ghana. But the type of democracy or institutions transporting the system has to be tailored to the culture, values, and traditions of such communities to enable the roots of democracy to be firmly established. We need to recognize these differences realistically, even while we continue to hope and work for democracy's spread around the world. After all, the democracy that is practiced in America or in Britain may not be the type that Ghana or Sweden or Denmark practices.

In political science literature, the best known definition of democracy—or what is termed poliyarchy—has been offered by Robert Dahl. Dahl's definition amplifies that of Schumpeter and Huntington but is very much in the same tradition and, again, closely tied to the Western experience. Dahl's definition emphasizes these aspects: (1) organized contestation through regular, free, and fair elections; (2) the right of virtually all adults to vote and contest for office; and (3) freedom of press, assembly, speech, petition, and organization.

What Are the Ingredients of Democracy?

Democracy is not just an abstract, theoretical, or philosophical issue anymore; instead, it has become a major policy issue with large interest groups, money, government, bureaucracies, and international actors and personnel involved. The actual existence of *democratic ideals* varies considerably from country to country, regardless of their names. A meaningful interpretation of democracy must include the following ideals: recognition of the dignity of every individual, equal protection of the laws for every individual, opportunity for everyone to participate in public decisions, and decision-making by majority rule, with everyone, no matter the person's status, having one vote. Democracy does not have the same meaning, the same socio-economic, cultural, or institutional base, or the same priority in every society. What democracy means, say, in the United States of America, may not be the same in Nigeria, just like how the Nigerian federal system is not the same as the American one. However, the belief is that there are certain universal ingredients that must be present to say that there is democracy. These include regular and competitive elections, political freedoms, and periodic changeovers of government. At the same time, however, the precise meaning, implications, importance, and cultural understanding of democracy may vary considerably.

Nevertheless, if there is anywhere in the world where the prospects for democracy have not been propitious, it is the African continent. First, has the colonial legacy of the continent and its colonialist political institutions all but guaranteed that the continent's experience with democracy will be less than successful? Second, as with the Middle East, we need to be aware of Africa's incredible poverty and underdevelopment, which suggests that much of the continent lacks the social, economic, and institutional foundation on which successful democracy can be established. Third, there was a time in the 1970s and 1980s when some countries of Africa experimented with indigenous or home-grown models of democracy, but often these were based on naïve, romantic, and unrealistic visions that lacked credibility and stood little chance of success. Hence, today, some of the more grandiose visions have been abandoned and more modest, and probably realistic, plans put in their place: some decentralization, better human rights, some privatization, investments, greater transparency in public accounts, education, respect for human rights, and peaceful coexistence with each other. The goal of democracy has not been abandoned, but a more realistic assessment of democracy's prospects and possibilities is needed; further, these modest steps now will help lay the groundwork for a more solid and widespread democracy later on. Democracy is both universal—in the sense that all people (almost all) want it and that it has certain core requirements that give it global applicability—and particularly in the sense that all countries and cultures are now attempting to conduct and practice democracy in their own way.

Public opinion surveys tell us that in country after country; most of the population prefers democracy. These assertions have become a reality because of the decline, overthrow, and discrediting of authoritarianism on the one hand and Marxism-Leninism on the other. The two major alternatives to democracy of the twentieth century seem to have the global playing field all to itself. In the modern world, no other system of government enjoys the legitimacy that democracy has; indeed, one can go further and say that democracy is now the only form of government that has global legitimacy. Today, democracy has triumphed in the world, and Winston Churchill's backhanded compliment 'Democracy is the worst form of government except for all the others' seems to have been borne out. As such, there seems to a substantial agreement on the core requirements of democracy, as the following illustrates.

Individual Dignity

The first underlying value of democracy is the dignity of the individual with regard to his liberty, right as a citizen, and freedom to choose, among others. Human beings are entitled to life and liberty, personal property, and equal protection under the law. These liberties are not granted by governments; they belong to every person born into the world. The English political philosopher John Locke (1632–1704) argued that a higher 'natural law' guaranteed liberty to every person and that this natural law was morally superior to all human laws and governments. Each individual possesses 'certain inalienable rights, among these are Life, Liberty, and Property' (see People in Politics: 'John Locke and the Justification of Revolution'). Individual dignity requires personal freedom. People who are directed by governments in every aspect of their lives, people who are collectivized and made into workers for the state, people who are enslaved—all are denied the personal dignity to which all human beings are entitled. In the above senses therefore, democratic governments try to minimize the role of government in the lives of their citizens.

Equality

Every true democracy requires equal protection of the law for every individual of that country. A practicing democratic country like Ghana cannot discriminate between ethnic groups, like the Nanumbas, Basaris, Fantes, Dagombas,

Asantes, Dagatis, Konkombas, Grusi, etc., rich and poor, or any groups of people, in applying the law. Not only must a democratic government refrain from discrimination itself, but it must also work to prevent discrimination in society generally. Today, our notion of equality extends to equality of opportunity for, say, women—the obligation of government to ensure that 40 per cent of women have an opportunity to develop their full potential under the National Democratic Congress (NDC) manifesto of 2009 (2008 National Democratic Congress manifesto, Accra). A case in point is the appointment of Mrs Marrietta Brew Appiah as attorney general and Minister of Justice; Ms Hannah Tetteh as the Minister for Foreign Affairs; Mrs Oye Lithur as the Minister for Women and Children, Gender and Social Protection, among other highly placed women in institutions of government.

Equality for all is the opportunity to share the land space in the country. Unlike situations in the three Northern regions, where during the reign of Colonel Kutu Acheampong (1978), land was allotted to only five ethnic groups in those parts of the country, which generates ethnic conflicts from time to time. Equality must provide a way of distributing land, economic benefits, and other social amenities that the central government would provide to everyone, irrespective of the persons' location or proximity.

Participating in Decision-Making

Democracy means individual participation in the decisions that affect individuals' lives. People should be free to choose for themselves how they want to live. Individual participation in government is necessary for individual dignity. People in a democracy should have decisions made for them by them. Even if they make mistakes, it is better that they be permitted to do so than to take away their rights to make their own decisions. The true democrat would reject even a wise and benevolent dictatorship because it would threaten the individual's character, self-reliance, and dignity. The argument for democracy is not that the people will always choose wise policies for themselves but that people who cannot choose for themselves are not really free.

Majority Rule: One Person, One Vote

Collective decision-making in democracies must be by majority rule, with each person having one vote. That is, each person's vote must be equal to every other person's, regardless of status, money, or fame. For example, Mr Abedi Pele, residing in an upper-class neighbourhood in East Legon, should have a vote equal to that of a truck pusher who resides in Agbogbloshie or Malam-Atta in Accra. Whenever any individual is denied political equality because of race, sex, or wealth, that government is not truly democratic. Majorities are not always right, but majority rule means that all persons have an equal say in decisions that affect them. If people are truly equal, their votes must count equally, and a majority vote must decide the issue, even if the majority decides foolishly.

The Paradox of Democracy

What if a majority of the people decides to attack the rights of some unpopular individuals or minority groups? What if hate, prejudice, or racism infects a majority of people and they vote for leaders who promise to get rid of, say, the minority groups in Ghana such as the Basaris or Nawuris from the Northern region of Ghana or 'put uneducated people in their place'. What if a majority of people vote to take away the property of wealthy people and distribute it among themselves? Do we abide by the principle of majority rule and allow the majority to do what it wants? Or do we defend the principle of individual liberty and limit the majority's power? If we enshrine the principle of majority rule, we are placing all our confidence in the wisdom and righteousness of the majority of the people. Yet, we do know that democracy means more than majority rule—that it also means freedom and dignity for the individual. How do we resolve this *paradox of democracy*—the potential for conflict between majority rule and individual freedom? The American founding fathers of democracy were not sure that freedom would be safe in the hands of the majority. In Ghana's quest for democracy, the majority must observe these paradoxes: Ghana's democracy must remain a *representative one*, in which elected leaders, rather than the people themselves, decide public issues. There must be *separation of powers*—in which each decision-making body—the Parliament, the presidents, and the Supreme Court—is selected by different means for different terms, so that a majority cannot change the nation's leadership easily or quickly—a *system of checks and balances*—so that each branch of government can restrain actions of other branches. Unitarism is where the national government in Accra decentralizes power to the ten regions of Ghana. And finally, *judicial review*— a process by which courts can declare laws and government actions that violate constitutional rights to be null and void.

More important than these structural arrangements for protecting individuals and groups from majorities is the principle of *limited government*. Limited government means that the power that government exercises over individuals is clearly limited, and that there are some personal liberties that even majorities cannot regulate, and that government itself is restrained by law. No government can be truly democratic if it directs every aspect of its citizens' lives. Individuals must be free to shape their own lives, free from the dictates of governments or even majorities of their fellow citizens. Indeed, we call a government with unlimited power over its citizens *totalitarian*. Under totalitarianism, the individual possesses no personal liberty. Totalitarian governments decide what people can say or write, what unions, churches, or parties they can join (if any), where people must live, what work they must do, what goods they can find in stores and what they will be allowed to buy and sell, whether citizens will be allowed to travel outside of their country, and so on. Under a totalitarian government, the total life of the individual is subject to government control.

Constitutions are *written* or *unwritten* social contracts or agreements that a nation formulates to police and guide its relationship with its citizens. Great Britain, Australia, Israel, New Zealand, and Canada have what are referred to as *uncodified constitutions*. Parts of the constitution come from *unwritten* sources. This is not to say that such countries do not have a constitution. These countries rely on several written and unwritten sources to construct their constitutional law. The Ghanaian constitution, which is a written one, sets forth the liberties of individuals and restrains government from interfering with these liberties. Consider, for example, the opening words of the First Amendment of the Ghana Constitution: 'In the Name of the Almighty God, We the People of Ghana . . . *in exercise* of our natural and inalienable right to establish a framework of government which shall secure for ourselves and posterity the blessing of liberty, equality of opportunity and prosperity; . . . *in a spirit* of friendship and peace with all peoples of the world: ... *and in solemn declaration and affirmation of our commitment to freedom, justice, probity and accountability; the principle that all powers of Government spring from the sovereign Will of the people; the principle of universal adult suffrage; the rule of law; the protection and preservation of fundamental human rights and freedoms, unity and stability for our Nation do hereby adopt, enact and give to ourselves this constitution.*' This first amendment in the 1992 constitution of Ghana places religious belief beyond the reach of government. Nonetheless, government cannot, even with the majority it can exert on the minority, interfere with the personal liberty of its people to worship as one wishes to. In addition, the courts, armed with the power of judicial review, can declare laws passed by majority vote of Parliament unconstitutional (see 'judicial powers' in chapter 7). Throughout this book, we will examine how all limited constitutional government succeeds in preserving individual liberty, and particularly in the case of Ghana. We will examine free speech and press, the mass media, religious freedom, the freedom to protest and demonstrate, and the freedom to support political candidates and interest groups of all kinds. We will examine how well the Ghana Constitution protects individuals from discrimination and inequality. We will also examine how far government can go in regulating work, homes, businesses, and the marketplace without destroying individual liberty.

Politics as a Policymaking Tool

In the broadest sense, politics includes the decision-making and decision-enforcing processes in any group that makes and enforces rules for its members. Several political scientists have studied these processes in non-governmental groups such as labour unions, business corporations, and medical associations. However, most political scientists have concentrated on the processes of governments rather than those of private associations. It therefore seems desirable to use the same focus in an introduction to political science. As the word will be used in this book, accordingly, *politics is the process of making government policies*. Let us see just what is involved in this definition.

When government officials are called upon to take some course of action (or inaction) on a particular matter, they are always faced with a number of alternatives they might pursue. They cannot, however, pursue all the alternatives simultaneously, if only because some would cancel out others. They have to select, from among the alternatives available, the few that they intend to put into effect. The course of action thus chosen becomes government *policy*. Therefore our definition is *the process by which policy makers choose which actions they will and will not take*, which is, according to our definition, *politics*. Politics, as we use the term in this book, is the process of making government policies (or public policies, which is another way of saying government decisions). But what is the nature of this process? What are its main characteristics? One is that politics everywhere involves conflict—that is, some form of struggle among people trying to achieve different goals and satisfy opposing interests. A basic, though perhaps painful, first step toward understanding the governing process is thus to face the fact that political conflict is not an unfortunate and temporary aberration from the normal state of perfect cooperation and harmony. Conflict arises from the very nature of human life itself.

Many political scientists emphasize a second universal characteristic of politics: the fact that the antagonists are rarely isolated individuals acting without reference to, or support from, other people. In most conflicts, a number of people on one or both sides of a political spectrum feel that they have a stake in the outcome and join forces with others who feel the same way. Most political conflict is thus best seen as conflict among groups rather than among individuals. For example, the New Patriotic Party (NPP) contest in 2007 among seventeen candidates for the party's presidential candidate was much more than a contest among those seventeen men alone. Each candidate was supported, opposed, and influenced by certain ethnic groups, business associations, and also by majorities of such unorganized but potent groups like workers, the youth, Makola market women, the middle class, and so forth. To describe the contest solely in terms of what the seventeen individuals said and did would present only a partial and misleading picture.

Tactics of Political Action

Politics, then, is a many-sided conflict among individuals and groups acting to get government to help them or keep government from doing harm. Political action is never easy. The stakes are high, the opposition is tough, and each competitor has to decide what combination of the following main tactics is most likely to bring success: lobbying, working inside political parties, mass propaganda, litigation, demonstrations, strikes and boycotts, nonviolent civil disobedience, and violence.

A *categoric group* (or social stratum, as some call it) is a number of individuals sharing one or more common characteristics (for example, people under twenty-one years of age, people earning more than GHC50,000 a year, residents of Community eleven in Tema, spare-part dealers at Konkompe, a suburb in Accra). The individuals in any particular categoric group may or may not be conscious of their common characteristics and may regard those characteristics as important and direct their behaviour accordingly. Few 'sakora' or bald-headed people, for example, feel strong bonds with other shaven-headed people or are acutely aware of a wide gulf between their own interests and the interests of shaven-headed people; thus, they are unlikely to unite with other similarly situated people to advance the cause of others.

A *pressure group* is an organized interest group that acts to achieve some of its goals by influencing government officials and policies. Political scientists often speak of a person's or group's political interest in a matter, meaning, as we have seen, the state of that person or group in what government does or fails to do. When people take action to protect or advance a common interest, they become a social force that has to be reckoned with. When one of their main activities is trying to induce government to do something they want or refrain from doing something they do not want, they become the kind of group on which we will concentrate in this book: a pressure group.

Lobbying—many legislative chambers have adjoining rooms, called lobbies, in which legislators (in Ghana—parliamentarians) and their guests meet and talk. At the time of writing this book (May 2013), work had begun (in 2011) for the renovation of the State House (Job 600) into offices for the parliamentarians. But a request for an additional GHC26 million (Ghana cedis) has been made for completion of the job. When that type of request is made, then offices and lobbies (if so earmarked) around the newly renovated Parliament House (around Job 600) can be termed lobbies designated for lawmakers and their clients. From this practice has emerged the term lobbying, which means *direct efforts by representatives of pressure groups to influence public officials to act as the groups wish.* Legislators or parliamentarians are the main targets of lobbying, but executives, administrators, and even judges are also frequently approached. The first prerequisite for successful lobbying is *access*, which is *the ability to get a hearing from government authorities.* Any group that cannot get a serious hearing from even one public official can hardly expect much success. A group's access depends on several things: for instance, its general prestige and social position and the reputation and skill of its lobbyists. A lobbyist whom the legislators (parliamentarians) have long known as reasonable, knowledgeable, and trustworthy is more likely to get a hearing than is one who is thought to be too aggressive, too careless with the facts, or too likely to talk out of turn.

After lobbyists gain access to one or more government authorities, they can use various techniques of persuasion. They can make a formal presentation of their group's position, marshalling facts, figures, and arguments to show it in the most favourable light; they can threaten an elected official with defeat at the next election and reinforce the threat by stimulating a flood of phone calls and letters from the parliamentarian's constituency; they can offer to trade their group's support of some pet project of the parliamentarian for his/her support of their proposal; and they can even offer bribes, either directly, in the form of cash, or indirectly, in the form of promises of well-paid jobs in private industry after the official has retired from office. In most modern nations, however, bribery has become so generally disapproved of, so hard to keep secret, and so dangerous that it is used far less frequently today than it was many years ago. In most modern countries, campaign contributions to candidates and parties are much better options of lobbying parliamentarians. Such contributions have become legal and all political parties and elected officials receive campaign donations to assist them in their re/elections.

Compared to What? Authoritarianism?

Authoritarianism is a form of government in which the rulers tolerate no public opposition and there are no legal means to remove these rulers from power. Some authoritarian regimes are dictatorships, where power is held by a single individual; others are juntas, where power is held by a small group of military officers. While authoritarian governments permit no challenges to their political rule, they generally allow people to go about their religious, social, business, and recreational activities relatively undisturbed.

Totalitarianism?

Totalitarianism is a form of authoritarian government in which the rulers recognize no limits to their authority and try to regulate virtually all aspects of social and economic life. The term *totalitarian* derives from the 'totality' of the rulers' ambitions; they tolerate no opposition in any sphere of life and aim for complete control of the society and its future.

Totalitarian governments are characterized by an elaborate ideology that covers every phase of the individual's life: a single political party that is identical with the government, widespread use of intimidation, complete control of mass media, monopoly control of weaponry and armed forces, and direction of the economy by the state bureaucracy. The most notable examples of totalitarian government are the three that were responsible for perhaps the most grotesque acts of genocide in history: Nazi Germany, Stalinist Russia, and Cambodia under the Khmer Rouge. In each case, terror was used as an instrument of policy, and millions of people were slaughtered at the whim of a regime that was utterly convinced of its own righteousness.

Conclusion

Politics is the process by which it is determined whose values will prevail in society. The basis of politics is conflict over scarce resources and competing values. Those who have power win out in this conflict and are able to control government authority and policy choices. The play of politics in Ghana takes place through rules of the game that include democracy, constitutionalism, and capitalism. Democracy is rule by the people, which, in practice, refers to a representative system of government in which the people rule through their elected officials. Constitutionalism refers to rules that limit the rightful power of government over citizens. Capitalism is an economic system based on a free-market principle that allows the government only a limited role in determining how economic costs and benefits will be allocated.

Feature Article 1—Why, in a constitutional democracy, government is still the *godfather*

Do you, as a Ghanaian, believe in justice? Have you ever felt at any time that justice has eluded you? That your civil liberties should be protected? That all Ghanaians should all be treated as equals? You would probably answer, 'Of course,' but do you also realize that if you are an avid supporter of public values like liberty, equality, fairness, and justice, then you should be an avid supporter of government? I am talking of central government, the Ghanaian government, because it is often the only institution that can make these kinds of core political values a reality. In fact, without an active and healthy public sector, these kinds of public values would be in very short supply. Take justice, for instance. It is not usually something provided by the marketplace or created by the actions of individuals. More often, it is something that can only be provided and sustained in the public sphere by the actions of government organizations like the courts and the legislature. In short, if we want a just society, we must work through government to get it. This argument—that government is an essential mechanism for realizing vital public values—is an important one in making the case for central government. Government is good not simply because it provides us, as individuals, with certain services and benefits, such as security, confidence, and sovereign guarantee as citizens of Ghana, for example, but also because it is the main way to promote important values that are good for us as a whole—values that are in the public interest. This view of government as the insurer of core democratic values is one that goes back to the very beginning of our national political institutions and the reasons for our constitutional instrument.

Major Concepts

Authority	Policy	Political culture
Capitalism	Political system	Politics

Democracy	Diversity	Equality
Individualism	Liberty	Self-government
Ideology	Polyarchy	Consolidation

Works Cited / Further Readings

Carey, Alex (1997), *Taking the Risk Out of Democracy: Corporate Propaganda versus Freedom and Liberty*, Andrew Lohrey, ed. (Urbana and Chicago: University of Illinois Press).

Crozier, Michael, Huntington, Samuel P., and Watanuki, Joji (1975), *The Crisis of Democracy: Report on the Governability of Democracies to the Trilateral Commission* (New York: New York University Press), pp. 113, 161.

Dahl, Robert A. (1971), *Polyarchy: Participation and Opposition* (New Haven: Yale University Press).

—— (1989), *Democracy and Its Critics* (New Haven: Yale University Press).

Diamond, Larry (1999), *Developing Democracy toward Consolidation* (Baltimore: Johns Hopkins University).

Haggard, Stephan and Kaufman, Robert R. (1995), *The Political Economy of Democratic Transition* (Princeton: Princeton University Press).

Kennan, George F. (1948), Policy Planning Study 23 (PPS23), *Foreign Relations of the United States (FRUS)*, quoted in Gilles d'Aymery, 'Context and Accuracy: George F. Kennan's Famous "Quotation"', *Swans Commentary*, 28 March 2005.

Lipset, Seymour Martin (1959), 'Some Social Requisites of Democracy: Economic Development and Political Legitimacy', *American Political Science Review* 53: 69–10.

Locke, John (1689), *First Treatise of Government*, the portion entitled 'Of Government: Book I'.

Samuels, Michael A. and William A. Douglas (1981), 'Promoting Democracy', *Washington Quarterly*, 4 (3): 52–66, quoted in William Robinson, *Promoting Polyarchy*.

Sussman, Gerald, *Branding Democracy*, p. 39, quoted in William Robinson, *Promoting Polyarchy*.

Zuckert, Michael P. (1994), *Natural Rights and the New Republicanism* (Princeton: Princeton University Press). Chapters 7–9 are a more extensive statement of the quasi-Hobbesian interpretation.

Chapter 2

CONSTITUTIONAL DEMOCRACY

Defining Democracy

Democracy is the kind of government that derives its authority from its citizens. The word *democracy* comes from two Greek words: *demos*, which means *the people*, and *kratos,* which means *authority* or *power.* Thus, *democracy* means government by the people, not government by one person (e.g. a monarch, dictator, the president, or high priest) or government by a few (oligarchy or aristocracy). The word *democracy,* from the import of ancient Athens and a few other Greek city-states and later on in the Roman republic (who practiced direct democracy), is a system in which citizens assemble to discuss and pass laws to select their officials. Most of these Greek city-states and Roman Republics later degenerated into mob rule while others resorted to dictatorships or rule by aristocrats. In the United States, when the constitution was formulated, the term *democracy* was used to describe unruly groups or mobs, and a system that encouraged leaders to gain power by appealing to the emotions and prejudices of the people. In 1787, James Madison, in the Federalist papers no. 10, reflected the view of many of the framers of the US constitution when he wrote, 'Such democracies [as the Greek and Roman] . . . have ever been found incompatible with personal security, or the rights of property; and have in general been as short in their lives, as they have been violent in their deaths.' James Madison feared that empowering citizens to decide policy directly would be dangerous to freedom, minorities, and property and would result in violence by one group against another. Thus, Ghana's democracy since independence has combined representative and direct democracy. *So what is a constitutional democracy?* A constitutional democracy means government by representative politicians. *Constitutional democracy is a system of government in which the limits of political authority are clearly stated and the electorate has the power to remove poor performing governments.* Countries that adhere to the political system of constitutional democracy usually have legal frameworks, such as a constitution (written or unwritten), which they use to rule over the country. Indeed, a central feature of democracy is that those who hold power do so only by winning a free and fair election. A constitutional democracy said to be stable and functioning is encouraged by various conditions, such as an educated citizenry, a healthy economy, and overlapping associations and groupings within a society in which major institutions interact to create a certain degree of consensus. Ghana seems to be at a crossroads, or can be described as struggling with the kind of democracy it practices, because of the mix or the strict maintenance of the colonial democracy left off by Ghana's colonial masters, the British. Moreover, the institutions deemed essential to the sustainability of its democracy are not strong enough, because of the frequency of demonstrations and strikes by workers in demand for their social rights.

More to the point, constitutionalism is a general label we apply to arrangements such as checks and balances, unitarism, separation of powers, due process, and the rights of individuals who vote for our leaders and representatives to listen, think, deliberate, bargain, and explain before they act and make laws. In a nutshell, a constitutional government enforces recognized and regularly applied limits on the powers of those who govern. But *democracy* is an often misused term, as it has many different meanings. We use *democracy* here to refer to a system of interacting values, interrelated political processes, and interdependent political structures. The vital principle of democracy is that a just government must derive its powers from the consent of the people, hence 'government by the people', and that this consent must be regularly renewed by free and fair elections at precise, stated intervals. Every four years in Ghana, the constitution says the government must subject itself to a referendum to determine if the people will endorse it or reject it and vote for another party. Ghana as a country has since the coming into force of the 1992 Constitution chosen the path of democratic governance. The president, as the head of the executive, and Members of Parliament are elected at regular intervals every four years. The principle of universal adult suffrage has firmly been established, giving every individual who is eighteen years and above the right to vote. The country has been divided into 10 regions, which are further divided into 275 constituencies, considering the population density in the country.

Limits to the Ghanaian Democracy

In the Ghanaian political system, the concentration of power within the executive (presidency) arm of government does not allow elected officials to mediate among factions, build coalitions, and work out compromises among and within the branches of the Ghanaian government to produce policy and action. Coalition building in parliament is nonexistent, as debates and mediation between the parties are done in an open and sometimes a confrontational manner on the floor. For example, in 2010, the National Democratic Congress majority in parliament forcibly passed an STX housing project without consensus from their counterparts, the National Patriotic Party (NPP), interest groups, and the general public. Without behind-the-scenes dialogue and discussions, the bill was quickly passed in parliament, but fell apart in June of 2011 when there was a realization that the Ghanaian partners with the Koreans (STX Korea) were embroiled in a court battle to establish the true ownership and identity of the project. If prior discussions and coalition building was initiated behind doors in Parliament, such a woeful disappointment in the eventual abrogation of the STX contract by the government of the housing project would have been avoided.

In a constitutional democracy, we expect politicians to operate within the rules of democracy and to be honest, well educated, humble, patriotic, compassionate, well informed, self-confident, and inspirational. Unfortunately, Ghanaians want politicians to have all the answers, and to have all the 'correct' values (as we perceive them). Ghanaians also want politicians to solve their personal problems, yet they insult politicians and make scapegoats of politicians for the things they dislike about government, such as government *rules and regulations*, especially when times are hard or difficult: *increase in taxes, limits on their freedoms, high crimes on the streets*, and *frequent power failures* (known as *dum sor, dum sor* in the Akan language). Many of these ideals are unrealistic, and no one can live up to all of them. Like all people, politicians live in a world in which perfection may be the goal, but compromise, ambition, fundraising, and self-promotion are necessary.

Ghanaians are beginning to learn that there are many facets of constitutional democracy practiced around the world. Ghanaians have long been sceptical of politicians and politics, as a result of the process by which governments are born in this country. After a brief democratic tenure of office of the first president of the first republic, Dr Kwame Nkrumah, in 1957, Ghana's democracy was shot down in February 1966 through a coup d'état by the Ghanaian Armed Forces. From 1966 until 1992, when Flight Lieutenant J. J. Rawlings re-established democracy, Ghana was frequently changing hands from one military junta to the other, with a brief spell of democratic governance by Dr Hilla Limann from 1977 to 1979. Yet, democracy has been a necessary and an important activity for the Ghanaian society. Indeed, politics and politicians are essentially indispensable in making the Ghanaian system of separate institutions and checks and balances to work. As earlier enumerated above, several attempts at democratizing the country began in the 1960s, but were soon taken over by military generals. A revolution in 1979, known as June 4th, had to be fought before a system of representative democracy could be tried and tested. It took several years, from 1979 until 1992, before a national constitution could be written, and the constitution has already been subjected (2010) to a review by the National Democratic Congress (NDC) government of the late president, Professor John Evans Atta Mills.

The democratic institution, the Electoral Commission (EC), which organizes election in Ghana, is still a work in progress, still in the process of being refined and improved as it is always being criticized by the opposition party, the New Patriotic Party. The 1992 Constitution provides that Ghana *shall not* be a one-party state and shall allow multiple political parties as well as independent candidates to contest elections. The Constitution elaborately provides for the right of each eligible individual to be registered, and the Electoral Commission allows for the review of the voters' register from time to time before elections. The Electoral Commission makes adequate provision for the conduct of elections every four years with budgetary support from the government. Articles 45 to 56 of the 1992 Constitution provide for the functions and powers of the Electoral Commission as well as the organization and supervision of political parties in the country. The 1992 Constitution, under article 11 sec. 25, gives the judiciary the mandate to administer justice. The judiciary, as an independent state institution, is vested with judicial power. Ghana, since the coming into force of the 1992 Constitution, has had five elections held in every four years. These elections have been relatively peaceful although there have been isolated instances of tension and disputes over some results. Fortunately, Ghana has not had the experience of conflicts resulting into violence after an election since 1992, as have been witnessed in some countries in the sub region. In the 2012 elections, the EC introduced the biometric system but the election was challenged by the flag bearers of the New Patriotic Party (NPP)—Nana Dankwa Akufo-Addo / Dr Mahamudu Bawumia—and the NPP party chairman (Jake Obetsebi Lamptey) for what they termed 'illegal malpractices' during the elections at the nation's highest court, the Supreme Court of Ghana. However, after eight months of intense battle at the Supreme Court of Ghana, the president, H.E. John Dramani Mahama, who took over shortly after the death of Professor J. E. A. Mills was eventually declared the winner of the challenge.

Under Ghanaian law, complaints or disputes are expressed in the nature of claims and described as election petitions that are filed before specified courts for determination. Petitions arising out of presidential elections are, in accordance with article 64 of the 1992 Constitution, to be determined by the Supreme Court, the highest court of the land and those in respect of parliamentary elections are, in accordance with article 99 of the 1992 Constitution, to be determined initially by the High Court. An appeal against the decision of the High Court in respect of parliamentary elections lies within the Court of Appeals, whose determination is final. Pursuant to section 17 of the Representation of the People Act 1992 (PNDCL 284), as amended, an election petition in a parliamentary election may be presented within twenty-one days from the publication of the results in the Gazette by one or more of the following: (a) a person who lawfully voted or had a right to vote at the election to which the election petition relates; (b) a person who claims that he had the right to have been elected at the election; (c) a person alleging to have been a candidate at the election; and (d) a person claiming to have had a right to be nominated as a candidate at the election. In the case of a challenge to presidential election, the 1992 Constitution, art. 64(1) provides that the validity of the election of the president may be challenged only by a citizen of Ghana by a petition presented to the Supreme Court within twenty-one days after the declaration of the results.

Therefore, an election petitioner must satisfy the court that he has the necessary capacity to initiate the petition. Once the court is satisfied that a petitioner is clothed with the capacity to institute the petition, the court can go ahead to commence hearing on the substantive petition. On the other hand, if the court is satisfied upon examination that the petitioner does not have the capacity to initiate the election petition, then there will be no need to entertain the petition. The petition should then be dismissed for lack of capacity on the part of the petitioner. Indeed, Ghana has shown much promise in conducting peaceful elections within the sub-Saharan region. From the above-discussed cases, it is evident that the courts of Ghana have contributed tremendously in ensuring peaceful elections. The judiciary must be lauded for its consistent effort to fairly adjudicate on election disputes. Moreover, the law pertaining to elections in Ghana has been fairly tested and the outcome promising, looking forward into the future. Amendments to election laws are done quite frequently and the judiciary must continue to safeguard the peace and stability that Ghana enjoys by rightly interpreting election statutes and fairly deciding on election disputes. This is an indispensable role that the judiciary must play if Ghana will continue to thrive on the peace it proudly boasts of. The most important examples of direct democracy is where voters, rather than party leaders or other elected officials, select who may run for office. Examples are the primaries usually conducted exclusively for parties like the NPP, the NDC, the CPP, and other parties to elect their party chairpersons, parliamentary candidates, and their presidential candidates. In the conduct of elections, these types of practices are known as *closed primaries*, where the election is open exclusively to the party (say, NPP or NDC) calling the election. An *open primary* is where anyone is allowed to vote and select, for example a parliamentary candidate, without restriction.

Other Constitutional Values

Direct democracy is the term used to describe particular forms of voting within any democratic system. The term *direct democracy* is commonly used to refer to three distinct types of vote: (1) *elections*, which are votes on a specific single issue, such as primary election for a political party or piece of legislation; (2) *citizen initiatives*, whereby citizens can propose new legislation or constitutional amendments by gathering enough signatures in a petition to force a vote on the proposal; and (3) *recalls*, under which citizens can force a vote on whether to oust an incumbent elected official by collecting enough signatures in a petition. The common characteristic of these mechanisms is that they place greater power in the hands of voters, as opposed to elected representatives. Direct democracy is, therefore, frequently seen as conflicting with representative democracy, in which voters elect representatives to make decisions on their behalf. By contrast, under direct democracy, voters can themselves make decisions about specific policies or issues.

Ghana's Political System

Today in Ghana, it would be impossible, even if it were desirable, to assemble the citizens of a village to make their laws or select their officials directly. Rather, the constitution calls for (closed) primaries for each party, to be supervised by the Electoral Commission of Ghana. Ghana practices a system of representative democracy, where the general population elects their leaders, who have constitutional authority and have their power directly or indirectly through free and fair elections in which all adult citizens are allowed to participate. The political system of Ghana takes place in a framework of a presidential representative democratic republic. As a result of this, the president of Ghana is both head of the state and head of the government, and of a pluriform multiparty system. The Ghanaian political system also has the government divided into three different branches, namely the executive, the legislature, and the judiciary. The seat of government, since President John Mahama took over from the late Professor John Atta Mills, is at the Flagstaff House, with the Parliament being unicameral in nature.

Ghana's Constitutional System

The constitution of Ghana was approved on 28 April 1992, though the country got its freedom a long time back, on 6 March 1957. The constitution of Ghana's political system declares Ghana as a unitary republic, with sovereignty residing in the Ghanaian people. The Constitution calls for a system of checks and balances, with powers shared between the presidents, its unicameral house called Parliament, the Council of State, and the judiciary. The constitution stipulates and anticipates the concept of power-sharing among these various arms of government.

The Executive Branch

Ghana is a member of the Commonwealth of Nations, and the president is the head of the country, with all the powers and privileges. He is elected for a term of four years by popular vote and is eligible for re-election for a second term of another four years, totalling eight years. John Agyekum Kufuor of the New Patriotic Party was the ninth president of the country from the 2000 election and was re-elected on 7 December 2004. The president of the Republic of Ghana also nominates members, subject to approval by Parliament, for the post of Council of Ministers. The vice president, like the president, is also elected for a term of four years (see chapter 6).

The Legislative Branch

All legislative functions of Ghana's political system are vested in the Parliament. It has a unicameral house with 275 members and a Speaker. The members of the Parliament are popularly elected by universal adult suffrage for a term of four years (see chapter 5).

The Judicial Branch

The judicial system of the Ghanaian government is independent from the two other branches of government. The Supreme Court is at the apex, with broad powers of judicial review. It has the power to rule on the constitutionality of any legislation or executive action at the request of any aggrieved citizen as authorized by the Constitution. This system of hierarchy of courts is largely derived from the British juridical system. The hierarchy is composed of the Supreme Court of Ghana, the Court of Appeal, the High Court of Justice, regional tribunals, and such lower courts or tribunals as Parliament may establish. Jurisdiction over all civil and criminal matters is held by the court (see chapter 7).

Constitutional Restraints on Political Power

In Ghana, the constitution calls for the protection of individual liberties and rights, the rule of law and press freedom. The constitution is more than a symbol in Ghana. It is regarded as the supreme and binding law that both grants and limits powers to the president of the country in the execution of his private and official duties. But as James Madison once wrote in the Federalist papers no. 51, 'in framing a government which is to be administered by men over men, the great difficulty lies in this: You must first enable the government to control the governed; and in the next place oblige it to control itself.' Therefore, Ghana's 1992 constitution is both a positive instrument for government to control the governed, and a restraint on government itself, which enables the ruled (people) to check the rulers (government). But then, how does the constitution serve as a great system of national unity and an instrument of the government? The secret therein is a provision within the constitution that calls for the separation of powers of government—being the executive, the legislature, and the judiciary—and a check-and-balance system that limits power with power. In terms of constitutional restraints on political power, government is the power structure of the society. This is the first and most important fact about the political agency, that it has the legal authority to coerce. The second thing is to inquire whether the power wielded by government is self-sprung, or delegated by a more comprehensive authority than being merely political. Does government rule autonomously or by divine right, or is the real power located elsewhere and merely loaned to government? The Ghanaian Constitution is clear on this point; that power is in the hands of the people to lay down the laws (through parliament), which government must implement for people to obey. In so doing, the restraints on political power determine how people initiate their own rules, as well as how the people want to be governed. A constitutional democracy is strengthened by an educated and prosperous public who have the ability to work out differences through the political process. A set of interacting values provides a foundation for that public confidence. Within the Ghanaian constitutional framework, there is still a struggle to understand such core values as:

Personal liberty is the essence of self-determination, where everyone has the opportunity to realize their own set of goals. We should, however, not forget that liberty is not simply the absence of external restraint on a person (freedom from something); it is also a person's freedom and capacity to reach his or her goals (freedom from something). Both history and reason suggest that individual liberty is the key to social progress. Indeed, the greater freedom that the people have, the greater the chance of discovering better ways of life to the betterment of all in the society.

Individualism is the idea that every person has the potential for common sense, rationality, and fairness in the pursuance of his life. Individuals have important rights collectively and those rights are the source of legitimate governmental authority and power. The concept here pervades democratic thought, and constitutional democracies make the person—rich or poor, male or female—which is the central measure of value.

Equality of opportunity—the democratic value of equality enhances the importance of the individual, such as 'all men (*tribes or ethnic groups*) are created equal, and from the equal creation, they derive rights inherent and unalienable, among which are the preservation of liberty and the pursuit of happiness.' In terms of Ghana's constitutional arrangement, what does equality mean? The question then might be, equality for whom? Does equality of opportunity mean that everyone should have the same place at the starting line? Or does it mean that the Ghanaian society should try to equalize the factors that determine a person's economic or social well-being? These enduring issues have witnessed situations in which certain ethnic groups, left without opportunity and denied their rights as equal citizens in Ghana, have fought wars in the immediate past to liberate themselves from artificial slavery.

Popular sovereignty is the idea that ultimate political authority rests with the people. This means that a just government must derive its powers from the consent of the people it governs, or by *popular consent*. It is a commitment to democracy that means a willingness to participate and make decisions in government for the benefit of all in that particular country.

Democratic Values in Conflict

The value of democracy is where the belief is that the values of democracy do not always coexist happily. Individualism may conflict with the collective welfare or the public good. Self-determination may conflict with equal opportunity. A media outlet's freedom to publish classified documents about foreign or defence policy may conflict with the government's constitutional requirement to provide for the common defence of the country. Therefore, much of what democracy derives is how to strike a balance among all these values.

Democracy as a System of Interrelated Values

In addition to having core democratic values, a successful democratic government requires a well-defined political process as well as a stable government structure. To make democratic values a reality, a nation must incorporate them into its political process, most importantly, in the form of free and fair elections, majority rule, freedom of expression, and the right of its citizens to peaceably assembly and protest at any time.

Free and Fair Elections

A democratic government can pride itself on free and fair elections held at an agreed interval, and frequently enough to make such elections relevant to policy choices. Elections are one of the most important devices for keeping officials and representatives accountable to the voters. The most important value attached to a country which prides itself as a democracy is that it encourages opposition political parties, which can exist, field candidates for all offices contested, and have a chance to replace those who currently hold public office. Thus, political competition and choice are crucial to the existence of democracy in a country that says it is democratic. Even though free and fair elections do not mean that everyone will have equal political influence, the value is that each citizen, whether the president or the plumber or carpenter on the street, has one—and only one—vote to cast at elections.

Majority and Plurality Rule

Governance according to the expressed preference of the majority, or majority rule, is the essence of democracy. The majority candidate or party is the one that receives more than half the votes and so wins the election and takes charge of the government until the next election. In practice, however, democracies often function by plurality rule. Here, the candidate or party with the most votes wins the election, even though the candidate or party may not have received more than half the votes because votes were divided among two or more candidates or parties.

Freedom of Expression

In constitutional democracies, free and fair elections depend on voters having access to facts, competing ideas, and the views of candidates. This means that competing, non-government-owned newspapers, radio stations, and television stations must be allowed to flourish. If the government controls what is said and how it is said, elections cannot be free and fair, and there is no democracy.

The Right to Assemble and Protest

In a democratic country, citizens must be free to organize for political purposes, assemble to discuss their grievances against the government in power, and be permitted to protest. The right to oppose government and to form opposition in order to seek reform and changes in attitude of the government should be permitted.

Democracy as a System of Interdependent Political Structures

Constitutional democracy is more than the values enumerated above. In discussing the last part, however, where the political structures that act as safeguards to the above values and processes, the constitutional democracy must set up structures that can grant and provide checks and balances to the system in order to curb governmental power. There must be a system of political parties, interest groups, media, and other institutions that intercede between the electorate and those who govern, reinforcing this constitutional structure and thus helping to maintain democratic stability. The Ghanaian constitutional structure provides for the separation of powers by the existence of the Parliament, the executive, and the judiciary, even though the executive somewhat controls Parliament because of the president's power to appoint ministers for his cabinet from Parliament. In terms of the checks and balances of the system, there is still a lot to be done by the agencies set up by the Office of the President to provide these. For instance, executive agencies like the Serious Fraud Office (EOCO), the Commission on Administrative Justice and Human Rights, and other offices are not currently effective because of their direct influence from the presidency. In Ghana, therefore, the constitutional arrangement does not clearly give each of these branches the constitutional means, the political independence, and the motives to check the powers of the other branches so that a relative balance of power between the branches endures and is judicially enforceable. We will discuss some of these limitations in chapter 7, when we deal more with the functions and responsibilities of the judiciary.

Ghana's Constitutional Framework

Ghana's constitutional framework is a set-up where all three branches of government have competing interests, which through their interactions require checks and balances. From the outside, the governed (i.e. the people) check the government through elections, petitions, protests, and amendments. The principle of separation of powers, in its traditional form, is a theory of governance that suggests that the legislature, the executive, and the judiciary, which are the three parts of a democracy, be made independent of each other in terms of functions and personnel. In order to prevent the abuse of power by any one of the branches of government, no one branch of the government must have absolute control or power over the other. Each body should have certain powers to serve as a check on the other branches. In his writings on government, the French philosopher, lawyer, and politician Baron de Montesquieu (1689–1755), gave vivid illustrations in his book *The Spirit of the Laws* (1748) about how a constitution should be framed void of despotism and the assurance of liberty and rights for citizens. Such principles, Montesquieu illustrated, must include the separation of the three branches of government, the legislature, the executive, and the judiciary, in order to function on their own without interference from the other two branches. The personnel who work for these branches must exist separately and distinctly. It is this limitation of the separation of powers that led to the incorporation of checks and balances. Checks and balances can be defined as *an arrangement for the functioning of government organs that allows a degree of checking on the powers of the others in their functions*. The interpretation of checks and balances can be demonstrated as follows: parliament enacts legislation, which the president must sign into law or veto. However, the Supreme Court can declare such laws passed (if they are challenged), or unconstitutional, even though it is the president who appoints the justices of the Supreme Court into offices (and promotes them). The president administers the laws, but parliament provides the money to run the government. Not only does each branch have some authority over the others, but also each is politically independent of the others.

In the Ghanaian context, it is impossible to practice such perfection since a rigid separation of powers would mean that no one of the three branches of government can ever participate in the functions of the other. The strict interpretation of this kind of checks and balances can slow down the government and bring the government machinery to a near standstill, for lack of consistency. The Ghanaian system, which is modelled after the British system, shows a union or a fusion of powers and exhibits a partial separation of powers. Like the British cabinet system, members of the Ghanaian president's cabinet or government are both members of the executive as well as the representatives of the constituencies that they serve as Members of Parliament. By this implication, they must be Members of Parliament first, before their selection or appointment as ministers, which is stipulated in the Constitution and even suggested 51 per cent as being members of Parliament who should be appointed into the cabinet. This is in contrast to the American system, where the ministers (secretaries) that are appointed are the *president's dream team*, and not members of Congress.

In Ghana, under delegated legislation, state ministers make laws, rules, and regulations for their ministries. They also issue orders with the force of law and even judge cases at administrative tribunals. As in Britain, the president of Ghana appoints the Chief Justice of the Supreme Court and approves of the appointments of High Court judges. The president also has the power of prerogative of mercy—that is, to pardon prisoners and forgive people for their crimes against the nation. The parliament approves the budget prepared by the executive and also approves treaties and major policies that the president enters into in the course of his duties as the chief executive of the country. The executive approves the salaries of the legislature, and on the other hand, all loans contracted on behalf of the country by the president must be brought to Parliament for approval. Does this not contradict and violate the theory of separation of powers / checks and balances? Indeed, modern constitutional democracies can be classified within the framework of three typologies, each of which consists of two contrasting categories of constitutional democratic political regimes: (1) *constitutional monarchy* and *constitutional republic*, (2) *parliamentary system* and *presidential system*, and (3) *majoritarian democracy* and *consensus democracy*. In the case of each typology, the American system of government falls into one category and the British system falls into the other category. Great Britain is a constitutional monarchy, while the USA is a constitutional republic. A parliamentary system operates in Britain, and a presidential system operates in the USA. The British governmental system is a majoritarian democracy, whereas the American system is a consensus democracy. What then is the Ghanaian system of government? The Ghanaian system is a combination of the British and the American systems, where we practice a constitutional republic but devoid of monarchy.

The Ghanaian political system is in contrast to the American system, where the American president's ministers (secretaries) that are appointed are the *president's dream team*, and not members of Congress. In Ghana, under delegated legislation, state ministers make laws, rules, and regulations for their ministries. They also issue orders with the force of law and even judge cases at administrative tribunals. As in Britain, the president of Ghana appoints the Chief Justice of the Supreme Court and approves of the appointments of High Court judges and justices. The president also has the power of prerogative of mercy—that is, to pardon prisoners and forgive people for their crimes against the nation. The Parliament approves the budget prepared by the executive and also approves treaties and major policies that the president enters into in the course of his duties as the chief executive of the country. The executive approves the salaries of the legislature, and on the other hand, all loans contracted on behalf of the country by the president are brought to Parliament for approval.

How does the American presidential system differ from the British parliamentary system?

Great Britain's *parliamentary system* and America's *presidential system* differ from each other, as regards eight political variables: (1) whether there is a constitutional *fusion* or *separation* of the legislative and executive powers of government, (2) the *nature and method of selection* of the top executive authority in the government, (3) whether the executive, institutionally, is *part of* or *separate* from the legislature, (4) whether the top executive office or organ is constitutionally *responsible to* or *independent of* the legislature, (5) whether the executive is the *agent of the legislature*, or the two institutions are *coordinate organs* of government, (6) the constitutional *relationship* between the positions of chief of state and head of government, (7) the possibility of *divided party control* of government, and (8) the nature of the *lines of political authority and responsibility*.

Under the British Constitution, there is a *fusion*, or *concentration*, of legislative and executive powers in the elective, lower house of Parliament, the House of Commons. The legislature (Parliament) and the top executive authority (the Cabinet) are not constitutionally separate and independent organs of government. The top executive authority, or Cabinet, emerges from and is a part of the legislature. The United States Constitution provides for an institutional *separation* between the legislature and the top executive authority. The legislature (Congress) and the chief executive (the president) are *separate and largely independent* branches or organs of government. Under the US Constitution, each of the separated branches or institutions of government has its own set of powers. However, the executive and the legislature also share certain powers. The British top executive organ of government is not elected separately from and independently of the legislature. The prime minister and most of the other members of the Cabinet are elected from local parliamentary election districts (like members of parliament in Ghana) as members of the House of Commons. *The majority in the House of Commons, in effect, chooses the Cabinet, mostly from its own membership in the Commons.* While a few Cabinet ministers are chosen from the House of Lords, they are chosen by the Commons majority from the ranks of its party members in the upper chamber.

Whenever a national election results in a new majority in the House of Commons, the monarch appoints as prime minister the clearly recognized top leader of the new majority party in the Commons. Then, the monarch, on the recommendation of the new prime minister, appoints the other members of the Cabinet. The monarch, in appointing the prime minister and other Cabinet ministers, does not exercise independent decision-making authority. As we have seen, conventions of the British Constitution dictate that the monarch always appoint as prime minister whoever is chief leader of the majority in the Commons and that the monarch always *follow* as well as receive the advice of the prime minister, including advice on Cabinet appointments. A person becomes prime minister by being the top leader of the political party that wins a majority of the seats in the House of Commons. A person becomes top leader of his party by being elected to that position by majority vote at a conference of the party MPs—a meeting of party members holding seats in Parliament. The newly elected top party leader, if his party has a clear majority in the Commons, is appointed prime minister by the Crown. The new prime minister advises the monarch on Cabinet appointments, after having conferred with the other leading members of his party in the Commons and having obtained their cooperation and support. Since the monarch must strictly observe the conventions of the Constitution, *the real choice of a prime minister and Cabinet is in the hands of the current majority in the Commons*. The functions performed by the monarch, including appointment of prime minister and Cabinet, are entirely ceremonial and symbolic. *The real power of government, including selection of the top executive authority, is in the hands of the Commons majority and its leadership elite.*

The formal ceremonial process of the monarch appointing a prime minister and automatically following the new prime minister's advice as regards appointment of the other Cabinet members, also occurs whenever the sitting Cabinet resigns, as a consequence of losing a vote of confidence in the Commons, and the prime minister does not advise the monarch to dissolve Parliament and call a new national election. When the Cabinet resigns under these circumstances, a conference of majority-party MPs is likely to elect a new top party leader, who, in strict accordance with constitutional convention, is then appointed prime minister by the monarch. Subsequently, the Crown, again in strict observance of convention, follows the new prime minister's advice regarding appointment of the other Cabinet ministers.

Under the United States Constitution, the Constitution provides for an independently elected national chief executive, the president. The president is not chosen by the national legislature. He is chosen in a national election which is separate from the congressional elections and which cannot be easily influenced and controlled by Congress. The president is not elected as a member of either house of Congress. He is elected as *chief executive* of the *whole nation*. The president is not elected as a member of the legislature from a single legislative election district by the voters of that district only. He is elected national chief executive by the voters throughout the entire nation, making their choice through the medium of the Electoral College.

In the government of the United Kingdom, there is no constitutional wall of separation between the legislature and the executive. The legislative and executive branches of government are united at the top—united in the form of the Cabinet, which is both the top executive authority in the government and the central leadership of the majority party in the legislature. The same group of people, the Cabinet, (1) are members of the legislature, (2) lead and manage the business of the legislature, (3) occupy the top offices in the executive branch, and (4) control and direct the executive branch. The top executive authority emerges from and continues to be part of the legislature. The prime minister and other Cabinet ministers simultaneously occupy the top executive offices in the government and hold seats in Parliament, speaking and voting on measures before their respective chambers.

Under the US Constitution, the president and other executive officers are not permitted to hold seats in the legislature at the same time they hold offices in the executive branch of the government. The Constitution requires a strict separation of the personnel of the executive and legislative organs of government. The same people may not simultaneously hold formal office in and exercise the authority of both branches of government. If a person occupying an executive or administrative office in the national government is elected to either chamber of Congress, he must resign the executive or administrative office before he can take his seat in the US Senate or House of Representatives. If an incumbent US senator or representative is elected president or vice president, he cannot be inaugurated as president or vice president until he resigns his seat in Congress. A member of either house of Congress cannot accept a presidential appointment as presidential staff officer, Cabinet-level department head, or other executive or administrative officer until he resigns his seat in the Senate or House of Representatives. Formally and legally, the president is not the majority party leader in the legislature. Under the Constitution, he is leader in neither of the two houses of Congress. On occasion, however, the president may function informally and unofficially as policy leader of one or both chambers of Congress in particular areas of national public policy.

In the United Kingdom, the tenure and prerogatives of the top executive authority, the Cabinet, are dependent upon the continuing support of a majority in the lower house of the legislature. To retain the position of top executive authority in the government, as well as the role of central leadership of the majority in the House of Commons, the Cabinet must continue to enjoy the confidence and support of the Commons majority. If the Cabinet loses a *vote of confidence* in the Commons, this means that the Cabinet no longer has the support of the majority in the Commons. Whenever this occurs, the sitting Cabinet has two alternative courses of action.

Alternative 1: The prime minister and other Cabinet ministers, acting jointly, resign their positions in the Cabinet (but not their seats in Parliament). This action is followed by a conference of MPs of the existing majority party—the party holding a majority of the seats in the Commons. The majority party conference elects a new chief party leader, who is then appointed prime minister by the monarch.

Alternative 2: The prime minister goes before the monarch and advises her to dissolve Parliament and call a new election, an action which the monarch, under the conventions of the Constitution, *must* take when advised to do so by the prime minister.

The second alternative course of action is very likely to be taken when the prime minister and other leading members of the Cabinet are convinced that

(1) currently, their leadership of the nation and its government has strong and widespread support among the voters throughout British society, as well as among the local constituency associations and rank-and-file members of their own party, and (2) if a national election is held within a relatively short period of time, their party, the current majority in the Commons, will have the better chance of winning the election, thereby retaining a majority of the seats in the Commons, remaining the governing party, and vindicating the policies of the existing prime minister and Cabinet. The Cabinet is *directly* responsible to the House of Commons. The Cabinet, including the prime minister, is collectively, or jointly, responsible to the Commons. The prime minister, *as prime minister*, is not *directly* responsible to the voters of the United Kingdom. The only voters to whom the prime minister is directly responsible, in a formal-legal sense, are the voters in the parliamentary election district where he was elected as a member of the House of Commons, and he is directly responsible to them *as a Member of Parliament (MP)*, not as prime minister.

The US Constitution provides America's national chief executive (the president) with a *separate and independent power base*, a power base separate from and independent of that of the national legislature. The tenure and prerogatives of the chief executive do not depend upon majority support in the legislature. Not only does the chief executive possess a separate set of powers granted by the Constitution, but he also serves during a fixed term of office. Under the Constitution, the president is elected to a four-year term and is eligible for re-election to a second four-year term. The president's tenure cannot be abruptly terminated by simple majority vote in either house of Congress or in both houses. The president cannot, against his will, be removed from office before the expiration of his term, except by the very difficult and cumbersome process of congressional impeachment, trial, and conviction, which requires a majority vote in the House of Representatives to pass the articles of impeachment and a two-thirds vote in the Senate to convict the president on the impeachment charges and remove him from office. The president, possessing a separate grant of constitutional authority and elected independently of Congress to a fixed term which the latter cannot easily cut short, is not primarily responsible to the legislature. Instead, he is directly and primarily responsible to the American voters. The executive is the agent of the legislature, or the executive and legislature as coordinate organs of government: The British Cabinet is the agent of the lower house of Parliament. The Cabinet is the executive and steering committee of the majority in the House of Commons.

In the US national government, the chief executive (the presidency) and the legislature are *equal* in rank. Neither organ of government is the agent of the other. Neither is subordinate to the other. The president and the Congress are *coordinate* organs of government—i.e. governmental organs equal in rank. The prime minister is the head of government in Great Britain. As chairman, or head, of the Cabinet, the prime minister leads and coordinates his colleagues in that body and, in terms of actual political power, is greatly elevated above them. The prime minister's position as head of the Cabinet, the top executive authority in the government, makes him the leading factor in shaping public policy as well as in supervising and directing the executive departments and agencies responsible for carrying out decisions on public policy. The prime minister, as chairman of the Cabinet and chief leader of the majority party in the House of Commons, is the link between Cabinet and monarch and the most important and most highly visible political leader in British society.

In Britain, the positions of head of government and chief of state are separate offices. While the prime minister is the effective head of government, the monarch is the chief of state and performs the purely symbolic and ceremonial functions of that office. In the US national government, the functions of chief of state and those of head of government are performed by a single popularly elected top executive officer, the president. The President is both ceremonial chief of state and effective head of government. The president is his own prime minister. There is no possibility of divided party control of the principal organs of British government, as long as the United Kingdom has a strong two-party system and the leading party has a clear and secure majority in the House of Commons. The party that has such a majority in and therefore controls the House of Commons, the more powerful chamber of the legislature, also controls the top executive organ, the Cabinet, which supervises and directs the executive departments and agencies. When one political party wins a majority of the seats in the Commons, that party's chosen top leader becomes prime minister. The other Cabinet ministers are selected mainly from among the leading members of the majority in the Commons, a few being chosen from among the members of the party in the House of Lords.

Unlike in Ghana-- in the United States of America, since the election of the president and the election of members of Congress are separate and independent elections, a political party's victory in the presidential election does not necessarily mean that the party will emerge victorious in the congressional elections. Conversely, the fact that a party has won a majority of the seats in one or both houses of Congress does not necessarily mean that it has also won the presidency. Therefore, control of the principal organs of the US national government may be divided between rival parties. The president, his staff officers, members of his Cabinet, and other high-ranking executive officers may be of one political party, while a majority in one or both chambers of Congress may be of the opposition party.

In the United Kingdom, voters elect the House of Commons, and the Commons, in effect, chooses the top executive authority, the Cabinet. The legislature derives its mandate to govern from and is directly responsible to the voters. The executive derives its mandate from and is directly responsible to the legislature. The result is a single, uninterrupted line of political authority running from the voters through the legislature to the executive as well as a single, uninterrupted line of political responsibility running from the executive through the legislature to the voters. The top executive authority, the president, is, in effect, elected by popular vote. Since the president is not chosen by Congress, the executive is not primarily responsible to the legislature. The chief executive, like the legislature, receives his mandate to govern from the voters and is thereby directly responsible to them. Moreover, the president, US Representatives, and US Senators are chosen by and responsible to different constituencies with varying and competing interests. The consequence is a multiple parliamentary and a presidential system, both evolving intermittently. In summary, most constitutional democracies in the world today are parliamentary systems. All modern constitutional monarchies are parliamentary systems. So are most modern constitutional republics. The governmental system of the USA, historically and traditionally, has been the one significant example of a presidential system. Since the establishment of the Fifth French Republic in 1958, France has had a system of government with both presidential and parliamentary features. However, the powers of the president under the 1958 De Gaulle Constitution were so overwhelming that the contemporary French government could be accurately referred to as a presidential system.

While Ghana's constitution and laws recognize and guarantee the rights of all persons, some segments of the population live in communities where culture and societal behaviour currently enable the perpetuation of harmful traditional practices. These include accusations of witchcraft leading to the exile of citizens, mostly older women, from their communities to so-called witch camps in Gambaga in the Northern region of Ghana. Other women are subjected to harmful widowhood rites, while some young girls continue to suffer the human rights violation of female genital mutilation. In responding to these challenges, USAID is providing support to Ghana's Ministry of Chieftaincy and Traditional Affairs and the National House of Chiefs to undertake field research and sensitization on harmful traditional practices with the goal of devising a strategy for eliminating such practices.

Government Accountability to Its People

Ghana pursues a decentralized government that can better provide the efficient, effective, and equitable local service delivery its citizens desire. However, lack of accountability continues to hamper the effectiveness of key government institutions. The government supports the Public Accounts Committee of Ghana's Parliament and broad groups of citizen associations to reduce corruption and strengthen incentives for elected officials and technical authorities to improve accountability. From 1957 when Ghana achieved its independence, Ghanaian elites have not been able to reconcile the British kind of representative democracy with its own indigenous political system for structural balance as has been done in Botswana and particularly in the American political system. The American political system is not like any other; it is unique in style and upon arrival in the North American continent, crafted their democracy, "the American way" or style and not according to what the British practiced when many left the United Kingdom for the Americas. In religiously following the British style of democracy and at times blending it with the American system, Ghana has disharmonized its political system, including an interruption of twenty-one years of gratuitous military rule through coups d'état and six years threatening one-party regime by the Convention People's Party (CPP) from independence until their overthrow in 1966. Daniel T. Osabu-Kle, a political scientist at Canada's Carleton University, elucidates in 'Compatible Cultural Democracy: The Key to Development in Africa' that 'instead of adapting the deeply embedded indigenous political cultures to achieve the appropriate political conditions, the [new African] nations, like Ghana, adopted alien democratic practices, which served to undermine the attainment of the political prerequisites for genuine decolonization. According to Osabu-Kle, such has divided the elites, stifled economic development and social cohesion, as well as, delayed the development and growth of most of these countries. In the midst of Ghanaian elites' inability to rethink a Ghanaian democracy drawn from within Ghanaian indigenous values, Ghana's democratic growth has suffered over the years. In its uncertainty, Ghana has created four constitutions since 1957 until now, and out of the four, three have been suspended; the 1956 constitution was suspended in February 1966, the 1969 constitution was suspended on 13 January 1972, the 1979 constitution was suspended on the hills of what can be described as the last coup d'état of Ghana on 31 December 1981—to usher in the constitution of 1992. In this regard, Ghana has seen painful meandering democratic administrations in the years 1957 until 1966, 1969 until 1972, 1979 until 1981, and 1993 to the present. Indeed, from 1958 until 1964, Ghana can be described as practicing a limited democracy under President Kwame Nkrumah, where the country was ruled intermittently as a one-party state.

The shortage of reasonable Ghanaian indigenous values in the British neo-liberal system occasionally created political volcanoes. There was powerful opposition to the ruling CPP not only from traditional chiefs, who had a running battle with the CPP over freedom issues, and big farmers but also the Ghana Congress Party that merged with other opposition parties to form the big United Party (UP[nowNPP]). Nkrumah escaped two assassination attempts; some of CPP's development projects were boomed to destruction, political bigwigs like J. B. Danquah, a leading figure of the UGCC, were jailed by the CPP. In 1959, Kofi Busia, as leader of the UP, felt his life was threatened and fled Ghana to England. With politics gone wild and violence swelling, the CPP enacted the much controversial detention orders from parliament, which allowed president Kwame Nkrumah to place in prison, his political enemies. In those days, the Nsawam prison was the home of most of these political enemies.

Ghana, as part of the universal democratic movement, has been evolving from direct democracy to representative and responsible democracy. However, the lack of mixture of Ghanaian indigenous values with the British democratic ideals hit at the contending issue of mass democracy, which Axworthy describes as the 'third milestone in democracy's evolution'. As Axworthy would ask, if the people were to choose their representative, who made up the people, in a piece published in the Toronto-based *National Post* that raised concerns about lower voter turnout. But in the various democratic practices, different democracies will answer Axworthy's question differently. In Ghana, part of answering Axworthy's question, as Osabu-Kle argues, is by 'modifying indigenous democracy', as part of the development process that will see the transfer of the traditional ideological symbol (or myth) of unity to the state from the coalition of the fifty-six ethnic groups that form the Ghana nation-state. Lack of the indigenous values has seen Ghana lose its mass in its democracy project and affected confidence-building measures as a progress issue. For 'before even the British came into contact with the Ghanaian people, Ghanaians were a developed people, having their own institutions, their own ideas of government' (quoted from Osabu-Kle in J. E. Casely Hayford), and Gold Coast (now Ghana) and nationalist. But there are attempts to correct this anomaly as Ghanaians become increasing convinced that the future progress rests with deepening democracy. From Flight Lieutenant Jerry John Rawlings to President John Agyekum Kufuor as presidents, democratic decentralization, as a mixture of the traditional with the Western neo-liberal, has been on the ascendancy. However, there have been calls by NPP's flag bearer Nana Akufo-Addo, who once proposed an Institute of Chieftaincy as a perfect laboratory to blend Ghanaian traditional values with that of the Western neo-liberal ideals for Ghana's democratic fruition. If his calls are anything to stand by, then this will be part of the calls to reform Ghana's democratic system and rebalance the power structures from traditional institutions to those at the national level. In view then of Axworthy's work on the modification of democracy, democracy can be said to be a work in progress as it evolves over time.

Conclusion

Ghana operates under a constitutional democracy. In the Ghanaian system of governance, the constitution lays out the basic rules of how politicians are to act to accomplish their different agendas. *Politics* is a broad term that can be used to describe what happens between these politicians in pursuit of their goals. *Government* is another broad term that encompasses the many different institutions enumerated by the constitution in which the politicians function. Political science studies the interaction among politics, politicians, the government, and within the Ghanaian context, our evolving constitutional democracy. The form of democracy practiced in Ghana is a representative democracy or republic. The politicians in parliament are elected from the 275 constituencies around the country. Representative democracy differs from direct democracy in the level of citizen participation. Several conditions can allow democratic government to form and consolidate. Among these conditions are equal access to the educational, economic, social, and ideological opportunities that are most important to the future progression of a country. These conditions further democratic values, such as a belief in personal liberty, respect for the individual, equality of opportunity, and popular consent. Our representative democracy functions through political structures including courts, legislature (parliament), the presidency, administrative agencies (civil service), and the principle of limited government.

Article 2—Federalist Papers

The Federalist papers are essays written in 1787 by James Madison, John Jay, and Alexander Hamilton under the pen name of Publius. Their purpose was to advocate the ratification of the new constitution by the states. They are an authoritative but unofficial explanation of American government by those who created it.

Madison wrote Federalist 10 to counter the argument that democracies inevitably dissolve into turmoil and disorder caused by factions which ignore the national interest in favour of their own interests. The consensus of late nineteenth-century political thought was that a monarchy was needed to restrain the destructive tendency of factions. Today, the opponents of democracy make similar arguments on behalf of undemocratic forms of government—that it is a number of citizens, either a minority or a majority, that are united by a common impulse or passion adverse to the rights of other citizens or the best interests of the community.

According to James Madison, factions are 'sown in the nature of man'. People have different opinions about religion, government, and political leaders. The most common cause of faction is the 'various and unequal distribution of property. Those who hold and those who are without property have ever formed distinct interests in society.' The most powerful faction will control the government and make decisions based not on the common good but to benefit itself. Both other groups and the common good will suffer. In a pure democracy, the people assemble and administer the government in person. Pure democracy can only exist in a small geographical area. Pure democracies inevitably fall victim to the mischief of faction. Pure democracies fail because they are unable to protect individual liberty and the rights of property.

Would Removing the Causes of Faction Solve the Problems?

No. Destroying the liberty that allows faction to develop is a cure worse than the disease. Giving everyone the same opinion is impractical. If a faction is less than a majority, then rely on majority rule to control it. If a faction is in the majority, then rely on the type of political system to control it. The cure to the problem of factions is a large republic.

Is a Republic Better Than a Pure Democracy?

In a republic, the citizens elect representatives to make policy decisions and administer the government on their behalf. A republic can be established in a larger country than can a pure democracy, because of its representative nature. A large republic provides a bigger candidate pool from which to select fit leaders. A large electorate is less likely to select undesirable leaders than is a small electorate. A larger territory will include a greater diversity of interests than will a smaller territory. A majority faction is therefore unlikely to emerge in a large territory. Madison wrote Federalist paper 10 to defend the Constitution against the charge that a faction would soon gain control, substituting its own interest for the national interest. The antidote to the problem of faction, Madison declared, is a large republic with a multiplicity of interests, making it unlikely that a majority faction will form.

Major Concepts

Direct democracy	Political power	Representative democracy
Constitutional framework	Checks and balances	Amendments
President's dream team	Equality of opportunity	Limited government

Works Cited / Further Readings

Adair, Douglass (1998), 'The Tenth Federalist Revisited' and '"That Politics May Be Reduced to a Science": David Hume, James Madison and the Tenth Federalist', in *Fame and the Founding Fathers* (Indianapolis: Liberty Fund).

Ackerman, Bruce and Fishkin, James S. (2004), *Deliberation Day* (Yale University Press).

Arato, Andrew (1995), 'Forms of Constitution Making and Theories of Democracy', *Cardozo Law Review* 17: 191–231.

Arjomand, Said Amir (2003), 'Law, Political Reconstruction and Constitutional Politics', *International Sociology* 18 (1): 7–32.

Bernstein, Richard B. (1987), *Are We to Be a Nation?* (Cambridge, MA: Harvard University Press).

Butler, D. and Ranney, A. (1994) (eds.), *Referendums Around the World*.

Callenbach, E. and Phillips, M. (1985), *A Citizen Legislature* (Berkeley, CA: Banyan Tree Books and Bodega, CA: Clear Glass).

Carey, Christopher (2000), *Democracy in Classical Athens* (Bristol Classical Press), 200.

'Constitutional Law—Referendum of Amendment to Federal Constitution', *The Virginia Law Register* 5, No. 6 (Oct. 1919): 468–470.

Elster Jon (1997), 'Ways of Constitution-making', in A. Hadenius (ed.) *Democracy's Victory and Crisis*, 123-

—— (2000a), 'Arguing and Bargaining in Two Constituent Assemblies', University of Pennsylvania *Journal of Constitutional Law* 2: 345–421.

—— (2000b), *Ulysses Unbound: Studies in Rationality, Recommitment, and Constraints* (New York: Cambridge University Press).

Elster, Jon (1998) (ed., *Deliberative Democracy*, part of Cambridge Studies in the Theory of Democracy, edited by A. Przeworski (Cambridge University Press).

Ghai, Y. (2001), 'Human Rights and Social Development: Toward Democratization and Social Justice', United Nations Research Institute for Social Development.

Hamilton, Alexander, Madison, James, and Jay, John (1961), *The Federalist*, edited by Jacob E. Cooke (Middletown, Conn.: Wesleyan University Press), 1982 edition.

Huntington, Samuel (1968), *Political Order in Changing Societies* (New Haven: Yale University Press).

Madison, James (1787), 'The Union as a safeguard against domestic faction and insurrection', New York, 23 Nov. 1787.

Magleby, David B. (1984), *Direct Legislation* (Johns Hopkins University Press).

Matsusaka, John G. (2004), *Many or the Few* (University of Chicago Press).

McCombs, M. and Reynolds, A. (1999) (eds.), *The Poll with a Human Face* (Lawrence Erlbaum Associates).

McGann, E. and Morris, D. (2007), *Outrage* (Harper Collins).

McGuire, R. Ohsfeldt, R. (1989b), 'Public Choice Analysis and the Ratification of the Constitution', in B. Grofman and D. Wittman (eds.), *The Federalist Papers and the New Institutionalism* (New York: Agathon), 175–204.

McLuhan, M., Fiore, Q., and Agel, J. (1967), *The Medium Is the Massage* (Gingko Press).

Merida, Kevin (1994), 'Americans Want a Direct Say in Political Decision-Making, Pollsters Find', *Washington Post*, 20 Apr. 1994, p. a.19.

Morgan, Edmund S. (1986), 'Safety in Numbers: Madison, Hume, and the Tenth "Federalist"', *Huntington Library Quarterly*, 49 (2): 95–112 in JSTOR.

Meyer, J. W. et al. (1987), *Institutional Structure: Constituting State, Society and the Individual* (Newbury Park, CA: Sage).

Therborn, Goran (1977), 'The Rule of Capital and the Rise of Democracy', *New Left Review*, 1/103 (May/June).

Woolsey, Lester H. (1910), 'A Comparative Study of the South African Constitution', *American Journal of International Law*, 4 (1): 1–82.

Wyler, Marcus (1949), 'The Development of the Brazilian Constitution (1891–1946)', *Journal of Comparative Legislation and International Law*, 31 (3/4): 53–60.

Ysaguire, Albert J. (1981), 'Belize', in A. P. Blaustein and G. H. Flanz (eds.), *Constitutions of the Countries of the World* (Dobbs Ferry, NY: Oceana Publications, Inc.).

Zartman, I. William (1971), 'Morocco', in A. P. Blaustein and G. H. Flanz (eds.), *Constitutions of the Countries of the World* (Dobbs Ferry, NY: Oceana Publications, Inc.).

Chapter 3

THE POLITICAL PROCESS

GOVERNMENTS AND GOVERNING

In Ghana, hardly a day passes without government playing a role in the day-to-day lives of its citizenry. Many anthropologists and some political scientists who specialize in studying societies such as the Inuit (Eskimo) of Alaska report that most of these societies are run more or less like mini governments. In Ghana, the Konkomba communities also operate like the Inuit of Alaska in terms of their leadership. The political system of the Inuit societies is like the Konkombas in Ghana and in respect of the Inuit, among the simplest known in North America. The Inuit (Eskimos) are scattered beginning from the Bering Straits to Greenland in smaller communities, each numbering around a hundred inhabitants, with most members of each community related by blood or marriage. There are only two specialized roles that are politically significant: those of the *shaman* and the *headman*. Both have mixed roles. The shaman is the religious leader, and in the Inuit custom the shaman is never a woman and can punish those who violate taboos of the Eskimos. In extreme cases, the shaman can even order an offender exiled, which in the Arctic area (with snow at its peak) may mean death. Like the Konkombas in Ghana, the headman is a task leader who is influential in making decisions about hunting, warfare, or the selection of places for settlement. However, if the other members of the community disagree with his recommendations, then he has no authority or power to impose his choices. Violations of order are handled mostly through fist fights and song duels or, in extreme cases, through family feuds. An individual who threatens the community by repeated acts of violence, murder, or theft may be dealt with by an executioner, who assumes the responsibility for the execution with the approval of the entire community.

Industrializing Communities

For the reader of this book, we are not in communities like those of the Inuit (the Eskimos). We live in nations such as those found in Africa, North and South America, Asia, and what we often refer to as the world. For those in what is known as industrialized, industrializing, this reference is made because the state of their economies is based on division of labour, mass production, and the heavy use of machines. Presumably, it is also because these societies are farther up some historical ladder of progress, though some political scientists reject both the label and its underlying point of view. The role of government is very different in these communities. Most of us who have had the opportunity to live in them have witnessed births and deaths in government-regulated hospitals and delivered by government-licensed physicians. Government protects its citizens against abuse by parents. Whether we like it or not, government regulates when and how the children go to school until the age of eighteen. We marry and divorce according to rules made by government. We take and leave jobs, set up businesses, engage in professions, buy and sell property, and retire according to rules set down by the government. Every year, we are compelled to pay taxes to government. We are recruited into the armed services to defend the government and to protect society from bad gangs, or to defend the country from external attacks. These relationships can go on and on because there is no escape from government. In Ghana, government plays a minor role in the lives of just about everyone who lives in it, but not exactly like in other advanced, industrialized, or industrializing societies in the world. Since this book is an introductory text in political science, we cannot possibly give equal attention to all kinds of societies and governments around the world, but can only concentrate mainly on the political and governmental institutions and processes of the society in which we live and through which we interact with government on a daily basis.

What Is Government?

Many of us are born into a family, and our parents tell us that we must drink our milk, brush our teeth in the morning, keep our rooms tidy at all times, and refrain from drawing on the walls in our rooms. We are placed into school, and teachers tell us that we have to attend classes, pass examinations, and say no to bad habits. We join a religious institution, as in the church, and our religious leaders will tell us the same things: attend services regularly, say your prayers, and live according to prescribed moral principles. We finally get jobs, and our bosses will tell us the same things: get to work on time, do your work, and remain at your desk until 5 p.m. And so it goes, all the days of our lives. Furthermore, each organization backs up its rules with sanctions, which are penalties that a group can impose on those who break its rules. Parents can spank us and ground us (restrict our movements) over a period of time; teachers can keep us after school, college professors can fail us, deans and presidents can throw us out of school, religious organizations can expel us from membership, bosses can fire us from work, and so on. The older we grow, however, the more we become aware of the rules and sanctions of another organization that claims even greater authority over us: the government.

Government Defined

The term *government* is often used in two related but distinct senses. Sometimes, it refers to a particular collection of people, each with individual idiosyncrasies, faults, and virtues, who perform certain functions in a particular society at a particular time. Sometimes, it refers to a particular set of institutions; that is, a series of accepted and regular procedures for performing those functions, procedures that persist over time, regardless of who happens to be performing them. Both senses are incorporated in the definition of government we will use in this book. *Government* is *the body of people and institutions that make and enforce laws for a society.* Government is undoubtedly one of humanity's oldest and most nearly universal institutions. Some political philosophers have speculated that the absence of government gives rise to what is known as a state of *anarchy*, which is *a society with no government.* Humanity's desire for a government has by no means led all people at all times and in all societies to establish the same kind of government. The striking fact about governments, whether they are past or present, is that they have always varied in complexity, all the way from the simple shaman-headman systems of the Inuit (Eskimo) to the highly complex system found in industrializing nations. Governments vary in the treatment of their people, all the way from the mass executions and brutality of General Idi Amin's days in Uganda to the mild and permissive welfare state of the Netherlands or the kingdom of Brunei. Evidently, then, different societies require different kinds of governments to satisfy their special needs. Yet, no matter how much some governments may differ from others, they all share certain characteristics that make them different from all other forms of human organizations.

Social Organizations

In advanced or industrializing societies, governments differ significantly from all other social organizations in a number of ways; among them are the following:

Involuntary Membership

In social organizations other than government, membership is voluntary; that is, people become members of an organization and place themselves under its rules only by conscious choice. One does not automatically become a Jehovah's Witness at birth because one's parents are Muslims or a Jehovah's Witness because one is Muslim, born in a Muslim or a Jehovah's Witness hospital. One officially joins an organization by going through certain formalities such as baptism and confirmation. Membership in a nation, however, is largely involuntary; that is, most people initially become citizens of a nation and subject to its rules without any deliberate choice or conscious act. Most times, all nations officially regard as citizens either all persons born in their territories or all children born of their citizens, or some combination of the two. Most nations also have procedures for non-citizens to acquire citizenship (a process generally called naturalization) and/or citizens to renounce it, but initial membership in a nation is involuntary.

Comprehensive Authority

Comprehensive authority comprises rules made by any social organization other than government that are intended to apply to members of that organization. For example, when the Ghana Telecom University College rules that all students must take a course in Ghanaian culture or business ethics before graduation, no one expects this rule to apply to students of the University of Ghana, Legon, or Central University College in Accra. On the other hand, the rules of the government of Ghana apply, and are intended to apply, to all members of the Ghanaian society. When Parliament approves new energy tariffs or new customs duties, every Ghanaian understands that it means precisely that such approval is obtained along with the consent of the president and the Supreme Court. The understanding is translated to mean that the approval commands governmental authority; that is, *the acknowledged power to make binding decisions and issue obligatory commands.*

Authoritative Rules

Authoritative rules are rules that are generally recognized; that is, they are generally considered to be more binding upon all members of a society than the rules of all other organizations. In any conflict between the laws of government and the rules of private organizations, there is general agreement that government laws should prevail. For instance, if a religious sect decrees human sacrifice as part of this ritual but such is forbidden by the government, most members of the society will regard the government's prohibition as more binding than the religious sect's ritual requirement. If the local building code stipulates that brick walls must be at least be twelve inches thick and local engineers think that eight inches is enough, most of the town's citizens, including most of its engineers, will obey the twelve-inch requirement, however misguided they may think it is. Therefore, in every democratic process, governments have the power to enforce rules, laws, and regulations over their people.

Who Has Overwhelming Force?

Not all government rules are obeyed by all citizens of a country; after all, every human organization has to deal with people who disobey its rules, and government is no exception. All organizations impose sanctions on rule breakers, but government differs from other organizations in the kind of sanctions it is authorized to impose. Private organizations are generally authorized to withhold certain privileges, impose fines, and require certain penances. Their ultimate legitimate weapon, however, is expulsion. If a member of a labour union or a member of a religious organization refuses to pay the union's dues or worship as the organization prescribes, the most extreme penalty either organization can impose is to expel the delinquent from membership.

Government can impose all those sanctions as well, but it can also impose two additional sanctions forbidden to private organizations. It can send lawbreakers to confinement (that is, to prison) and it can also take lives (exact the death penalty) of offenders in certain criminal acts. It is important to recognize that governments are not the only organizations that in fact impose life-and-death sanctions. Gangsters and drug dealers sometimes kill people who violate their rules, and terrorists sometimes kidnap airline passengers and kill patrons of airports and restaurants.

The point of distinction is that government alone has the *legitimate* power to execute criminals or convicted criminals, i.e. *rule breakers*. The concept of *legitimacy* is crucial here, and it means the general belief of the member of a society that the government's power to make and enforce rules is proper, lawful, and entitled to obedience. In every political system, most people believe that if any agency must rightfully use the ultimate sanction of execution, then government should be the only entity. Any private organization or person that uses such power is committing murder. Government differs from other social organizations, not because it occasionally uses force to enforce its rules, but because it can muster maximum force. The rocks and pistols that private organizations can use are feeble indeed compared with the armed police and military force available to governments.

Basic Duties of Government

Government authorities in most nations around the world believe that the basic duty of any government, whether democratic or authoritarian, is to ensure the nation's survival. That survival involves two fundamental tasks: defending the country against external enemies, and keeping internal conflicts from becoming so bitter that they lead to secession and civil war. To accomplish the second task, the government must satisfy the needs that made the people decide to accept a government in the first place. Government must comb through the many political demands constantly besieging it, blend demands into public policies, and enforce those policies in such a way that no group of citizens feels compelled to disobey or attempt to destroy the country. National survival is thus the ultimate test of any government. There is no universal or infallible method for accomplishing this basic task of government, nor a surest way to prevent civil wars or win foreign wars. Throughout this book, we will review the wide range of policies usually pursued by modern governments in their quest to be good guardians of their citizens. Additionally, we note that all governments rely upon combinations, varying in emphasis from time to time and from government to government, of a few basic tools, which are discussed below.

Interest Aggregation—The term *interest aggregation* means the process of combining the demands of different interest groups into public policies. Essentially, the aggregating process consists of adjusting and combining demands so that they do not cancel each other out and that each major group is reasonably happy with what it gets. Some political demands inevitably conflict with others, and there is no way a government can fully satisfy each and every demand made on it. Governments can hope to deal adequately with the demands only if the demands are aggregated in some way. However, much aggregation of interest occurs outside formal government, in discussions among individuals and in negotiations and deals within and among pressure groups and political parties. Considerable aggregation also takes place in the legislative, executive, and administrative agencies of government. However, in whatever way that interest aggregation is achieved, it is necessary for any political system as a vital tool of government.

Interest Articulation—In every society, the population is divided into many groups distinct from one another in one or more significant respects. Among other things, a society can be divided into gender, racial, and ethnic identity; education; occupation; and income. Just about every one of those groups and the people who compose them have a political interest—a concept that plays a leading role in political analysis. We define a *political interest* as *the stake of a person or group in government policy, something of value to be gained or lost by what government does or does not do.* The important thing to note here is that politics boils down to a great many interest groups making demands (articulating interests) that the government performs an act to assist them or refrains from an act that hurts them. The first challenge to President John Mahama's administration was in March 2013, in which a strike action by members of GNAT, NAGRAT, and TEWU through an interest articulation for payment of their car maintenance allowance was intercepted by the president himself, which eventually aborted the ill intentions of the strikers. The essence of governing is responding to these demands in one way or another. If, for example, the Ghana government does not know what demands Ghanaians are making, it can hardly deal effectively with those demands. If government is dimly aware of the demands but unaware of their variety or intensity, it is not likely to deal very well with the demands. If government does not cope effectively with the most urgent and widely supported demands, it risks anger, alienation, and perhaps even rebellion from the groups it so ignores. Consequently, governments need effective methods for the articulation of interests. *Interest articulation*, as political scientists use the term, means *the process of forming and expressing demands by political interest groups and transiting the demands to government authorities.* Later in the book, we will look at some of the principal devices by which interests are articulated in modern nations, such as propaganda, protest, public opinion polls, lobbying, and campaigns and elections. But it suffices here to note that every political system needs an effective way for the authorities to know and understand its citizens' strongly felt political demands from time to time.

Coercion and Compromise

The Ghanaian government, like every government in the world, whether democratic or authoritarian, perpetually faces the key question of how to achieve acceptance of its policies and compliance with its laws. One obvious and important answer, of course, is government *coercion*, which is *the threat or imposition of force and other sanctions to get compliance.* A government can apply many kinds and forms of sanctions to lawbreakers: economic (fines), physical, violent, non-violent, and even psychological. Governments can also deny citizens license to engage in businesses or professions, take away the right to vote and hold public office, withdraw financial aid, revoke citizenship, deport, and exile citizens. Of course, governments can fine, imprison, brainwash, torture, and even kill. As noted earlier, government's legitimate monopoly of the death penalty is a prime difference between it and all other social organizations.

Governments generally use coercion to achieve one or both of two main objectives: (a) to make an example that will convince potential lawbreakers that the consequence of breaking the law will be worse than any likely gains, and (b) to take out of circulation any person who, undeterred by those threats, breaks the law anyway. No doubt an element of revenge often exists as well, but the principal justification for government coercion is deterrence. However, no government can rely on coercion alone. It is plainly impossible to imprison massive numbers of citizens. Hence, large-scale and determined resistance to a law simply cannot be overcome by coercion alone. A policy that receives only sullen, foot-dragging, minimal compliance is not likely to be very effective. Therefore, willing compliance by many people is necessary for any policy to be successful, and enthusiastic popular support can make up for a good many technical deficiencies in any policy. Any government, however brutal and ruthless it is prepared to be, depends upon this kind of voluntary compliance for most of its policies most of the time.

So, how do governments obtain voluntary compliance? There are many ways, but to some degree, all are variations on the basic theme of compromise. Conflicting interests and incompatible demands are inevitable, and so for every political 'winner', there is bound to be a 'loser'. No government can escape this hard fact of life, but it can try to shape the content and impact of each policy so that the 'losers' will feel that continuing to live under the existing regime, though perhaps far from ideal, is at least bearable. A government can best keep its competing interest groups sufficiently satisfied not to rebel by giving each group something of what it wants. Thus, no group experiences total 'defeat' or the despairing feeling that the whole system is rigged against it so that its wishes and needs will never receive serious consideration. To do that, the government must deny total victory to the 'winners' by watering down the maximum demands of all clashing interests. The resulting policies are likely to contain some logically inconsistent provisions and may even appear ridiculous when judged by the rules of logic. However, every government is more concerned with preserving its society than with being logically consistent, and if a policy helps to achieve such a government's basic tool, no one will care much about its lack of neatness or logical symmetry.

Nationalism and the Birth and Death of Nations

In this world, every person lives under the authority of a government at several different levels—villages, towns, cities, regions, and the like—but the most important level is the national level. The world's population is divided among independent and sovereign nations, each of which has complete legal authority within its particular territory and none of which acknowledges a government legally superior to its own. So what are nations like? How do they begin? How do they fold up?

Nature of Nations

Nations, by nature, can be grouped into the dates they were accorded the legal status of nationhood. For example, from January 1995, there were about 185 political units generally called nations. The number included an increase of at least 19 others after 1990, following the break-up of the Soviet Union and Yugoslavia. There are, of course, great differences among those nations on many dimensions: population size, natural resources endowment, economic productivity, military power, and many other attributes.

Definite Population

Each nation regards certain people as its citizens and all others are alien to that country. A *citizen* is *a person who has the legal status of being a full member of a particular nation.* This status includes being loyal to that nation above all others, receiving its protection, and enjoying the right to participate in its political process. By the same token, each nation regards any non-citizen as an *alien*; that is, *a person who is neither a citizen nor a national of the nation in which he or she is present.*

Government: Unitary and Federal

Each nation has an officially designated set of persons and institutions authorized to make and enforce laws for all people within its territory. The governing systems are usually classified as one of two types, according to how their powers are distributed between national and regional levels (such as regions, municipalities, and districts).

A *federal government* is a setting in which power is formally divided between the national government and certain regional governments, each of which is legally supreme in its own sphere. The constitutions of those nations usually specify the matters over which the national governments and the regional governments have authority and stipulate that neither level is subordinate to the other. The United States is the oldest example of a federal setting, in this regard. Other federations include countries like Germany, Switzerland, Nigeria, Canada, and Australia. Some scholars contend that other nations—for example, Mexico, India, and Austria—should also be included and predict that the independent but associated nations of the European Community will ultimately form a federation in the near future if they continue to aggregate their fiscal policies.

A *unitary government* is one in which the national government is legally supreme over regional and local governments. The powers that such subnational governments have are granted by the national government, and such legal authority can be taken away by the national government if it wishes. Most of the world's governments are of this type, and include such nations as Japan, Sweden, France, Britain, and Ghana, among others.

Other Forms of Government

Communism is a system of government in which each commune or community is virtually an independent state. It is found in a state where people tend to show and demonstrate strong ties or allegiance to their ethnic or tribal group rather than act as citizens of a state. Under such a system, property is collectively owned and used.

Communism is the extreme of socialism. It is a political and economic theory that states that all economic and social activities should be owned by the government or the state and not by private individuals. Communism is a system whereby the social organization of all economic and social activities is controlled by a totalitarian state dominated by a single political party. The founder of communism is Karl Marx. Communism shares several characteristics with fascism and Nazism; all three systems are totalitarian dictatorships.

Fascism is a totalitarian system of government led by a dictator and emphasizes aggressive nationalism with a blend of racism. It is a system of forced governance, exhibited by the ruler to his people, which does not tolerate political opposition. Examples of this type of political regime occurred during the time of Benito Mussolini of Italy, and in South Africa before 1994, called the apartheid system of government.

Nazism is a system of political and economic principles held and put into practice by the Nationalist Socialist Party in Germany under the rule of Adolf Hitler. The system is totalitarian in nature, where the control of all industries is under the state. There is also a general feeling that the Germans (being the predominant group) are racially superior and that the *Fuhrer* or *leader* of the Nazis was the ultimate leader. There are still remnants of Nazism in Germany today, where young people and some adults maintain shaven heads to symbolize their continued existence. Such groups are called neo-Nazis.

Monarchy is a system of government in which the control and management of the country is in the hands of a king or a queen. In a monarchical government, succession to the throne is only by inheritance and the monarch reigns until he/she dies. The United Kingdom (Britain) practices a constitutional monarchy whereby the queen has only advisory and ceremonial responsibilities, but is not directly in charge of the day-to-day administration of the country.

Feudalism is a social, economic, and political system that is based on land ownership, where the land is owned by the monarch or the lord within his domain and his tenants. This system in medieval Europe placed the class of tenants, vassals, and serfs at the bottom.

Oligarchy is a form of government in which a few people rule in their own interest or on behalf of their class.

Statocracy is a form of government in which political power is vested in the army or military class.

Aristocracy is a form of government in the hands of a few privileged, noble, or most able men. It is considered a government by the highest social order or class in that country.

Dictatorship is a government by one person or a small clique of people who are accountable to nobody but themselves. An example of dictatorships is during military regimes. The regime of General Idi Amin in Uganda was a notable example of a dictatorship.

Nationalism

Most nations in this world are rooted in what is termed *nationalism*, which refers to people's psychological attachment to a particular normality, based upon a common history, common language and literature, common culture, common norms, and a desire for political independence. For many of the world's inhabitants, especially those in the long-established nations, nationalism is the highest allegiance. Many people are more loyal to their nations than to their religions, their social classes, their races, and even their families. The most striking evidence of nationalism's power over human thought and behaviour is the fact that modern-day wars, the supreme test of people's loyalties, are fought mainly among nations, and not among races or religious institutions or social classes, as they once were. When the United States fought against Germany, US workers, capitalists, Roman Catholics, and Lutherans killed and were killed by German workers, capitalists, Roman Catholics, and Lutherans. Some political analysts feel that nationalism and national sovereignty are old-fashioned and dangerous principles in a modern, highly interdependent world in which a number of nations have nuclear weapons. Be that as it may, nationalism has never been stronger than it is right now. For example, of the over 185 generally recognized nations today, no fewer than 138—nearly three-quarters—have achieved their independence since the end of World War II in 1945. Indeed, 62 per cent, or around 115, of these countries have come into existence since 1960. Since 1960, it is in Africa that new nations have been created—a total of about 44 out of the 48 nations have since gone through such phenomena.

Formal Independence

Every nation has sovereignty, which is the full and exclusive legal power to make and enforce laws for a particular people in a particular territory. This means that each nation, large or small, strong or weak, has supreme legal authority over its own affairs and in that respect is fully equal to every other nation. Note that this is a purely legal principle in international law known as the *principle of the sovereign equality of nations*. However, some nations are more subject to influence by foreign nations than are others. For example, the USA cannot be equated to Iraq, Grenada, and other countries that were invaded and their sovereignties infringed upon.

Conclusion

Although many world governments claim to act in the best interests of the people they govern, only democracies actually represent the will of the people. Elections give voice and agency to every person in the political community and allow all interested citizens to directly engage in politics and participate in the discussion of how the society will be ruled. Elections are therefore the most fundamental component of democracies. Not all elections are the same. In fact, national, regional, and local governments employ a variety of voting systems to meet their constituents' needs. Also important is the question of which people in the community are allowed to vote. Elections can serve different purposes too, for that matter. Some elections determine who will lead the community, whereas other elections ask voters to express their opinions on specific laws, taxes, and other issues. For these reasons, understanding elections and voting systems is essential to understanding democratic systems of government.

Article 3—The Living Constitution

The constitution of Ghana grants and limits powers. In Ghana, those who were invited to write the constitution are not always ordinary people. The writers of the constitution were highly educated men, unlike those of the United States, where ordinary men, such as farmers, fishermen, etc., were invited to assist in writing the constitution of the United States of America. The framers of any constitution are always concerned with creating a national government strong enough to solve national problems. Thus, they give the national government substantial grants of power, but these grants are made with such narrow strokes that it becomes impossible for the constitutional system to remain flexible and adapt to changing conditions. Like the constitution of the United States of America, every good constitution must ensure a *judicial review*.

A *judicial review* is the power of the courts to strike down acts of parliament, the executive branch, and the state as unconstitutional. It is one of the unique features a good constitution must impose unto itself as a check. Although the Ghanaian government system has its roots in British traditions, our separation of powers and checks-and-balances systems differ sharply from the British system of concentrated power.

Although adaptable, a living constitution itself needs to be altered from time to time, and the document provides a procedure for its own amendment. An amendment must be both proposed and ratified: proposed by either two-thirds vote in parliament or by a national convention called by the president, ratified either by the legislatures and voted by three-fourths of the parliamentarians.

Major Concepts

Federalism	Checks and balances	Communism	Coercion
Judicial review	Sovereignty	Amendment	Nationalism
Alien	Apartheid	Stratocracy	Oligarchy
Monarchy	Neo-Nazi	Compromise	Interest aggregation
Legitimacy	Advanced countries	Industrialized countries	

Works Cited / Further Readings

Banks, Jeffrey S. and Hanushek, Eric Allen (1995), *Modern Political Economy: Old Topics, New Directions* (Cambridge UP).

Best, Michael H. and Connolly, William E. (1982), *The Politicized Economy* (D. C. Heath).

Dahl, Robert and Lindblom Charles E., *Politics, Economics, and Welfare*.

Drazen, Allan (2000), *Political Economy in Macroeconomics* (Princeton).

Foss, Murray and Stein, Herbert (2000), *An Illustrated Guide to the American Economy: A Hundred Key Issues*, 3rd ed. (AEI).

Kant, Immanuel (2006), *Toward Perpetual Peace and Other Writings on Politics, Peace, and History (Rethinking the Western Tradition)*, ed. Pauline Kleingeld, trans. David L. Colclasure (New Haven, CT: Yale University Press).

Krugman, Paul (1997), *The Age of Diminished Expectations*, 3rd ed. (Cambridge: MIT Press).

Kumar, Krishna (1998) (ed.), *Postconflict Elections, Democratization and International Assistance* (Boulder, CO: Lynne Rienner), 5; Reilly.

Lindblom, Charles E. (1997), *Politics and Markets: The World's Political-Economic Systems* (Basic Books) and *The Market System* (Yale UP), 2001.

Peretz, Paul (1996) (ed.), *The Politics of American Economic Policymaking* 2nd ed. (M. E. Sharpe).

Persson, Torsten and Tabellini, Guido (2000), *Political Economics: Explaining Economic Policy* (MIT Press).

Pouligny, Beatrice (2000), 'Promoting Democratic Institutions in Post-Conflict Societies: Giving Diversity a Chance', *International Peacekeeping* 7 (3): 17–18.

Commission of the European Communities, *Communication from the Commission*.

Silk, Leonard, *Economics in the Real World* (Simon and Schuster).

Staniland, Martin (1985), *What Is Political Economy? A Study of Social Theory and Underdevelopment* (Yale).

UN (2000), 'Support by the United Nations System of the Efforts of Governments to Promote and Consolidate New or Restored Democracies', UN Doc. A/55/489 (2000), sec. 30.

—— (1948), Universal Declaration of Human Rights, Article 21.1.

Weingast, Barry R. and Wittman, Donald A. (2008), *The Oxford Handbook of Political Economy* (Oxford UP).

Chapter 4

POLITICAL PARTIES

What Is a Political Party?

Defining political parties is a task that seems relatively simple. In 1984, Robert Huckshorn provided what he called a pragmatic definition. In his description of what constitutes a political party, Huckshorn explained that a political party is an autonomous group of citizens having the purpose of making nominations and contesting elections in the hope of gaining control over governmental power through the capture of public offices and the establishment of a government. Nevertheless, embedded within any definition of a political party are several normative assumptions about what parties are and are not—and, even more frequently, what they should be. Taking cognizance of this definition, political parties are described as mediating institutions between the governors and the governed. But questions would arise: What tasks should they be performing? Should they be election facilitators who provide candidates with ballot access? Or, do they exist to promote ideas? What of the voters or the electorate? Do they, or should they, behave in an entirely rational manner, thereby making parties objects of political utility? Or, do voters eschew parties altogether and bring other considerations into making their ballot selections?

Alternatively, Anthony Downs (1957) defined a political party as *a team of men and women seeking to control the governing apparatus by gaining office in a duly constituted election*. Despite the struggle that political parties go through in Ghana, they do a variety of things. There are *five main functions* that political parties have. *Recruiting candidates* for public office is one of the most important functions that political parties do very well. An important goal of political parties is *to gain control of the government*, and to do this, parties must work to recruit candidates for all elected offices. For example, if a constituency has a bye-election due to the death or removal of a parliamentarian, each political party would try and find a person they can support to run for that position. Political parties also actively try to *gather volunteers to help register voters* as well as *organize* voters for general elections. The hope is that the more people that are involved in helping with the election, the more interest there will be in the outcome, which should increase *voter turnout*. The ultimate goal is to get the person the party supports *to win an election*. While political parties do end up endorsing or supporting individual candidates, they do so because those people share very similar ideals and political positions of the entire party. Thus, another function of political parties is *to present alternative policies to the electorate*, called their political platform. A *political platform* is the ideals and positions of a political party. Thus, we often learn of the ideals a political party has from the members that support it. When a member of a political party wins an elected position, they in essence take the responsibility of running the country's government. This includes *staffing positions* with loyal party supporters and developing connections among other elected officials to gain support for policies and their implementations. For example, our current president, His Excellency, John Mahama did so when he named the Flagstaff House staff members, cabinet members, and other appointed officials. The president also does so when there is a reshuffle of state and cabinet members of the government. The last function of a political party is to put its policies and oppose the winning party, when appropriate if the party did not win an elected position. The purpose of this is to promote healthy debate so that the winning party remains fair in the policies that they promote.

Legislation Governing Political Parties

In Ghana, the main documents governing political parties is the 1992 constitution; the Political Parties Law (PNDCL 281) of 1992, amended in 2000; the Representation of the People Law (PNDCL 284) of 1992, amended in 2000; the Public Elections Regulations (CI 15) of 1996; the Political Parties Act of 2000 (Act 574); and the Political Parties Code of Conduct of 2000, amended in 2004. The Political Parties Code of Conduct, as its name implies, is not a legal document and thus is not binding. Instead, it is a code of conduct drawn up by civil society groups in collaboration with the political parties and the Electoral Commission. The purpose of the code is to guide political parties in their day-to-day activities, especially during campaign periods. Ghana has a dual electoral system. Parliamentary elections use the first-past-the-post system—that is, the candidate who wins the highest number of votes is declared the winner. The same system is used for district-level elections, but district assembly elections are officially non-partisan. In presidential elections, the winning candidate must obtain at least 50 per cent plus 1 of the votes cast. When no candidate wins the required number, the constitution requires that another election be held for the two candidates with the highest vote count within twenty-one working days of the first election. This process is called a *run-off* election. The 1992 constitution does not set a quota for the representation of any group, whether its members are women, ethnic minorities or disabled persons. It does, however, stipulate that all citizens should have equal opportunity, irrespective of ethnic background, religion, or gender. The constitution requires regional balance in ministerial appointments and specifies that a majority of ministers of state are to be appointed from among Members of Parliament (MPs).

Internal Party Functions

The internal functions of political parties in Ghana are governed by the Political Parties Act 2000, Act 574, Section 9 (a–f) and Section 17 (1 and 2). This stipulates that a party's internal organization should be consistent with democratic principles and that it should not represent an ethnic, religious, or sectoral interest. Hence parties are supposed to be national in character and have offices in all of the country's constituencies.

Registration of Parties and Nomination of Candidates for Elections

The Electoral Commission of Ghana has sole responsibility for registering political parties in Ghana. The parties' candidates for general elections are nominated by the parties themselves. The commission determines the dates, the procedures for the filing of nominations, and the fees or deposits to be paid. The foregoing factors are governed by the Representation of the People Law of 1992, PNDCL 284 Section 11 (5) (a–c). The Public Elections Regulations 1996, CI 15 (4 and 5), Section 4, specifies the number of signatories and fees to be paid; Section 5 deals with presidential candidates and elections.

Election Campaigns and Observation

In Ghana, political activities can be conducted year-round, but the Electoral Commission of Ghana's official campaign period is normally six months before the elections. The Inter-Party Advisory Council (IPAC) is a committee comprising the Electoral Commission, registered political parties, and representatives of donor agencies, who sometimes attend the meeting as observers. The IPAC meets periodically to discuss issues affecting political parties and elections. It contributes to various aspects of the election process, although the final decision is the sole preserve of the commission. All registered political parties may be represented during the compilation of the electoral roll, on polling day, during the vote-counting process, and at the tabulations of elections' results in the constituency polling stations and the headquarters of the Electoral Commission. The commission's presiding officers must consult party agents in making decisions on ballots' eligibility and on spoiled ballots. The final results at the polling stations and the compilation centres are to be signed by party agents. If they refuse or fail to do so, however, the result is not invalidated. If they object to any aspect of the process, they may complete a complaint form to be forwarded to the Electoral Commission for investigation and action. Copies of declared results in the polling stations are made available to party agents. The latter may also compile their own results on the basis of those declared at the polling stations. The Electoral Commission, however, has the final authority to declare a candidate or a party as a winner.

Purpose of a Political Party

A political party typically seeks to attain and maintain political power within government, usually by participating in electoral campaigns, educational outreach, or protest actions. Political parties perform various tasks in a democratic society, such as aggregating and articulating needs and problems identified by members and supporters, socializing and educating voters and citizens in the functioning of the political and electoral system and the generation of general political values, balancing opposing demands and converting them into general policies, activating and mobilizing citizens into participating in political decisions and transforming their opinions into viable policy options, channelling public opinion from citizens to government, and recruiting and training candidates as well as selecting them for public office.

Democracy is the will of the people. Political parties are therefore expected to play major roles as institutionalized mediators between civil society and those who decide and implement decisions. In doing so, they enable their members' and supporters' demands to be represented in parliament and in government. In other words, they are expected to behave and be involved in a cordial relationship with the people. Political parties should work for social and political change. They are to be important in making changes happen. For the sake of argument, Nelson Mandela and ANC played a leading role in ending apartheid in South Africa.

At whatever level they serve in society, political party leaders and authority must themselves be led by *divine* inspiration and must seek God's guidance. They must maintain the spirit of nationhood and must ensure that, in their search for national leadership, people do not suffer prejudice and discrimination, and that the true spirit of nationhood is not broken. Political parties must promote the participation of minorities and women. They must be a major institutional factor against the skewed under-representation of minorities and women. Political parties should be at the forefront in championing electoral reforms that would produce a parliament that would represent the majorities and authorities in the community. The following principles guide legislation and practices regarding political parties and candidates. The first three derive directly from basic civil and political rights, while the other seven relate to what is needed in practice for a political system to function democratically.

Freedom of organization

In this context, the freedom of organization refers to the freedom to form and join political parties and other political organizations. It also refers to the legal rights of such parties and organizations to, for example, have their name and logo protected, to be legally registered and recognized by the government, and to be treated fairly regardless of political conviction, ethnicity, language, religion, or gender of its members.

Freedom to stand for election

The freedom to stand for election refers to an individual's ability to stand for election and to be duly elected to office. This may be either as an independent candidate or as a candidate of a political party or other organization. Principles to take into consideration when restricting individuals' freedom to stand for election include non-discrimination, relevance, reason, and objectivity. It is critical to ensure that the restrictions on and process of nomination are clearly stated in the electoral law.

Freedom of speech and assembly

Freedom of speech and assembly refers to the right of citizens to express their opinions freely, individually, or with others. It also refers to the ability for political parties and candidates to hold meetings and rallies and to freely and openly conduct public election campaigns. If restrictions are imposed, they tend to address issues of protection from, for example, hate speech or incitement of hatred and violence.

Fair and peaceful competition

For the electoral competition to be fair and peaceful, political parties, candidates, and other electoral actors need to agree on the rules of the game. Such rules may include refraining from practices of hate speech, electoral violence, and defamation. This agreement can be informal, through a voluntary Code of Conduct, and/or supported through a legal framework with enforceable sanctions and is usually contained within the Electoral Code duly established and recognized by the Inter-party Advisory Committee (IPAC).

Plurality

In order for voters to have a real and meaningful choice on Election Day, the political and legal system of a given country usually considers establishing and maintaining a multiparty electoral system. This system usually includes provision for independent candidates to stand for election—in order for voters to have a choice among several political parties and/or independent candidates.

Inclusion in the electoral process

In all aspects of an election—changes to electoral laws, election administration, codes of conduct, etc.—countries need to decide what kind of involvement they want from political parties, candidates, voters, and other key stakeholders. The involvement can take different forms ranging from being informed to being consulted, part of decision-making, or free to observe voting, vote counting, and collation of results. In some countries, this may include active participation of political parties in the election cycle prior to Election Day when the Election Commission (EC of Ghana) or other electoral governing body is deliberating and determining the content and character of the electoral code.

Level playing field

Political, cultural, legal, and financial realities might lead to a situation where some political parties or candidates have (or are perceived to have) an unfair advantage over others. Equal access to media legislation can help to ensure that all candidates (and their respective parties) receive airtime and press access. Additional measures such as party registration, freedom of assembly, ability to promote party platform in the media, and quotas to enhance the participation of under-represented groups may also be applied.

Media access and reporting

The media are a key channel for voters, political parties, candidates, and other stakeholders to receive information related to an election. Legal frameworks should protect media freedom to report and scrutinize the workings of political parties and other actors in the electoral process, and should also address ways to ensure that parties and candidates receive an equitable access to and coverage in publicly owned media.

Transparent and accountable political finance

Money is a key element in modern political campaigning, and legal frameworks and administrative practices often regulate party and campaign finance. Regulations may cover possible access to public funds, restrictions on (mis)use of public resources (by the incumbent party or candidate), provisions for the finances of political parties and candidates to be transparent, or prohibitions on certain sources of funds. In Ghana, political parties seldom account for their finances. Despite the law requesting all political parties to present to the Electoral Commission of Ghana on a yearly basis their financial expenditure, no political party does so.

Internal party democracy

If a political party would like the democratic principles of electoral politics to be applied within the party, it may consider practices like internal information and consultation processes, internal (formal or informal) rules and structures for the organization and decision-making within the party, and transparency in its functioning at all levels. Party members may also take on more formal roles in the decision-making like participating in internal elections for leadership positions or in selecting the party's candidate(s) for the upcoming elections. Many parties also work actively to enhance the role of traditionally under-represented groups in their parties. In Ghana, the New Patriotic Party since 2000 has gained support from the Konkomba people in particular for recognizing them in the appointments of Ministers of State against the National Democratic Congress (NDC), who only until recently appointed a Konkomba as a deputy chief of staff (operations), which some believe is not enough to compensate the ever-growing influence and political power of the Konkombas in the Northern, Brong Ahafo, Northern Volta, and Ashanti regions of Ghana. Contradictions between different principles also occur. Take for example societies with a history of severe intercommunity violence, where laws are sometimes passed to discourage or even prohibit political parties that are based on ethnicity or religion. It may be very difficult to draw the line between safeguarding the principle of fair and peaceful competition and violating the principles of freedom of organization and freedom to stand for election.

Different Types of Party Systems

One-Party System: a one-party system cannot produce a political system as we would identify in political science. One party cannot produce any system other than autocratic/dictatorial power. A state where one party rules in the world today would include the remaining communist states of the world (Cuba, North Korea, and China). The old Soviet Union was a one-party state until its reforms in 1989 when the Cold War between her and the United States ended. One of the more common features of a one-party state is that the position of the ruling party is guaranteed in a constitution and all forms of political opposition are banned by law. The ruling party controls all aspects of life within that state. The belief that a ruling party is all-important to a state came from Lenin, who believed that only one party—the communists—could take the workers to their ultimate destiny and that the involvement of other parties would hinder this progress.

Two-Party System: as the title indicates, is a state in which just two parties dominate. Other parties might exist but they have no political importance. America has the most obvious two-party political systems, with the Republicans and Democrats dominating the political scene. Ghana, after the 1992 constitution, has stayed that way with the National Democratic Congress (NDC) and the New Patriotic Party (NPP) emerging as the two dominant parties. For the system to work peacefully, without interruptions, one of the parties must obtain a sufficient working majority after an election and that party must be in a position to govern without the support from the other party. A rotation of power is expected in this system. In terms of the dominance of the Democratic Party (the Democrats) and the Republican Party (the Republicans) in America, the victory of George W. Bush in the November 2000 election fulfils this aspect of the definition. In Ghana, the victory of the NDC II in the 2012 parliamentary and presidential elections, with the election of HE John Dramani Mahama as the president, also confirms the assertion that Ghana is gradually becoming a two-party state like the United States of America and Britain, should that trend continue in the 2016 general elections.

The Two-Party Mechanism

The two-party system works by providing a system of voting that punishes voters for supporting the choice that best represents them, and rewards voters that support one of the two dominant political power camps. Its purpose is to aggregate power to a small group while giving the appearance of choice to the electorate. Unlike a one-party system, the members of the two dominant parties are willing to surrender political power from time to time to the other party in return for the appearance of legitimacy in the eyes of those over whom they wield power. This yields a very stable system of government. The political parties are themselves indirectly influenced by their investors, which are often the same for the two parties. The two-party system is therefore a stable means for one class to exercise indirect control over the government. Because access to power is indirect, the system permits government to occasionally act contrary to the interests of the investors, providing a safety valve that can effect changes *strongly* supported by the electorate, thereby increasing the appearance of legitimacy and providing additional stability. The two-party system reinforces the appearance of choice to the electorate by promoting the concept of a political spectrum, and rhetoric that positions the two parties at separate points along this one-dimensional abstraction of political choice and attempts to force most voters to characterize themselves by a point on this spectrum, thereby aggrandizing power from one issue to others. Indeed, the two-party system presents the voter with a simple choice and it is believed that the system promotes political moderation as the incumbent party must be able to appeal to the 'floating voters' or what can also be called independent or undecided voters within that country. Those who do not support the system claim that it leads to unnecessary policy reversals if a party loses an election, as the newly elected government seeks to impose its mark on the country that has just elected it to power. Such sweeping reversals, it is claimed, cannot benefit the state in the short and long terms.

The Multiparty System

A multiparty system is a system in which multiple political parties across the political spectrum run for national election, and all have a similar or equal chance of gaining control of government offices, separately or in coalition government. Alternatively, a *multiparty system* in politics is a *system* of government in which more than two political *parties* truly have a chance to get real political power. This means that more than two *parties* have a chance to either govern on their own or to be part of a coalition government. A multiparty system can lead to coalition governments such as those experienced by Germany, Israel, and Italy. In Germany, this has provided reasonably stable governments, and a successful coalition can introduce an effective system of checks and balances on the government, which promotes political moderation. Many policy decisions also take into account all views and interests. In Italy, coalition governments have not been a success; many have lasted less than one year. In Israel, recent governments have relied on the support of extreme minority groups to form a coalition government and this has created its own problems with such support being withdrawn on a whim, excuse, or occurrence or if those extreme parties feel that their own specific views are not being given enough support.

Dominant-Party System is different from a one-party system. A party is quite capable, within the political structure of a state, to become dominant to such an extent that victory at elections is considered a formality. In this case the National Democratic Congress (NDC) cannot be described as a dominant party in Ghanaian politics. This is because the New Patriotic Party is always poised to wrestle political power from them at any given political calendar. Perhaps the 7 December, 2016 elections, if won by the National Democratic Congress, can open up a debate to the extent that Ghana could be turning up a dominant party in the case of the NDC. A dominant-party system can only be described as existent during the tenure of the British conservative governments of Margaret Thatcher and John Major. For eighteen years (1979 to 1997), one party dominated politics in the United Kingdom. In theory, the Conservatives could have lost any election during these eighteen years. But such was the disarray of the opposition parties—especially Labour—that electoral victory was all but guaranteed. The elections of the 1980s and 1990s were fought with competition from other parties; hence, there can be no comparison with a one-party state. During an extended stay in power, a dominant party can shape society through its policies. During the Thatcher era, health, education, the state ownership of industry, etc. were all massively changed and reshaped. Society changed as a result of these political changes and this can only be done by one party having an extended stay in office.

Types of Electoral Systems and Their Influence on Parties

The multiparty system has many variants, representing the history of the struggle for democracy in different countries. While political parties in democratic countries are generally allowed to develop on their own, without specific constitutional provisions defining their number or nature, partisan patterns are strongly influenced by a country's electoral framework. In the United States, the United Kingdom, and Ghana, elections are conducted under a 'first past the post' system in which the candidate with the most votes wins, and legislative contests are held in geographically defined, single-member districts. In Ghana, the single-member districts are referred to as constituencies, 275 in all. This arrangement favours the development of a small number of large parties, since minor parties have difficulty contesting multiple districts and outpolling all of their rivals in any given district. Under proportional representation (PR) systems, used in many other countries (except Ghana), legislative seats are allocated according to a party's percentage of the vote nationally or regionally, meaning smaller parties can gain representation without actually defeating larger parties. Because multiple parties take seats in the legislature, coalitions of two or more parties are often needed to obtain a majority. There are many forms of PR. Some divide the vote into regional multi-seat districts, require parties to win a minimum percentage of the ballots to gain representation, or use complicated formulas to convert vote percentages into seats. Aside from the respective electoral frameworks that help to create them, there is no clear dividing line between two-party systems like that of the United States and systems with many parties. Even though two large parties may dominate in some countries, they must represent broad interests and sometimes have a number of shifting factions within them. Third and fourth parties may also arise from time to time as alternative outlets. Meanwhile, in countries with many parties, two larger, broad-based parties routinely serve as the cores of rival coalitions, finding allies among smaller groups with narrow concerns or constituencies in order to form a governing majority or a united opposition bloc.

What Do Political Parties Do?

Parties are a vehicle whereby people with similar ideas can join with others to express their opinions. However, there are factions within parties because not all people think alike; therefore, conflict and differences of opinion that seem to be natural to humanity occasionally arise within parties from time to time. Suppressing disagreement, or prohibiting peaceful forms of conflict, can often lead to a loss of liberty. If dissenting views are denied the right to be heard, violence can be the alternative. No one side will always win and some people will disagree with the majority. If everyone has a say, however, and the rights of the minority are respected, then most people are willing to accept the decisions made, using peaceful means to express any differences that may remain.

Organization of Political Parties

Political scientists say that organized political parties serve two major purposes: (a) *interest articulation* and (b) *interest aggregation*. The political organization process usually results in two major centres of political power. They might be the US two-party system, or they may be like the shifting majority and opposition coalitions seen in the multiparty systems of many European nations such as Italy and in Israel. This process does not always work perfectly. In Ghana and most of Africa, the appearance of strong third parties is usually a sign that the major parties have become unresponsive to the public. New parties are often very effective at *interest articulation*. They tend to be very visible and assertive about expressing what they believe in. Independents and third parties in the US, however, have traditionally suffered from not having enough members to be effective at *interest aggregation*. They can express their views, but have trouble creating the *big tent* or *rallies* that the major parties use to bring about change.

Institutional Characteristics of a Party

Like other institutions of government—parliament, the judiciary, and the executive—political parties have procedures, rules, and organizational structure. The supreme authority in major political parties is the *national party congress*, which meets at a determined number of years and for a stipulated number of days to nominate candidates for president, to ratify the party manifesto or platform, and to amend or adopt rules. When a party is not yet assembled or has chosen its candidate, the *national party committee* or national executive committee (NEC) is in charge. In recent times, almost all the parties in Ghana—NDC, NPP, CPP, and PNC—and to a large extent the other smaller ones have strengthened the role of their *national party committees* (central party committees) and also enhanced their influence.

Each party has a *national chairman* as its top official. The national chairman and other officers of the party are elected at the national party congress, which is organized once every two years or once every four years. The contest for the national chairman and other offices within the political party is very competitive. At a national party congress, other officers of the party are elected. Those positions that are usually hotly contested are the vice chairmanship, the general secretary, the deputy general secretary (sometimes two general deputy secretaries), treasurer, propaganda secretary, and national vice chairmen, who could number from four to fifteen, depending on the size of the party. Apart from the election of the national party secretariat, there are also national parliamentary committees. These committees work to recruit candidates, train them, make limited contributions to them, and spend time directing the ways and means of getting their party elected to office in the next general elections.

Party Manifestos or Platforms

Although national party committees exist primarily to win elections and gain control of government, policy goals are also important to the party. Every four years or so, each party adopts a manifesto or platform at the national nominating congress. The typical party platform or manifesto is the official statement of party policy, which is often a vague and ponderous document, derived after many meetings and compromises between groups and individuals of their party. Manifestos are ambiguous by design, giving voters few obvious reasons to vote for the party. Besides, many politicians contend that manifestos rarely help elect anyone, but manifesto positions can hurt a presidential candidate if the policy choices are wrongly interpreted by the opponent. This is because the presidential nominee does not always control the manifesto-drafting process. Once elected, politicians are rarely reminded what their manifesto or platform positions were on a given issue. In reality, though, the wining party actually seeks to enact much of its party platform or manifesto so as to convey its achievements over its tenure of office. An example of this behaviour is what divided the National Democratic Congress after their 2008 victory at the polls. Whereas the party founder felt the party was elected by the people based on the platform or manifesto that they presented, the president, on the other hand, felt it was his *Better Ghana*

Agenda and not the values and principles of *justice, probity, and accountability* that brought the NDC back to power. The division of the NDC prior to the 2012 elections with the formation of the National Democratic Party (NDP) demonstrates the ideological tensions that can exist among members of the same party.

Parties at the Regional and Constituency Levels

The two major parties in the country are the National Democratic Congress (NDC) and the New Patriotic Party (NPP) and are decentralized. They have organizations for each level of government: regional, district, and even at the ward (polling station) level and organize these for elections. The regional and district levels (constituency levels) are structured much like the national level. Each region has a regional committee headed by a regional chairman. Regional laws determine the composition of the regional committees and regulate them. Members of the regional committee are usually elected from the ward upward to the region. Lately, in politics, regional party offices have become very powerful because of the contribution in seats and votes that they represent in parliament. Despite much region-to-region variation, the trend is toward stronger regional organizations of parties, with the NDC and the NPP typically being much better funded. Below the regional committees are the *constituency committees*, which vary widely in functions and powers. The constituency level functions like a regional committee, whose responsibility is to recruit candidates to run for parliament. For a party that rarely wins an election, the constituency committee has to struggle to find someone willing to run. When the chance of winning is greater, primaries, not the party leaders, usually decide the winner. Many constituency organizations are active, distributing campaign literature, organizing telephone campaigns, putting up posters, and canvassing house to house for votes on behalf of the candidate and the presidential candidate. Other constituency committees do not function at all, and many party leaders are just figureheads.

Political Parties in Ghana

Political Parties in Ghana can be traced to 1957 when Ghana achieved its independence. The political parties formed at the time included United Gold

Coast Convention (UGCC), United Party (UP), and Convention People's Party (CPP). The parties were formed primarily to contest competitive elections nationwide. Those parties adopted symbols and colours which identify each other. The candidates who emerged winners from competitive general elections were mandated to rule the country for a period of time as enshrined in the then-drafted independence constitution of Ghana in 1957. Thereafter, there were varied military governments, including the National Liberation Council (NLC), the National Redemption Council (NRC), the Supreme Military Council (SMC) and the Armed Forces Revolutionary Council (AFRC) interventions for years 1966–1982. Political party formation activities became operational in the mid 1992 after a ten year ban by Rawlings's Provisional National Defense Council (PNDC) military government, which took power from a democratically elected government of the People's National Party (PNP) in 1981. The election of December 1992 followed an eleven-year hiatus in political party activity. The formation of political parties had been banned by the Provisional National Defense Council (PNDC) that ruled the country from December 1981 to early January 1993. The major political parties that took part in the 1992 elections were the New Patriotic Party (NPP), the National Democratic Congress (NDC), the National Independence Party (NIP), the People's Heritage Party (PHP), and the National Convention Party (NCP). The elections were supervised by the Interim National Electoral Commission (INEC) under Justice Josiah Ofori-Boateng.

The Structure of Political Parties

According to the Electoral Commission of Ghana data on political parties (2012), there are now twenty-eight registered political parties under the fourth republic, the major ones being the National Democratic Congress(NDC), which won presidential and parliamentary elections in 1992, 1996, 2008, and 2012 respectively, and the New Patriotic Party (NPP), which won elections in 2000 and 2004; the Convention People's Party (CPP) and the Peoples' National Convention (PNC) are, however, yet to win any general election since 1992.

Ghanaian political parties can be described as 'weak' parties. They seem to lack not only a stable and functioning party apparatus, but also a clear programmatic appeal. Because of these weaknesses, their possible contribution to democratic development is often questioned. In fact, many political parties in Ghana do not conform to the ideal of effective mass parties which perform democracy-promoting functions such as candidate nomination, electoral mobilization, societal representation, or interest aggregation. Political parties, however, do operate under very difficult conditions such as uneven and weakly developed infrastructure, low living standards and low levels of education, lack of party offices in the regional capitals as well as in the districts. Against this background, it is questionable whether the Western European model of the mass-based party is applicable at all. Yet, not all parties are weak in the study of political parties in Ghana because, by African standards, the NDC and the NPP clearly stand out as credible ones.

In Ghana, parties are objects of passionate support from the people. The party system is dominated by the two major parties NDC (National Democratic Congress) and NPP (New Patriotic Party). Both of them are comparatively well organized on the ground and possess a network of party branches all over the country. Although ideological competition may not take centre stage in elections, both parties have relatively clear programmatic appeals. The NPP claims to stands for the rule of law, (liberal) democracy/good governance, and freedom of business and of the individual. The NDC in contrast portrays itself as centre-left on the political spectrum, or social-democratic party that is focused on the poor, vulnerable, and socially disadvantaged. Political analysts believe state intervention is critical to securing basic social services and therefore the pure-liberalism orientation of the NPP is outwardly rejected. This does not necessarily mean that there are substantial ideological differences between the parties: in practice, the NPP embraces social-democratic policies and the NDC is not principally against market reform. However, the master narratives of both parties are opposed to each other and thus play a role in the structuring of political competition.

While parties in Ghana have very few institutionalized contacts to civil society groups, they have developed alternative strategies to reach out to rural voters. Both NDC and NPP try to win over influential people on the local level who are supposed to deliver the votes of their respective communities. These can be chiefs (who are however not allowed to be openly involved in party politics), or other local 'big men'. Another way of mobilizing voters at the grass-roots level is so-called house-to-house campaigns. Typically, such campaigns come not only with a political message, but also with a small gift (cola, water, food, as well as drinks and cash for the elders). In addition, parties take advantage of any occasion where people come together, such as funerals, local festivals, marriages and naming ceremonies, communal labour exercises, and many more to canvass for votes.

The other aspect of these localized mobilization strategies is the fact that they often go together with clientelistic relationships. This is also obvious in the candidate selection processes where irregularities, vote buying, and other forms of manipulation prevail within the political system of Ghana. While the interference from above is one factor that distorts the nomination process, financial capability is another. Local candidates receive little or no support from the central party and so they usually have to finance their campaigns from their own funds. This excludes candidates with little capital from even contesting their own party's primaries. While the expenditures in the primaries and parliamentary elections are enormous, they are exorbitant in the competition for the presidential slot. As a consequence, the top-level positions in the political system are reserved to a small circle of extremely wealthy individuals while the poor are excluded from rising in the party hierarchy. This means that while Ghanaian parties nominally fulfil the function of candidate nomination, they do not always nominate the most able candidates but rather those who are rich enough to engage in the political game.

To sum up, Ghanaian political parties are weak, as presented. But two of the bunch, the NDC and NPP are organized all over the country, mobilize substantial numbers of voters at each election, and provide at least a rough ideological orientation to the electorate. It is also worth noting that parties in Ghana have successfully adapted to the context in which they exist. The socio-economic context coupled with the fact that there is no public funding for political activities, however, has some wider implication for political participation and democratic development. First, it distorts political competition by disadvantaging small parties with few resources. Secondly, it keeps the rural and urban poor outside of the active decision-making process. Thus, political parties in Ghana still have some deficits in the realm of internal democracy and vertical accountability—to a certain extent they 'belong' to those who finance them. Finally, political parties seem to rely heavily on state money to finance their political activities when such parties are in government. It suffices here to catalogue the various political parties in Ghana at this time.

Second Republic (1969–1972)
All People's Republican Party
Justice Party
National Alliance of Liberals—offshoot of CPP
People's Action Party
Progress Party—Danquah/Busia tradition
United Nationalist Party

Third Republic (1979–1981)
Action Congress Party
People's National Party
Popular Front Party (PFP)—Danquah/Busia tradition
Social Democratic Party (SDP)
Third Force Party (TFP)
United National Convention (UNC)

Fourth Republic (1992–present)
People's National Convention (PNC)
Progressive People's Party (PPP)
Ghana National Party (GNP)
Independent People's Party (IPP)
National Democratic Congress (NDC)—the ruling party 2009–2012/2013–2016
National Democratic Party (NDP)
National Patriotic Party (NPP)—Danquah/Busia tradition
National Reform Party (NRP)
New Vision Party (NVP)
Ghana Freedom Party (GFP)
Great Consolidated Popular Party (GCPP)
Every Ghanaian Living Everywhere Party (EGLE)
Ghana Democratic Republic Party (GDRP)

Democratic People's Party (DPP)
Democratic Freedom Party (DFP)
Peoples Heritage Party (PHP)—merged with NIP to form PCP
National Independence Party (NIP)—merged with PHP to form PCP
People's Convention Party (PCP)—merged with NCP to form CPP
National Convention Party (NCP)—merged with PCP to form CPP
Convention People's Party (CPP)
United Front Party (UFP)
Yes People's Party (YPP)
United Renaissance Party (URP)
Ghana Redevelopment Party (GRP)
United Progressive Party (UPP)—formed in May 2015
All People's Party (APC) – formed in February 2016

Political Parties and Governance

Political parties are central to the operations of any modern government. They help bridge the separation of powers and facilitate coordination between the three levels of government, as follows:

a. *In the legislative branch*—Members of Parliament take their partisanship seriously, at least while in Accra. Their power and influence are determined by whether their party is in control of Parliament and, of course, the executive branch of government. The chairmanship of all standing committees in Congress comes from the majority party, as do the presiding officials of parliament. In committees and subcommittees, Members of Parliament sit together with fellow partisan members to decide on a bill or to discuss rules or regulations to be adopted on the floor of Parliament. Political parties help bridge the separation of powers between the legislative and executive branches by creating partisan incentives to cooperate. Partisanship can also help unify the two houses of Parliament. Parliamentary staff is non-partisan, except those directly working under the parliamentarians such as interns, support staff in the Member of Parliament's office, and particularly, drivers of the Member of Parliament.

b. *In the executive branch*—The president selects all members of his/her staff and also cabinet members from his own party. In addition, presidents typically surround themselves with advisers who have campaigned with them and proved their party loyalty. Partisanship is also important in presidential appointments to the highest levels of the national workforce. Party commitment, including making campaign contributions, is expected of those who seek these positions. However, presidents usually fill at least one or two senior posts with members of the opposition party, such as selecting the opposition for the Second Deputy Speaker position in parliament. When this is done, it is considered a way of describing bipartisanship in Parliament in their deliberations and enactment of bills.

c. *In the judicial branch*—The judicial branch of the national government is limited by a retirement age and political independence. The judiciary is designed to operate in an expressly non-partisan manner. Judges, unlike parliamentarians, do not sit together by political party. Nevertheless, the appointment process for judges has been partisan from the beginning of our country. As alleged recently, most judges who were appointed during the NPP era favour the NPP and arrive at decisions meant to favour the party.

d. *At the regional and district levels*—The importance of party in the operation of regions and districts is the same across the country. In most regional and district offices of the major political parties, contracts in the feeding of schoolchildren (school feeding programs), awards to build school structures, feeder roads, and other contracts from the national government are all partisan when the allocations are being made.

Duties of Political Parties

Parties in the Electorate

Political parties would be of little significance if they did not have meaning to the electorate. In every political system, those who follow the political trend are drawn to the party of their choice by a combination of certain factors: their stand on issues; personal or party history; religious, ethnic, or social peer grouping; and the appeal of their candidates. The emphases among these factors change over time, but they are remarkably consistent with those that political scientists identified over the last forty years.

Membership

Membership of parties is open to all Ghanaians aged eighteen and older who are of sound mind and who subscribe to the parties' ideologies and programs. Parties keep membership registers at all levels of the party structure but neither is able to indicate party membership. The explanation offered usually by political parties is that the register is not a true reflection of voter membership, since a significant number of party 'members' neither register officially nor hold party cards. Despite the lack of accurate data, all parties have claimed and continue to claim an increase, over the years, of their members.

Members of parties are expected to pay monthly dues, but only a few actually do so. That circumstance is attributed to poverty, and to a lack of appreciation for the role of political parties in the development of the country and the individual. The parties have clear channels of communication (both horizontally and vertically) between members and the executive. What constitutes unethical behaviour and breaches of conduct is clearly defined in each party's constitution or regulations, as are the procedures for investigating alleged misconduct and the sanctions to be applied. The parties carry out regular membership drives and train their members, especially party activists, executives, and those who represent the party during voter registration and on polling day.

Party Registration—For most citizens in this country, 'party' has a particular legal meaning—registration prior to an election. When voters register to vote in the country, they are fulfilling their civic duty as citizens. The purpose of registration is to increase the number of voters within a party in order to win an election. Registration is also mandatory to enable those who have turned eighteen years and those who could not register in the previous registration exercise to do so. As a constitutional requirement, the Electoral Commission of Ghana conducts a registration exercise every fourth year to register all those who are not registered or those who have reached the required voter registration age. But this exercise ought to be done on an annual basis in various government organizations such as the Driver and Licensing Authority (DVLA), police stations, and other outposts across the country.

Party Activist—People who invest time and effort in political parties are often called party activists. They tend to fall into three broad categories: party regulars, candidate activists, and issue activists. *Party regulars* place the party first. They are those who value winning elections and understand that compromise and moderation are necessary to reach that goal. They also believe that it is important to keep the party together because a fractured party only helps the opposition. *Candidate activists* are those who follow a particular candidate and do everything possible for him or her to win, in particular, those running for parliament at the constituency level. *Issue activists* want to push or navigate the parties in a particular direction on a single issue or a narrow range of issues. To issue activists, the party manifesto is an important battleground because they want the party to endorse their position rather than other equally relevant or important positions.

Party Identification

Party identification refers to the political party with which an individual identifies. Party identification is typically determined by the political party that an individual most commonly supports (by voting or other means). In Ghana and most democratic countries, political parties consist of three parts: *the party as government* (members of the party who hold public office), *the party as organization* (committees, leaders, and activists who work to promote the party and the candidates), and *the party as electorate* (citizens who support the party through party identification).

Citizens in the general population who identify with a particular party make up *the party as electorate*. Party identifiers (partisans) could be described by their support in the following ways:

- They have a higher voter turnout in primary elections than the general population.
- They register and remain loyal members of the particular party.
- When surveyed, they identify themselves as member of a particular party.
- They are inclined to support policies endorsed by that particular party.

- They volunteer for campaigns to support party candidates more than the general population.
- They show a strong tendency to vote for candidates in their preferred party in most elections.

Political scientists view party identification as *a form of social identity*, in the same way that a person identifies with a religious or ethnic group. This identity develops early in a person's life, mainly through family and social influence. This description would make party identification a stable perspective, which develops as a consequence of personal, family, social, and environmental factors. Other researchers consider party identification to be more flexible and more of a conscious choice. Researchers see it as a position and choice based on the continued assessment of the political, economic, and social environment. Party identification can increase or even shift with motivating events or conditions in the country.

Characteristics of Party Identification

a. *Childhood influences*—Childhood influence is one of the main factors behind formation of party identification. During childhood, the main political influence comes from parents, other close family members, and close surroundings such the immediate community. Children remember events that happened during their childhood and associate them with the political party, whether or not they were connected with those events. For example, a child growing up in the 1970s would associate with the Progress Party (PP) of Busia, who was referred to as 'party papa' in the Twi language, or Dr Kwame Nkrumah's Young Pioneers in the early 1960s.

b. *Adulthood influences*—People can begin to adjust their party loyalties according to their personal experiences. The longer an individual holds a party identification, the stronger that attachment to the party becomes. Older adults are more likely to hold strong party attachments, and less likely to change them when compared with young adults.

c. *Change influences*—Party identification changes can occur in times of party coalition change or realignment. During this time, party coalitions themselves are being transformed, and as a result, people are more likely to desert the party of their parents. There was a probability that the election of Hon. Samia Nkrumah of the CPP as the party chairperson would encourage older people who once were with CPP to leave other parties and go to the CPP, but this has not yet occurred. She stepped down (as at September 2015) as the chairperson after rather causing diminishing returns to the CPP as a chairperson. In fighting to become the presidential candidate in the 2016 primaries of the CPP, Ms Samia Nkrumah was humiliated with the election of a lesser known candidate and party national secretary, Mr Ivan Greenstreet, who has pledged to unite once more the fractured party. The problems within the NDC after the 2008 elections and the near loss of the party in 2012 can be another factor, where most people who have been left out or sidelined will begin to jump ship if their conditions are not met.

Political Parties in Government (1992–present)

Two rival parties, the NPP and the NDC, dominate the political system. Ghana's multiparty system provides ample opportunity for the meaningful participation of opposition parties in the political process. The country has experienced two peaceful, democratic transfers of power between presidents from the opposing NPP and NDC, in 2000 and in 2008. Moreover, the legal framework provides for equal participation in political life for the country's various cultural, religious, and ethnic minorities.

Patriotic Party (NPP) is a liberal democratic and conservative party in Ghana and one of two dominant parties in Ghanaian politics. The party is centre-right, its leading rival being the National Democratic Congress (NDC). It supplied former president John Agyekum Kufuor. At the elections held on 7 December 2004, the party won 129 out of 230 seats. The NPP candidate was John Kufuor, who was re-elected president with 52.75 per cent of the vote on 7 December 2014. The party symbol is the elephant and the party colours are red, white, and blue. In the Ghanaian general election, in 2008, the NPP candidate, Nana Akufo-Addo, lost the presidential election in a closely contested runoff, with Akufo-Addo receiving 49.77 per cent of the votes versus 50.23 per cent for John Atta Mills, the NDC flag bearer. In the Ghanaian general election in 2012, the party faced a similar situation. Akufo-Addo lost the election with 47.74 per cent of the vote, while incumbent president of Ghana John Mahama won 50.7 per cent.

National Democratic Congress

NDC chairman Mr Kofi Portuphy is also the chief executive officer (chairman) of the National Disaster Organization. The general secretary is Mr Johnson Asiedu Nketia. The NDC is a social democratic political party in Ghana, founded by Jerry John Rawlings, who was head of state of Ghana from 1981 to 1993 and the president of Ghana from 1993 to 2001. The NDC was formed ahead of elections in 1992 and in 1996 returned Rawlings to power. Rawlings's second term ended in 2001. The NDC lost the presidency in the 2000 election, and it was not until the 2008 election that they regained it with candidate John Atta Mills. The NDC's party symbol is an umbrella with an eagle's head on top of the umbrella. Party colours of the NDC are red, white, green, and black. Internationally, the NDC is a member of Socialist International. On 9 December 2012, the Electoral Commission of Ghana announced NDC's candidate John Dramani Mahama president-elect after a hotly contested race in which he won with 50.7 per cent of votes cast.

In all, there were about twenty-three political parties in Ghana at the close of the 2012 elections. The active ones during the 2012 elections were the NDC, the NPP, the CPP, the PPP, the PNC, and an independent party.

Political Parties and Their 2012 Presidential Candidates

New Patriotic Party—NPP
Nana Dankwa Akufo-Addo

National Democratic Congress—NDC
John Dramani Mahama

People's National Convention—PNC
Mahama Ayariga

Convention People's Party—CPP

Dr Abu Sakara Foster

Progressive People's Party—PPP
Dr Paa Kwesi Nduom

Democratic Freedom Party—DFP
Emmanuel Ansah-Antwi

Democratic People's Party
Thomas Ward-Brew

Reformed Patriotic Party
Kwabena Adjei

Independent Candidate
Kwesi Amoafo-Yeboah

In summary, political parties are often portrayed in the popular media and culture as corrupt or incompetent. This is the case not just in the United States, but in Ghana, where citizens have generally been sceptical of political parties. In Europe, however, parties have had higher levels of support and public trust. Such negative views, however, overlook the essential importance of political parties as representative institutions. In fact, political parties reflect the spectrum of the people's views and needs, from their highest ideals to their basest instincts. They act together to create a balance or compromise between extremes, as the nineteenth-century British philosopher John Stuart Mill suggests in the quote above. Political parties have also been the vehicle for inspiring voters to support fundamental political change when it is needed. Thus, even in jaded times, idealistic citizens seeking change turn to political parties to make a difference. It is evident from the last two centuries of history that no democracy can survive without a multiparty system in which the people are free to organize themselves politically. Absent the organization of free and independent political parties, power has been exploited by narrow cliques that pursue their own interests or monopolized by a single party that suppresses dissent and dispenses patronage to supporters as is taking place in Libya after the overthrow of Col. Muammar al-Qaddafi.

Conclusion

Political parties are often a standard by which a country's political freedom can be measured. Some countries have only one political party. In China, for example, there is only one party, the Communist Party. Under such a system, people who do not agree with the party in power cannot express their objections by voting for another group. Often, the ruling party holds absolute power over all segments of the country's political, social, and economic institutions. Canada also has two major parties, the Conservatives and the Liberals. Multiparty systems are common in Europe and other parts of the world. In this system, three or more parties each enjoy substantial support from voters. France, Germany, Israel, and South Africa are just a few examples. In these countries, there may be many parties representing a wide range of political views. Because of the number of competing parties, it is sometimes difficult to come up with a clear winner after a general election; in that case the two or more of the parties form what is known as a coalition government. Democracies usually operate under either a two-party or a multiparty system. Like the United States, Britain has a two-party system. Ghana is gradually becoming a two-party system despite the poor performance of the Convention People's Party and other newly formed cluster parties.

Article 4—Value-Oriented Vision of Government

In Ghana, I don't know how many people share this value-oriented vision of government. Do we have Ghanaians who are value-oriented? The kind people or Ghanaians who get involved in politics and the governing process not because of what they want for themselves but because they want to promote certain democratic values—such as equality, entrenching the notion of freedom and justice, fairness, and providing security—that they feel are important. They have a vision of what a good society is and they try to use government to make that vision a reality. How many Ghanaians think this way or come to Parliament as legislators to make sure this thinking prevails in society? In return, members of society vote for candidates and lobby the government not simply to line their own pockets but in order to encourage government to do what is right for society as a whole. Many people participate in the democratic process because they want to promote principles and values that they believe are in the public interest for the advancement of peace and harmony in the country, but how many do so? To really appreciate the unique role that government plays in promoting these basic political principles, we need to take a more careful look at some of these key values and see how they can be ensured only by government and how they are embodied in particular policies and programs of central government. Let's begin with *justice and fairness*. 'Life isn't fair' is a favourite saying among people considered to be thinking conservatively. And the often unspoken corollary is 'So get used to it.' But most people do not want to get used to it. In fact, fairness is what everybody desires. We get riled up when people are not treated fairly and we think something should be done about it. And more often than not, the place that people turn to try to right these wrongs—to make life fairer for themselves and others—is government. This is because government is the major producer of justice and fairness in Ghana. Therefore, many government policies and institutions are explicitly designed to promote these important public values.

The most obvious manifestation of this is the criminal and civil justice system. It is the primary way we, as a society, ensure that criminals are punished and that wrongs are righted. This kind of legal justice is not something that can be reliably provided by the private sector. We would not want, for instance, for a market in legal justice to exist. We would not want this justice to be something provided to the highest bidder. In fact, those times when our current justice system does take on the characteristics of a market—such as when the rich are able to get off because they can afford to hire the most talented and expensive lawyers—are exactly the times when we think the justice system has broken down. *Justice should not be for sale*; it must be available to *all people equally*, and *only government can provide that*. Nor can we rely on people acting outside of the law, either individually or in private groups, to provide justice in our society. All too often, the result of this kind of an approach is *revenge killings in society, the lynch mob*, or the civil wars that often revisit us and divide us as a country. Justice administered outside of government and outside of the law is almost always arbitrary, inappropriate, violent, and out of control. For justice to be true justice, it must be ordered by law and administered by the government. It is revealing that even libertarians and other anti-government ideologues admit that the criminal and civil justice systems are parts of government that are absolutely necessary and cannot be done away with. They argue that running the police, the courts, and prisons are legitimate public endeavours that must be maintained, even in a final version of government. In short, if we cherish important public values like justice and equality, we need a public sector strong enough and well-funded enough to make these things a reality, *and that is government.*

Key Terms

Autonomous groups	Canvassing	Minority groups	Majority groups
Non-partisan	Two-party system	One-party system	
Manifesto	Ideological	Interest articulation	Socialization
Partisan	Undecided voters	Independent voters	Public offices

Works Referenced / Further Reading

Ames, Barry (1995), 'Electoral Rules, Constituency Pressures, and Pork Barrel: Bases of Voting in the Brazilian Congress', *Journal of Politics*, 57: 324–343.

Brancati, Dawn (2008), 'The Origins and Strengths of Regional Parties', *British Journal of Political Science*, 38: 135–159.

Chhibber, Pradeep and Kollman, Ken (1998), 'Party Aggregation and the Number of Parties in India and the United States', *American Political Science Review*, 92: 329–342. Doi:10.2307/2585667.

Huckshorn, Robert Jack (1984), *Political Parties in America* (Brooks Cole Pub. Co.).

Charles J. Pattie is Senior Lecturer in Geography, University of Sheffield, Sheffield SIO

Ronald J. Johnston is Professor of Geography, University of Bristol, Bristol BS8 1SS, United Kingdom

Edward A. Fieldhouse is Research Fellow in the Census Microdata Unit, University of Manchester, Manchester M13 9PL, United Kingdom.

Robert D. (1988), 'Diplomacy and domestic politics: the logic of two-level games', *International Organization*, 42.

Sartori, G. (1962, 1965), *Democratic Theory* (Detroit / New York).

Chapter 5

THE PARLIAMENT (LEGISLATURE)

Establishment and Mission

The current Parliamentary Service was established in 1993 by the Parliamentary Service Act (Act 460), pursuant to article 124 of the 1992 Constitution. It has a governing board composed of six members with the Speaker of Parliament as the chairman. The head of the service is the Clerk to Parliament, who is assisted by three deputies, heads of departments, unit heads, and other specialized officers. The Parliamentary Service exists to facilitate the work of Parliament through the provision of support services to the House, including its committees and agencies for the purpose of ensuring full and effective exercise of the powers of Parliament. Furthermore, it works to enhance the dignity of the House and adequately inform the public on parliamentary activities. In discharging its functions, the service ensures transparency, non-partisanship, and a high sense of professionalism. Before we delve into the functions of the Ghanaian parliament, a look at the historic background of the legislature is in order.

Historical Background

Ghana achieved independence on 6 March 1957. The political struggle that preceded this historic event dates back over a hundred years. The early period of nationalist struggle for political independence created political awareness and desire to assert the right of self-determination both for the individual and the State. As far back as 1850, Ghana, then the Gold Coast, was given its own Legislative Council to advise the colonial governor to enact legislation mainly in the form of ordinances '*for the peace, order, and good government of the subjects'*. By 1954, the Gold Coast government, with the agreement of the Secretary of State, decided on its constitutional future. The great majority of recommendations received from the chiefs and people across the country, in the words of Ronald E. Wraith (1), wanted an arrangement in which Ghana would have a two-chamber system.

The Exercise of Legislative Power (1837–1901)

Legislative power was first exercised in the Gold Cost during the reign of Queen Victoria of England (1837–1901). Beginning from 1850 to 1865, the Gold Coast was allowed to constitute its own Legislative Council. It consisted of the governor and at least two other persons designated by Royal Instructions from England. It was required to make 'all such laws, institutions, and ordinances as may from time to time be necessary for the peace, order, and good government of our subjects and others within the said present or future Forts (castle) and settlements in the Gold Coast', subject to rules and regulations made by Order in Council and to the right of the Crown to disallow any such ordinance, either in whole or in part, and with a saving for the future exercise of legislative power by an Act of Parliament or Order in Council.

The Style of the Ordinances

All ordinances enacted by the governor of the forts and settlements in the Gold Coast were to have the advice and consent of the Legislative Council. The governor was required to withhold assent to any ordinance that was repugnant to any Act of British Parliament or to the Royal Charter or Royal Instructions, or which interfered with Christian worship, diminished public divorce, etc. With few exceptions, no ordinance was to come into effect until the pleasure of the Crown had been signified. In 1850, the Gold Coast became a separate dependency of the British Crown. Its governor was responsible to London. In that year, it established a Legislative Council and selected Africans to serve on it. Between 1866 and 1874, the Gold Coast was reunited with the West African Settlements and its Legislative Council was reduced in size. By 1874, however, the Gold Coast was given a separate government. It was from then on that the steady growth of the legislature began, but even quite near the end of the nineteenth century, the powers of the legislature were still limited and its area of authority undefined. By 1946, the constitutional provision called for an elective legislature. The Ashanti region was the first to be given representation. In 1949, the Legislative Council was given jurisdiction over Southern Togoland under United Kingdom trusteeship. In 1951, the Legislative Council also became the legislature of the Northern Territories. Before these changes, legislative jurisdiction over these areas resided exclusively with the governor.

The Legislative Council was purely advisory, as the governor exercised all legislative and executive powers. In 1916, for the first time in the history of the Gold Coast, the Legislative Council was reconstituted to include nine nominated officials, six of whom were Africans, as opposed to eleven officials and the governor. The first Legislative Council elections ever to be held took place in 1925 under the Guggisberg Constitution. Under this arrangement, the governor still retained complete control of legislation. Under the 1946 Bums Constitution, which replaced the Guggisberg Constitution, the representatives of the people formed the majority in the Legislative Council. The governor ceased to be ex-officio president of the Legislative Council and an unofficial member was appointed president. This system continued until 1951, when the legislature elected its first Speaker under the 1950 Constitution. In 1951, the first large-scale elections to the Legislative Assembly took place when seventy-five members were elected. There were three nominated ex-official members and six special members representing commercial and mining interests.

In 1954, a transitional Constitution provided for an assembly of a Speaker and 104 Members elected on party lines on the basis of universal adult suffrage. In 1957, when Ghana achieved full political independence, the constitution was fashioned after the Westminster model. In June 1960, ten women were elected by the National Assembly to fill specially created seats. This was done to expose women for the first time to parliamentary life. This system of election was not intended to be permanent. However, the Act made no provision for filling a vacancy caused by death, resignation, or expulsion of a woman Member. On 1 July 1960, Ghana became a sovereign unitary republic, the first of such countries in sub-Saharan Africa.

In February 1964, Ghana adopted a one-party system of government. The First National Assembly of the Republic was dissolved in 1965 and a general election was held, in which all the 198 Members—all of them members of the national party, the convention People's Party (CPP)—were elected unopposed. The 1964 Constitutional Amendments, among other things, increased the powers and prerogatives of the president. In February 1966, the first republican government was overthrown by a military coup, which installed a military government that remained in power up to September 1969 when, on its own volition, it handed over power to another constitutionally elected government, and thereby restored parliamentary rule once again. After only twenty-two months in office, the second parliamentary democracy also succumbed to another military rule between January 1972 and October 1979 when, under much political pressure, that military government was compelled to usher in the third republican parliamentary system.

The Trek to Nationhood

In opting for a unitary or federal constitution in Ghana, many factors were taken into consideration; among them were history, culture, and size of the country. A constitution is defined as a body of laws that determines how a state is governed. It sets out the structure and functions of the organs of government and declares the principles that regulate its operations and the bonds between the citizen and the state. For example, Article 4(1) of the 1992 Constitution states that the sovereign state of Ghana is a unitary republic consisting of those territories comprised in the regions that, immediately before coming into force of this Constitution (7 January 1993), existed in Ghana, including territorial sea and air space. Subject to this provision, the president, under Art 5 (1), may, by constitutional instrument: (a) create a new region, (b) alter the boundaries of a region, or (c) provide for the merger of two or more regions, if (2) on the advice of the Council of State, a substantial demand for it is demonstrated.

Legislative authority in Ghana has been vested in Parliament, which has exercised it in varying degrees under the four constitutions of Ghana since independence in 1957. The transitional constitution of 1954 provided for the direct election of 104 members of legislative assembly on the basis of universal adult suffrage. As far as the legislature was concerned, the difference between the Transitional Constitution of 1954 and the Independence Constitution of 1957 lay not so much in detailed provision as in the character of the Assembly. The former constitution gave the country an advanced colonial legislature, and at independence, the country attained a sovereign parliament. The 1957 Constitution introduced a parliamentary system like the Westminster system, which the prime minister and all Ministers of State were Members of Parliament elected on party lines. An important feature of this constitution has been an attempt to decentralize the administration of the country by the creation of regional assemblies.

Functions of Parliament

It is well known that Parliament's basic function is lawmaking. However, a number of functions are incidental to the performance of this function. Among others, the following can be clearly identified as functions performed by the Parliament of Ghana: *legislative, financial, oversight of the executive, representational,* and *deliberative.*

Legislative

Lawmaking is considered to be the most important function of Parliament. Under article 93(2) of the 1992 Constitution, the legislative power of Ghana is vested in Parliament and is exercised in accordance with the Constitution. No person or body other than Parliament has the power to pass any measure with the force of law, except by or under the authority conferred by an Act of Parliament. The legislative function consists of passing bills and scrutinizing statutory instruments and deciding whether to annul them or allow them to take effect by the passing or expiration (effluxion) of time. According to Edmund Burke on 3 November 1774, regarding the duties of Parliament to citizens of their respective constituents, parliament is not a congress of ambassadors from different hostile interests, which interests each must maintain, or as an agent and advocate, against other agents and advocates; but parliament is a deliberative assembly of one nation, with one interest, that of the whole, where, not local purposes, not local prejudices ought to guide, but the general good, resulting from the general reason of the whole. A constituent chooses a member indeed; but when such a member is chosen, he/she is no more a member of, say,

Bunkpurugu Yoyo (Northern region), Takoradi West constituency (Western region), or Ametefe East constituency, but a member of Ghana's parliament.

Financial Control or the Power of the Purse

Chapter 13 of the 1992 Constitution variously vests the control of all public funds (power of the public purse) in Parliament. In specific terms, this means (a) No tax can be imposed without the authority of Parliament (art. 174); (b) Apart from monies charged directly on the Consolidated Fund by the Constitution, no monies can be withdrawn from the Fund without the authority of Parliament (art. 178); and (c) Parliament has the power and duty to monitor the expenditure of public funds to ensure that the monies it has authorized are used for the purposes for which they are intended by taking appropriate actions on the Auditor-General's reports. In addition to these functions enumerated above, Parliament's financial powers include the following:

- Authorizing the granting or receiving of loans (cf. article 181)
- Monitoring the country's foreign exchange receipts and payments or transfers (article 184)
- Authorizing the waiver/exemption or variation of taxes to non-governmental organizations (NGOs), or non-taxable entities under article 174 of the Constitution.
- Appointing an auditor to audit and report on the accounts of the Auditor-General's office (article 187[15]). In effect, the executive is free to propose various expenditure levels and how revenue should be raised to meet them. Parliament is, however, empowered to control the expenditure of public funds.

Oversight of the Executive Branch of Government

As the embodiment of the sovereign will of the people of Ghana, Parliament exercises oversight of the Executive. Parliament keeps watch over the performance of the Executive, which controls the public services, to ensure that the implementation of public policy conforms to the approved developmental agenda of the state and expenditure incurred is in accordance with parliamentary authorizations. Parliament exercises this function (oversight) by way of scrutiny of policy measures and executive conduct through its committees, questions to ministers, motions, and censorship of ministers, among others. Parliament also exercises this power through the approval or otherwise of presidential nominees for appointment as Ministers, Deputy Ministers, the Chief Justice, and other justices of the Supreme Court, members of the Council of State, and other public offices as specified by law.

Representational

Parliament is the supreme forum for the ventilation of grievances aimed at seeking redress by the citizens of Ghana. The Member of Parliament (MP) is the communication link between his constituent and government. Through parliamentary mechanisms/tools such as question time, statements, motions, and debate on policy/bills, among others, an MP has the opportunity to draw attention to developments in his constituency and explore avenues for socio-economic development of the constituency through the district/municipal/metropolitan assembly.

Deliberative Function

In the execution of its functions, the House of Parliament undertakes deliberations through debate on matters before it. More specifically, however, the deliberative function of Parliament enables it to debate an array of policy issues, some of which result in the passage of resolutions. Deliberations may throw light on underlying tensions in society and help to foster consensus, compromise, and reconciliation. The deliberative function is exercised mainly through the mechanism of statements, motions, questions, and ceremonial speeches, etc.

How a Bill Becomes Law

According to Article 106, clause (2) of the constitution, 'No bill . . . shall be introduced in Parliament unless it has been published in the Gazette *at least 14 days* before the date of its introduction in Parliament.' The bill, as published in the Gazette is introduced in Parliament. The legislative process in Parliament can be classified in four stages: first reading, second reading, committee or consideration stage, and third reading. The first reading is the first time the bill appears before Parliament. The Speaker reads the long title of the bill and the sponsoring minister then rises and bows to the Speaker. The bill is then referred to the relevant committee. This same committee investigates and examines the bill. During the following deliberation, the committee produces a report that forms the basis for the second reading. During the second reading, Parliament debates the principles and policies of the bill. The Sector Minister delivers a speech explaining the implications of the bill and argues for its passage. The minority party will also debate the bill. Debates of the parliament are recorded verbatim by the Hansard Department of the Office of the Clerk of Parliament. These recordings, and other Parliamentary materials including bills, are published as an official report in the *Hansard* of the Parliament of Ghana from time to time.

Committee Stages of a Bill under Consideration

In the committee or consideration stage, the bill is discussed clause by clause and all concerns are debated and voted upon. The Speaker states each clause of the bill and members note their questions and concerns. Finally, changes or amendments are voted upon. The attorney general's department then takes the accepted amendments and redrafts the bill. In an attempt to describe how a bill is passed in the Ghanaian legislature, a retired justice of the Supreme Court of Ghana, Justice V.C.R.A.C. Crabbe illustrated the proceedings at the consideration stage as follows: After the formal debate, the Speaker puts the question that clause 1 for example, stands part of the bill. Those in favour say aye, those against say no, thus the affirmative response is aye and the negative response is no. Then he says the ayes have it and waits whether there is a demand for division. Where there is no demand for division, the Speaker says the ayes have it or the nos have it if there is an objection. In the event that a member calls for revision, the Speaker asks for votes to be counted. Tellers are then appointed and the House goes into division for the actual numbers to be taken and tallied. Names are then taken for a roll-call. The names of the ayes and nos present in the chamber of parliament are then published in the *Hansard* of parliament as a record and circulated accordingly. According to Justice V.C.R.A.C. Crabbe, different political manoeuvres could be used at the committee stage to keep Parliament on schedule: the Winnowing Session, the Guillotine, and the Kangaroo. The Winnowing Session is the only one of these procedures that is clearly detailed in the Standing Orders of Parliament. The Standing Orders state, 'Where after a bill has been read a second time, more than wenty (20) amendments are proposed to it, any Member proposing an amendment may appear before the Committee dealing with the subject matter to defend his or her amendment(s) and the Committee shall submit a Report to the House on the result of this exercise before the consideration stage of the bill is taken.' In these sessions, members consolidate the questions on particular clauses. The next procedure, the Guillotine, is used to prevent filibusters. For example, if parliament has five days to end a session and ten bills to work on, the opposition may opt to filibuster, because they know they will lose. The Speaker combats the filibuster by creating a timeline, and regardless of the progress, when the deadline arrives, the bill will pass. If even only ten out of fifty clauses may have been discussed, the bill will still pass. Finally, when Parliament wants to expedite the process, the Kangaroo procedure is exercised. In the Kangaroo procedure, the Speaker sets a time for a set of clauses in the bill and at that time the Speaker puts the question that the relevant clauses stand part of the bill and they are voted on. The next set of clauses is then taken. So like the kangaroo, members jump from a set of clauses to another. In the third reading, Parliament continues to debate the principles and policies of the bill. If a Member of Parliament indicates that a clause was not properly reviewed, the bill is recommitted to the committee stage. If there are no objections, all present parliamentarians vote for or against the bill's passage. Following the vote, the Clerk examines the votes of the proceedings to determine which amendments have been made and incorporates them into the bill. The Clerk sends the final bill with all amendments to the Government Printer.

Duties of a Member of Parliament

Ghana's parliament has 275 members, elected for a four-year term in single-seat constituencies. The vice president or a minister or deputy minister, who is not a member of Parliament, shall be entitled to participate in the proceedings of Parliament and shall be accorded all the privileges of a member of Parliament except that he is not entitled to vote or to hold an office in Parliament. Ghana's parliament is a representative institution, which reflects the dictum 'government of the people, by the people and for the people'. Therefore, Parliament is the hub of the country's democratic governance. It has a responsibility to foster public awareness of the basic tenets of democracy.

The MP, as an elected representative of his constituents, is an agent for the realization of the aspirations of his people and the nation at large. The MP finds himself/herself in a web of onerous duties such as service to the nation, to the constituents, and to their respective political parties.

Duties to the Nation

A member of Ghana's parliament (MP) has a fiduciary duty to his people. An MP exercises the legislative power of the state in accordance with the Constitution. This is done through the introduction and passage of bills. The MP also participates in all deliberations on matters of national and international importance. Parliament exercises constitutional authority over the use of public funds and the operations of ministries, departments, and agencies through inquiries and investigations. It is the duty of an MP to assist the House to execute this mandate through committees that enable MPs to examine, in greater detail, legislative and fiscal proposals from the Executive and its agencies. Effective participation in committee deliberations enables MPs to specialize in particular subject areas and this enhances Parliament's exercise of oversight responsibility of ministries, departments, and agencies (MDAs). Mechanisms such as Statements and Question Time present MPs with the opportunity to draw attention to issues of public or national importance. These mechanisms also serve as a means of obtaining assurances from ministers on actions being taken on the issues raised.

Duties to Constituents

An MP is a representative of all his/her constituents regardless of their party affiliations. The MP must find time to interact with his constituents at regular intervals. As a non-voting ex-officio member of the District Assembly, he/she is required to monitor programs and projects that the Assembly initiates in his constituency. It is the duty of a Member to explain to his constituents the laws passed by Parliament and policies being pursued by the government. The law demands such to be done periodically by the Member of Parliament to his/her people. In this regard, a Member is enjoined to advocate both in Parliament and the District Assembly the concerns of his constituents. A member of Parliament may use his/her portion of the District Assemblies' Common

Fund and other funding to assist directly in solving some of the developmental problems of his/her constituency.

Duties to the Party

An MP owes allegiance to the political party to which he/she belongs. His/her general performance must reflect the trust reposed in him/her by his/her party. While the majority group endeavours to implement its manifesto, the minority group is expected to offer constructive alternative programs. An MP's loyalty to his/her party may be expressed in the following ways:

- mobilizing support for his party's policies through intelligent contributions to debates both in the House and at committees;
- offering constructive criticism to the party's policies as and when appropriate;
- enhancing the party's image at both national and constituency levels.

Parliamentary Service Board

The Parliamentary Service is governed by the Parliamentary Service Board, which is composed of (a) the Speaker of Parliament, who by Constitution acts as chairman; (b) four other members appointed by the Speaker, but acting in accordance with the advice of a committee of Parliament; and (c) the Clerk of Parliament. The board has the responsibility of promoting the welfare of MPs and staff of the service. It also has general control of the management of the service in matters of policy. The Speaker has ultimate responsibility for the service. With the prior approval of Parliament, the Board makes regulations prescribing the terms and conditions of service of officers and other employees for the effective and efficient administration of the service. The Parliamentary Service Board appoints the Clerk to Parliament and other members of staff of the service in consultation with the Public Services Commission.

Clerk of Parliament

The Clerk to Parliament is the principal advisor to the Speaker of Parliament and MPs on matters of privilege, practice, and procedure. As head of the

Parliamentary Service, it is the duty of the Clerk to (a) arrange sittings of the House, (b) prepare the Order Paper, (c) keep the Minutes Book. All bills passed by the House are authenticated by the Clerk for presidential assent. The Clerk to Parliament presides over the first sitting of a newly elected Parliament for the purpose of electing the Speaker of Parliament. The Clerk also presides over the Management Committee comprising the three deputy clerks and heads of departments. The Clerk demonstrates non-partisanship and impartiality in the discharge of his/her duties to Parliament.

Committees within the Legislature of Ghana

A *standing committee* is a group of members of a larger body, such as a legislature or membership association, appointed for a specific purpose and, usually, a specific period of time. It can also be described as a society, etc., intended to consider all matters pertaining to a designated subject. In Ghana, Parliament establishes many standing committees, each with its own specific jurisdiction. For example, the parliamentary committee on education is a standing committee that reviews all proposed legislation regarding educational matters in the country.

Select Committees

In Ghana, *select committees* are legislative (or parliamentary) ones which deliberate upon complex issues and/or scrutinize the executive on issues broader than legislation. They may invite written and oral evidence from witnesses, deliberate, and make reports with recommendations to the House. Their membership is determined in proportion to party strength in the House, and their members normally serve for a full parliamentary term. Members attempt to work on a non-partisan basis and it is normal for some select committee chairs to go to members of the opposition parties. Select committees, nevertheless, are criticized for lacking information in undertaking inquiries to complete their tasks on schedule. In the United States, however, the House and Senate *select committees* are usually formed for limited periods and for limited purposes. Although there are exceptions, most have not been given legislative power—that is, the authority to consider and report legislation to the full chamber. After completing its purpose, such as an investigation of a government activity and making a related report, the select committee disbands. Recently, however, the chambers have allowed select committees to continue to exist over extended periods. Some, such as the House and Senate Select Committees on Intelligence, have been granted legislative authority.

A. *Select Committees*
(1) Foreign Affairs, (2) Health, (3) Local Government and Rural Development, (4) Environment, Science, and Technology, (5) Works and Housing (6) Employment, Social Welfare, and State Defense and the Interior, (7) Mines and Energy, (8) Lands and Forestry, (9) Constitutional, Legal, and Parliamentary Affairs, (10) Communications, (11) Poverty Reduction Strategy, (12) Education, Youth, Sports, and Culture, (13) Roads and Transport

B. *Standing Committees*
(1) Public Accounts, (2) Privileges, (3) Standing Orders, (4) Special Budget, (5) Judiciary, (6) Finance, (7) Business, (8) Selection Subsidiary Legislation, (9) Appointments, (10) Committee on Members Holding Offices of Profit, (11) Committee on Government Assurances, (13) Committee on Gender and Children, (14) Education Committee, (15) House Committee

Parliamentary Leadership and Committees

The Constitution of Ghana allows for a legislature, parliament, political parties, and the local government—the District Assembly, which sees to the enactment of laws and policies for the development and well-being of the nation.

The Ghanaian parliament is composed of representatives of the various political parties currently registered with the Electoral Commission of Ghana. The Ghanaian Members of parliament, called parliamentarians, as they are often referred to, are elected every four years in very competitive elections. Parliament is made up of representatives of political parties, called Members of Parliament (MPs). The 2012 general elections produced the following results:

Majority:	NDC	(148)
Minority:	NPP	(122)
PNC		(1)

CPP   (1)
Independent candidates   (4)
Total: 275
Government Majority   21

Leadership in Ghana's Parliament
Speaker of Parliament:
Hon. Joe Adjaho
Speaker of Parliament:
Rt. Hon. Edward K. Doe Adjaho – former Member of Parliament
First Deputy Speaker:

Hon. Ebo Barton Oduro	- NDC MP Cape Coast North – Central Region

Second Deputy Speaker:

Hon. Joe Ghartey	- NPP MP Essikado-Ketan - Western Region

Majority Leader:

Hon. Alban Sumana Kingsford Bagbin	NDC MP Nadowli West - Upper West Region

Minority Leader:

Hon. Osei Kyei-Mensah-Bonsu	NPP MP Suame - Ashanti Region

Deputy Minority Leader:

Hon. Dominic Aduna Nitiwul	NPP MP Bimbilla - Northern Region
Hon. Barton Oduro	NDC

Second Deputy Speaker

Hon.	NPP

Majority Leader

Hon. Alban Sumana Kingsford Bagbin	NDC

Minority Leader

Hon. Osei Kyei-Mensah Bonsu	NPP

Deputy Minority Speaker
Dominic Nitiwul

Publication

The *Hansard* is the official nearly verbatim report of proceedings of the House. It is a repository and reflection of the legislative activities of Parliament.

Summary

Ghana's parliament is organized into a unicameral legislature. There is only one parliament, which exercises all primary legislative functions. Article 11 of the 1992 Constitution of Ghana states, 'The laws of Ghana shall comprise (a) this Constitution; (b) enactments made by or under the authority of the Parliament established by this Constitution; (c) any Orders, Rules, and Regulations made by any person or authority under a power conferred by this Constitution; (d) existing law; and (e) common law.' Therefore, chief legislative power has been vested in the Parliament of Ghana. Although the current constitution vests principal legislative power in parliament, this appropriation of authority was not always the case. In 1850, the first Legislative Council was established to advise the colonial governor in enacting legislation. Although this council prevented direct involvement of the people, it served with its enlargement in 1916 under Sir Hugh Clifford as a representation chamber (see Political History of Ghana, Kimble, p. 433 et sec.) as a precursor to today's representative democracy.

Conclusion

The legislative branch of the Ghanaian government passes bills which are assented to by the president, and become the laws which protect the constitutional rights of the citizens of Ghana. The elected body consists of no less than 275 members. A Member of Parliament must be a citizen of Ghana and must have attained the age of twenty-one years and be a registered voter. Article 94 further states, 'A Member of Parliament must hold current residence in the area he or she represents or has lived in the area for at least 5 of the 10 years preceding his or her election.' A candidate vying to become a Member of Parliament must have paid all taxes due to the state. Besides, criminal cases, bankruptcy, or other judicial issues can prevent a citizen from becoming a Member of Parliament. Article 94 of the 1992 Constitution outlines possible reasons for someone not being qualified to become a Member of Parliament: (1) A person shall not be qualified to be a Member of Parliament if he (a) owes allegiance to a country other than Ghana, or (b) has been adjudged or otherwise declared bankrupt under any law in force in Ghana. Other provisions of the constitution outline possible reasons for the ineligibility of candidates for Parliament. If, for instance, a person is a member of the Police Service, the Prisons Service, the Armed Forces, the Judicial Service, the Legal Service, the Civil Service, the Audit Service, or any other service listed in Article 94 of the 1992 Constitution, he is ineligible to become a Member of Parliament. It is very important to note that even after being elected, a Member of Parliament can lose his or her seat for a number of reasons. Such reasons include, but are not limited to 'if he is elected as Speaker of Parliament, if he is absent without the permission in writing of the Speaker, if he is expelled [after being] found guilty of contempt of Parliament, [or] if he leaves the party of which he was a member at the time of his election to join another party or seeks to remain as an independent.' One of the most important clauses in Article 97 pertains to the act of changing political parties following an election. Although this has not been much of an issue now within Ghana as in the past, other countries have suffered from such acts. Currently, many parties exist within Parliament, including the National Democratic Congress (NDC), which is the majority party, and the New Patriotic Party (NPP), which is the minority party. Other political parties within Parliament are the Convention People's Party (CPP), the People's National Convention (PNC), and independent candidates. The current Parliament of Ghana has 275 members.

Key Terms

Hansard   Manifesto   Ex-officio member   Oversight   Constitutional

Legislative instrument   Minority party   Majority party

Judicial review   Political process   System lapses

Service select committees   Non-partisanship   Chief legislative power

Manuscripts   Standing committees   Clerk of Parliament   Chief whip

Ombudsman Notaries   Minority leader   Majority leader   Speaker

Works Cited / Further Readings

Constitution of the Republic of Ghana (1992), Article 94, Article 97.

Hansard (2000–2015), Parliament House, Accra.

National Democratic Congress (1992, 2004, 2008), The NDC Handbook.

New Patriotic Party (1992, 2006, 2012), The NPP Handbook.

Chapter 6

THE PRESIDENCY (EXECUTIVE)

The Presidency

Ghana's political system can be described as presidentialism since the emergence of the fourth republic. Presidentialism in a country suggests that there is an individual who combines the functions of head of state and head of government. Aside from his/her juggernaut role in setting the national agenda as head of government, the president also functions as chief legislator, chief diplomat, and commander-in-chief. Presidential governments have features that distinguish them from parliamentary political systems. Though Ghana's Constitution allows the office of the presidency to be controlled by a nationally elected president, in practice, the political system is semi-presidential or a hybrid political system, because the same fundamental law requires more than 50 per cent of the cabinet to be selected from Parliament. In other words, there is compatibility between membership of cabinet and the legislature—a system where the president is elected with Members of Parliament on the same ballot— compatibility between membership of cabinet and the legislature. Unlike the strict presidentialism, as in the United States and Nigeria, this system hardly ever produces a deadlock between the executive and the legislative branches of government, since some politicians simultaneously play key roles in both branches of government, the Parliament and the executive, as ministers of departments and ministries. The literature on types of government systems, especially as it relates to the composition of the executive, has been explicit on the adverse effects that face any country that adopts a particular system, for instance, relating to how the two main systems of government, presidentialism and parliamentarism, enhance the stability of democracies. Linz (1996) argues that while parliamentary government gives flexibility to the political system, presidentialism makes the system rigid. On the other hand, the central role of separation of powers and checks and balances in presidential governments serve as a check on executive powers and, consequently, makes the executive branch more accountable to the legislature. In practice, the integration of both systems in Ghana since 1992 serves as a catalyst to the minimization of the disadvantages inherent in any particular system. Indeed, it serves to maximize the advantages of both systems in the delivery of democracy to its citizens. In Ghana, presidentialism has made the presidency far more superior than the other branches of government. The legislative branch does not have the political clout to serve as an institutional check on corruption within executive departments. This brand of governance is what Prempeh (2007) describes as the imperial president in Africa. According to Prempeh (2007), the *imperial* president received recognition following the decolonization of the continent in the 1960s, which led to the newly emergent African leaders' use of supra-constitutional measures to enhance their legitimacy. Ghana's governing system can thus be described as an *imperial presidency*, which has its roots in the Ghanaian Constitution, where the executive appears more powerful than the legislature. Some basic provisions of the Constitution, such as the wide latitude given the president to appoint not only cabinet ministers, but also chief executives of local government, municipal, and metropolitan agencies, as well as the chief executives and board members of many state organizations, undergird the predominance of the president in setting the national agenda. As applied to Ghana's political and policy processes, the imperial presidency paints a picture of presidential dominance. By and large, presidentialism, as it relates to the dominance of the executive branch of government in setting the national policy agenda, has made the presidency the most respected and recognized institution in the country.

The Executive

The power of the executive branch is vested in the president of the Republic of Ghana, who also acts as head of state and commander-in-chief of the Ghana Armed Forces (GAF). The president is responsible for implementing and enforcing the laws written by Parliament and, to that end, appoints ministers, including the Cabinet. The vice president is also part of the executive branch, ready to assume the presidency should the need arise. Presidents often face what is termed a 'damned if they do, damned if they don't' dilemma in the execution of their duties. They are expected to make decisions on the basis of available information without necessarily knowing how complete, accurate, or up to date it is. Presidents are expected to act in accordance with their previously stated goals (i.e. platforms or manifesto pledges) and positions, even though circumstances may have changed. Presidents are expected to be sensitive to public opinion even though that opinion (e.g. gay and lesbian rights in Ghana) may be divided or ambiguous or totally outrageous. And they are expected to solve problems even though they do not control all or even most of the factors that generated them. Moreover, if the problems persist, they are normally criticized, and their capacity to lead in the future may be impaired. Presidents also have a persistent leadership problem. The roots of problem lie in the Ghanaian system of government. To achieve their goals, the Ghanaian president requires the cooperation of many individuals over whom he/she may have little or no influence. Yet, the Constitution, by its derivatives divides authority, share power among several institutions, despite the fact that political parties lack cohesion and long-term policy positions by their orientation.

The pluralistic nature of Ghanaian society is another source of the problem. Presidents are required to do what is best for the country. Yet, assessments of their actions depend on how those actions affect individuals and groups within the society. The leadership problem has been aggravated in the last two decades by the proliferation of single-issue groups like Alliance for Accountable Governance (AFAG), Occupy Ghana Alliance (OGA), Let My Vote Count Alliance (LMVCA), gay and lesbian groups, Ghana Integrity Initiative, Amnesty International, ethnic youth associations, Graduate Unemployment Association, etc. The range of groups with an interest in most public policy issues has forced contemporary presidents to devote increasing amounts of time and energy to mobilizing support for their priorities. How can presidents overcome their leadership problems? The key to presidential success is the skilful use of legal, institutional, and political powers. In Ghana, the president, by virtue of being the head of government and the president, deserves respect to the highest order. In view of these legal aspects of powers conferred on the presidency, the occupant of that position is often referred to as His Excellency.

The Many Roles of the President

The Constitution of Ghana speaks briefly about the duties and obligations of the president. Based on this brief list of powers and on the precedents of history, the presidency has grown into a very complicated job that requires balancing at least five constitutional roles. These are (1) head of state, (2) chief executive, (3) commander-in-chief of the armed forces, (4) chief diplomat, and (5) chief legislator of Ghana. Here, we examine each of these significant presidential functions, or roles. It is worth noting here that one person plays all these roles simultaneously and that the needs of these roles may at times be in conflict.

President as Head of State

Every nation has at least one person who is the ceremonial head of state. In most democratic governments, the role of head of state is given to someone other than the chief executive, who leads the executive branch of government. In Britain, for example, the head of state is the Queen; and there is a prime minister, who executes the day-to-day activities of the country as the president. In much of Europe, the prime minister is the chief executive, and the head of state is the president (e.g. Federal Republic of Germany, being the chancellor). In the United States, the president is both chief executive and head of state, just as in Ghana, Nigeria, Togo, Benin, and many other countries practicing the executive system of governance. As head of state, the president engages in a number of activities that are largely symbolic or ceremonial:

a. Receiving visiting heads of state at the Flagstaff House
b. Going on official state visits to other countries
c. Making personal telephone calls to other heads of state on behalf of Ghana
d. Representing the nation at times of national mourning, such as the Melcom departmental store building collapse in Accra in 2011 and the flood disaster which occurred in Ghana around the Kwame Nkrumah Circle, claiming sixty lives, and property.

However, some scholars of African politics believe that having the president serve as both the chief executive and the head of state drastically limits the time available to do the 'real' work of the president. Not all presidents agree with this conclusion or notion; however, presidents who have skilfully blended these two roles with their role as politician have excelled. His Excellency, President John Mahama, in late 2012 combined his role as a newly sworn-in president of Ghana and also as a presidential candidate for the National Democratic Congress (NDC). Being head of state gives the president tremendous public exposure; this can be an important asset in a campaign for re-election. When that exposure is positive, it helps the president deal with parliament over proposed legislation and increases the chances of being re-elected, or getting the candidates of the president's party elected. This statement can be attributed to the elections for parliamentary candidates and president in Ghana in the 2012 general elections. After the death of President J. E. A. Mills of the NDC and the assertion to the presidency of then Vice President John Dramani Mahama, it was amply demonstrated in the popularity he received from Ghanaians on the thank-you tour and successor to the throne before embarking for his own re-election to the post of president.

President as Chief Executive

According to Article 57 of the 1992 Constitution of Ghana, the executive power shall be vested in a president elected by the people of Ghana in a general referendum. As chief executive, the president is constitutionally bound to enforce the acts of Parliament, the judgments of Supreme Court of Ghana, and treaties signed by Ghana. The duty to faithfully execute the laws has been a source of constitutional power for presidents. To assist in the various tasks of the chief executive, the president has a national bureaucracy (see chapter 8).

The Power of Appointment and Removal

One might think that the president, as head of the civil service or the bureaucracy, wields enormous power. The president, however, only nominally runs the executive bureaucracy. Most government positions are filled by civil service employees, who generally gain government employment through a merit system (civil service examinations) rather than presidential appointment. Therefore, even though the president has important appointive power, it is limited to cabinet and sub-cabinet jobs, such as ministers and deputy ministers and chief executive officers of government companies and corporations like the Volta River Authority (VRA), the Ghana Supply Company (GSCL), the Savannah Accelerated Development Authority (SADA), the Electricity Company of Ghana (ECG), the Ghana Grid Company (GRIDCO), judgeships, and other lesser jobs. This means that most of the civil service employees owe no political allegiance to the president. They are likely to owe loyalty to parliamentary committees or to interest groups representing the sector of the society that they serve.

The Power to Grant Reprieves and Pardons

The Constitution of Ghana Article 72 (1), Section (a), (b), and (c) gives the president the power to grant reprieves and pardons for offenses against Ghana, except in case of impeachment. All pardons are administered through the Minister of Justice and the attorney-general department. In principle, a pardon is granted to remedy a mistake made in a conviction. Examples of pardons that can be described in this light are those of Mr Tsatsu Tsikata and others, but not that of the convicted Bawku Member of Parliament, who lied about his nationality and was convicted to Nsawam prisons. His pardon smacks justice and fairness and constitutes why people continue to be dishonest about issues within the Ghanaian jurisprudence.

President as Commander-in-Chief

The president, according to the Constitution, 'shall be commander-in-chief of the army, air force, and navy of Ghana, the police, the immigration, Prison Service, Fire Service, when called into active service of Ghana'. In order words, the armed forces of Ghana are under civilian control rather than military control.

Wartime Powers of the President

Even though presidents are not expected to lead soldiers into battle, presidents as commanders-in-chief have wielded dramatic powers, such as calling the nation into emergency situations in times of national crisis such as emergencies and war. The president as commander-in-chief of the GAF can sent Ghana's armed forces to war with another country even before seeking parliamentary approval.

Democracy and peace—Some political scientists have claimed that the statement 'Democracies do not go to war with each other' is so true that it can be called a law of political science. It follows that a democratic world would be a world without war. Some observers, however, do not believe that nations have to be democratic to remain at peace with one another. Since they became independent, the nations of both South America and Africa have experienced constant dictatorships until now.

President as Chief Diplomat

The constitution gives the president the power to recognize foreign governments, to make treaties with the advice and consent of parliament, and to make special agreements with other heads of state that do not require parliamentary approval. In addition, the president nominates ambassadors. As chief diplomat, the president dominates Ghanaian foreign policy, by the appointment and approval by parliament of a Foreign Minister.

Diplomatic Recognition. An important power of the president as chief diplomat is that of diplomatic recognition, or the power to recognize—or not to recognize—foreign governments. In the role of ceremonial head of state, the president receives foreign diplomats and presidents on state visits to Ghana. In modern times, the simple act of receiving a foreign diplomat has been equivalent to accrediting the diplomat and officially recognizing his or her government. Such recognition of the legitimacy of another country's government is a prerequisite to diplomatic relations or treaties between that country and Ghana. A case in point during the inaugural ceremony of Ghana's president John Dramani Mahama, under the fifth republic, was the trooping in of African heads of state (about twenty-five) to Ghana on 7 January 2013. Another example is the recognition given to the Palestinian Authority and its diplomatic mission in Ghana.

Proposal and Ratification of Treaties. The president has the sole power to negotiate treaties with other nations. These treaties must be presented to

Ghana's parliament, where they may be modified and must be approved by a two-thirds majority vote.

Executive Agreements. A presidential power in foreign affairs is enhanced greatly by the use of executive agreements made between the president and other heads of state. These agreements do not require parliamentary approval, although parliament may choose to strike out a budget to fund or implement this type of initiative.

President as Chief Legislator

One of the crucial jobs of the president under the constitution is to recommend legislation that the president deems necessary for parliament. As a chief legislator, the president sets an agenda for the year through what is termed the State of the Nation address to parliament. The presentation of the State of the Nation address is a constitutional requirement under Article 67 of the 1992 Constitution of Ghana. It is a broad, comprehensive view of what the president wishes Parliament to accomplish during its session. It is as much a message to the Ghanaian people and to the world as it is to Parliament. Its impact on public opinion can determine the way in which Parliament responds to the president's agenda.

Getting Legislation Passed. The president proposes legislation to parliament under the constitution. Even though parliamentarians can themselves propose legislation, the practice is not common under any of the previous sittings of parliament. Through the nation's address, the president is able to use the power of persuasion, combined with his majority leadership in parliament, to introduce bills and get them passed. With the winner-takes-all system and a majority in parliament, it is normally easier for the president to exercise legislative leadership through the parliamentarians of that party. A president whose party holds a large majority in parliament may have an easier time getting legislation passed than when the majority is very slim in parliament.

The President's Veto Powers

According to Article 106, clause 7 of the Constitution, 'where a bill passed by parliament is presented to the president for assent, he shall signify, within seven days after the presentation to the Speaker that he assents to the bill or that he refuses to assent to the bill, unless the bill has been referred by the President to the Council of State under article 90 of [the] Constitution'. Within *seven days*, the president informs the Speaker of Parliament of his assent, refusal, or referral of the bill. If the president assents, the bill becomes law. The new law is published in the Gazette and enters into force. If the president refuses to assent to the bill, according to Article 106, clause (8) (a), he must 'within *fourteen days* after the refusal, state in a memorandum to the Speaker any specific provisions of the bill which in his opinion should be reconsidered by parliament, including his recommendations for amendments, if any'. In accordance with clause 9 of the same article, parliament reviews the bill, considering the president's comments. Subsequently, parliament votes for or against passing the resolution. According to Article 106, clause 10, 'where a bill reconsidered under clause 9 of this Article is passed by parliament by a resolution supported by the votes of not less than two-thirds of all the Members of Parliament, the president shall assent to it within thirty days after passing the resolution'. Because the president does not have the power to refuse or refer the bill at this point, the bill becomes law with the president's obligatory assent. Within presidential powers, referral to the Council of State exists as a measure to assent or refuse. The Council of State is a small body of prominent citizens of proven character that advises the president on national issues'. In Article 106, clause 8, 'the President [can refer], allow the president to refer a bill to the Council of State for consideration and comment'. If the president refers a bill to the Council of State, consideration of the bill must be *done thirty days* after the third reading of Parliament. This rule stands under all circumstances, except if the bill is introduced under a Certificate of Urgency. When a bill is introduced under a Certificate of Urgency, the Council of State has seventy-two hours to consider and to make subsequent recommendations. If the Council of State does not propose any amendments, the chairman must send a certificate of the council's decision to the president within seven days. If the Council decides to include proposed amendments, the chairman must send a memorandum of the proposed amendments to the president within *fifteen days* after the council's decision. Upon receipt of the certificate or memorandum, parliament considers the comments and recommendations of the council and casts a vote. *A two-thirds vote passes the resolution.* The bill is then sent for the president's assent. When the bill receives assent, it becomes law and is published in the Gazette. The Gazette is, therefore, a source for locating bills or proposed legislation in Ghana.

Other Presidential Powers

The powers of the president just discussed are called *constitutional powers*. Constitutional powers are those derived from the Constitution of Ghana. There are other powers established by law, or statute, such as the ability to declare national emergencies. These are called *statutory powers*. Both constitutional and statutory powers can be labelled or called *expressed powers* of the president, because they are expressly written in the Constitution or into law. The president also has what is known as *inherent powers*. These powers depend on the statements in the Constitution that the executive power shall be vested in a president and that the president should take care that the laws be faithfully executed. The most common example of inherent powers are those emergency powers invoked by the president during civil unrest in the country, for example, like the curfews that were imposed in Bawku in the Upper East region between 2009 to 2011 and the ones in Nkonya-Alavanyo-Hohoe in the Volta region of Ghana in 2012, as well as those in Bimbilla in the Northern region over chieftaincy issues.

The President as Party Chief and 'Super-politician'

Presidents are by no means above political partisanship, and one of their many roles is that of chief of party (leader of the party). Although the Constitution says nothing about the function of the president within a political party, they are leaders of their respective political parties. Within the political parties, presidents or presidential candidates are also automatic leaders, who control the directions of their parties.

As party leader, the president chooses the national committee chairpersons and, with the assistance of other party leadership, disciplines party members who fail to support presidential policies. One way of exerting political power within the party is through patronage—appointment of individuals to government or public jobs. This power has become very extensive today. The president appoints several thousand individuals to jobs in the cabinet, the Flagstaff House, and the national regulatory agencies and boards.

Perhaps the most important partisan role that the president plays is that of raising funds during a campaign year. The president is able to raise large amounts for his party through dinners, speaking engagements, and other social occasions. Presidents have a number of other ways of exerting influence as party chief. The president may appoint a Member of Parliament because the member is supportive of his vision in Parliament or dismiss an MP as a minister for sabotaging his government. The only problem with raising such funds for his party in Ghana is that such funds are not regulated or accounted for under the electoral laws of the country.

Constituencies and Public Approval

All politicians worry about their constituencies, and presidents are no exception. Just as a Member of Parliament worries about occurrences in his constituency, the president worries about negative public comments or incidents around the country. Presidents are also concerned with public approval ratings or public perception of his leadership. Presidents have many constituencies. In principle, they are beholden to the entire electorate—the public of Ghana—even those who did not vote at all. They are certainly beholden to their party because its members helped to put them in office. The president's constituency also includes members of the opposing party whose cooperation the president needs to get certain pieces of legislation passed in parliament. Finally, the president must take into consideration a constituency that has come to be called the *Accra (the capital city) community*. This community consists of individuals who—whether in or out of political office—are intimately familiar with the workings of government, thrive on gossip, and measure on a daily basis the political power of the president.

Public Approval

All these constituencies are impressed by presidents who maintain a high level of public approval, partly because this is very difficult to accomplish. Presidential popularity, as measured by national polls, gives the president an extra political resource to use in persuading parliament or bureaucrats to pass legislation. After all, refusing to do so might go against public sentiments and the country's constitution.

Going Public

Presidents can also go over the State of the Nation address and political elite by appealing to the people of the country directly. The term 'going public' gives the president additional power through the ability to persuade and manipulate public opinion over a proposed legislation. By identifying their own positions so clearly, presidents make compromises with parliament much more difficult and weaken the parliamentarians' position—whether they are in the president's party or on the side of the opposition. Giving importance of the media as the major source of political information for citizens and elites, presidents will continue to use public opinion as part of their arsenal of weapons to gain support from parliament and to achieve their policy goals. Can admitting to a mistake ever help a president gain public support in Ghana?

Special Uses of Presidential Power

Presidents also have at their disposal a variety of special powers and privileges not available in the other branches of the Ghanaian government. These include (1) emergency powers, (2) executive orders, and (3) executive privilege.

Emergency Powers

Emergency powers are inherent powers exercised by the president during a period of national crisis. If one were to read the Constitution of Ghana, one would find no mention of additional powers that the executive office may exercise during national emergencies. Indeed, emergency powers are used by presidents to safeguard national security or situations that threaten the peace of the country.

Other Powers of the President

a. *Legal powers.* Presidents can utilize the formal authority that is vested in the presidency. They command legal powers by virtue of constitutional and statutory powers as well as being the commander-in-chief of the Ghana Armed Forces (GAF).
b. *Institutional powers.* Presidents can utilize subordinates in the executive branch for the performance of their duties. Here, they delegate to others the job of collecting information and assessing opinions while reserving the critical decisions for themselves. Such assistants are referred to as presidential aides or staffers/advisors.
c. *Political powers.* Presidents can also utilize the informal powers of the presidency by persuasion. This political power is based on their elected positions, their political reputation, and public approval. Another important aspect of presidential power focuses on those powers and the environment in which they are exercised. We begin by exploring the legal basis of presidential authority, the creation of the executive by the constitution, and the evolution of presidential powers through stature and precedent. Next, we look at presidential leadership and the institutional and personal resources necessary to achieve it. We conclude by examining how presidents use their political powers to try to get things done and how they attempt to make, sell, and implement public policy.

Executive Powers

Executive powers are rules or regulations issued by the president that has the effect of law. Executive orders can implement and give administrative effect to provisions in the Constitution, to treaties, and to statutes. Executive orders can do the following: (1) enforce legislative statutes, (2) enforce the Constitution or treaties with foreign nations, and (3) establish or modify rules and practices of executive administrative agencies. Executive orders then represent the president's legislative power. Executive orders have been used to establish procedures to appoint non-career administrators, to implement national affirmative action regulations, to restructure civil service, to ration consumer goods, to administer wage and price controls under emergency conditions, to classify government information as secret, to regulate the export of restricted items, and to establish military tribunals for suspected terrorists.

Executive Privilege

Another inherent executive power that has been claimed by presidents concerns the ability of the president and the president's executive officials to withhold certain information from the public or refuse to appear before parliament or the courts to give out such information. Executive privilege is the right of executive officials to withhold information from or to refuse to appear before parliament or the courts to testify to such information. When presidents feel that the information to be testified or that they are about to release is so secret and of national importance, or could in a way jeopardize the security of the country, they can invoke what is termed an executive privilege.

Executive Power and Impeachment

Presidents normally leave office either because their first term has expired and they have not sought (or won) re-election or because, having served two full terms, they are not allowed to be elected for a third term because of constitutional limitations. The Constitution of Ghana limits the tenure of presidents to only two four-year terms, which means that a president in Ghana can only be re-elected once. In Ghana, one president, Professor John Evans Atta Mills, died in office in July of 2012, but there is still another way for a president to leave office, and this could be by impeachment and conviction. The Ghanaian Constitution, in Article 69, clause 1 authorizes Parliament and the Supreme Court to remove the president, the vice president, or other civil officers of Ghana for committing treason, bribery, or other high crimes and misdemeanours. An impeachment is to accuse (charge) a person, whether the president, vice president, or other civil officers of the country. An impeachment process draws up articles of impeachment and submits them to the Supreme Court, which conducts the actual trial and thereby removes the accused (impeached) executive officer.

The Executive Organization—Staff of the Flagstaff House

The executive organization of the Flagstaff House (FSH) office staff has steadily grown beyond what we had when the seat of government was at the Castle, Osu. The staff of the Flagstaff House also includes some workers who have no access to the president and are not concerned with the administration's political success. The staff of the Flagstaff House—apart from those appointed to assisting positions, such as the executive secretary to the president, the cabinet secretary, the chief of staff and his deputies, among others—are referred to as presidential staff and were probably working with the president in his election campaign. These assistants are most concerned with preserving the president's reputation. Also included in the president's staff are a number of councils and advisory organizations, such as the National Security Council, the National Economic Council, the Economic Crimes Office (EOCO), Bureau of National Investigations (BNI), and others. Although the individuals who hold staff positions in these offices are appointed by the president, they are really more concerned with their own areas than with the president's overall success. The group of appointees who perhaps are most helpful to the president is the cabinet; each member of the president's cabinet is the principal officer of a government department or ministry.

The Cabinet

The Constitution does not explicitly use the word *cabinet*, but it does state that the president 'should require the opinion, in writing, of the principal officers in each of the executive departments to which the president turns for counsel'.

Members of the Cabinet. The cabinet does not have an exact number. It depends on each president and what that particular session of cabinet he meets wants to discuss. Originally, the cabinet consisted of principally four officials—the Minister of Foreign Affairs, the Finance Minister, the Attorney General, and the Minister of Justice, and the Minister for Defence. However, the president can constitute a cabinet number from fourteen departments to a maximum of seventeen, depending on his agenda for the country and the issues prevailing in the country. The cabinet may include others as well. The president, at his or her discretion, can ascribe cabinet rank, for example, to the vice president, the head of civil service, the chairman, and other officers of the president's party, the national security advisor, an ambassador, or to many others.

Kitchen Cabinet. A kitchen cabinet is a group of informal advisors to the president. A president uses a kitchen cabinet to replace the formal cabinet as a major source of advice. The term *kitchen cabinet* originated with the use of close friends by American presidents, who drew and met with a few close friends in the kitchen of the White House to agree or disagree on issues important to the president before they are brought into the open. A *kitchen cabinet* is a very informal group of advisers, usually friends with whom the president worked before his election as president of the country.

Presidential Use of Cabinet

The Constitution in Ghana states that the president should consult with the cabinet in the approval of certain pieces of legislation before it is sent to parliament. Some presidents have relied on the counsel of their cabinet more than others. More often, presidents have solicited the opinions of their cabinet and then did what they wanted to do anyway. But when that is detected, the president can face what is called high crimes. It is not surprising that presidents tend not to rely on their cabinet members' advice. Often, the ministers of the various ministries are more responsive to the wishes of the president and serve at the president's pleasure. They are concerned with obtaining and fulfilling the agenda so as to achieve the overall objectives of the president. So, there is often a strong relation of interest between president and cabinet ministers in pursuit of the government's overall agenda.

The Executive Office of the President

The *executive office of the president* is an organization established to assist the president carry out major duties of his position. As a result of this establishment, the president coordinates the executive bureaucracy. Most of the offices under the executive office of the president are sometimes not within the premises of the Flagstaff House, such as the Offices of Coordinator of Microfinance (MASLOC). The offices and agencies that can be found under the executive offices of the presidency are:

Council of Economic Advisers	Office of Narcotics and Drugs Board
National Security Council	National Planning Commission
Office of National AIDS Policy	Office of the Vice President
Flagstaff House Military Office	Office of the President
MASLOC	Ghana AIDS Commission

He was popularly elected in an election conducted by Ghana's Electoral Commission on 7 December 2012. This is his first term as president (7 January 2013–6 January 2017), despite serving the remaining five months of the late President J. E. A. Mills's term.

President John Mahama ascended to the Office of President after the untimely demise of the late president—His Excellency Professor John Evans Atta Mills on 24 July 2012. President Mahama had previously served as the vice president, and on the passing of President Mills, he took over the reins of government and led the country to bid a befitting farewell to a leader who was much loved, respected, and can be described as a father for all. The Ghanaian Constitution of 1992 provides in Article 60 (6), 'Whenever the President dies, resigns, or is removed from office, the Vice President shall assume office as President for the unexpired term of office of the President with effect from the date of the death, resignation, or removal of the President.' President Mahama therefore assumed the role of head of state, head of government, and commander-in-chief of the Armed Forces of Ghana from the time of the passing of the late president. He was sworn into office on the same day by the Chief Justice, and Ghana accomplished a peaceful transition that demonstrated the strength and robustness of the country's democratic institutions.

Presidential Succession

In Ghana, the Constitution clearly states that there shall be a presidential succession. This succession can only take place when a president dies or when a president is impeached and removed from office. In Ghana, there has only been one occurrence of succession, which took place after the demise of president John Atta Mills in July of 2012. His successor, then vice president, took over when he was sworn in as president and subsequently became the president after the December 2012 elections the following year 2013. At the time of writing this book, the president was due for re-election. Elections are scheduled for 7 November 2016, shifted from its usual constitutional date of December 7th since 1992, because of a constitutional amendment in 2015. But on 22 July 2016, the Ghanaian parliament rejected a proposed amendment to shift the voting date from the usual date of 7 December to 7 November.

The Vice President and Succession

The Constitution of Ghana states clearly the issue of how the president should fill a vacant vice presidency: 'Whenever there is a vacancy in the office of the Vice President, the President shall nominate a Vice President upon confirmation by a majority vote of Parliament.' This is exactly what occurred and the first (in history) for Ghana, when President John Mahama had to nominate the former governor of the Bank of Ghana in late 2012 to become his vice president when the then president, Professor John Atta Mills, passed on. He nominated the former governor of the Bank of Ghana, Mr Kwesi Amissah-Arthur, as the vice presidential nominee, who was subsequently vetted and approved by the Parliament in late 2012. However, the question of who shall be president if both the president and vice president die at the same time is answered by the Constitution. If the president and the vice president should die, or resign, at the same time, then the Speaker of Parliament assumes the presidency and shall become president, after resigning from Parliament.

Why Is the Presidency Important Today in Ghana?

Political scholars have suggested that the presidency is virtually in your face these days in terms of the relationship it maintains with the general public.

Certainly, the media is responsible for this relationship, with every single activity in which the president is involved reported to the public. Most of the media coverage of the president provides entertainment value only; yet, it can generally be said that no other country in Africa puts its head of state under such a microscope as Ghana does. It is true that no Ghanaian can escape the actions of the president of the country because of his constitutional powers which can affect you, your family, or your business and friends on a daily basis. As already enumerated before, the president can veto legislation and acts as chief legislator by submitting proposed legislation to Parliament. The president also has the ability to act while Parliament is not in session, through the use of emergency powers as well as executive orders.

Why Should You Care?

As a Ghanaian, should you care about sending a message to the president if you sincerely believe certain policies of the government are not achieving their intended impact? There are reasons why you might want to engage in this form of political participation. Presidents typically claim that they do not set their policies or reverse their stand on policies by looking at the reactions of the public. Yet, presidents pay attention to public opinion, and many presidents have been able to avoid changing policy when the public is pressing them to do so. President John Dramani Mahama, in the heat of the 2012 general elections, had to call Parliament to attention when he suspended salary increases from GHC3,300 to a high of GHC7,500 for legislators and GHC9,000 for the president. What are some of the issues you would write to the president about? Fuel hikes? School fees hikes? The rampant power outages by the Electricity Company of Ghana? Or higher utility bills?

Conclusion

Ghana has been a stable democracy since the introduction of constitutional democracy in 1992. Changes of government between the two dominant parties, National Democratic Congress (NDC) and the New Patriotic Party (NPP) have generally been smooth. Campaigns have been heating up since 2004 and the same can be said of the campaigns of 2008 and 2012. The 2012 election results were disputed and finally had to be adjudicated upon by the nation's highest court, the Supreme Court of Ghana, and in NDC's favour. After a few turbulent decades following independence in 1957, Flight Lieutenant J. J. Rawlings completed the country's fifth military coup in 1981, with the declared aim to lay the foundations for a modern democratic state. Rawlings won the subsequent presidential elections in 1992 and 1996 for the NDC, which he had founded. He stayed in power until 2000 when the presidential election was won by the NPP presidential candidate John Kufuor. Kufuor stayed in office until 2008, after re-election in 2004. Presidential and parliamentary elections were held on 7 December 2012. John Dramani Mahama won the presidential elections in the first round with 50.7 per cent of the votes and NDC retained parliamentary majority. The elections were generally hailed as free and peaceful. The opposition party NPP, citing electoral irregularities, contested the election results at the Supreme Court. In August 2013 the Supreme Court ruled that John Mahama rightfully won the elections. The opposition leader Nana Akufo-Addo immediately recognized the ruling.

The next elections are due to be held in December of 2016. At the 18 October 2014 NPP Super Delegates Congress, Nana Akufo-Addo was elected the party's presidential candidate for the third time, receiving over 80 per cent of the vote. Akufo-Addo is expected to the run against NDC incumbent, His Excellency, John Dramani Mahama at the next elections. In 2009 the government of Ghana proposed the revision of aspects of the 1992 Constitution of Ghana. A Constitution Review Commission presented its recommendations to the government of Ghana in 2011. A referendum on constitutional reform is currently postponed because of a civil court case. The impending district assembly elections will take place without the referendum on the constitutional reform provisions, because of the case still in court for a constitutional interpretation; however, the local assembly elections came on as expected on 3 March 2015. Although Ghana's government has declared zero tolerance toward corruption, studies show that corruption occurs, especially in the police, customs, and judiciary system, but also in the education and health sectors. In 2014 Ghana was ranked 61 out of 175 on Transparency International's Corruption Perception Index. Among African countries, Ghana was rated number 8. Ghana was also ranked 7 out of 52 African countries on the 2014 Mo Ibrahim Index, which ranks security, good governance, the economy, social sectors, and human rights.

Key Terms

Constitution   Commission   Recommendations   Provisions   Customs

Mo Ibrahim Index   Human rights   Referendum Reforms   Review

Commission   Proposal   Delegates   Congress   Transitions   Amendments

Presidential assent   Pardons   Clemency   Bail-out   Good governance

Works Cited / Further Readings

'Ghana gets a New Presidential Jet', http://www.adeparadio.com/ghana-gets-a-new-presidential-jet/ retrieved 7 June 2013.

'Ghana Unveils Presidential Palace', BBC News Online 2008 retrieved 7 June 2013

'Profile: Ghana President John Atta-Mills', BBC World News, 3 January 2009

'Ghana's President John Atta Mills dies', BBC World News, 24 July 2014.

Constitution of the Republic of Ghana (1992), The Oath of Allegiance.

Judiciary of Ghana, http://www.judicial.gov.gh

'President Mahama Moves to the Flagstaff House', http://presidency.gov.gh/node/77

Ghana Institute of Journalism (1995), 'Informational Brochure' (Accra).

'Ghana Journalists Association Thinks Big, Vendors Cry Foul.' *Accra Mail*, 11 March 2002.

'Ghanaian Diplomat, Journalist Discuss Media in Recent Elections.' *Accra Mail*, 14 March 2001.

Hasty, Jennifer (1999), 'Big Language and Brown Envelopes: The Press and Political Culture in Ghana', Ph.D. dissertation, Duke University.

'Hope for Media in the New Democracy.' *IPI Report*, Vol. 42, No. 8, Aug. 1993, p. 7.

'Independent Radio on the Rise in Ghana.' *Billboard*, 109 (2): 45.

Chapter 7

THE COURTS (JUDICIARY)

The Origins and Background of Ghana Courts

1969–1972

The constitution of the second republic began in 1969, inter alia, the offices of the president and prime minister with a Cabinet; and this is where we shall begin the study of the courts in Ghana. Art. 53 of the then constitution (1969) provided for a Council of State to aid and counsel the president. Provision was made for a Parliament consisting of the president and a National Assembly. The National Assembly consisted then of about 140 members. The structure of the judiciary of Ghana is found in chapter 11 of the Constitution of the Republic of Ghana, 1992 (to be referred here as the Constitution, or the 1992 Constitution). The 1992 Constitution is and remains the primary source of law in the country of Ghana today. This is enhanced by the Courts Act, 1993 (Act 459) which was enacted 'to incorporate into the law relating to the courts, the provisions of . . . the Constitution; to provide for their composition'. Act 459 was amended on 13 April 2002 by Act 620 and on 1 November 2004 by Act 674. The judiciary, according to Article 126 of the 1992 Constitution, consists of the Superior Courts of Judicature and lower courts or tribunals as Parliament may by law establish. Indeed, the common law in force in Ghana today is based on common law—doctrines of equity and general statutes in force in England in 1874—as modified by subsequent ordinances. Over time, the Ghanaian customary law has become the basis of most personal, domestic, and contractual relationships. Criminal law is based on the criminal procedure code, 1960, derived from English criminal law, and since amended.

The origins of the Ghanaian system started when the Bond of 1844 was signed between Commander H. Hill and the local Fanti chiefs in Cape Coast. The signing of the bond was to acknowledge the power and jurisdiction which had been de facto exercised in the territories around the British forts and settlements of the then Gold Coast (now Ghana). The signing of the bond for the first time indicated the protection of individuals and property and stipulated, for the first time, the further protecting of people from sacrifices, beheading, panyarring (or the kidnapping of hostages for debt), and other customs contrary to law. The bond indeed permitted the trial of serious crimes by the (British) Queen's judicial officers sitting with the chiefs for the first time to frame the general principles of British law.

Furthermore, the Supreme Court Ordinance of 1853 established the Supreme Court of Her Majesty's forts and settlements because of the separation of the court from Sierra Leone under Governor H. Hill. In 1866, a commission was created to revoke where the Gold Coast, together with Sierra Leone, Lagos, and Gambia, were created under 'the Governor of Goaur West African Settlements'. In doing so, the existing Gold Coast ordinances were preserved, as well as the Legislative Council. Because of these creations, the Executive Council ceased to exist and the Supreme Court was abolished in 1866 and replaced by the Court of Civil and Criminal Justice presided over by a chief magistrate.

The Ghana legal system, like so many other institutions in our state, is a direct product of our colonial past. After a few false starts, the Supreme Court of Judicature for the Gold Coast Colony was established by ordinance by the imperial Parliament in Westminster in 1876. It consisted of a Chief Justice and not more than four puisne judges. Provision was further made for a full court consisting of the Chief Justice and one or two puisne judges, who acted as a Court of Appeal sitting in Accra and Lagos, then administered as part of the Gold Coast Colony. The Supreme Court was vested with the same jurisdiction in civil and criminal matters as was exercisable by the Court of Queen's Bench, the Court of Common Pleas, and the Court of Exchequer. It can be properly said that the establishment of the Supreme Court constituted the commencement of the legal profession in the country. Hence, the Ghana Bar Association's claim to be the most senior of the professions in the nation is quite a valid one in the judiciary history of Ghana.

The Court System—Ghana, the UK, and Australia

In the United Kingdom, the structure of the courts in all the three jurisdictions (England and Wales, Scotland, and Northern Ireland) tends to be arranged according to the subject matter of cases brought before the courts, rather than the source of the laws to be applied. Laws are the ones that dictate how a nation/country functions and are politically, economically, and societally focused. Law serves as the mediator between all peoples living in the state. Without rules, there would never be concordance among all the citizens. The law is thus the basis for decision-making as it regulates the events, and movement of manpower, monetary and natural resources to be used for the development of the country and welfare of all men. Law indeed sets out details of the rights and responsibilities and regulates the conduct of every citizen living in the country.

A lawless country, therefore, might find it difficult to develop in peace, as the most affluent and strong individuals within the state are more likely to offend with impunity. In the United Kingdom or England, the more serious criminal cases are tried on the basis of a document called the indictment. Here, the defendant is indicted on criminal charges specified in the indictment by the prosecutor. In most cases, the prosecution is on behalf of the Crown (the state) and is handled by an official agency called the Crown Prosecution Service, which takes the case over from the police, who have already investigated most of the evidence. The first stage will be to decide whether, prima facie, there is a case to answer. This process—called committal—is dealt with by a magistrate on the basis of evidence disclosed in papers provided by the prosecutor. If the case proceeds, it is heard in the Crown Court (there is only one Crown Court, but it has about 70 centres around the jurisdiction).

Here, the trial is before a judge and jury. The judge presides over the trial process by attempting to ensure clarity and fairness. The judge must also consider and decide on legal issues (such as whether a piece of evidence is admissible—should be put before the jury) and also instruct the jury as to the correct view of the law relevant to the case. This is termed as jury direction. The jury decides the facts—whose story is more believable—and applies the law to those facts. So, it is the jury, not the judge, which reaches a verdict on the guilt or innocence of the defendant. In criminal cases, the prosecution has the burden of proof—it must prove guilt, rather than the defendant having to prove innocence. The standard (level) of proof is heavy—guilt must be proven beyond reasonable doubt.

In less serious criminal cases, which according to Home Office Research and Statistics Directorate website for statistics (the 1996 British Crime Survey) comprise over 90 per cent of criminal cases, the case is sent for summary trial in one of over 400 magistrates' courts (this 400 figure might be lower because of the current economic climate). A summary trial means there is no committal and no jury. The trial is before a bench of magistrates. In most cases, there are three magistrates who are laypersons—in other words, they are not professional judges, nor are they lawyers, but like the jury, they are persons from the local community. Apart from travel and subsistence expenses, magistrates, also known as Justices of the Peace or JPs, are unpaid volunteers and come from all walks of life and backgrounds, and can be any age from eighteen to seventy. They retire at seventy and are usually expected to serve for at least five years. One won't normally be appointed JP if s/he is over sixty-five.

The selection and the roles of UK magistrates are not within the scope of this work. There are an increasing number of stipendiary magistrates—paid magistrates who are qualified lawyers. We mention in passing that magistrates sit in courts in their local area and hear criminal cases and help solve disputes—civil and family litigations. With experience and extra training, magistrates can go on to deal with cases such as child custody and taking children into care in family courts. Thus, magistrates don't just deal with crimes but also hear some civil cases, over things such as unpaid council tax and appeals against licensing decisions. Those defendants who are dissatisfied by the verdict may be able to appeal, from the magistrates' courts. There is an appeal to the Crown Court on matters of fact or law. From the Crown Court, it might be possible to appeal to the Criminal Division of the Court of Appeal on matters of fact or law. Certain legal disputes arising in the magistrates' courts or the Crown Court can be taken before the Divisional Court of the High Court.

It is suggested that the majority of cases sent by the magistrates to the Crown Court that result in a sentence receive a punishment within the existing powers of magistrates. The argument had been that by sending defendants to the Crown Court, the magistrates presumably thought they deserved a higher sentence. The main features of the British magistracy are the identification of the legal facts from fictions, not forgetting its community focus and commonsense approach to access to justice. At present, there is a general limit on the sentencing powers of magistrates' courts, which, according to part 12, clauses 137–138: magistrates' sentencing powers prevent JPs from imposing more than six months' imprisonment for any one offence. See also Magistrates' Court Act 1980, s 31(1). The limit for consecutive terms of imprisonment is also six months, unless the sentence relates to two or more either way offences (e.g. theft, burglary), in which case the limit is twelve months. The Courts of Ghana interpret and apply the laws of Ghana and decide cases/disputes among and between individuals within the state, as well as those of special republican interest. Like in the UK, legally argued, all cases are likely to begin at the Magistrates' Court and end at the Supreme Court. The Supreme Court of Ghana is the highest court of appeal on all matters that have some element of constitutional interpretations, whether decided at the magistrates' or High Court. In the UK, matters of important legal dispute arising in the Crown Court or Divisional Court may be appealed to the House of Lords.

In civil cases, the litigation is commenced by a plaintiff (a private person or company or a public authority) against a defendant. The plaintiff must try to prove the liability of the defendant on the balance of probabilities. The sorts of claims arising in the civil courts are typically about contracts (most common of all), torts (civil wrongs such as causing a road accident through negligence, damaging a person's reputation through defamation, or affecting the enjoyment of their property through causing a nuisance such as by pollution), and land disputes. The choice of court depends in most cases on the value of the claim. Claims of lesser value (small claims—not more than £5,000) will start in a county court. The UK magistrates, for example, have jurisdiction over £5,000 fines.

In Australia, the Federal Court's jurisdiction is broad, covering almost all civil matters arising under Australian federal law and some summary criminal matters. The court also has substantial and diverse appellate jurisdiction, including over the decisions of single judges of the Federal Court and the

Federal Magistrates Court (in non-family-law matters) and some decisions of the state and territory courts. The Family Court is Australia's superior court in family law. Through its specialist judges and staff, the court helps to resolve complex family disputes. It also covers specialized areas such as cases relating to The Hague Convention on International Child Abductions (which came into force in Australia in December 1998) and the international relocation of children by parents or guardians. The Federal Magistrates Court was established by the federal parliament in 1999 and conducted its first sittings in July 2000. Its jurisdiction includes family law, bankruptcy, unlawful discrimination, consumer protection and trade practices, privacy, migration, copyright and industrial law.

According to the report, each state and territory court system operates independently. All states have supreme courts and some also have courts of criminal appeal, which are the highest appellate courts at the state level. Courts known as district or county courts hear the more serious cases, with a judge presiding over the court to interpret and determine the law. For more serious charges, it is usual for a jury (usually of twelve people) to determine the guilt or innocence of defendants. Serious offences such as murder, rape, and armed robbery are usually tried in a higher court. Lesser offences are dealt with in lower courts, known as local or magistrates' courts (or courts of petty sessions), where magistrates determine the guilt or innocence of defendants. In all cases, defendants are considered to be innocent until proven guilty beyond all reasonable doubt. Australia has no death penalty. Ghana's Independence Constitution of 1957—see Ghana (Constitution) Order in Council, 22 February 1957—established a unitary system of government, with powers vested in the state.

The unitary laws apply to the whole of the Republic of Ghana and define exclusive powers—imbuing the National Assembly (legislature) and government with the exclusive power to make laws on matters such as trade and commerce, taxation, defence, external affairs, and immigration and citizenship. Unlike the 1960 Republican Constitution, which expressly established two superior courts—the Supreme Court and the High Court—the 1969 Constitution established three superior courts: the Supreme Court of Ghana, the Court of Appeal, and the High Court of Justice. In addition, Parliament had, by law, power to establish other inferior and traditional courts. This provided accommodation for such inferior courts as circuit courts as well as for local courts. Thus, there had been the desire in Ghana that the judicial power of the state must be vested not only in the superior courts but also in such inferior courts as may be provided for by law. In consequence, there were also circuit courts, district courts, juvenile courts, and local courts operating as law enforcement institutions during the first republic.

The Divisions of the Courts

The Superior Court of Judicature comprises a Supreme Court, a Court of Appeal, a High Court, and a Regional Tribunal. Inferior courts include circuit courts, circuit tribunals, community tribunals, and such other courts as may be designated by the law. It is worth mentioning that the judicial system is competent and impartial. Ghanaian courts have acted with increased autonomy under the 1992 constitution, but are still subject to governmental influence. The judicial system has not yet reached an appreciable level of capacity to handle the judicial function. As in many African countries, and in Ghana, the waiting time is excessive while an accused waits in jail for trial.

In Ghana, defendants are presumed innocent, trials are public, and defendants have a right to be present, to be represented by an attorney (at public expense if necessary), and to cross-examine witnesses. Defendants and their attorneys have access to government-held evidence relevant to their cases and have a right to appeal. Defendants have the right also to present witnesses and evidence. Juries are used in murder trials. In practice, authorities generally respect these safeguards. Authorities routinely fail to notify prisoners' families of their incarceration; such information often was obtained only by chance. The court has unlimited discretion to set bail, which is often prohibitively high. The court may refuse to release prisoners on bail and instead remand them without charge for an indefinite period, subject to weekly review by judicial authorities. But on many occasions, particularly in remote areas of the country, police extort money from suspects as a precondition for their release on bail, even though this act is illegal and unacceptable in law.

According to the constitution of Ghana, justice emanates from the people and shall be administered in the name of the republic by the judiciary, which shall be independent and subject only to this Constitution. Ghanaian courts have acted with increased autonomy under the 1992 constitution. Citizens may exercise popular participation in the administration of justice through the institutions of public and customary tribunals and the jury and assessor systems. The judicial power of Ghana is vested in the judiciary; accordingly, neither the president nor Parliament nor any organ or agency of the president or Parliament shall have or be given final judicial power.

The Supreme Court is constituted by the Chief Justice (CJ) and no less than nine other Justices of the Supreme Court (JSC). JSCs are appointed from lawyers of no less than fifteen years standing, with high moral character and proven integrity, by the president of the Republic of Ghana.

Current Composition of the Supreme Court of Ghana 2013–

Per the constitution of Ghana, the composition of the justices of the supreme court of Ghana is headed by Georgina T. Wood (Mrs), as Chief Justice. Other members constituting the court include the following:

Justice W. A. Atuguba
Justice S. A. B. Akuffo (Ms)
Justice Prof. S. K. Date-Bah
Justice S. A. Brobbey
Justice J. J. Ansah
Justice S. O. Adinyira (Mrs)
Justice R. C. Owusu
Justice J. V. M. Dotse
Justice Anin-Yeboah
Justice P. Baffoe-Bonnie
Justice B. T. Aryeetey
Justice N. S. Gbadegbe
Justice V. Akoto-Bamfo (Mrs)

Evaluation of Ghana's Legal System

The Republic of Ghana has one legal system: Parliament makes the laws, the executive government administers the laws, and the judiciary independently interprets and applies them. The common-law system, as developed in the United Kingdom, forms the basis of Ghanaian jurisprudence. This means that Ghana has, legally speaking, a good legal system. According to justicediary.com, a good legal system is one that provides fair justice without any partiality. It should be transparent and proceedings must be made public to make the judgment unbiased. Research shows, however, that corruption is the biggest enemy of the good judiciary system and that governments should ensure that it is kept at bay. A good legal system is one that has little or no influence over the judiciary. A good legal system must speed up the proceedings instead of postponing the hearing dates because it is said that justice delayed is justice denied. What, then, can be said of the Ghanaian legal system?

The state is governed and ruled by laws established by the legislature. A legal system consists of judges, lawyers, and clients. It is said that it is the responsibility of everyone to act ethically and morally so the legal system works well. It is also very important that a client must state the truth to the lawyer and lawyer must be equally honest with the client. Thus, a good legal system requires the lawyer to be very honest with the job so that right justice is delivered. Judges should be free from any influence so that they can write the judgment without any bias. In a common-law country such as ours, writing a judicial opinion or judgment that could be relied on in future decisions could be, arguably, the basis for honest delivery and administration of justice, fairness, and equality. Indeed, laws are created by human beings who are members of the legislative or judicial body and, therefore, are not free from flaws, errors, and future scrutiny. So, it is prudent that laws are created or formulated according to the needs and changing demands of the society it serves. Thus, with time, laws might be unnecessary, incomplete, or even inappropriate. It is from this premise that the judicial system or the judicature is created to evaluate, analyze, and interpret laws that are brought before it.

The Chief Justice

The Chief Justice shall, subject to this Constitution, be the head of the judiciary and shall be responsible for the administration and supervision of the judiciary. The judiciary shall have jurisdiction in all matters civil and criminal, including matters relating to this Constitution, and such other jurisdiction as Parliament may, by law, confer on it. The judiciary shall consist of the Superior Courts of Judicature comprising (1) the Supreme Court, (2) the Court of Appeal, and (3) the High Court and regional tribunals.

According to the constitution, the Supreme Court shall consist of the Chief Justice and not less than nine other justices of the Supreme Court. At present, the Supreme Court of Ghana, which consists of the Chief Justice and ten other justices, is the final court of appeal and has jurisdiction over matters relating to the enforcement or the interpretation of constitutional law.

List of Chief Justices of the Supreme Court

Since its inception in 1876, the Supreme Court has had twenty-four Chief Justices, including twelve in the Gold Coast era.

Chief Justices of the Supreme Court of the Gold Coast

Chief Justice	Time frame	Period
Sir David Patrick Chambers	1876–1878	Gold Coast
P. A. Smith	1878–1879	Gold Coast
Sir James Marshall	1880–1882	Gold Coast
N. Lessingham Bailey	1882–1886	Gold Coast
H. W. Macleod	1886–1889	Gold Coast
Sir Joseph Turner Hutchinson	1889–1895	Gold Coast
Sir William Bradford Griffith	1895–1911	Gold Coast
Phillip Crampton Smyly	1911–1928	Gold Coast
Sir George Campbell Deane	1929–1935	Gold Coast
Sir Phillip Bertie Petrides	1936–1943	Gold Coast
Sir Walter Harragin	1943–1947	Gold Coast
Sir Mark Wilson	1948–1956	Gold Coast
Sir Kobina Arku Korsah	1956–5 March 1957	Gold Coast

Chief Justices of Ghana

Chief Justice	Time frame	Period
Sir Kobina Arku Korsah	6 March 1957–1963	Ghana—1st republic
J. Sarkodee-Addo	1964–1966	
Edward Akufo-Addo	1966–1969	military rule (1966–1969)
	1969–1970	
Edmund Alexander Lanquaye Bannerman	1970–1972	2nd republic
Samuel Azu Crabbe	1973–1977	military rule
Fred Kwasi Apaloo	1977–1986	military rule (1977–1979) 3rd republic (24 September 1979–31 December 1981) military rule (31 December 1981 – 1986)
E. N. P. Sowah	1986–1990	military rule
Phillip Edward Archer	1991–1993	military rule (1991–1993)
	1993–1995	
Isaac Kobina Abban	1995–21 April 2001	
Edward Kwame Wiredu	2001–2003	4th republic
George Kingsley Acquah	4 July 2003–25 March 2007	
Georgina Theodora Wood	15 June 2007—incumbent	

The Court of Appeal, established under the (1992) Constitution, Articles 136–138 to Act 459 subsection (ss) 10–13, includes the chief justice and not fewer than ten other judges and has jurisdiction to hear and to determine appeals from any judgment, decree, or High Court of Justice order. The Court of Appeal determines appeals from the High Court of Justice (with the exception of treason and high treason cases), regional tribunal, and the circuit court in all matters civil or criminal. The court is composed of not less than ten justices of the Court of Appeal. Justices of the Court of Appeal are appointed from lawyers of not less than twelve years standing and of high moral character and proven integrity. There are three Courts of Appeal in Ghana, located in Accra, Kumasi, and Cape Coast.

The High Court of Justice was established under the 1992 Constitution: Articles 139–141 and Act 459 ss 14–22, which consist of the Chief Justice and not fewer than twenty other justices, and such other justice of the Superior Court of Judicature as the Chief Justice may, by writing signed by him, request to sit as High Court Justice for any period. The high court has jurisdiction in all matters, civil and criminal, other than those involving treason. Lower Courts and any lower courts or tribunals as Parliament may by law establish. The High Court has original jurisdiction, subject to other provisions of the Constitution, in all matters civil and criminal, jurisdiction to enforce fundamental human rights and freedoms guaranteed by the Constitution, jurisdiction conferred in relation to infants, jurisdiction over persons of unsound mind, and maritime matters. The High Court has appellate jurisdiction in criminal matters from the circuit court, appellate jurisdiction over the district and juvenile courts, and any other jurisdiction conferred pursuant to the Constitution. It has exclusive jurisdiction over piracy, but has no jurisdiction in matters of treason or high treason. It also has supervisory jurisdiction over all lower courts and all lower adjudicating authorities. The High Court is to consist of the Chief Justice, no less than 20 Justices of the High Court, and such other Justices of the Supreme Court, Court of Appeal and Chairmen of Regional Tribunals as the Chief Justice may from time to time assign to sit as Justices of the High Court. Justices of the High Court shall be lawyers of not less than ten years standing and of high moral character and proven integrity. High Courts are presently established in twenty localities: Accra, Tema, Cape Coast, Koforidua, Amim Oda, Nkawkaw, Agona Swedru, Sekondi, Tarkwa, Sefiwi Wiawso, Denu, Ho, Hohoe, Asante Mampong, Kumasi, Sunyani, Wenchi, Tamale, Bolgata, and Wa (capital of the Upper West region).

Regional tribunals, under the 1992 Constitution, are found under Articles 142–143, Act 459 ss 23–27 and shall consist of the Chief Justice, one chairman, and such members who may or may not be lawyers as shall designated by the Chief Justice to sit as panel members of a regional tribunal and for such period as shall be specified in writing by the Chief Justice. A regional tribunal has concurrent original jurisdiction with the High Court in criminal matters. A regional tribunal is especially empowered by the Courts Act to try matters falling under chapter 4 of part III of the Criminal Code 1960 (Act 29), offences arising from the Customs, Excise, and Preventive Services Management Law

1993 (PNDCL 330), Income Tax Decree 1975 (SMCD 5), Narcotic Drugs (Control, Enforcement and Sanctions) Law 1990 (PNDCL 236), and any other offence involving serious economic fraud or loss of state funds or property.

A regional tribunal consists of the Chief Justice, a chairman, and such members of the panel as the Chief Justice may appoint from time to time. While members of the panel may not be lawyers, a person can only be appointed as a chairman if he or she is qualified to be a Justice of the High Court, namely of no less than ten years' standing as a lawyer and of high moral character and proven integrity. The CJ or any other Justice of the Supreme Court, Court of Appeal, and the High Court may be appointed to sit as a chairman of a regional tribunal. The panel members are appointed by the CJ in consultation with the Regional Coordinating Council and on the advice of the Judicial Council. In relation to lower courts, the Courts Act, 1993 (Act 459), as amended by the Courts Act (Amendment), 2002 (Act 620), and further by Act 620, provides for the circuit court, district court, juvenile court, National House of Chiefs, Regional House of Chiefs, and traditional councils.

The Ghanaian court system has a *Judicial Council (JC)*, which comprises the following persons: the Chief Justice (who is chairman), the attorney general, a Justice of the Supreme Court nominated by the Justices of the Supreme Court, a Justice of the Court of Appeal nominated by the Justices of the Court of Appeal, a Justice of the High Court nominated by the Justices of the High Court, two representatives of the Ghana Bar Association (one of whom shall be a person of not less than twelve years' standing as a lawyer), a representative of the chairmen of regional tribunals nominated by the chairmen, a representative of the lower courts or tribunals, the Judge Advocate-General of the Ghana Armed Forces, the head of the Legal Directorate of the Police Service, the editor of the Ghana Law Reports, a representative of the Judicial Service Staff Association nominated by the association, a chief nominated by the National House of Chiefs, and four other persons who are not lawyers, appointed by the president.

Duties of the JC

Functions of the Judicial Council are to propose, for the consideration of government, judicial reforms to improve the level of administration of justice and efficiency in the judiciary, to be a forum for consideration and discussion of matters relating to the discharge of the functions of the judiciary and thereby assist the Chief Justice in the performance of his duties with a view to ensuring efficiency and effective realization of justice, and to perform any other functions conferred on it by or under this Constitution or any other law not inconsistent with this Constitution.

Circuit Court—The circuit court is established under the 1992 constitution and under Act 620 ss 40–44. The circuit court has original jurisdiction in civil matters (1) in personal actions where the amount claimed is not more than GHC10 million; (2) in landlord and tenancy matters for the possession of land claimed under lease; (3) in matters involving the ownership, possession, occupation of or title to land; (4) to appoint guardians of infants and to make orders for the custody of infants; (5) to grant injunctions or orders to stay waste, or alienation or for the detention and preservation of any property or to restrain breaches of contract or the commission of any tort; (6) in claims of relief by way of interpleader in respect of land or other property attached in execution of an order made by a circuit court; and (7) in applications for the grant of probate or letters of administration in respect of the estate of a deceased person, and in causes and matters relating to succession to property of a deceased person, who had at the time of his death a fixed place of abode within the area of jurisdiction of the circuit court and the value of the estate or property in question does not exceed GHC10 million. The Circuit Court also has jurisdiction in all criminal matters other than treason, offences triable on indictment, and offences punishable by death.

The Chief Justice is empowered to specify the jurisdiction of a circuit court in each region. A circuit court judge, being a lawyer of no less than five years' standing, shall be appointed and assigned to a circuit who may hold sittings in parts of the circuit the Chief Justice decides on. The Chief Justice and any justice of a superior court may be assigned to sit as a circuit court judge. About fifty-two circuit courts are currently operating in regional and district capitals of the country.

District Court (Act 620 ss 45–53) → (Act 674 amends section 46)

The district court has original jurisdiction in civil matters: (1) in personal actions where the amount claimed does not exceed GHC5 million; (2) to grant injunctions or orders to stay waste or alienation or for the detention and preservation of any property, or restrain breaches of contracts or the commission of any tort; (3) in claims for relief by way of interpleaded in respect of land or other property attached in execution of a decree made by the district court; (4) in landlord and tenancy matters; (5) in actions relating to ownership, possession, or occupation of land where the value of the land does not exceed GHC50 million; (6) in divorce and other matrimonial causes or matters and actions for paternity and custody of children; (7) in applications for the grant of probate or letters of administration in respect of the estate of a deceased person, and in causes and matters relating to succession to property of a deceased person, where the value of the estate or property in question does not exceed GHC5 million; and (8) in juvenile matters.

A district court has jurisdiction to determine any action under the Children's Act, 1998 and exercises powers conferred on the Family Tribunal under that Act. The District Court has jurisdiction in criminal matters to try summarily an offence, an attempt to commit an offence, abetment or conspiracy in respect of an offence punishable by a fine not exceeding 500 penalty points or imprisonment for a term not exceeding two years or both; any other offence except an offence punishable by death or by life imprisonment or an offence declared to be a first degree felony. *District court magistrates* may be lawyers or persons with such judicial or legal knowledge as the Chief Justice shall on the advice of the Judicial Council determine. About 140 district courts are currently operating in various towns in Ghana.

Juvenile Court → (Act 459 ss 49–50 as amended by Act 620) and Act 674 Jurisdiction of District Courts in Juvenile Matters under section 49 of Act 459, as amended, the Chief Justice may designate a district court as a juvenile court. A juvenile court has power to hear and determine any matter, civil or criminal, that involves a person under the age of eighteen. The juvenile court shall be composed of the district magistrate, presiding, and two other persons one of whom shall be a social welfare officer and the other a person of not less than twenty-five years. Other lower courts provided for in the Courts Act are:

1. The National House of Chiefs,
2. Regional Houses of Chiefs,
3. Traditional Councils, and
4. Such other lower courts and tribunals as Parliament may establish.

The Attorney General

Under the Constitution of Ghana, there is an attorney general of Ghana who is a Minister of State and the principal legal adviser to the government.

The attorney general discharges such other duties of a legal nature as may be referred or assigned to him by the president, or imposed on him by the Constitution or any other law.

The attorney general is responsible for the initiation and conduct of all prosecutions of criminal offences against individuals and entities on behalf of the state. In furtherance of its statutory role, the Ministry of Justice and Attorney General's Department implements seven core objectives, viz.

- Develop the capacity of the legal system to enhance speedy and affordable access to justice for all.
- Review 1992 Constitution and conflicting Acts of Parliament toward amendment where necessary.
- Promote transparency and accountability and reduce opportunity for rent-seeking.
- Effect public awareness creation on laws for the protection of vulnerable and excluded
- Improve accessibility and use of existing database for policy formulation, analysis, and decision-making.
- Ensure efficient internal revenue generation leading to financial autonomy of districts.

The foregoing objectives are to enable the ministry to achieve its goals of being principal legal adviser of the government, to initiate and conduct all prosecutions of criminal offences in the most efficient and cost-effective manner to support the attainment of the national goal. All offences prosecuted in the name of the Republic of Ghana are at the suit of the attorney general or any other person authorized by him in accordance with any law. The attorney general is responsible for the institution and conduct of all civil cases on behalf of the state; and all civil proceedings against the State shall be instituted against the attorney general as defendant. The attorney general has audience in all courts in Ghana.

In conclusion, within the judicial system of Ghana, the courts interpret and apply the laws of Ghana, decide cases/disputes among and between individuals within the state and as well as those of special republican interest. Like the UK, all cases are likely to begin at the magistrates' courts and end at the Supreme Court. The Supreme Court of Ghana is the highest court of appeal on all matters that have some element of constitutional interpretations, whether decided at the magistrates' or High Court. In civil cases, the litigation is commenced by a plaintiff (a private person or company or a public authority) against a defendant. The plaintiff must try to prove the liability of the defendant on the balance of probabilities. The sorts of claims arising in the civil courts are typically about contracts (most common of all), torts (civil wrongs such as the causing a road accident through negligence, damaging a person's reputation through defamation, or affecting the enjoyment of their property through causing a nuisance such as by pollution), and land disputes.

The unitary laws apply to the whole of the Republic of Ghana and defined exclusive powers—imbuing the National Assembly (legislature) and government with the exclusive power to make laws on matters such as trade and commerce, taxation, defence, external affairs, and immigration and citizenship. Unlike the 1960 Republican Constitution which expressly established two superior courts, the Supreme Court and the High Court, the 1969 Constitution established three superior courts: the Supreme Court of Ghana, the Court of Appeal, and the High Court of Justice. In addition, Parliament had, by law, power to establish other inferior and traditional courts. This provided accommodation for such inferior courts as circuit courts as well as for local courts. Thus there had been the desire in Ghana that the judicial power of the state must be vested not only in the superior courts but also in such inferior courts as may be provided for by law. In consequence there were also circuit courts, district courts, juvenile courts, and local courts operating as law enforcement institutions during the first republic.

The 2015 Judicial Scandal in Ghana

In 2015, twenty-two judges and magistrates were cited in a corruption exposé by ace journalist Anas Aremeyaw Anas and suspended by the Judicial Council. The decision was taken after the Chief Justice Mrs Georgina Wood and the Judicial Council examined the video evidence of malfeasance brought against the judges by Mr Anas Aremeyaw Anas. The judicial council of the Judiciary Service of Ghana established a disciplinary committee of the Judicial Council to investigate the petition against the twenty-two judges and magistrates. The committee was a five-member committee chaired by a justice of the Supreme Court. On 7 September 2015, the circuit judges and magistrates were served with letters stating the allegations against them and asked to submit their responses by 9 September 2015. The Judicial Council further decided that upon receipt of the responses, the twenty-two judges and magistrates would be suspended with effect from Thursday, 10 September 2015, which did come to pass. A total of thirty-four judges faced impeachment as the video was aired on 22 September 2015, which entangled them in the damning corruption scandal. One of the high-profile judges, Justice John Ajet-Nassam, a High Court judge, who freed Alfred Agbesi Woyome in the controversial GHC51 million judgment debt scandal, was videotaped and audio recorded in separate conversations with suspects or persons acting as agents of suspects before him to compromise big cases. Other judges were Human Rights Court judge Kofi Essel Mensah and Charles Quist, a High Court judge. The over two years' painstaking investigations by ace investigative journalist Mr Anas Aremeyaw Anas were released in full in the coming weeks, ahead of a premiere at the Accra International Conference Centre.

At an emergency meeting of the council on Monday, 7 December 2015, the Council unanimously decided to remove from office twenty out of the twenty-two judges and magistrates cited in the petition filed by Tiger Eye PI accusing them of taking bribes to influence judgments of the court. Made up of eight circuit court judges and thirteen district magistrates, they were removed for stated misbehaviour under article 151 (1) of the 1992 Constitution. Some of them were removed from office without their end of service benefits and others with benefits. The Chief Justice, Mrs Georgina Theodora Wood, made this known at a press briefing in Accra on Monday evening. One of the indicted, Samuel Essel Walker of Bolgatanga District Court, was reprimanded in a written letter since there was no adverse finding against him during the JC investigations. The council resolved that he should be given a written reprimand since the disciplinary committee, chaired by a justice of the Supreme Court, Her Ladyship, Justice Sophia Adinyira, did not find that his conduct warranted removal from office.

Those removed with benefits according to the Judicial Council showed remorse when they appeared before the disciplinary committee and apologized profusely to the people of Ghana and the judiciary for bringing the name of the institution into disrepute by their conduct. However, those who were removed without benefits, were said to have shown no remorse when they appeared before the disciplinary committee, hence they went home with nothing. Tiger Eye PI petitioned the Judicial Council for the removal from office of twenty-two members of the Lower Bench, on grounds of stated misbehaviour, pursuant to article 151 of the 1992 Constitution. Two of them had been elevated to the High Court as of April 2015 and therefore could not be dealt with under the said article 151. Later, Tiger Eye submitted another name, Emmanuel Pare, to put the total number at twenty-three.

Judges Dismissed (without benefits)

The names of those removed without benefits were given as Frank Kingley Oppong of the Kasoa District Court, Alfred K. A. Mensah of the Somanya District Court, Alex Obeng Asante of Tarkwa Circuit Court, Emmanuel K. Sunu of Bolgatanga Circuit Court, Baptist Kodwo Filson of Bibiani Circuit Court, and Emmanuel Opare of Techiman Circuit Court. Others are Florence Otoo Ninepence of Tema Circuit Court, Isaac B. Akwantey of Wa Circuit Court, Samuel Ahiabor of Adidome Circuit Court, William Baffoe of Cape Coast Circuit Court, Michael Boamah Gyamfi of Mampongten District Court, and Jacob Amponsah of Ejisu District Court.

Judges Dismissed (with benefits)

Those removed with benefits are Benjamin Y. Osei of Juaben Circuit Court, Seyram Tsatsu Azumah of Akropong Circuit Court, Paul K. Alhassan of Agona District Court, Albert Zoogah of Ashiaman Circuit Court, and Courage Ofori Afriyie of Offinso District Court.

Conclusion

From Ghana's independence in 1957, the courts system, headed by the Chief Justice, has demonstrated extraordinary independence and resilience. The structure and jurisdiction of the courts, defined by the Courts Act of 1971, established the Supreme Court of Ghana (or simply the Supreme Court). The same act established the Court of Appeal (Appellate Court) with two divisions—ordinary bench and full bench, and the High Court of Justice (or simply the High Court), a court with both appellate and original jurisdiction. The act also established the so-called inferior and traditional courts, which, along with the above courts, constituted the judiciary of Ghana according to the 1960, 1979, and 1992 constitutions. Until mid-1993, the inferior courts in descending order of importance were the circuit courts, the district courts (magistrate courts) grades I and II, and juvenile courts. Such courts existed mostly in cities and large urban centres. In mid-1993, however, Parliament created a new system of lower courts, consisting of circuit tribunals and community tribunals in place of the former circuit courts and district (magistrate) courts. The traditional courts are the National House of Chiefs, the Regional Houses of Chiefs, and traditional councils. The traditional courts are constituted by the judicial committees of the various houses and councils. All courts, both superior and inferior, with the exception of the traditional courts, are vested with jurisdiction in civil and criminal matters. The traditional courts have exclusive power to adjudicate any cause or matter affecting chieftaincy as defined by the Chieftaincy Act of 1971.

Key Terms

Tribunals   Violations   Chieftaincy Act Chieftaincy Amnesty Superior courts

Frivolous   Appellate courts   Vested interest   Exclusive   Human rights

Traditional Courts   Economic Courts   Adjudicate   Inferior courts Higher courts

Jurisdiction   Traditional councils   Bench Committees Judicial council

Works Cited/Further Readings

Appiah, Edwin (2015), 'Scandal: Let's celebrate incorruptible judges in Anas exposé', *Joy Online* [website], http://www.myjoyonline.com/news/2015/september-11th/scandal-lets-celebrate-incorruptible-judges-in-anas-expose.php

Association of Commonwealth Criminal Lawyers (2011), 'Ghanaian Criminal Court system', retrieved 2011.

BBC News (2015), 'Accused Ghana judges shown bribe videos', http://www.bbc.com/news/world-africa-34210925 retrieved 2015.

Boakye-Yiadom, Nana (2015), 'Chief Justice cracks whip: 22 "corrupt" judges suspended', *Citi 97.3 FM* [website], http://www.citifmonline.com/2015/09/09/chief-justice-cracks-whip-22-corrupt-judges-suspended/ retrieved 2015.

Fredua-Kwarteng, Y. (2005), 'Our Judges Still Wearing Wigs', *Modern Ghana* [website], http://www.modernghana.com/news/117909/1/our-judges-still-wearing-wigs.html retrieved 2014.

Laary, Dasmani (2015), '22 Ghanaian judges suspended over corruption scandal', *The Africa Report* [website], http://www.theafricareport.com/West-Africa/22-ghanaian-judges-suspended-over-corruption-scandal.html

Open Society Initiative for West Africa (2007), 'Ghana: Justice Sector and the Rule of Law'

Chapter 8

CIVIL SERVICE SYSTEM

Understanding Ghana's Civil Service System

In modern political history, every president has proclaimed that his or her administration was going to fix government, change government (as in 'real changes coming'), minimize government spending, or work hard to accomplish set goals, particularly those enumerated in the party's manifesto. Also, all modern presidents have put forth plans to rid the government of corruption and end government waste and inefficiency. Notwithstanding, presidents have been powerless to affect the structure and operation of the national bureaucracy significantly. The national bureaucracy or civil service system, as it is called in Ghana, is the name given to a large organization that is structured hierarchically to carry out specific functions within a government. Generally, most bureaucracies are characterized by an organization chart. The units of the organization are divided according to the specialization and expertise of the employees. In Ghana, the national bureaucracy is called the civil service system and headed by the head of the Civil Service.

Public and Private Bureaucracies

Bureaucracies are not unique to governments. One can think of any large corporation or university as a bureaucratic organization. This is because the handling of complex problems requires a division of labour as well as specialization. Bureaucracy requires the congregation of individuals who concentrate their skills on specific, well-defined aspects of a problem and depend on others to solve the rest of it. Public or government bureaucracies differ from private organizations in some important ways. A private corporation, such as Melcom Department Store, has a single set of leaders—its board of directors.

Public bureaucracies, in contrast, do not have a single set of leaders. Although the president is the chief administrator of the national civil service system, all bureaucratic agencies are subject to parliament for their funding, staffing, and indeed, their continued existence. Additionally, public bureaucracies are set up to serve the public. One important difference between private corporations and government bureaucracies is that government bureaucracies are not organized to make a profit. Rather, they are supposed to perform their functions as efficiently as possible to conserve the taxpayer money. It is this important aspect of the expectations of the public toward government bureaucracies that usually rouses the citizens' hostility when they experience inefficacy and red tape in services.

The Historical Origins of Bureaucracy (Civil Service)

There are several theories that can help us to understand the origins of the word *bureaucracy* and the ways in which bureaucracy works. Each of these theories that follow focuses on specific features of bureaucracies. The *classic model*, or what is called the *Weberian model*, is one of the modern bureaucratic systems and proposed by a German sociologist, Max Weber. Weber stipulated that the increasingly complex nature of modern life, coupled with the steadily growing demands placed on governments by the citizens, necessitated the formation of bureaucracies. According to Weber, most bureaucracies—whether in the public or private sector—are organized hierarchically and governed by formal procedures. The power in a bureaucracy flows from the top to the bottom (downward). Decision-making processes in bureaucracies are shaped by detailed technical rules that promote similar decisions in similar situations. Civil servants (bureaucrats) are specialists who attempt to resolve problems through logical reasoning and data analysis instead of guesswork. Individual advancement in bureaucracies is supposed to be based on merit rather than political considerations or connections. Indeed, the modern bureaucracy, according to Weber, should be an apolitical organization and everything that has to do with recruiting and staffing must eschew nepotism, selfishness, and tribal/ethnic considerations, among others.

The *acquisitive model* and other theories do not view bureaucracies in terms as benign as Weber does. Among the theorists, some believe that bureaucracies are acquisitive in nature. Proponents of the *acquisitive model* argue that top-level bureaucrats will always try to expand—or at least to avoid any reductions in—the size of their budgets. Although government bureaucracies are not-for-profit enterprises, bureaucrats want to maximize the size of their budgets and staff, because these things are the most visible trappings of power in the public sector. These efforts are also prompted by the desire of bureaucrats to 'sell' their products—national defence, public housing, agricultural subsidies, and so on—to both parliament and the citizens of the country.

The *monopolistic model* is that of theorists who believe that since government bureaucracies do not compete with each other, they can be explained best by a monopolistic model. The analysis is similar to that used by economists to examine the behaviour of monopolistic firms. Monopolistic bureaucracies—like monopolistic firms—essentially have no competitors and act accordingly. Because monopolistic bureaucracies usually are not penalized for chronic inefficiency, they have little reason to adopt cost-saving measures or to make more productive use of their resources. Some economists have argued that such problems can be cured only privatizing certain bureaucratic functions.

Civil Service Reform Initiatives

One major reform activity that changed the role and functions of the then-colonial civil service and led to its modernization was the *Africanization policy and programme* introduced by Governor Gordon Guggisberg between 1925 and 1926. This was the first comprehensive plan for the development of an indigenous civil service. The Africanization plan was aimed at (a) increasing the number of Africans holding European appointments, (b) reducing the high cost of employing Europeans, and (c) creating local machinery for accelerated development. In furtherance of the Africanization program, a series of initiatives were undertaken; among them were:

Lynch Commission (1941). This commission carried out a survey of government departments and this led to (a) the establishment of a scholarship program which ensured the training of both juniors and seniors, (b) the establishment of an interim Public Services Commission in 1948 to advise the governor on appointments and promotions in the public service, (c) the drawing up of a scheme for the progressive education and training of Africans to take up senior appointments in the civil service.

Harragin Commission. This commission introduced the negotiation of terms and conditions of service of the civil services of British West Africa. It introduced the idea of two levels of staff consultations, one for the junior service and the other for the senior service.

Colonial Civil Service

The history of the Ghana Civil Service is linked with the establishment of the British Colonial Service in the Gold Coast. Its origin can be traced to 1843 when the Crown, after taking over the administration of the forts and settlements from the London Committee of Merchants, started appointing various prominent citizens to public office. The service was established as the main instrument of the British imperial policy concerned with *maintenance of law and order, imposition and collection of taxes,* and *exploitation of the rich mineral deposits and other natural resources of the colony.*

The focal point of the administrative machinery was the secretariat of the governor in colonial Gold Coast. Apart from the formulation of policy, this secretariat became the agency for supervising and co-coordinating all governmental activities. The governor was at the apex. Next to the governor was the colonial secretary. The secretariat served as the nerve centre of the administration. Below the colonial secretary and within the secretariat were the financial secretary, the attorney general, and the auditor general.

Directly under the secretariat were the various departments, such as Posts and Telegraphs, Education, Health, Agriculture, and Customs. These departments also formed part of the headquarters organization and worked under the overall direction of the colonial secretary. Advice to the governor from the various heads of departments was channelled through the colonial secretary, and it was through the colonial secretary that rulings and directives of the governor were conveyed to the officers concerned.

The following legal instruments and constitutional provisions have, over the years, affected the organization and work of the Civil Service. First in the line of actions were the following:

Republican Constitution 1960. This constitution abolished the Public Services Commission and replaced it with a Civil Service Act 1960 (CA 5). This Act provided for the following: (a) creation of civil service posts, (b) setting up of ministries and departments, (c) appointment and retirement of civil servants and other matters relating to the civil service, (d) Civil Service Interim Regulations 1960 (LI 147). The regulations provided for the following: (a) creation of a Ghana Civil Service Commission, (b) structure of the Ghana Civil Service, and (c) filling of vacancies in the Ghana Civil Service, among others.

The second provision was the *Civil Service Amendment Act 1965 (Act 303)*. This Act abolished the Civil Service Commission and transferred its powers to an establishment secretariat. The members of the commission were styled establishment officers while the secretariat was brought under the personal control of the head of state and government.

The third was the *1992 Constitution Articles 19 (1) and (2)*. These articles describe the civil service as part of the public services of Ghana and comprise service in both central and local government. Article 19 (1) also hived off the International Revenue Service (IRS), the Police Service, the Immigration Service, etc. Local Government Act 462 and Local Government Service Act 656 set up and governed the operations of the local government system and service.

Ghana's Civil Service System

The object of the civil service, as detailed in the legislation PNDCL 327 is primarily to assist the government in the formulation and implementation of government policies and programs for the development of the country. Its objectives are accomplished through advising on government plans, undertaking research for effective formulation and implementation of government policies, and monitoring, co-coordinating, evaluating, and reviewing government policies and plans. It also ensures that policies are translated into practical and cost-effective programs and projects, and maintains vigilant oversight of the implementation of policies by the various government departments and agencies assigned such responsibility. In addition, other responsibilities are assigned to it from time to time. The duties and responsibilities of the civil service are set by the direction the government wants to take the country.

One critical role of the Ghana Civil Service is its stabilizing influence on political life of the country. During transition periods (i.e. changes of governments), the civil service holds the fort in the interim before the incoming governments assume office.

The object of the civil service as detailed in the legislation PNDCL 327 is primarily to assist the government in the formulation and implementation of government policies and programs for the development of the country.

In Ghana, there is somewhere between fourteen and seventeen cabinet ministries, which can be described as the major service organizations of the Ghanaian government. These cabinet ministries can also be called line organizations. This means that they are directly accountable to the president of the country and are responsible for performing major government functions, such as printing and distribution of money (Ministry of Finance and Economic Planning) in the country to the recruitment and training of the manpower that the country needs (Ministry of Labour and Manpower Development) for development. All departments were created by acts of parliament. A president might ask that a new department be created, aligned to another, or take on an emerging need in serving the people; that is, in 2013, President John Dramani Mahama realigned two ministries. The addition was made from that of the Ministry of Tourism to Tourism and Creative Arts and the Ministry of Women and Children to that of Women and Protective Services. The president has no power to do so, however, without legislative approval from Parliament.

Each ministry is headed by a Minister of State (except for the Ministry of Justice, which is headed by an attorney general). Each ministry has several levels of directors, with the chief director closest to the minister serving as the chief policy and budget advisor. Presidents theoretically have considerable control over the cabinet ministries; because presidents are able to appoint or fire (dismiss) all of the top officials. One reason that presidents are not happy about the structure of ministries or civil service is that the entire bureaucratic structure below the top political levels of the minister and his deputy minister is staffed by permanent employees, many of whom are committed to established programs or procedures and who resist change. Each ministry employs individuals but only a handful of them are under the president. The most recently created ministry in Ghana is the Ministry of Gender, Children, and Protective Services.

Independent Executive Agencies

Independent executive agencies are bureaucratic organizations that are not located within a ministry but report directly to the president, who appoints their senior officers. When a new independent agency is created—the President's Office of Policy Evaluation and Research—parliament decides where it will be located in the bureaucracy. In recent times, presidents often have asked that a new organization be kept separate or independent rather than added to an existing ministry, particularly if a ministry may be hostile to the agency's creation. A clear example of this is the creation of the Ghana National Gas Company—created to harness and build pipelines from the jubilee fields of Ghana's oil and gas platforms to the point of consumption. This agency has not been placed under the Ministry of Energy by the government of the late Professor Atta Mills for probably the reasons enumerated above.

The purpose and nature of regulatory agencies is that they are administered independently of all three branches of government. They are set up because parliament believes it is unable to handle the complexities and technicalities required to carry out specific laws in the public interest. The regulatory commission in fact combines some functions of all three branches of government—the executive, the legislature, and the judiciary. First, independent regulatory agencies are legislative in the sense that they make rules that have the force of law. They are also executive in the sense that they provide for the enforcement of those rules. They are judicial in the sense that they decide disputes involving the rules they make if those rules are questioned (challenged) in the law courts.

Members of regulatory agency boards or commissions are appointed by the president with the consent of the parliament, and report to the president of the republic. By law, the members of regulatory agencies cannot all be from the same political party. Presidents can influence regulatory agency behaviour by appointing people of their own parties or individuals who share their political views when vacancies occur, in particular when the chairman position or the chief executive position is vacant. These persons can be removed or dismissed by the president for causes specified in the law creating the agency. The independent regulatory agencies are typically responsible for a specific type of public policy. Their function is to make and implement rules and regulations in a particular sphere of action to protect the public interest. Independent regulatory agencies typically make technical, non-political decisions about rates, profits, and rules that would be for the benefit of all and do not require parliamentary legislation. In the years that followed the creation of the National Utilities Regulatory Commission, other agencies were formed to regulate communication (the National Communications Commission) and others.

Agency Capture: Over the last few years, some observers have concluded that these agencies, although nominally independent, may in fact not always be so. They contend that many independent regulatory agencies have been *captured* by the very industries and firms that they were supposed to regulate. An example is the Ghana Standards Board and children's favourite meal producers Indomie noodle company's relationship regarding inspections and standards in Ghana. The results have been less competition rather than more competition, high prices rather than lower prices, and less choice rather than more choice for consumers.

Government Corporations

Another form of bureaucratic organization in Ghana is the government corporation. Although the concept is borrowed from the world of business, distinct differences exist between public and private corporations. A private corporation has shareholders (stockholders) who elect a board of directors, who in turn choose the corporate officers, such as chief executive and deputy chief executive. When a private corporation makes a profit, it must pay taxes (unless it avoids them through various legal loopholes). It either distributes part or all of the after-tax profits to shareholders as dividends or ploughs the profits back into the corporation to make new investments. A government corporation or company has a board of directors and managers, but it does not have any stockholders. For example, the Ghana National Petroleum Corporation (GNPC) was created to see if Ghana has oil and gas deposits along its coast. Corporations have the board of directors, and the government becomes their shareholders or stockholders.

Categories of Government Bureaucracy

Government Corporations
Ghana Broadcasting Corporation
New Times Corporations
Tema Development Corporation
Ghana Railway Development Corporation

Government Companies
Precious Minerals Marketing Company Limited
Volta Lake Transport Company
Ghana Publishing Company Limited
Ghana Water Company Limited
Ghana Supply Company Limited
Ghana Post Company Limited
Ghana Airports Company Limited
State Housing Company Limited
GIHOC Distilleries Company Limited
Electricity Company of Ghana
Bulk Oil Storage & Transport Company Limited
Ghana Cylinder Manufacturing Company Limited
Ghana Railway Company Limited
Ghana National Gas Company
National Food Buffer Stock Company Limited

Other Government Agencies
Grains and Legumes Development Board
National theatre of Ghana
Airport Clinic
ICOUR Limited
Architectural and Engineering Services Limited
GNPA Limited
Tema Oil Refinery

Staffing the Civil Service

There are two categories of bureaucrats: political appointees and civil servants. As noted earlier, the president is able to make political appointments to most of the top jobs in the national bureaucracy. The president also can appoint ambassadors to foreign posts. All these jobs are considered political plums and are usually given to those that are politically connected. The rest of the national government's employees belong to the civil service and obtain their jobs through a much more formal process by taking exams called the civil service exams.

Political Appointees

Political appointments are usually positions the president offers to pay off outstanding political debts. However, the president may take into consideration such things as the candidate's work experience, intelligence, political affiliation, and personal characteristics. Presidents have differed in the importance they attach to appointing women and minorities to plum positions. Presidents often use ambassadorships, however, to reward individuals for their campaign contributions.

The Bottlenecks within the Civil Service

Political appointees are in some sense the aristocracy of the national bureaucracy. But their powers, although appearing formidable on paper, are often exaggerated by what they cannot do. Like the president, a political appointee often leaves office when he or she is detected; but in principle, they are supposed to leave office before the president's term of office ends. In fact, the average term of service for political appointees should be less than three years. But this is not the case in Ghana. As a result, most appointees have little or no background for their positions and may be mere *figureheads*—a situation often referred to as square pegs in round holes. Often, they respond to the paperwork that flows up from below the chain of command of the ministry. Additionally, the professional civil servants who make up the permanent civil service may not feel compelled to carry out their current boss's directives quickly, because they know that he or she will not be around for long, due of course to the fact that the president has a term limit of either four years (one term) or eight years maximum.

The Difficulty in Firing Civil Servants

Whether civil servants perform below expectations or not, their dismissal often sparks controversy. This inertia is compounded by the fact that it is very difficult to sack or discharge civil servants. In recent years, calls have been made to the fact that the civil service of Ghana is overstaffed, redundant, or that most civil servants are incompetent. But the difficulty is that discharged employees may appeal their dismissals, and many months or even years can pass before the issue is resolved conclusively. This occupational rigidity helps to ensure that most political appointees, no matter how competent or driven, will not be able to exact much meaningful influence over their subordinates, let alone implement drastic changes in the bureaucracy itself.

The Modern Civil Service

The civil service derives its existence (legal status) from the 1992 Constitution of the fourth republic. It is one of the public service institutions listed in the Constitution. Until the establishment of the Local Government Service, it comprised the central and local administrative machinery of government. In short, the civil service was instituted by the 1992 Constitution, with the vision to serve Ghana. The vision of the civil service is to be a compact, professional, and transparent service, playing a pivotal role in the formulation and implementation of programs and projects for the achievement of the government's development and transformation agenda.

Objectives and Functions of the Civil Service

The objectives and functions of the civil service are carried out through sector ministries which are responsible for policy issues, manpower, and financial matters as well as exercising overall supervisory, monitoring, and coordinating powers over technical departments in their respective sectors. To ensure that they play their roles efficiently and effectively, a ministry is organized into four broad areas: (a) general administration and finance; (b) planning, budgeting, coordination, monitoring, and evaluation; (c) human resource management; and (d) research, statistics, information, and public relations.

Who Is a Civil Servant?

According to section 4 of the Civil Service Law, 1993, PNDC Law 327, the following are members of the service: a person serving in a civil capacity in a post designated as a Ghana Civil Service post by or under the law in the Office of the President; a ministry; a government department/agency at the national, regional and district levels; any other civil service department established by or under the authority of the law the emoluments attached to which are paid directly from the Consolidated Fund or any other source approved by the government. The calibre of individuals within the service is high, diverse, and in many respects comparable with their private sector counterparts. There are administrators, planners, management analysts, engineers, geologists, surveyors, agriculturists, lawyers, architects, archivists, scientists, secretaries, etc. There are core values that guide the work of the civil service. The strength of the civil service lies in its values and ethics stated in the Civil Service Code of Conduct, such as permanence, continuity, impartiality, objectivity and non-partisanship, integrity, anonymity, knowledge and competence, efficiency.

Pre-Independence Civil Service: This was the first real attempt made to reform the structures of the machinery of government and the public service. It made wide-ranging recommendations, namely (a) redesigning of the structure of the machinery of government, (b) restructuring of the civil service, (c) establishment of statutory corporations to assume certain functions of government, and (d) new salary structure and conditions of service. For the restructuring of the civil service, the commission adopted the British system as a model. As a result, the departments and portfolios in the Colonial Office were converted into ministries when the Gold Coast gained internal self-government in 1951. Since then, many ministries and government departments have been created, restructured, or realigned to suit the needs of the times.

The independence of Ghana heralded an era when emphasis was placed on development and public welfare. Civil servants therefore became the main instruments for executing implementing this agenda. In line with the 1960 first republican constitution, a new charter for the civil service was published. It defined the functions of the civil service, its control and administration in order to ensure that it is efficiently designed and properly equipped to support and to take its full share in the development of the country in line with the vision of the government and the aspirations of the people. In addition, the Civil Service Act 1960 (CA5) was passed. The law provided for the following: (a) the creation of the civil service post, (b) the setting up of ministries and departments, (c) the appointment and retirement of civil servants, and (d) conditions of service, disciplinary proceedings, and other matters relating to the civil service. The Civil Service Act 1960 (Act CA5) was later complemented by the Civil Service (Interim) Regulations, 1960 (LI47), which provided for the following: (a) the creation of a Ghana Civil Service Commission, (b) the structure of the Ghana Civil Service, and (c) the filling of vacancies in the Ghana Civil Service, among others.

In September 1965, the Civil Service (Amendment) Act, 1965 (Act 303) was passed. One important feature of this law was the establishment of the Establishment Secretariat and the creation of the position of Head of Civil Service and Secretary to the Cabinet. This Act subsisted until the promulgation of the 1992 Constitution and the Civil Service Law 1993 (PNDCL 327). Both pieces of legislation made the Ghana Civil Service part of the Public Services of Ghana and defined the service as comprising service in a civil office of government. This Mills Odoi Commission was established in 1966 by the National Liberation Council (NLC) to review the structure and organization of the public services, so as to gear the machinery of government to the rapid social and economic development of the country, and recommend new salary structures for the public services in line with the general economic circumstances of the country at that time, among others. Its recommendations were adopted, particularly its reform of the machinery of government, i.e. the policy of decentralization and salary recommendations.

Another important milestone in the history of Ghana's civil service was the establishment of the Okoh Commission. This was a reform initiative undertaken in 1974 by the National Redemption Council (NRC). Its main terms of reference were to investigate the organization and structure of the civil service and its methods of operation and to make recommendations for reforms with special regard to the need to transform the civil service into a dynamic instrument of social change and economic development. Its major recommendations were to the effect that (1) a new and separate post of Head of Civil Service should be created and appointment made from the regular civil service to fill the post, which should remain a career post for civil servants; (2) the head of civil service should have direct access at all times to the head of government and report to him on civil service matters; (3) the principal secretary post should no longer be the preserve of members of the administrative class. It should be open to all civil servants and to persons outside the civil service; (4) there should be established a civil service department to provide professional support service required for effective central management of the civil service, among others; (5) the Public Administration Restructuring and Decentralization Implementation Committee (PARDIC) was set up by the PNDC to review the earlier reforms, particularly the decentralization program and to accelerate its implementation. One major recommendation of PARDIC is the introduction of four functional areas for Ministries and limiting the Ministries to policy formulation, monitoring and evaluation.

Management of the Civil Service

Civil Service Council (CSC): At the apex of the structure is the Civil Service Council. This is the governing board for the entire Ghana Civil Service. It gives policy direction on human resource issues and approvals for human resource management decisions in the Ghana Civil Service. Immediately below the council is the head of the Ghana Civil Service who, as the name suggests, is the head of the entire Ghana civil service. He is answerable to the president through the Civil Service Council. He implements the decisions of the Civil Service Council. On a day-to-day basis, he manages the entire service through Management Services Division (MSD), PRAAD, and the various directorates at OHCS. The Civil Service Council is the governing body of the civil service. It is supported by the head of civil service, who, prior to the Okoh Commission, was both the head of civil service and secretary to the Cabinet. The OHCS was created in 1980 as a successor to the Establishment Secretariat, with Mr J. H. Sackey as the first head. The office was created as a centre for human resource management for the entire Ghana Civil Service. This strategically placed the OHCS under the purview of the presidency.

The composition and functions of the directorate of OHCS under Section 5(3) states, 'The composition and function of directorates, divisions, and units shall be determined by the head of the civil service.' In the exercise of this authority, the head of the civil service over the years have undertaken reorganization and realignment resulting in the creation of the following directorates:

The Chief Director: Below the head of civil service is the Chief Director, the bureaucratic head and the spending officer of the OHCS. The Chief Director is the chief advisor to the head of the civil service on all matters relating to the smooth operations of the OHCS in particular and the civil service in general. The Chief Director also coordinates the activities of the various directorates and units of the OHCS.

Below the Chief Director are the following directorates and departments:

1. Research Statistical Information Management (RSIM)—This directorate is responsible for providing data/information on human resource issues for evidence-based policy formulation and decision-making.
2. Recruitment and Training Directorate (RTD)—This directorate is the focal point for the recruitment of qualified and competent personnel as well as their training.
3. Career Management Directorate (CMD)—This directorate provides leadership and guidance for effective career management in the civil service.
4. Policy and Standards Directorate (PSD)—This directorate is responsible for the initiation, formulation, and review of administrative instructions, rules, and regulations in the civil service.
5. Policy Monitoring and Evaluation Directorate (PMED)—This directorate is responsible for facilitating the strengthening of institutional capacity of MDAs through the formulation of performance improvement and monitoring policies.
6. Finance and Administration Directorate (FAD)—This directorate is responsible for providing administrative and financial support services for the efficient running of the all the directorates of OHCS.
7. Public Records and Archives Administration Department (PRAAD)—This department manages the records of the entire civil service. It facilitates and promotes good record-keeping practices in all MDAs.

Bureaucrats as Politicians and Policymakers

In theory, whether they are independent executive, regulatory, or corporations, administrative agencies are created to serve a governmental purpose by acts of parliament. This is because parliament is unable to oversee the day-to-day administration of its programs; it must delegate certain powers to administrative agencies. Parliament delegates the power to implement legislation to agencies through what is called *enabling legislation*. The enabling legislation generally specifies the name, purpose, composition, functions, and powers of the agency. This means that these agencies themselves must decide how best to carry out the wishes of parliament. The discretion given to administrative agencies is not accidental. Parliament has long realized that it lacks the technical expertise and the resources to monitor the implementation of its laws. Hence, the administrative agency is created to fill the gaps. These gap-filling roles require the agency to formulate administrative rules (regulations) to put flesh on the bones of the law. This kind of delegation of power from parliament to the independent executive, regulatory, or corporations forces such agencies to become unelected policymakers.

The Rule-making Environment

The term *rule-making* is a process by which rules and regulations are made by parliament and implemented by a government agency. The process does not occur in a vacuum because suppose that parliament passes a new air pollution law, how will such a law be implemented? Since air pollution falls under the jurisdiction of the Ghana Environmental Protection Agency (EPA), the agency might decide to implement the new law through a technical regulation on factory emissions. This proposed regulation would be published in a national register so that interested parties would have an opportunity to comment on it. Individuals and companies that oppose parts or the entire rule might then try to convince the EPA to revise or redraft the regulation. Some parties might try to persuade the agency to withdraw the proposed regulation altogether. In any event, the EPA would consider these comments in drafting the final version of the regulation, following the expiration of the comment period.

Once the final regulation has been published in the national register, there is a period given to allow the law's effect or when the law can be enforced.

During that period, businesses, individuals, and state and local government can ask parliament to overturn the regulation. After that stipulated period has lapsed, the regulation can still be challenged in court by a party having a direct interest in the rule, such as a company that expects to incur significant costs in complying with it. The company could argue that the rule misinterprets the applicable law or goes beyond the agency's statutory purview. An allegation by the company that the EPA made a mistake in judgment probably would not be enough to convince the court to throw out the rule. The company instead would have to demonstrate that the rule itself was arbitrary and capricious. To meet this standard, the company would have to show that the rule reflected a serious flaw in the EPA's judgment.

There is, however, what is called a *negotiated rule-making*. A negotiated rule-making occurs when those to be affected by a rule become directly involved in drafting the regulations. Agencies hope that such participation may help to prevent later courtroom battles over the meaning, applicability, and legal effect of the regulations. For example, if an agency chooses to engage in negotiated rule-making, it must publish in the national register the subject and scope of the rule to be developed, the parties affected significantly by the rule, and other information. Representatives of the affected groups and other interested parties then may apply to be members of the negotiation committee. The agency is represented on the committee, but a neutral third party (not the agency) presides over the proceedings. Once the committee members have reached agreement on the terms of the proposed rule, a notice is published in the national register, followed by a period for comments by any person or organization interested in the proposed rule. Negotiated rule-making often is conducted under the condition that the participants promise not to challenge in court the outcome of any agreement to which they were a party.

As Policymakers: In the past, theories of public administration once assumed that bureaucrats do not make policy decisions but only implement the laws and policies promulgated by the president and parliamentary bodies. Many people continue to make these same assumptions today. A more realistic view, which is now held by most bureaucrats and elected officials, is that the agencies and departments of government play important roles in policymaking. As we have seen, many government rules, regulations, and programs are in fact initiated by the bureaucracy, based on its expertise and scientific studies. How a law passed by parliament eventually is translated into concrete action—say, from the forms to be filled out to the decisions about who gets the benefits—usually is determined within each agency or department. Even the evaluation of whether a policy has achieved its intended purpose usually is based on studies that are commissioned and interpreted by the agency administering the program. To this effect, the bureaucratic policymaking role often has been depicted by what traditionally has been called the *iron triangles*. Recently, the concept of an *issue network* has been viewed as a more accurate description of the policymaking process.

Iron Triangle: Previously, scholars describe the bureaucracy's role in the policymaking process by using the concept of an iron triangle—a three-way alliance among legislators in parliament, bureaucrats, and interest groups. Consider, as an example, the development of a communication policy of cell phone number portability in Ghana in 2009. Parliament, as one component of the triangle, would include two major committees concerned with communications policy, such as the House Committee on Communications and the Ministry of Communications. These groups will then sit as the 'iron triangle' to draft rules guarding the introduction of cell phone portability and its administration. Number portability or cell phone portability is the ability of a customer of, say, the Air Tel network to carry over his/her number to, say, the Vodafone network without penalties exacted to the telephone user.

Issue Networks: The following discussion presents a much simplified picture of how the iron triangle works. With the growth in the complexity of government, policymaking also has become more complicated. The bureaucracy is larger, Parliament has more committees and subcommittees, and interest groups are more aggressive in Ghana today than before. Although iron triangles still exist, often they are inadequate as descriptions of how policy is actually made. Frequently, different interest groups concerned about a certain area of policy have conflicting demands, which makes agency decision-making difficult. However, many scholars now use the term *issue network* to describe the policymaking process. An issue network consists of individuals or organizations that support a particular policy position on, say, the environment, taxation, consumer safety, or communications. Typically, an issue network includes parliamentarians and or their staff members, interest groups, bureaucrats, scholars, and other experts and representatives from the media. Members of a particular issue network work together to influence the president, Members of Parliament, administrative agencies, and the courts to affect public policy on a specific issue. Each policy issue may involve conflicting positions taken by two or more issue networks.

Parliamentary Control of the Bureaucracy

In Ghana, the issue at stake is whether parliament or acts of parliament must be obeyed by government agencies and corporations. Do many of the government agencies even know that their setting up was by the act of parliament and that parliament can overhaul or even terminate their existence? Many forget that parliament specifies in an agency's enabling legislation the powers of the agency and the parameters within which it can operate. Indeed, that parliament has the power of the purse and theoretically could refuse to authorize or appropriate funds for a particular agency. Whether parliament would actually take such a drastic measure would depend on the circumstances. It is clear, however, that parliament does have the legal authority to decide whether to fund or not to fund administrative agencies. Parliament can also exercise oversight over agencies through investigations and hearings; in essence parliament has investigation and supervisory (oversight) functions over government agencies, departments, and corporations. More to the point here is that parliamentary committees conduct investigations and hold hearings to oversee an agency's actions, reviewing them to ensure compliance with parliamentary intentions and objectives. The government agency's officers and employees can be ordered to testify before a committee or subcommittee of parliament about the details of an action. Through these oversight activities, especially in the questions and comments of members of the legislature during the hearings, parliament indicates its position on specific programs and issues.

Conclusion

A bureaucracy is an organization of non-elected officials of a governmental or organizations who implement the rules, laws, and functions of their institution, and may be characterized by officialism and red tape. The *Weberian bureaucracy* has its origin in the works by Max Weber (1864–1920), who was a notable German sociologist, political economist and administrative scholar who had contributed immensely to the study of bureaucracy and administrative discourses and literatures, during the mid 1800s and early 1900s. Max Weber belongs to the scientific school of thought, who among others, discussed intensely on subject matter such as specialization of job scope, merit system, uniform principles, structure and hierarchy, to name a few. Among the scholars of his contemporaries are Frederick Taylor (1856–1915), Henri Fayol (1841–1925), Elton Mayo (1880–1949), and later scholars, such as Herbert Simon (1916–2001), Dwight Waldo (1913–2000), and others. Weber listed several preconditions for the emergence of the bureaucracy. The growth in space and population being administered and the growth in complexity of the administrative tasks being carried out and the existence of a monetary economy resulted in a need for a more efficient administrative system. Development of communication and transportation technologies made more efficient administration possible but also in popular demand, and democratization and rationalization of culture resulted in demands that the new system treat everybody equally.

Weber's ideal bureaucracy is characterized by hierarchical organization, delineated lines of authority in a fixed area of activity, action taken on the basis of and recorded in written rules; bureaucratic officials need expert training, rules are implemented by neutral officials, and career advancement depends on technical qualifications judged by organization, not individuals.

In everyday language, we use the word *bureaucracy* as an insult. For most people, the term conjures long lines of angry people, piles of papers just about to tip over, and workers asleep at their desks. The truth is that every government needs a bureaucracy in order to function properly. In fact, the national government of the Ghana employs roughly half a million of Ghana's population, within its bureaucracy. The Department of Motor Vehicles (DVLA), the Bureau of National Investigations (BNI), the Student Loans Office, the Office of Government Ethics, the Ghana Police, and the Small Business Administration of Ghana are all part of the Ghanaian bureaucracy, but so are religious groups, businesses, and educational institutions. For better or worse, a bureaucracy is the best way to organize large numbers of people working toward the same goal.

Key Terms

Independent regulatory agencies   Independent executive agencies

Bureaucrats   Monopolistic model   Civil service   Kitchen cabinet

Administrative agency   Legislature   Parliamentary subcommittees

Weberian model Oversight Bureaucracy   Rule-making   Issue networks

Works Cited / Further Readings

Elliott de Saez, Eileen (2002), *Marketing Concepts for Libraries and Information Services* (London: Facet Publishing).

Ghana Population and Housing Census (2002)

Gilmore, A. (2003), *Service Marketing and Management* (London: Sage Publications Ltd).

Hall, Richard (1962), 'Intra Organizational Structural Variation: Application of Bureaucratic Model', *Administrative Science Quarterly* No. 7.

Heady, Ferrel (1996), *Public Administration: A Comparative Perspective*, 5th edition (New York).

Kernaghan, K. and Siegel, D. (1999), *Public Administration in Canada*, 4th edition (Ontario).

Kotler, P. and Zaltman, G. (1971), 'Social Marketing: An Approach to Planned Social Change', *Journal of Marketing*, 35.

—— Lee N. and Zaltman G (1971), Marketing in the Public Sector

Chapter 9

INTEREST GROUPS

What Is an Interest Group?

An interest group may be identified as a pressure group, a special interest group, or a lobby group seeking to achieve a purpose. It is an organization whose members share common views and objectives to promote their interest. Interest groups participate in activities designed to influence government officials and policy decisions. Parent groups, teacher organizations, and school board associations all actively lobby for more money from the central government. In Ghana, examples of interest groups include professional bodies like the Trades Union Congress (TUC) of Ghana, the Ghana National Association of Teachers (GNAT), the Ghana Bar Association (GBA), the Polytechnic Teachers Association of Ghana (POTAG), the University Teachers Association of Ghana (UTAG), the Civil and Local Government Staff Association of Ghana (CLOGSAG), WANEP, Ghana Integrity Initiative (GII), and NAGRAT, among many others.

The Intent of an Interest Group

Politics typically focuses on the nomination and election of citizens of a country or state to public office. There is, however, much more to this election of citizens and opponents within a party. Politics is perhaps best understood as the process of influencing public policy decisions to protect and preserve a group, to achieve the group's goals, and to distribute benefits to the group's members. Organized citizens demand policies that promote their financial security, education, health, welfare, and protection. Government makes and enforces public policy decisions; so it is not surprising that people try to influence officials who make and apply society's rules or policies. History shows that people who organize for political action tend to be more effective in achieving their goals when compared to persons acting alone. This is particularly true if a group is well resourced in terms of money and human resource. Money plays a big role in state government and state elections, and groups that help politicians finance their campaigns often achieve their goals when the party wins and takes control of the government machinery. When people attempt to influence political decisions or the selection of the men and women who make such decisions, they usually turn either to political parties (examined in chapter 4, 'Political Parties') or to interest groups (the subject of this chapter). In Ghana, there is not much interest group participation in the political process, because of the evolving nature of the country's democracy. Most of the interest articulation in Ghana is unionized and their activities are usually that of challenging government over salaries and emoluments, as well as protests/demonstrations over salary arrears or benefits associated with such.

Political Parties and Interest Groups

Although political parties and interest groups both attempt to influence political decisions by government officials, they differ in their methods. The principal purpose of party activity is to increase the numbers of its members who are elected or appointed to public offices, in order to gain control of government and to achieve party goals. In contrast, an interest group seeks to influence government officials (regardless of their party affiliation) to the advantage of the group. As such, interest groups try to influence policy decision in the following ways: by using persuasion to mobilize members and supporters, by attempting to sway public opinion, by building coalitions with other groups with identical or closely related interests in one or more issues, by obtaining access to key decision makers, and by influencing elections.

Generally, an interest group wants government to create and implement policies that benefit the group without necessarily placing its own members in public office. Part of the purpose of economic groups (for example, the Ghana Consumers Protection Agency) and professional groups (such as the Chartered Accountants Association of Ghana, or the Ghana Bar Association) is to make their policy preferences known to government officials. Interest groups act as intermediaries for people who share common interests and reside throughout the state. In this way, they add to the formal system of geographic representation used by the group to elect many of their office holders. In essence, these organizations serve the interests of their members by providing functional representation within the political system. They offer a form of protection by voicing the interests of these groups as business people, labourers, farmers, Roman Catholics, teachers, physicians, and university students across the nation. These are groups that are composed of people who have similar interests but may not in themselves constitute a majority in any region, city, town, or district.

Reasons for Interest Groups

The growth and diversity of interest groups in Ghana continues unabated. Ghana is emerging as a complex society which has much to do with the rate of proliferation of interest groups and within the ethnic make-up of the country. Because of legal and cultural reasons, interest groups are becoming a norm in Ghana today. They are growing from professional associations and more lethal in their roles. First, the Constitution of Ghana recognizes the right of association as part of the right of assembly. This right has greatly facilitated the development of interest groups, ensuring the right of citizens to organize for political, economic, religious, and social reasons. The nation's political culture has traditionally encouraged citizens to organize themselves into a bewildering array of associations, whether religious, fraternal, professional, or recreational, among others. Ghanaians have responded by creating literally hundreds of these groups over the course of our independence. In Ghana, controversies over social issues of late (the issues with homosexuals and gay rights), education policy issues (e.g. school funding), and the issues of fair wages for workers (e.g. under the single spine salary) have sparked new groups and revitalized existing interest groups. For instance, in 2010, the Ghana Consumer Protection Association and Alliance for Accountable Governance (AFAG) were formed to raise issues concerning the treatment of consumers and to challenge government on several political issues. As a political action committee (PAC), the group raises several important issues concerning the passing of appropriation and revenue bills in parliament and sometimes goes out to direct their displeasure against government policies.

The second reason is that because of the unitary system of governance in Ghana and the levels of decentralization within the structures in Ghana, interest groups have also created offices in the regional capitals and districts of the country. In a decentralized government, power is not concentrated at the highest level; it is achieved in two principal ways. First is the devolution of power from the national government to the regional coordinating councils (RCCs). In turn, each regional coordinating council shares its power with a wide variety of local assemblies, including towns and wards. Second, within each level of government, power is separated into the three branches of government practiced at the national level. But in the case of Ghana, the unitary system of governance does not provide that kind of strict observance of separation because of the Westminster kind of government that Ghana practices. Indeed, a decentralized structure increases the ability of interest groups to influence governmental activities. This structure provides different access points for groups to fight their battles at different levels of government and within different branches at each level. However, in the case of Ghana, interest groups exert pressure on government only for the wrong reasons.

The Don'ts of Interest Groups in Ghana

In a universally recognized part of the democratic process, pressure groups or interest groups are by definition the collection of people with a common interest who influence socio-political structures and strengthen the democratic process by giving a voice to a variety of the citizenry. They achieve this through advocacy, public awareness programs, policy research, lobbying of parliament, public opinion polls, and organized protests. The whole idea of kicking up a stink against policies and organizations in a bid for positive change or prodding policies in the right direction away from disaster is practically non-existent in Ghana; and here are a few of the don'ts of pressure groups.

In Ghana, trade unions are too busy staging demonstrations and strikes for pay rises for their members. However, they do not focus on say the taxation levels and how it affects the Ghanaian people. Second, interest groups in Ghana do not come out against government acquisitions, stake holds, and government trade agreements with foreign investors and ask for transparency and citizenry input and acceptance of the nature of the deals before it goes ahead. Third, you will not find interest groups in the corridors of the House of Parliament presenting proposals or getting State Ministers to read their finding on conflicting issues to the general public. Fourth is that the Ghanaian media associations are too busy chasing politicians to find out who just had a gold tooth fitted, which minister is driving a Mercedes Benz, a BMW, or the latest Jaguar. The media barely have the time to advocate for, say, *decentralization* or raise awareness through the electronic and print medium about certain salient national policies, such as citizens' duty to pay taxes to the state, which will go a long way to educate and enlighten people about socio-political policies and associated issues. Moreso, the Ghanaian media would not sumit a white paper on the collective opinion on a policy they have gathered from across the country to parliament regarding a particular national sentiment which may perhaps help parliament to know how the electorate really feels about that policy. This action by interest groups will help shed some insight into the repercussions if it goes against the will of the people. Fifth, the bar associations are too scared to challenge the status quo and stand up on behalf of citizens and lobby parliament in a bid for transparency in the public accounts system and the passage of the right to information act. Lastly, and not the exhaustive list of don'ts, the farmers associations are always making appeals but do not realize that they have a right to call on their members to march with cutlasses and hoes, fishing rods and cattle whips in hand to sway policy and raise awareness that they deserve better incentives and conditions of work under the commercialization of agriculture in Ghana program.

The Strength of the Party System and Political Ideologies

Two other factors have precipitated interest group activity: the strength of the party system and political ideologies. First, the absence of unified and responsible political parties magnifies opportunities for influential interest group action. A lack of strong, organized political parties can particularly affect policymakers (both at the regional level and at the district level). By contrast, a united, cohesive party can provide policymakers with a concrete agenda and political strength to resist pressure from well-organized interest groups. Nevertheless, interest groups continue to exert heavy influence over state officials. Second, ideologies—developed systems of political, social, and economic beliefs—traditionally have not been strong factors in Ghanaian politics. Ghana voters do not typically act in accordance with their commitment to ideological beliefs, although recently church groups and other social conservative political ideas have increased in importance regarding the demands by gay and lesbians that Ghana should recognize their rights to assembly in the country. The Christian Coalition and similar organizations have spurred political activism to pressure the government to keep the demands of lesbians and gays at bay, since they will never give in to homosexuality in the country.

Organization of Interest Groups

Citizens may join an interest group for a variety of reasons, whether financial, professional, or social. In some cases, they join an interest group simply because they want to be part of a network of like-minded people working for a cause. The interest group often provides members with information and benefits and usually tries to involve them in the political process. This description suggests that any organization becomes an interest group when it influences or attempts to influence governmental decisions. There are almost as many organizational patterns as there are interest groups. This variety arises from the fact that, in addition to lobbying, most interest groups carry on non-political functions of paramount importance to their members. A religious organization, for example, emphasizes charitable and spiritual activities, but it may also undertake political activity. Some interest groups are highly centralized organizations that take the form of a single controlling body without affiliated local or regional units. Some examples of centralized groups currently operating in Ghana are the Ghana Pharmaceutical Association, Ghana Medical Council, and others. Other groups are decentralized, consisting of loose alliances of local and regional subgroups. Their activities may be directed at the local, regional, or national level. Many trade associations (such as those affiliated with the Ghana Trades Union Congress, the Textiles Workers' Union, say, of Akosombo Textile Limited) are examples of decentralized organizations in Ghana. Groups with national organization, including the National Association of Teachers and the Civil and Local Government Staff Association of Ghana, usually have both regional and district offices across the country.

Membership and Leadership—Interest groups are chiefly composed of persons from professional and managerial occupations. They tend to have greater resources than most people possess. For instance, members are more likely to be homeowners with high levels of income and formal education who enjoy a high standard of living. Participation, especially active participation, varies. Many citizens are not affiliated with any group, whereas others are members of several interest groups.

An organized group of any size is usually composed of an active minority and a passive majority. As a result, decision makers may range from a few elected officers to a larger body of delegates representing the entire membership. Organizations generally leave decision-making and other leadership activities to a few people. Widespread apathy among rank-and-file members and the difficulty of dislodging entrenched leaders probably account for limited participation in most group decisions. Other factors influence group leadership; these include the financial resources of the group (members who contribute most heavily usually have greater weight in making decisions), time-consuming leadership duties (only a few people can afford to devote much of their time without compensation), and the personality traits of leaders (some individuals have greater leadership ability and motivation than others).

Characteristics of Interest Groups

The increasing diversity of interest groups in Ghana at the national, regional, and district levels of government permits them to be classified in several ways. Not only can they be studied by organizational patterns (as discussed earlier), they can also be categorized according to the level or branch of government to which they direct their attention. Some groups exert influence at all levels of government and on legislative, executive (including administrative), and judicial officials. Others may try to spread their views among the general public and may best be classified according to the subject matter they represent. Some groups do not fit readily into any category, whereas others fit into more than one. In the next section, various types of interest groups are examined—from economic groups, professional and government employee groups, and social groups to public interest groups.

Economic Groups—Many interest groups exist primarily to promote their members' economic self-interest. These organizations are commonly known as economic interest groups. Traditionally, many people contribute significant amounts of money and time to obtain financial benefits. Thus, some organizations exist to further the economic interests of a broad group, for example, trade associations such as hairdressers' associations. The Ghana Chamber of Commerce is an example of a broader type of interest group, known as an umbrella organization. There are individual corporations, such as the Ghana Consumer Protection Agency, that use the political process to promote a company's particular economic interests, which pressures the government to ease price controls to the general public.

Business Groups—Business people understand they have common interests that may be promoted by collective action. They were among the first to organize and press the state and local government to adopt favourable public policies. Business organizations typically advocate lower taxes, a lessening or elimination of price and quality controls by government, and minimal concessions to labour unions. At the national level, business organizations most often take the form of trade associations (groups that act on behalf of an industry). The Kantamanto Used Clothes Traders Association and the Kokompe Spare Parts Traders Association are among interest groups that have lobbied parliament, and particularly the Ministry of Finance, for their interests. Two of the many other Ghana trade associations are the Greater Accra Builders Associations (GREDA) and the Ghana Private Road Transport Union (GPRTU).

Labour Groups—Unions representing Ghana workers, although relatively active, are not as numerous or powerful as business-related groups. The nation's labour organizations pursue, among other goals, government intervention to increase wages, obtain adequate health insurance coverage, provide unemployment insurance, and promote safe working conditions for their members. Ghanaians are traditionally sensitive to the potential political power of organized labour, but certain industrial labour organizations are generally regarded as significant in Ghanaian government. The most important labour organization in Ghana is the Trades Union Congress (TUC) and their affiliates. For a highly industrialized nation with a large population, union membership in Ghana is small compared with that of other countries.

Professional/Career Groups—Closely related to economic interest groups are groups dedicated to furthering the interest of a profession or an occupation or career. The standard of admission to a profession or an occupation and the licensing of practitioners concerns professional groups. Examples of Ghana professional and occupation associations are the Ghana Medical Association, the Ghana Bar Association, and the Ghana Dental Council, for a list of some of the more important Ghana professional and occupational associations. Medical doctors in Ghana have always been spoon-fed by the government, even without collectively bargaining, for some of the benefits they enjoy. Government has found it very difficult to get some of the doctors to serve in rural areas, and besides that, most leave the country without serving their probation period after being taken care of by the public purse. In recent years, doctors have been given cars by the government to improve their performance and service to the Ghanaian public, but they still believe their remunerations are low compared to other countries in the world.

Table 1: Professional and Occupational Associations
Ghana Medical Association
Ghana Dental Association
Ghana Pharmaceutical Council
Ghana Nurses and Midwives Council
Ghana Physiotherapists Association

Table 2: Education-Related Associations
Ghana Union of Ghana Students (NUGS)
National Union of Polytechnic Students (GNUPS)

Government Employee Groups—Government employee groups include officers and employees of national and local governments organized to obtain better working conditions, higher wages, more fringe benefits, and better retirement packages. The Ghana Civil and Local Government Staff Association (CLOGSAG), for instance, lobbies for legislation that prevents job cuts and increases pay and healthcare for their members. Teacher groups made headway when the National Democratic Congress government came into office regarding the single spine salary implementation. Building on their momentum, teacher groups successfully pushed the government to implement an executive order from the previous government—the National Patriotic Party (NPP)—for the implementation of the single spine salaries. The agitation from the Concerned Teachers Association was particularly effective; this group mounted pressure on the Ghana National Association of Teachers (GNAT) on a weekly basis to push government for the implementation of the single spine salary (SSS) for its members.

Social Group—Ghana has a wide array of social interest groups. These include ethnic and traditional organizations, civil rights organizations, gender-based organizations, religious-based organizations, and several public interest groups.

Ethnic Group—Leaders of ethnic groups recognize that only through effective organizations can they hope to achieve their cherished goals. In a country with more than forty-four ethnic groupings, there is the need to form groups in order to demand fair treatment and justice in areas where these groups find government not forthcoming in its orientation as the guardian of rights for all. Examples of these goals include eliminating ethnic discrimination in opportunities in areas of employment, allocation of public schools, increasing educational opportunities, and obtaining greater representation in national government, national legislature, regional coordinating councils, district assemblies, and other policymaking bodies of government. Several formidable groups exist in Ghana and are formed on ethnic and tribal lines. These groups are too numerous to mention here, as every tribal group or ethnic group has an organization. Examples of some of these groupings are the Asanteman Union, the Dagomba Youth Association, the Konkomba Youth Association, the Basari Youth Association, the Frafra Youth Association, the Ga Youth Association, the Volta Youth Association, and many more. These organizations fight against ethnic discrimination on the basis of a group as opposed to the individual's behaviour or information identifying the individual as engaged in criminal activity.

Unlike most interest groups, public interest groups claim to promote the general interests of society rather than narrower private or corporate interests. Environmental, consumer, political participation, and public morality organizations are often identified as public interest groups. Public interest organizations pursue diverse goals. The Ghana Integrity Initiative, for example, focuses primarily on governmental and institutional reform. It advocates open-meeting laws, public financing of political campaigns, stricter financial disclosure laws, and recording the extent of corruption in the country. It supports efforts toward campaign finance reform, such as government funding of political campaigns to avoid the extent of corruption usually associated with vote buying during elections.

In Ghana, of all the politically active pressure groups or organizations, the Trades Union Congress (TUC) has always had the largest following, with a total membership in the early 1990s to 2012 of more than 600,000. This figure includes workers and salaried employees in the public and the private sectors who are members of the seventeen unions that are affiliated with the TUC. Since independence, successive governments have made repeated attempts to control or manipulate it but the Trades Union Congress has always been successful in avoiding the pitfalls. Former military ruler and later president Jerry John Rawlings enjoyed the support of the TUC during the first two years of Provisional National Defense Council (PNDC) rule, but the stringent austerity measures introduced in the Economic Reform Program (ERP) in 1983 led to discontent among union members adversely affected by devaluation, wage restraints, and lay-offs. By 1985 the original support enjoyed by the PNDC in labour circles had all but disappeared. The PNDC worked hard to regain union support, however, and the National Democratic Congress government of the fourth republic has continued to woo the unions through tripartite consultations involving itself, the TUC, and employers. From the inception to the end of PNDC rule in 1992, the Christian Council of Ghana (CCG), the Catholic Bishops Conference (CBC), the Ghana Bar Association (GBA), National Union of Ghana Students (NUGS), and the National House of Chiefs (NHC) played prominent roles in the transition to democracy. These organizations took the provisional nature of the PNDC regime quite literally, calling for a quick return to democratic national government. Although NUGS and the GBA consistently demanded a return to multiparty democracy, the CCG, the CBC, and the national and regional houses of chiefs favoured a non-partisan national government. While the NUGS and GBA leadership used methods that frequently provoked confrontation with the PNDC, the CBC and the national and regional houses of chiefs adopted a more conciliatory method of political change, but emphasizing on national unity.

The Christian Council of Ghana, the Catholic Bishops Conference, and the national and regional houses of chiefs function openly as independent national lobbies to promote common rather than special interests. They insist on negotiation and mediation in the management of national disputes, and they advocate policy alternatives that stress the long-term needs of society. In the past, they have taken bold initiatives to attain the abrogation of state measures and legislation that violate human rights or that threaten law and order. All three bodies share a commitment to democracy, the rule of law, and the creation of political institutions that reflect Ghanaian cultural traditions.

The GBA, like the other professional associations in Ghana, is concerned, among other things, with maintaining the dignity of the legal profession through a code of professional ethics and with promoting further learning and research in the profession. The main objectives of the GBA according to its constitution include the defence of freedom and justice, the maintenance of judicial independence, and the protection of human rights and fundamental freedoms as defined under the United Nations Universal Declaration of Human Rights and Fundamental Freedoms. These objectives, by definition, have inevitably pitted the GBA against both military regimes and one-party governments, which on their part have considered the GBA at best a necessary evil.

NUGS and its national executives represent all tertiary institution in Ghana's polytechnics, and universities across the country are among the most vocal and articulate pressure groups. By reason of their higher education, in a largely illiterate society, students have often been in a position to agitate for far-reaching political, economic, and social change. Indeed, students have been in the forefront of political activism in Ghana since independence. NUGS was most vocal in its support of Rawlings and the PNDC in 1982, but this changed as the PNDC adopted policies that NUGS considered to be against the welfare of students in particular and of Ghanaians in general.

Conclusion

An *interest group* (also called an advocacy group, lobbying group, pressure group, or special interest) is a group, however loosely or tightly organized, that is determined to encourage or prevent changes in public policy without trying to be elected. Most textbook used in class define *interest group* as 'an organization of people with shared ideas and attitudes who attempt to influence public policy'. All interest groups share a desire to affect government policy in order to benefit themselves or their causes. Their goal could be a policy that exclusively benefits group members or one segment of society (e.g. government subsidies for farmers) or a policy that advances a broader public purpose (e.g. improving air quality). They attempt to achieve their goals by lobbying—that is, by attempting to bring pressure to bear on policymakers to gain policy outcomes in their favour.

In conclusion, the term *interest* rather than *interest group* is often used to denote broad or less-formalized political constituencies, such as the agricultural interest and the environmental interest—segments of society that may include many formal interest groups. Similarly, *interest* is often used when considering government entities working to influence other governments (e.g. a local government seeking to secure funding from the national government). In authoritarian and developing societies, where formal interest groups are restricted or not as well developed, *interest* is often used to designate broader groupings such as government elites and tribal leaders.

In their non-political role, interest groups may have several functions, but when they become enmeshed in the political sphere, they have one overriding goal: to gain favourable outcomes from public policy decisions. In the political realm, interest groups perform important functions, particularly in a democracy but also in an authoritarian regime. These include aggregating and representing the interests of groups of individuals in a way that a single individual would not be able to do, helping to facilitate government by providing policymakers with information that is essential to making laws, and educating their members on issues and perhaps giving them political experience for entering politics. In addition to providing this political experience, groups sometimes actively recruit candidates for public office, with the hope that, once elected, these individuals will support their cause. Interest groups in most democracies are also a source of financial support for election campaigns. In the United States the development of political action committees (PACs) after World War II was geared to providing money to candidates running for public office. In Western Europe, campaign funding is provided by many interest groups, particularly trade unions, for social democratic parties as in Sweden and Germany. Mass parties in authoritarian regimes also often rely on interest groups for support. For example, in Argentina, Juan Peron used the General Confederation of Labor (CGT), the trade union peak associations to gain and maintain the presidency of that country from 1946 to 1955. In addition to financial resources, members of interest groups are important resources for grass-roots campaigning, such as operating telephone banks to call prospective voters, canvassing neighbourhoods door to door, and organizing get-out-the-vote efforts on Election Day. But in Ghana, interest groups are basically interests who function to demand for their economic interest; they are yet to aggregate themselves to seek for political favours as is practiced in other affluent countries such as the United States of America, Britain, Sweden, Argentina, and many others.

Key Terms

Public opinion Lobbying Pluralism Government Political party Geeks

State Organizations Non-profit Non-governmental organization (NGO) Academy

Political machine think tank Authoritarian regimes Interest groups

Democracies Authoritarian Primitive societies

Fundamental freedoms Human rights Platform

Works Cited/Further Readings

Afrifa, Akwasi A. (1966), *The Ghana Coup* (London: Cass).

Agbodeka, Francis (1971), *African Politics and British Policy in the Gold Coast, 1868–1900* (Evanston, Illinois: Northwestern University Press).

Alexander, H. T. (1966), *African Tightrope: My Two Years as Nkrumah's Chief of Staff* (New York: Praeger).

Allman, Jean Marie (1993), *The Quills of the Porcupine: Asante Nationalism in an Emergent Ghana* (Madison: University of Wisconsin Press).

Busia, Kofi Abrefa (1951). *The Position of the Chief in the Modern Political System of Ashanti* (London: Oxford University Press).

Chazan, Naomi (1983), *An Anatomy of Ghanaian Politics: Managing Political Recession, 1969–1982* (Boulder, Colorado: Westview Press).

Crowder, Michael and J. F. Ade Ajayi (1972) (eds.), *History of West Africa* (New York: Columbia University Press).

Curtin, Philip D. (1969), *The Atlantic Slave Trade: A Census* (Madison: University of Wisconsin Press).

Kraus, Jon (1970), 'Arms and Politics in Ghana', pages 154–221 in Claude E. Welch, Jr. (ed.), *Soldier and State in Africa: A Comparative Analysis of Military Intervention and Political Change* (Evanston, Illinois: Northwestern University Press).

Ladouceur, Paul Andre (1979), *Chiefs and Politicians: The Politics of Regionalism in Northern Ghana* (London: Longman).

Lawrence, Arnold Walter (1964), *Trade, Castles, and Forts of West Africa* (Stanford: Stanford University Press).

Davidson, Basil (1989), *Black Star: A View of the Life and Times of Kwame Nkrumah* (Boulder, Colorado: Westview Press).

Chapter 10

CIVIL SOCIETY ORGANIZATIONS (CSOS)

Becoming a Good Citizen

Who is a good citizen? What does it take to be a good citizen of a country that one lives in? The year was 1980, January. That year was the beginning of the Ghanaian revolution, which brought about the overthrow of Dr Hilla Limann's administration and the establishment of what came to be known as the June 4th Revolution, led by Flight Lieutenant Jerry John Rawlings. The short story goes like this: Ghana was suffering a severe shortage of essential commodities such as sugar, milk, bath soap, washing soap, sardines, mackerel, and whatnot. Soldiers had taken over stores and subjected store owners to searches and seizures of their commodities. The owners were accused of commodities hoarding and their commodities were forcibly sold at what was known as controlled prices. But one store owner who knew that the penalty for failure to comply with the orders of the soldiers was death by firing squad refused to heed this call. He locked up his store and refused to open his store for inspection when the soldiers ordered everybody to avail themselves and allow them to auction goods that were being hoarded. Acting under this law, his son, a young boy of sixteen years, reported this father to the soldiers for concealing and hoarding goods. The father was apprehended by these soldiers, shot by firing squad for hoarding, and all the goods in the store were liquidated to the general public. Soon after, the boy was himself killed by a group of people, led by the boy's uncle, who was outraged that the boy had betrayed his own father. The government, taking a radically different view of the affair, extolled the boy as a patriotic martyr. What is your view?

What are we to make of the historical incident described in the preceding paragraph? 'The excellence of citizens', declares Aristotle in one of his writings, the *Politics*, 'is relative to the political order under which they live.' In other words, different political regimes define the requirements of good citizenship in different ways. Thus a good *citizen* in Ghana in the 1980s would have been a person whose first loyalty was to the revolution. That person would willingly and happily blend into the crowd. In defining who is a good citizen, the closest here is that *the true test of good citizenship would be the capacity to subordinate all personal convictions and even family loyalties to the dictates of political authority*. This definition of good citizenship, which is a common one under totalitarian regimes, stands in marked contrast to the usual standards of citizenship characteristic of constitutional democracies. Unlike their totalitarian counterparts, democratic nations generally prize and safeguard an individual's freedom of conscience, as well as the right of citizens to express personal opinions. Throughout history, people of diverse moral character have laid claim to the title of good citizenship. The obvious relationship between citizens' moral character and different forms of government underscores Aristotle's observation that the true measure of a political system is the kind of citizen it produces. According to this view, a good state is one whose good citizens are good people; a bad state is one whose good citizens are bad people. As simple as this formulation sounds, it offers a striking insight into the relationship between governments and citizens and points up that civic virtue cannot be divorced from questions of moral character in general.

Political Socialization

Though the proper definition of citizenship may be disputed, almost everyone agrees that good citizens are made, not born. Children grow up to be responsible citizens through the interplay of various influences and institutions—including the family, schools, peer groups, the mass media, and the law—that help to shape the individual's sense of civic duty and political self-confidence. The process of being conditioned to think and behave in a socially acceptable manner is called socialization. *Political socialization* is the process whereby citizens develop the values, attitudes, beliefs, and opinions that enable them to relate to the political system. Every self-sustaining society inculcates in its citizens certain basic values. Unquestionably, shared beliefs are the necessary building blocks of any state, even so staunch an individualist as the British philosopher John Stuart Mill (1806–1873) acknowledged that the sense of citizen loyalty or allegiance may vary in its objects and is not confined to any particular form of government; but whether in a democracy or in a monarch, its essence is always the same, viz. that there be in the constitution of the state something which is settled, something permanent, and not to be called into question, something which, by general agreement, has a right to be where it is, and to be secure against disturbance, whatever else may change. It follows that no government, however legitimate, can afford to ignore the way in which its citizens develop their political beliefs. This process begins in the family.

Contrasting Definitions

But different political states embrace different definitions of citizenship. In many authoritarian states, people can be classified as citizens only in the narrowest sense of the word—that is, they reside within the territory of a certain state and are subject to its laws. Their relationship with the government is a one-way street: They pay taxes and bribe corrupt officials and that is it. As ordinary citizens, they have no voice in deciding who rules or how they are ruled. Generally, the government leaves them alone as long as they acquiesce to the system. By contrast, in totalitarian states, where the government seeks to transform society and create a new kind of citizen, people are compelled to participate in the political system. From the standpoint of citizenship, however, this kind of participation is meaningless because it is not voluntary and stresses duties without corresponding rights. Loyalty and zealotry form the core of good citizenship under such regimes, and citizens may be forced to carry out orders that contradict their personal beliefs.

But in democratic societies like the United States, the United Kingdom, Europe, and others around the world, people view citizenship in different ways. Elementary schoolteachers consider a good citizen to be a pupil who causes a minimum of trouble during class periods, sets a good example, respects others, and studies diligently. Newscasters and political scientists commonly attribute good citizenship to adults who take their civic obligations seriously by obeying the laws, paying taxes, and voting regularly. Many individuals, including civil libertarians, emphasized that the essence of citizenship lies in the rights that individuals may exercise within society. It is worth noting that the formal requirements of citizenship in the United States are minimal, even though the rewards are envied by people the world over (hence the steady flow of immigrants into the United States, compared to the trickle of US citizens emigrating to other countries). According to the Fourteenth Amendment of the American constitution, 'All persons born or naturalized in the United States, and subject to the jurisdiction thereof, are citizens of the united States, and of the State in which they reside.' Note that in the United States, citizenship is constitutionally defined. Note, too, that citizens of the United States are distinguished from non-citizens not on the basis of how they act or what they have done but simply by their place of birth. The underlying presumption here is that once a citizen, always a citizen, barring some extraordinary misdeed (such as treason) or a voluntary renunciation of citizenship. In the United States, in peacetime, the demands of citizenship are usually quite limited. In Ghana, citizenship is not particularly defined since indigenous ethnic groups are mostly discriminated through the allocation of land rights to equally situated ethnic groups in the Northern, Volta, and similarly situated regions of the country.

What Is Civil Society?

A *civil society* is defined as that vast web of intermediary associations (labour unions, farm groups, business associations, Boy and Girl Scouts, religious bodies, etc.) that occupy the ground between individual citizens and the state and that serve as transmission belts between them. A civil society group or organization has long been thought of as essential to democracy. The concept of civil society has a long and distinguished history in Western political thought and practice. Let us note some contributions of CSOs here: first, while civil society is indisputably part of the Western tradition, its meaning and implications have varied enormously over time, in different historical contexts, and from country to country; and second, while civil society is tied to and closely a part of the distinctively Western tradition, with its emphasis at least in modern time on individualism, absence of feudal or semi-feudal restraints, freedom of association, liberty, participatory and pluralist politics and middle-class, entrepreneurial, and free-market economics, we must question whether and how much it has relevance in many developing countries like Ghana, with quite a different culture, divided among over forty-four different tribes in the country. But questions that must be asked are the following: Is civil society such a genuinely universal concept that it is applicable to all countries in approximately the same form? These are the issues I am trying to wrestle with in relation to the Ghanaian society and whether civil groups are really playing their part in Ghana's new-found democratic dispensation.

Ghana does not have strong civil society groups nor has it been very liberal; instead, civil societies for most of their recent histories have been corporatist and authoritarian. Liberalism means a system of free and unfettered associability, pluralism, and a largely unregulated civil society, interest groups, or non-governmental organizations (NGO) activity, whereas corporatism (not to be equated with one of its variants, racism) means state regulation and control of interest group/NGO activity and even the creation of official, state-run associational life. Now, as the economy of Ghana is being deregulated, and as authoritarianism is giving way to democracy, numerous societies and the political system are similarly transitioning from corporatism to free association, civil society, and greater societal and political pluralism. This process is still ongoing in Ghana. The activities of civil society are still incomplete and partial. There are often limits on NGO / civil society activities or the new groups must compete, often unfairly, with official, state-sponsored organizations. This is because there is fear in Ghana and particularly in many other developing countries that unfettered, unregulated interest group activity will produce chaos and breakdown. Many governments, while dismantling corporatism formally, are nevertheless continuing its practices, or even though repudiating corporatism at the national level, governments are recreating controls at the local levels—precisely where many NGOs and civil society groups operate. There is a delicate balance between wanting democracy and pluralism, and the reality that many developing countries may unravel, break down, and prove ungovernable if that process proceeds too rapidly.

Liberalism and free associability have not been the sole, inevitable, or universal outcomes of recent modernization processes in Ghana. Instead, corporatism and various mixed forms of state control/freedom have predominated. But while economic reform and democratization (parties and elections) have received a great deal of attention from scholars, policymakers, and the NGO civil society community, almost no one is analyzing the arena from corporatism to free associability. For if democracy is to flourish beyond the mere formal level, a free, unfettered associability, genuine social and political pluralism, and civil society must also be encouraged, enhanced, and nurtured. If we are wise, that transition can be managed smoothly; if we are not, it can produce upheaval, instability, fragmentation, and a likely return to the authoritarianism of the 1970s and 1980s.

This chapter explores the political processes involved as Ghana's societies transition from authoritarianism and statism to democracy, and from corporatism to free associability. I am referring here to the legacy and frequently still present reality of state or government controls over NGO / civil society activity during the transition process. The chapter here is not only stating this based on academic analysis, but is interested in the practical policy implications: How can the dismantling of authoritarianism and corporatism be sped up (if that is the case) and made more complete? How can we be sensitive to local mores, institutions, and ways of doing things during the crucial transitional stage? How can civil society / NGOs operate more effectively in the transitional phases and in the interstices between corporatism and liberalism or democracy? What can be done when governments seek to re-establish statist controls either at national or local levels? How can civil society be made more effective and democracy, therefore, hopefully sustainable in Ghana?

The main impacts of civil society groups in Ghana are on influencing public policy, empowering citizens, and responding to social interests. CSOs in Ghana have been known to influence public policy in three main ways: through being at the table during the early stages of policy formulation, advocacy, and indirectly, by influencing the choices made by political actors. CSOs in Ghana also empower people to better their lives physically and economically, and help them to engage better or participate in community and state issues, in two main ways: capacity building and awareness creation. Another area of impact is in the ability of CSOs to respond to social interests. CSOs in Ghana undertake this function in three main ways: providing social amenities, undertaking voluntary work, and influencing social norms and attitudes. However, impact can be slow to see. For example, CSOs advocated for some years before family planning was added to the National Health Insurance Bill. CSOs' input is visible in governance and education issues.

The Family

The family exerts the first and most important influence on the formation of individual values. Different political regimes view the family in different ways. Some governments support and nurture the family; others choose to be indifferent to it. A few seek to undermine it, regarding the love and loyalty that flow from family ties as subversive to the state. Despite these varying reactions, however, no government would deny the importance of the family in the socialization process. In the family, children first learn what they should (or should not) do; rewards and punishments reinforce daily behaviour. In this manner, children's obligations to the family are made clear. Slowly, they become citizens of the family, often with clearly defined responsibilities and occasionally with rights or privileges. Moral ground rules are emphasized even if the reason for them is sometimes not specified ('Do it because I said so'). Trust, cooperation, and self-esteem, which are generally rooted in family relations, all bear on the behavioural and moral development of individuals. These factors also help to determine the direction children's ultimate political socialization takes and how easily that socialization is accepted.

Children usually derive their initial political orientation from their parents. Often, specific party affiliation also drives from the family, especially when both parents belong to the same party. In addition, the family exerts a powerful influence on religious persuasion, which tends to correlate highly with party affiliation as well as with certain political opinions (Catholics tend to oppose abortion, Muslims tend to circumcise their children one week after birth, Jews tend to support Israel, and so on). Of course, parental influences have their limits. In Ghana, for example, only about 40 per cent of children whose parents have the same party affiliation tend to affiliate with their parents' party. In other words, even in circumstances highly favourable to political influence, a significant number of children do not follow in their parents' political footsteps. Similarly, studies have indicated that when it comes to opinion about more abstract political issues, parents' influence over their children is quite limited. So although children are influenced by their parents' values, in no sense are their opinions predetermined by their upbringing.

Issues and Controversies

Civil society has become a topic of increasing interest in recent years in the developing world. Scholars have examined its historical, theoretical, and philosophic foundations. The US government has built civil society requirements into many of its foreign aid programs as well as overall foreign policy, and the foundations and international lending agencies have settled on civil society as their latest 'discovery' to solve the problems of the world. Many non-governmental organizations are similarly integrating civil society concepts into their programs; civil society is being touted by the developing world as holding great promise for assisting democratization and national development efforts. Still others see civil society grandiosely as saving the world. Several studies have indicated that patterns of political socialization vary with the social class of the parents, though not to a great extent. Middle- and upper-class children are more likely to become actively involved in politics than are lower-class children. Observers account for this by citing statistics showing that a family's interest in politics increases as its social standing improves. Children from lower-class families, by contrast, tend to be badly informed about politics and consequently participate less in political activities.

Why Civil Society?

One can readily understand why the notion of civil society is so attractive, particularly to scholars, foundations, policy advocates, and the NGO community. First, it has a nice ring to it: *civil society* as a term sounds lofty, non-partisan, citizen-oriented, participatory, and democratic, and who could argue with those attributes? Second, civil society conjures up images of Madisonian, Tocquevillian pluralism, town meetings, grass-roots participation, checks and balances, and countervailing yet ultimately harmonious interest group competition and democratic public policy. The images most of us have of civil society include bowling leagues, parent–teacher associations (PTAs), soccer moms, Girl and Boy Scouts, neighbourhood associations, town meetings, and peaceful, harmonious collective bargaining. A third reason why civil society is so attractive is that it holds the promise of taking public policymaking out of the hands of often corrupt, venal bureaucracies, governments, and 'evil' international organizations like the World Trade Organization (WTO) or the

International Monetary Fund (IMF), and placing it directly in the hands of popular organizations, or 'the people'. Fourth (and this by no means exhausts the list), civil society is popular because it looks 'just like us' or at least what we imagine ourselves to be: democratic, grass-roots oriented, participatory, pluralist. It avoids all of Ghana's bad attributes (the influence of money in politics, boos from the legislative bench in parliament between the executive and legislative branches, large, impersonal bureaucracy, and so on) and restores an earlier, more pristine form of citizen participation, interest-group balance, and direct democracy. Civil society has thus taken on aspects of a civic renewal, the apparent rediscovery of our long-lost and better attributes, even in some quarters a quasi-religious crusade and reconversion.

Over the last two decades, policymakers have also recognized the importance of civil society and have seized upon it as an instrument of foreign policy. For example, in the 1980s and 1990s, the Ghanaian government and others used emerging civil society organizations to assist in the ouster of discredited authoritarian regimes (Thomas Sankara of Burkina Faso, Samuel Doe of Liberia, etc.) as well as, through solidarity and other organizations, in the overthrow of communist regimes in Togo. Recognizing the incapacity and/or corruption of central government, civil society organizations have been used to carry out policies in the areas of family planning, education, environmentalism, and democratization. Civil society has proved a means to think globally but act locally on a variety of policy fronts; civil society has also proved to be a useful conduit for Ghana for overseas and other foreign assistance programs.

Civil Society Organizations in Ghana

Specifically, the key freedoms concerning CSOs are listed under Article 21 as follows:

All persons shall have the right to freedom of speech and expression, which shall include

- freedom of the press and other media;
- freedom of thought, conscience and belief, which shall include academic freedom;

- freedom to practice any religion and to manifest such practice;
- freedom of assembly including freedom to take part in processions and demonstrations;
- freedom of association, which shall include freedom to form or join trade unions or other associations, national or international, for the protection of their interest;
- information, subject to such qualifications and laws as are necessary in a democratic society; and
- freedom of movement which means the right to move freely in Ghana, the right to leave and to enter Ghana and immunity from expulsion from Ghana.

Additionally, Article 37 of the 1992 Constitution forces the state to enact appropriate laws to ensure 'the enjoyment of rights of access to agencies and officials of the state' and 'freedom to form organizations to engage in self-help and income-generating projects; and the freedom to raise funds to support these activities'. Notwithstanding the clear wording of Article 37, no new laws have been enacted governing the CSO sector since the 1992 Constitution, though it is universally agreed that the legal regime governing the sector is antiquated. Currently, the law under which a vast majority of relevant organizations are governed is the Companies Code, Act 179 of 1963, Section 10. This act allows for the establishment of companies limited by guarantee (or guarantee companies) as non-profit companies. Other statutes that govern CSOs include the Trustees (Incorporation) Act, 1962 (Act 106) and the Professional Bodies Registration Decree (NRCD 143) of 1976.

The constitution of professional bodies registered under this statute should include a statement of (a) the objects of that body, and (b) rules regulating discipline of members of the specific profession and the manner of enforcing such rules. Professional bodies registered under this statute can act as bodies corporate, and can sue and be sued, and hold and dispose of property. The statute allows for only one professional body per vocation. It also requires the professional body to have at least fifty members. The professional bodies, though not public agencies, therefore play an indirect gate keeping role. Though this statute permits the government to regulate and scrutinize registered bodies, there is in practice very little direct government involvement in the activities of professional bodies. It is unclear if such involvement would withstand constitutional inquiry. The National Redemption Council, the military government that passed this decree in the 1970s, and subsequent military regimes placed a much higher value on involvement in the activities of these professional bodies than the current civilian administrations do.

All three kinds of organizations are treated similarly for tax purposes. The Internal Revenue Act of 2000 permits the exemption of income not derived from business activities. However, actually obtaining this exemption is a long and complex process. In 1997, the government suspended automatic tax exemptions for CSOs in response to suspected abuses and fraud in respect to the exemptions that were being received. Until then, the government had only taxed CSOs for staff income, and had exempted imports linked to CSO projects from customs duties. Today, tax-exempt status is granted on a case-by-case basis. Qualification as an exempt organization requires a fairly discretionary ruling from the internal revenue commissioner. Thus, beyond the possibility of tax-exempt status, there is little advantage in incorporating under these organizational forms.

One of the primary pieces of evidence required for tax-exempt status is a listing with the Department of Social Welfare (DSW) as a charity, interjecting another level of government bureaucracy. Registration with the DSW requires an exempt organization to show, for example, that it operates within the framework of the National Development Policy. In addition, the DSW requires a general account of the organization's activities, as well as evidence that its members are able to manage and control it. Registration with the DSW also requires applicants to submit four copies of the registrar general's certification of incorporation and four copies of the organization's constitution and by-laws, as well as any brochure or newspaper reports on the activities of the organization. There are relatively few barriers to the formation of CSOs. There are many single issue-based, unregistered advocacy groups that operate without any difficulties. There are no sanctions that exist merely for holding oneself as a group or organization, and indeed, any such sanction would be a violation of the constitutional right to freedom of association. There are also very few barriers to the creation of non-profits. No initial capital outlay is required, beyond a filing fee of less than GHC200 for guarantee companies. There are also no restrictions on the kind of persons that can be directors of CSOs. However, there are some reports that bureaucratic barriers have been put in place to deny or to frustrate the creation of CSOs. It has been reported, for example, that an application for registration of a CSO to conduct research in national security and defence policy was turned down on the grounds that the subject matter was inappropriate for civilians. Also, it is widely believed that while the registration process itself may be relatively uncomplicated, the process of obtaining tax-exempt status is arbitrary and susceptible to negative political or pecuniary influences.

Weaknesses of Civil Society Groups

There are four main weaknesses of CSOs in Ghana. First is the lack of a common voice from CSOs, and CSOs seeing each other as competitors rather than partners. Second is the lack of downward accountability by CSOs, which means that CSOs often undertake projects without input from constituents. Third is the overdependence on funds from foreign donors, to the extent that Ghanaian CSOs have failed to seek other ways of sustaining themselves, calling into question their sustainability, and finally, the lack of staff members with sufficient training to carry out their functions, whether in advocacy or service provision. In view of these weaknesses, civil society groups in Ghana should realize that they are partners and not competitors; civil society groups need to find new ways of generating funds locally to fund their activities, pay their staff, and sustain their organizations. Additionally, civil society organizations should harmonize their activities and develop their human resource functions to redress the impact of high attrition levels, do more to build the capacity of staff members internally, and make every effort to attract and retain experienced staff.

Conclusion

Ghana has a long tradition of active civil society engagement. By 1897, civil society organizations (CSOs), such as the Aborigines Rights Protection Society, became some of the earliest advocates for the independence of Ghana (then called the Gold Coast) from British rule. In the post–World War II period, a number of volunteers, farmers, trade unions, religious groups, and town improvement organizations and associations served as important organizations in the struggle for independence. The event that many believe precipitated the drive toward independence was the 1948 violent suppression of a demonstration conducted by the Gold Coast Ex-Servicemen's Union, a noted CSO. In addition, some of the major political parties that emerged when pre-independence colonial authorities opened the democratic space began as civil society organizations.

Despite the number and range of CSOs that have existed historically in Ghana, their actual influence in society and on public discourse has often been a function of the amount of political space they have been given to operate. Since independence in 1957, Ghana's record as an open, liberal democratic state has been mixed. First, the Independence Constitution of 1957, which created British-style parliamentary and legal institutions and processes, was replaced with the Republican Constitution in 1960, which designated the role of an executive president. Second, Dr Kwame Nkrumah, the country's first president, worked quickly to amend the constitution to abolish opposition parties, and gave himself the power to override acts of Parliament and dismiss judges. Because of his actions, Ghana became a single-party state by 1964. A military coup in 1966 ultimately resulted in the abrogation of the 1960 Republican Constitution and the promulgation in 1969 of a new, more liberal democratic constitution with a Bill of Rights.

Key Terms

Civil society   Information   Civil war   Foreign sources   Independence Evil

Domestic policy Environmental policy Economic policy Social policy   Rules

Regulations   Bureaucracy   Fourth arm of government Civil service

Government

World Trade Organization (WTO) International Monetary Fund (IMF)

Banks

Civil Society Organizations (CSOs)

Non-governmental organizations (NGOs)

Works Cited / Further Readings

The Trustee's Act replaced the Land (Perpetual Succession) Southern Ghana and Ashanti Ordinance (Cap. 137), which permitted groups of families or other individuals to hold and alienate land collectively. See also Kuma & Another v Koi-Larbi (1991)1 GLR 537–549.

Darkwah, A., Civicus Report, Supra.

Gyimah Boadi, E. and Oquaye, Mike, 'Civil Society and Domestic Policy Environment in Ghana', CDD-Ghana Research Paper 7 (Sept. 2000). Information on the history of NGOs was also compiled from IDEG and APRM.

Paffenholz, T. and Spurk, C. (2006), 'Civil Society, Civic Engagement, and Peace building', *Social Development Papers: Conflict Prevention and Reconstruction*, 36.

'West African Civil Society Position on the Millennium Development Goals and Their Implementation', paper presented in West African Civil Society Forum on Millennium Development Goals, Dakar, 2003.

'We the People, 2004, A Call to Action for the UN Millennium Declaration', World Federation of United Nations Associations and the North–South Institute.

World Bank (2004), 'Issues and Options for Improving Engagement Between the World Bank and Civil Society Organizations', Civil Society Team, External Affairs, Vice Presidency, Environmentally and Socially Sustainable Development Vice Presidency.

World Development Report (1990), 'Poverty' World Development indicators, World Bank.

World Development Report (2004), 'Making Services Work for Poor People', World Bank.

Yanacopulos, Helen, 'The Strategies that Bind: NGO Coalitions and Their Influence', cited in Çakmak, C. (2007), 'Coalition Building in World Politics: Definitions, Conceptions, and Examples', *Perceptions*, Winter 2007.

Chapter 11

CIVIL RIGHTS

The Basis for Equality and Equal Rights

Civil rights are a class of rights that protect an individual from unwarranted infringements by the government and private organizations, and to ensure that a person's ability to participate in the civil and political life of the country is without repression or discrimination. In other words, civil rights include the protection of one's physical integrity and safety, as well as the protection of a person from discrimination on grounds such as physical or mental disability, gender, religion, race, national origin, age, sexual orientation, or gender identity. Also relevant to civil rights are individual rights such as the freedoms of thought and conscience, speech and expression, religion, the press, and the freedom of movement.

Political rights can be defined as rights of the accused embedded in natural justice (procedural fairness). In law or in legal terms, it can also be described as the rights of the accused, including rights such as the right to a fair trial, due process, the right to seek redress or a legal remedy, and rights of participation in civil society and politics like the freedom of association, the right to assemble, the right to petition, and the right of self-defence. Civil and political rights form the original and main part of international human rights law. These laws comprise the first part of the 1948 Universal Declaration of Human Rights, with economic, social, and cultural rights comprising the second portion. The theory of three generations of human rights considers this group of rights to be first-generation rights, and the theory of negative and positive rights considers them to be generally negative rights. The phrase 'civil rights' is a translation of Latin *ius civis* (rights of citizens). Roman citizens could be either free (*libertas*) or servile (*servitus*), but they all had rights in law.

Historical Development of Civil Rights

In early-nineteenth-century Britain, the phrase 'civil rights' most commonly referred to the problem of legal discrimination against Catholics. In the House of Commons, support for the British civil rights movement was divided; many more largely known politicians supported the discrimination toward Catholics. Independent MPs (such as Lewis Eves and Matthew Mountford) applied pressure on the larger parties to pass the civil rights act of the 1920s. But in the 1860s, Americans adapted this usage to newly freed blacks. Congress subsequently enacted civil rights acts in 1866, 1871, 1875, 1957, 1960, 1964, 1968, and 1991. In Ghana, civil rights are a part of the 1992 Constitution, which grants freedom of association and rights to the citizens of Ghana, but they are not as entrenched as those in the United States of America.

Ancient and Modern Citizenship

The idea of equal citizenship can be traced back to Aristotle's political philosophy and his claim that true citizens take turns ruling and being ruled (*Politics*: 1252a16). But in modern society, as in Ghana, the idea has been transformed, in part by the development of representative government and its system of elections. For modern liberal thought, by contrast, citizenship is no longer a matter of having a direct and equal share in governance, but rather consists in a legal status that confers a certain package of rights that guarantees to an individual a voice, a vote, and a zone of private autonomy. The other crucial differences between modern liberalism and earlier political theories concern the range of human beings who are regarded as having the capacity for citizenship and the scope of private autonomy to which each citizen is entitled as a matter of basic rights. Modern liberal theory is more expansive on both counts than its ancient and medieval forerunners.

The Civil-Political Distinction

Until the middle of the twentieth century, civil rights were usually distinguished from political rights. The former included the rights to own property, make and enforce contracts, receive due process of law, and worship in one's religion. Civil rights also covered freedom of speech and the press (Amar 1998: 216–17), but they did not include the right to hold public office, vote, or to testify in court. The latter were political rights, reserved to for adult males.

The civil-political distinction was conceptually and morally unstable insofar as it was used to sort citizens into different categories. It was part of an ideology that classified women as citizens who were entitled to certain rights but not to the full panoply to which men were entitled. As that ideology broke down, the civil-political distinction began to unravel. The idea that a certain segment of the adult citizenry could legitimately possess one bundle of rights while another segment would have to make do with an inferior bundle became increasingly implausible. In the end, the civil-political distinction could not survive the cogency of the principle that all citizens of a liberal democracy were entitled, and in Rawls's words, to 'a fully adequate scheme of equal basic liberties' (2001: 42). It may be possible to retain the distinction strictly as one for sorting rights, rather than sorting citizens (Marshall 1965; Waldron 1993). It is difficult, however, to give a convincing account of the principles by which the sorting is done. It seems neater and cleaner simply to think of civil rights as the general category of basic rights needed for free and equal citizenship.

Three Generations of Rights

The claims for which the American civil rights movement initially fought belong to the first generation of civil rights. Those claims included the pre-twentieth-century set of civil rights—such as the rights to receive due process and to make and enforce contracts—but covered political rights as well. However, many thinkers and activists argued that these first-generation claims were too narrow to define the scope of free and equal citizenship. They contended that citizenship could be realized only by honouring an additional set of claims, including rights to food, shelter, medical care, and employment. This second generation of economic welfare rights, the argument went, helped to ensure that the political, economic, and legal rights belonging to the first generation could be made effective in protecting the vital interests of citizens and were not simply paper guarantees from the government of the day. Yet, some scholars have argued that these second-generation rights should not be subsumed under the category of civil rights. According to Cranston (1967), traditional political and civil rights can be readily secured by legislation. And since the rights are, for the most part, rights against government interference, the legislation required is to restrain the executive's own arm.

In the United States, however, the law does not treat issues of economic well-being per se as civil rights matters. The law will only treat rights insofar as economic inequality or deprivation is linked to race, gender, or some other traditional category of anti-discrimination law is it considered to be a question of civil rights. In legal terms, poverty is not a suspect classification. On the other hand, welfare rights are protected as a matter of constitutional principle in other democracies. For example, section 75 of the Danish Constitution provides that any person unable to support himself or his dependents shall, where no other person is responsible for his or their maintenance, be entitled to receive public assistance. And the International Covenant on Economic, Social, and Cultural rights provides that the state parties to the agreement 'recognize the right of everyone to an adequate standard of living for himself and his family, including adequate food, clothing, and housing, and to the continuous improvement of living conditions'.

In Ghana, a third generation of claims, which is absent in the 1992 Constitution but has received considerable attention in recent years, is what may be broadly termed 'rights of cultural membership'. These include language rights for members of cultural minorities and the rights of indigenous peoples to preserve their cultural institutions and practices and to exercise some measure of political autonomy. There is some overlap with the first-generation rights, such as that of religious liberty, but rights of cultural membership are broader and more controversial. Article 27 of the International Covenant on Civil and Political Rights declares that third-generation rights ought to be protected.

In contemporary political thought, the term 'civil rights' is indissolubly linked to the struggle for equality of opportunity of American blacks during the 1950s and '60s in the United States of America. The aim of that struggle was to secure the status of equal citizenship in a liberal democratic state. *Civil rights* are the basic legal rights a person must possess in order to have such a status. They are the rights that constitute free and equal citizenship and include personal, political, and economic rights. No contemporary thinker of significance holds that such rights can be legitimately denied to a person on the basis of race, colour, sex, religion, national origin, or disability. Anti-discrimination principles are thus a common ground in contemporary political discussion. However, there is much disagreement in the scholarly literature over the basis and scope of these principles and the ways in which they ought to be implemented in law and policy. In addition, debate exists over the legitimacy of civil rights, including sexual orientation among the other categories traditionally protected by civil rights law. Moreover, there is an emerging literature examining issues of how best to understand discrimination based on disability.

Civil rights are the rights of individuals to receive equal treatment (and to be free from unfair treatment or discrimination) in a number of settings, including education, employment, housing, and more, and based on certain legally protected characteristics. Historically, the civil rights movement refers to efforts toward achieving true equality for African Americans in all facets of society, but today, particularly in Ghanaian politics, the term 'civil rights' is also used to describe the advancement of equality for all people regardless of ethnicity, race, sex, age, disability, national origin, religion, or certain other characteristics.

Civil Rights vs. Civil Liberties

Civil rights are different from civil liberties. Traditionally, the concept of civil rights has revolved around the basic right to be free from unequal treatment based on certain protected characteristics (ethnicity, race, gender, disability, etc.), while civil liberties are more broad-based rights and freedoms that a country extends to its people.

The Idea of Discrimination

In liberal democracies, civil rights claims are typically conceptualized in terms of the idea of discrimination. Persons who make these claims assert that they are the victims of discrimination. In order to gain an understanding of current discussion and debate regarding civil rights, it is important to disentangle the various descriptive and normative senses of *discrimination*. In one of its central descriptive senses, *discrimination* means the differential treatment of persons, however justifiable or unjustifiable the treatment may be. In a distinct but still primarily descriptive sense, it means the disadvantageous (or, less commonly, the advantageous) treatment of some persons relative to others. This sense is not purely descriptive in that an evaluative judgment is involved in determining what counts as a disadvantage. But the sense is descriptive insofar as no evaluative judgment is made regarding the justifiability of the disadvantageous treatment.

In addition to its descriptive senses, there are two normative senses of *discrimination*. In the first, it means any differential treatment of the individual that is morally objectionable. In the second sense, *discrimination* means the wrongful denial or abridgement of the civil rights of some persons in a context where others enjoy their full set of rights. The two normative senses are distinct because there can be morally objectionable forms of differential treatment that do not involve the wrongful denial or abridgement of civil rights. Discrimination that does deny civil rights is a double wrong against its victims. The denial of civil rights is in itself a wrong, whether or not others have such rights. When others do have such rights, the denial of civil rights to persons who are entitled to them involves the additional wrong of unjustified differential treatment. On the other hand, if everyone is denied his civil rights, then the idea of discrimination would be misapplied to the situation. A despot who oppresses everyone equally is not guilty of discrimination in any of its senses. In contrast, discrimination is a kind of wrong that is found in systems that are liberal democratic but imperfectly so: it is the characteristic injustice of liberal democracy.

It is a notable feature of civil rights law that its prohibitions do not protect only citizens. Any person within a given jurisdiction, citizen or not, can claim the protection of the law, at least within certain limits. Thus, non-citizens in Ghana too are protected by fair housing and equal employment statutes, among other anti-discrimination laws. Non-citizens can also claim the legal protections of due process if charged with a crime. Even illegal aliens have limited due-process rights if they are within the legal jurisdiction of the country. On the other hand, non-citizens cannot claim under Ghana law that the denial of political rights amounts to wrongful discrimination. Non-citizens can vote in local and regional elections in certain countries, but not in Ghana, but the denial of equal political rights would seem to be central to the very status of non-citizen.

The application of much of civil rights law to non-citizens indicates that many of the rights in question are deeper than simply the rights that constitute citizenship. They are genuine human rights to which every person is entitled, whether he/she is in a location where she has a right to citizenship or not. And civil rights issues are, for that reason, regarded as broader in scope than issues regarding the treatment of citizens.

Why Discrimination Is Unjust

Given the principle of equal citizenship, discrimination in the sense of the denial of civil rights is an injustice that denies certain citizens the rights to which they are entitled. But it is not obvious that the principle entails that discrimination in the sense of differential treatment is unjust, even if the differential treatment disadvantages persons based on their race, sex, or another paradigmatic civil rights category. The common view is that such differential treatment is (at least prima facie) an injustice that violates the basic rights of the individual. In other words, the view is that it is a civil right to not be treated disadvantageously on account of one's race or sexual orientation.

There are two main approaches to providing an account of the injustice of discrimination based on race, ethnicity, and sex. The first is individualistic in that it seeks to explain the injustice in a way that abstracts from the broader social and political context in which the differential treatment occurs. The second is systemic in that it seeks to explain the injustice in a way that links the differential treatment to social patterns that reduce, or threaten to reduce, the members of certain groups to second-class citizenship.

Often people will insist that the injustice of racial, ethnicity, or sex discrimination stems from the connection between those forms of discrimination and the reliance on stereotypes. It is not just that race is irrelevant but that those who act on race-based grounds are using inaccurate stereotypes instead of treating a person 'as an individual', as the phrase goes. However, if being treated as an individual means that others must take into account all of the potentially relevant information about the person in their behaviour toward her, then there is no plausibility to the claim that anyone has a right to such treatment. Life's scarcity of time and resources undermines the idea that there is such a right.

Ghana Constitutional Reforms toward Civil and Political Rights

In the light of the gross human rights violations that characterized past military regimes in Ghana's political history, one key feature of the 1992 Constitution of the fourth republic was a strong emphasis on the protection of people's natural rights. Chapter 5 of Ghana's Constitution is entitled 'Fundamental Human Rights and Freedoms' and is dedicated to the protection and promotion of a wide range of rights, including civil and political rights as well as economic, social, and cultural rights (see appendix 3). In recognition of the discrimination against vulnerable groups, the Constitution mandates the state to enact appropriate laws to ensure 'protection and promotion of all other basic human rights and freedoms, including the rights of the disabled, the aged, children, and other vulnerable groups in the development process'. The rights of women are also protected to some extent, with Article 27 of the Constitution, entitled 'Women's Rights', providing for maternity leave, pre- and postnatal care for mothers, and equal rights of training and promotion for women. Beyond these constitutional provisions, the government has undertaken a number of reforms aimed at giving formal legal protection to the rights of certain socially disadvantaged groups and individuals, including women, children, and the disabled. Among these reforms are the passage of the Human Trafficking Act of 2005 (Act 694) to combat the growing trafficking of children for forced labour, Disability Act of 2006 (Act 715) to protect and promote the rights of persons living with disability, and more recently, the Domestic Violence Act of 2007 (Act 732) to protect women and girls from all forms of violence at all places. In 1998, the then NDC government also established Women and Juvenile Units (WAJU) in the Ghana Police Service to give special attention to addressing discriminatory acts against women and children.

Equal Rights Ghana

Ghana's commitment to human rights protection is also reflected in the country's ratification of important human rights treaties at both international and regional levels. At the international level, Ghana is a party to the International Covenant on Economic, Social, and Cultural Rights, the International Covenant on Civil and Political Rights, and the Convention on the Elimination of All Forms of Discrimination Against Women (CEDAW), among others. In January 1990, Ghana became the first country in the world to sign the Convention on the Rights of the Child (OSIWA and IDEG 2007b: 18). At the regional level, Ghana has also acceded to the African Charter on Human and Peoples' Rights, including its protocol establishing a human rights court, and the African Charter on the Rights of the Child (OSIWA and IDEG 2007b: 19). Finally, Ghana's commitment to human rights promotion was demonstrated by the establishment of a National Reconciliation Commission (NRC) in 2002 to investigate and address past human rights abuses during the country's periods of unconstitutional government between 1957 and 1993. In its final report submitted to the government in October 2004, the NRC recommended a comprehensive reparations package that covers a range of acts, including a formal presidential apology to victims of human rights abuses.

In Ghana, freedom of expression is constitutionally guaranteed and generally respected. Numerous private radio stations operate, and many independent newspapers and magazines are published in Accra. However, in 2009, there were a large number of assaults on and acts of intimidation against journalists, often perpetrated by NPP or NDC supporters. Internet access is unrestricted. Religious freedom is protected by law and generally respected. While relations between Ghana's Christian majority and Muslim minority are generally peaceful, Muslims often report feeling politically and socially excluded, and there are few Muslims in the top levels of government. Both domestic and international human rights observers have reported a high incidence of exorcism-related physical abuse at Pentecostal prayer camps. Academic freedom is legally guaranteed and upheld in practice. In 2005, the government removed all fees for access to primary and secondary education, and in 2009 it was reported that primary school enrolment was as high as 85 per cent for boys and 78 per cent for girls. At the same time, many teachers have complained of neglect by President Atta Mills, citing low salaries and recent reductions in some of their allowances. Similarly, the story today is no different for teacher groups—the National Association of Teachers (GNAT), the National Association of Graduate Teachers (NAGRAT).

Indeed, the rights to peaceful assembly and association are constitutionally guaranteed, and permits are required for meetings or demonstrations from the Ghana Police Service (GPS). Once the permit is approved, the group will be guided by the police to stage a peaceful march along approved routes by the Ghana Police. Under the constitution and 2003 labour laws, which conform to International Labour Organization (ILO) conventions, workers have the right to form or join trade unions. However, the government forbids industrial action in a number of essential industries, including fuel distribution, public transportation, and the prison system. Ghanaian courts have acted with increased autonomy under the 1992 constitution, but corruption remains a problem. Scarce resources compromise the judicial process, and poorly paid judges are tempted by bribes. The Ghanaian Fast Track High Courts are specifically tasked with hearing corruption cases involving former government officials, but many observers raise doubts about its impartiality and respect for due process under the Kufuor administration. It remains to be seen whether its performance will improve under subsequent governments. While Atta Mills pardoned 1,021 prisoners in 2009 to celebrate the birthday of Dr Kwame Nkrumah, easing the strain on prison infrastructure, prisons remain seriously overcrowded and often feature life-threatening conditions. While communal and ethnic violence occasionally flares in Ghana, often because of tribal rivalries in the north, no such violence was reported in 2009 and 2010, but with a much coordinated effort by the regional minister, Hon. Woyongo, he was able to put aside the crisis in favour of peace in the Upper East. Ghanaians are generally free to travel throughout the country, despite occasional police-imposed curfews and roadblocks erected by security forces or civilians seeking payments from motorists. Road conditions are dismal, and car accidents are one of the leading causes of death in the country. According to the United Nations' Integrated Regional Information Networks (IRIN), 602 people died in road accidents between January and March 2009, up from 399 in the same period in 2008.

Ghana's Constitutional Provisions—General Emergency Powers

The fundamental human rights and freedoms are enshrined in Ghana's constitution and can be found in chapter 12.1 of the General/Emergency Powers. It states that all persons in Ghana shall be respected and the powers upheld by the executive, legislature, and judiciary and all other organs of government and its agencies and, where applicable, by all natural and legal persons in Ghana, and shall be enforceable by the courts as provided for in the Constitution.

Equal Rights and Women

Despite their equal rights under the law, women suffer societal discrimination, especially in rural areas where opportunities for education and wage employment are limited. And although a domestic violence law was passed in 2007, few victims report such crimes because of the persistent stigma attached to them. However, women's enrolment in universities is increasing, and there are a number of high-ranking women in the current government. For the first time, women have held the positions of speaker of Parliament, police inspector general, Trade and Industry, and are currently heading the ministries of Foreign Affairs, Transport, and the attorney general. The country serves as a source and transit point for human trafficking, including for child labour and sexual exploitation. In 2009, following undercover work conducted by a journalist working for the *New Crusading Guide* newspaper, three Chinese nationals were sentenced to a combined 36 years of hard labour for trafficking fellow Chinese for prostitution in Ghana.

Equal Rights under Ghanaian Law

Section 12(2) of chapter 5 of the Constitution of Ghana provides that 'every person in Ghana, whatever his race, place of origin, political opinion, colour of skin, religion, creed or gender shall be entitled to the fundamental human rights and freedoms but subject to respect for the rights and freedoms of others and for the public interest.' However, lesbian, gay, bisexual, and transgendered (LGBT) persons face widespread discrimination in Ghana, as well as police harassment and extortion attempts. Gay men in prison are often subjected to sexual and other physical abuse in Ghana. In June 2010, more than 1,000 protesters in Takoradi, Western region marched in a peaceful rally against reports of gay and lesbian activities in their city. This was reportedly the first such protest in the country since independence in 1957. As a result of this the government held an HIV/AIDS training workshop in Takoradi for healthcare workers in May of 2010. After the workshop, *The Daily Graphic* announced that 8,000 gay persons had been 'registered' in the Western and Central Regions. However, experts in the field denied that there had been any such registration. After the workshop, there was significant negative reporting in the media about homosexuality. In a June 2010 interview with *The Daily Graphic*, the Western region minister called on the government to take steps to combat homosexuality. He included the possibility of police raids on locales frequented by gay men and lesbians, efforts by community leaders to 'wean young people' away from homosexuality, and a public condemnation by the government. However, no arrests of persons were made in connection with his comments by year's end, and he has since then not repeated his call. It was reported that four men who worked within the community of gay men were arrested in May 2010 in connection with an alleged sexual assault and were later charged with sodomy. The case was first brought to the Takoradi Circuit Court on August 24; however, it had not been heard since then.

Conclusion

Ghana has ratified the main UN conventions on human rights and freedom of the press. However, human rights issues exist in the area of trafficking in persons, exploitive child labour, lesbian, gays, transsexuals, societal discrimination against women, and harsh and life-threatening prison conditions. Conditions in prisons are unsatisfactory and the government has promised to improve the conditions for the inmates. The Constitution provides freedom of religion and Ghana is a good example of how Christians and Muslims can live side by side in respect of each other's religion. The Constitution also guarantees freedom of speech and assembly and it forbids the use of torture. There are furthermore proscriptions against discrimination against race, sex, disability, linguistic and social status. However, homosexuality remains a sensitive topic in Ghana, and up till this point, no legislative instrument exists to guide security authorities regarding the protection of these people and their rights as citizens.

Ghana was recently elected to the Human Rights Council for the 2015–2017 period. The Human Rights Council is an intergovernmental body within the United Nations system responsible for strengthening the promotion and protection of human rights around the world, as well as addressing human rights violations and making recommendations on them. Ghana was one of the first members of the African Union to sign up to the African Peer Review Mechanism, and welcomed the Universal Periodic Review system. The advancement of women, protection of children and people with disabilities has been among Ghana's priorities in the area of human rights.

Key Terms

Human rights   Equal rights   Violations   Disabilities

Universal Periodic Review   Homosexuality   Gay rights   Bisexuality

Legislative instrument   Lesbianism   Heterosexuality   Unnatural canal

Ethnicity   Tribalism   Multiculturalism   Biased   Superiority   Abuse

Works Cited / Further Readings

Ansbro, John J. *Martin Luther King, Jr.: Nonviolent Strategies and Tactics for Social Change* (Madison Books).

Baldwin, Lewis (1991), *There Is a Balm in Gilead* (Fortress Press).

—— (1992), *To Make the Wounded Whole* (Fortress Press).

—— (2010), *Never to Leave Us Alone: The Prayer Life of Martin Luther King Jr.* (Fortress Press).

King, Coretta Scott (1969), *My Life with Martin Luther King, Jr.* (New York: Henry Holt and Company) Revised edition copyright 1993 by Coretta Scott King.

'Regional Minister on a war path with Gays and Lesbians', *The Daily Graphic*, July 21, 2011.

United Nations (1966), 'United Nations Treaty Collection: Chapter IV. Human Rights: 5 Optional Protocol to the International Covenant on Civil and Political Rights' (New York) 16 December 1966 https://

treaties.un.org/Pages/ViewDetails.aspx?src=IND&mtdsg_no=IV-5&chapter=4&lang=en Retrieved 2012.

United Nations, 'United Nations Treaty Collection: Chapter IV: Human Rights: 8,9,10, & 11', Convention on the rights of the child, New York, 20 November 1989.

Chapter 12

CIVIL LIBERTIES

The Basis for Civil Liberties in Ghana

Civil liberties are freedoms that are guaranteed to people to protect them from an over-powerful government. Civil liberties are used to limit the power of a coercive government. Originally introduced by framers of American Constitution, *civil liberties* are rights guaranteed to citizens of the United States under the Constitution of the United States, as interpreted and clarified by its Supreme Court. Freedom of speech, protected by the First Amendment of the United States Constitution, allows people the freedom to express themselves and enjoy the expressions of others in nearly all instances. A definition of civil liberties can be stated as 'individual legal and constitutional protections against the government'. But governments have adopted civil liberties around the world, particularly countries that are becoming democratic and attempting to offer their citizens more rights and freedoms. Civil liberties are found in democratic states such as Great Britain, Ghana, Japan, Canada, Argentina—to describe such countries is to say 'countries that are practicing democracy'—but are not found in undemocratic states such as Iraq under Saddam Hussein and Iran under Ayatollah Khomeini and North Korea under its current and former leadership. Examples of civil liberties (some nations might refer to them as civil rights) are:

- Freedom from arbitrary arrest
- Freedom from arbitrary detention
- The right to a fair trial
- Freedom of association
- Freedom of assembly
- Freedom of movement

- Freedom of conscience
- Freedom of religion
- Freedom of speech within the parameters of the law

Because these rights are part of the fabric of human society, we tend to take them for granted. On rare occasions, governments may take action against a small group of people that, it could be argued, infringes on their civil liberties. Since September 2001, after the American terrorist event called 9/11, various anti- acts have given the police a far greater ability to 'trespass' on people's individual rights. The American government argued that those actions were necessary to ensure the safety of the country. Groups such as Liberty for All, a kind of pressure group in the United States, have argued that governments have overstepped the mark and have gone past the acceptable line of what a government can and cannot do within a representative democracy.

One of the most complicated areas of civil rights is when a civil liberty that one person enjoys causes offence and trespasses on the civil liberties of another. This happened when Salman Rushdie published *The Satanic Verses*. British Muslims were incensed by what they considered to be blasphemy against their religion and asked the government to ban the book. Rushdie claimed that he had a right to produce what his conscience supported, even if it did cause offence. The government decided that a ban of the book would be the equivalent of censorship and, as a democratic nation, did not want to go down that road.

Where Do Civil Rights Come From?

Most laws prohibiting discrimination, and many legal definitions of discriminatory acts, originated at the American federal level through either:

- *Federal legislation*, such as the Civil Rights Act of 1964 and the Americans with Disabilities Act of 1992. Other federal acts (supplemented by court decisions) prohibit discrimination in voting rights, housing, extension of credit, public education, and access to public facilities.
- *Federal court decisions*, such as the US Supreme Court case *Brown v. Board of Education*, which was the impetus for nationwide racial

desegregation of public schools. Other Supreme Court cases have shaped the definition of civil rights violations like sexual harassment, and the legality of anti-discrimination remedies such as affirmative action programs.

Civil Rights vs. Civil Liberties

It is important to note the difference between civil rights and civil liberties. The legal area known as civil rights has traditionally revolved around the basic right to be free from unequal treatment based on certain protected characteristics (race, gender, disability, etc.) in settings such as employment and housing. Civil liberties concern basic rights and freedoms that are guaranteed—either explicitly identified in the Bill of Rights within the American constitution or, in the case of Ghana, the 1992 constitution, or interpreted through the years by courts and lawmakers. Civil liberties include:

- Freedom of speech
- The right to privacy
- The right to be free from unreasonable searches of your home
- The right to a fair court trial
- The right to marry
- The right to vote

One way to consider the difference between civil rights and civil liberties is to look at (1) what right is affected, and (2) whose right is affected. For example, as an employee, you do not have the legal right to a promotion, mainly because getting a promotion is not a guaranteed civil liberty. But, as a *female* employee you *do* have the legal right to be free from discrimination in being considered for that promotion—you cannot legally be denied the promotion based on your gender (or race, ethnicity, disability, etc.). By choosing not to promote a female worker solely because of the employee's gender, or by denying a Bulsa man from the Upper East a promotion simply because of his ethnicity, the employer has committed a civil rights violation and has engaged in unlawful employment discrimination based on gender or ethnicity.

What Is Discrimination?

In plain English, to discriminate means to distinguish, single out, or make a distinction. In everyday life, when faced with more than one option, we discriminate in arriving at almost every decision we make. But in the context of civil rights law, unlawful discrimination refers to unfair or unequal treatment of an individual (or group) based on certain characteristics, including:

- Age
- Disability
- Ethnicity
- Gender
- Marital status
- National origin
- Sexuality
- Race
- Ethnicity
- Religion

Lawful vs. Unlawful Discrimination

Not all types of discrimination will violate national laws that prohibit discrimination. Some types of unequal treatment are perfectly legal, and cannot form the basis for a civil rights case alleging discrimination. The examples below illustrate the difference between lawful and unlawful discrimination.

Example 1: *Applicant 1*, an owner of two dogs, fills out an application to lease an apartment from Landlord. Upon learning that Applicant 1 is a dog owner, Landlord refuses to lease the apartment to her, because he does not want dogs in his building. Here, Landlord has not committed a civil rights violation by discriminating against Applicant 1 based solely on her status as a pet owner. Landlord is free to reject apartment applicants who own pets.

Example 2: *Applicant 2*, a student of the University of Professional Studies (UPS) in Accra, fills out an application to lease an apartment from a landlord around East Legon. Upon learning that Applicant 2 is a student, Landlord refuses to lease the apartment to him, because he prefers to have a worker-tenant in his only single room left in the house. Here, Landlord has committed a civil rights violation by discriminating against Applicant 2 based solely on his status. Under national civil rights laws on fair housing and anti-discrimination, Landlord may not reject apartment applicants because of their status.

Where Can Discrimination Occur?

Other national civil rights laws prohibit discrimination against members of protected groups (identified above) in a number of settings, including:

- Education
- Employment
- Housing
- Government benefits and services
- Healthcare services
- Land use / zoning
- Lending and credit
- Public accommodations (access to buildings and businesses)
- Transportation
- Voting

Discrimination: Getting a Lawyer's Help

If you believe you have suffered a civil rights violation such as discrimination, the best place to start is to speak with an experienced discrimination lawyer. Important decisions related to your case can be complicated—including which laws apply to your situation, and who is responsible for the discrimination and any harm you suffered. A discrimination lawyer will evaluate all aspects of your case and explain all options available to you, in order to ensure the best possible outcome for your case.

Constitutional Freedoms

The 1992 constitution of Ghana declares in no equivocal terms that all persons shall have the right to freedom of speech and expression, which shall include freedom of the press and other media. The constitution guarantees that the press and every individual in Ghana have the right to say anything that they want, whenever they want, and wherever they want. But there are limits to every expression of freedoms. Furthermore the Universal Declaration of Human Rights (UDHR) adopted by the United Nations General Assembly, and to which Ghana is a signatory, also states in Article 19 that everyone has the right to freedom of opinion and expression; this right includes freedom to hold opinions without interference and to seek, receive and impart information and ideas through any media and regardless of frontiers. Hence the freedom to express one's opinion without any kind of censorship is a natural right guaranteed by the highest law of our land, the Constitution, and also guaranteed by the entire human race through the Universal Declaration of Human Rights. There should be no confusion about this freedom. This right to freely express ourselves is not contingent on the whims and caprice of any government.

Contrary to popular misconception, Ghanaians are not granted this right in exchange for any kind of responsibility. This right can be revoked if not used with responsibility. The only time that this right may be revoked is when it's used by an individual who threatens the very life of another individual. Short of that, the right is sacred and inviolable. In 1960, Kwame Nkrumah with the ruling CPP, in an attempt to strengthen their hold on power in Ghana, passed a criminal code in which section 208 criminalized 'any statement, rumor or report which was likely to cause fear and alarm to the public or to disturb the public peace, knowing or having reason to believe that the statement, rumor or report was false'. This law was repugnant and contradicts the spirit of the 1992 constitution which enshrines free speech in Ghana today. The greatest problem with this law, however, is the fact that it is liable to abuse by any government that does not believe in free speech.

What Is Due Process in the Ghanaian Sense of the Law?

What then are those standards of treatment which must be accorded a person who has been restricted, arrested, or detained? Or has otherwise been invited by, say, the Ghana Police Service (GPS), Bureau of National Investigations (BNI), the Economic and Organized Crime Office (EOCO), or even CHRAJ for some questioning in relation to a matter being investigated by them? The most fundamental requirements of due process are notice and hearing, or the right to be heard. Notice implies that a person who is arrested or detained must be informed immediately of the reasons for his arrest or detention, and also that the one who is invited for questioning must be given sufficient prior notification. It also means generally that where a person had the right or privilege of enjoying a facility, then he should be given advance notification of an intention or decision to terminate the enjoyment of that facility. Hearing (i.e. the right to be heard), on the other hand, simply means that no person should be condemned or otherwise deprived of any right until he has been given the right to challenge such deprivation in a properly conducted trial or other process recognized by law. These are fundamental principles of justice which underlie any civilized legal system.

Other correlative due process guarantees which are aimed at securing fair hearing for an accused person in a criminal proceeding are *the right to be presumed innocent until proven guilty, the privilege against self incrimination, the rule against double jeopardy*, and most importantly *the right to counsel*, which I intend to devote a little more attention to in this piece. A person who is arrested, restricted, detained or who is under some investigation for a wrongdoing has *a right to be presumed innocent until his guilt is proven and pronounced by a competent court* or until he himself admits his complicity in the matter. Because of this, no person has any right to treat a person against whom an accusation has been made as though he has already been convicted of the offence. If the reverse were the case, then governments could detain individuals indefinitely without bringing them before any court, or the police could shoot and kill persons whom they suspect to have committed a serious offence like murder or armed robbery, without any court proceeding.

Privacy Rights

The 1992 Constitution guarantees the human rights of all individuals found within the territorial boundaries of the Republic of Ghana. Chapter 5 of the 1992 Constitution, titled 'Fundamental Human Rights and Freedoms', provides for rights such as right to life, economic rights, and women's rights. The entire chapter 5 is entrenched clauses, and as such, they can only be amended by the people of Ghana voting at a referendum where at least 40 per cent of registered voters cast their votes; and of those voting, at least 75 per cent vote in favour of the amendment. What is the position of the law in Ghana as far as due process of law is concerned? Does our Constitution recognize due process much the same way as it is applied in the United States? The answer is yes! Even though the 1992 Constitution of Ghana does not specifically use the phrase 'due process of law', the entire package of legal entitlements which constitute due process as applied in the US is enshrined in our Constitution of 1992.

Rights of Criminal Suspects

Indeed, articles 14 and 19 of the Constitution are just two examples of the many provisions which expressly enact in the Constitution very extensive guarantees of due process including the right to be presumed innocent until proven guilty, the privilege against self-incrimination, the rule against double jeopardy, and the right to counsel, all of which are subsumed under the general right to fair trial. What is even more interesting is that guarantee of due process entitlements is not peculiar to the 1992 Constitution; both the 1969 and 1979 Constitutions also contained provisions in very similar terms to what we have in the 1992 Constitution.

Conclusion

Civil liberties are personal guarantees and freedoms that the government cannot abridge, either by law or by judicial interpretation. Though the scope of the term differs amongst various countries, some examples of civil liberties include the freedom from torture, freedom from forced disappearance, freedom of conscience, freedom of press, freedom of religion, freedom of expression, freedom of assembly, the right to security and liberty, freedom of speech, the right to privacy, the right to equal treatment and due process, the right to a fair trial, and the right to life. Other civil liberties include the right to own property, the right to defend oneself, and the right to bodily integrity, what is referred to as privacy. Within the distinctions between civil liberties and other types of liberty, distinctions exist between positive liberty / positive rights and negative liberty / negative rights.

Freedom of expression is constitutionally guaranteed and generally respected in practice. Ghana has a diverse and vibrant media landscape that includes state and privately owned television and radio stations, and several independent newspapers and magazines. However, the government occasionally restricts press freedom through harassment and arrests of journalists reporting on politically sensitive issues. In March, 2015 two photojournalists from state-owned newspapers were brutally beaten by security officials while they were taking photos during Ghana's Independence Day celebrations. The Ghana Journalist Association (GJA) and the Media Foundation for West Africa condemned the attack and demanded an immediate probe. The Ghana Armed Forces conducted an investigation of the incident and in April exonerated the military personnel involved of any misconduct. However, public uproar over the exoneration led the country's chief of defence staff in May to apologize to the photojournalists and say they would be compensated.

Key Terms

Civil rights   Harassment   Exoneration   Integrity   Privacy   Liberty

Incrimination   Preservations   Privy   Fractured landscape   Discriminations

Exonerated   Investigations   Misconduct   Photojournalists Chief of defence

Privacy rights Constitutional rights Liberalism   Constitutionalism

Works Consulted / Further Readings

Constitution of the Republic of Ghana (1992), Chapter 6, Article 40 and Chapter 8, Article 73.

Dershowitz, Alan (2001), 'Preserving Civil Liberties: Reflections on the Fractured Landscape', spec. sec. of Chronicle of Higher Education, *Chronicle Review*, 28 September 2001. Accessed 11 August 2006.

Millennium Development Authority Ghana Fact Sheet, Kotoka International Airport Perishable Cargo Center, 20072013.

Millennium Development Authority Ghana Fact Sheet, Volta Lake Transport Services Ltd, 2007–2013.

New International IDEA Handbook, Electoral System Design: International Institute for Democracy and Electoral Assistance 2005.

Ofori-Atta, Ken (2013), 'Democracy looks to Ghana's Supreme Court', *The Africa Report*, 7 June 2013.

Rakner, L., Menocal, A. R., and Fritz, V. (2007), 'Democratization's Third Wave and the Challenges of Democratic Deepening: Assessing International Democracy Assistance and Lessons Learned', A Research Project of the Advisory Board for Irish Aid.

Schedler, Andreas (1997), 'Concepts of Democratic Consolidation', paper prepared for delivery at the 1997 meeting of the Latin American Studies Association (LASA), Continental Plaza Hotel, Guadalajara, Mexico, 17–19 April 1997.

Schumpeter, Joseph (1947), *Capitalism, Socialism, and Democracy*, 2d ed. (New York: Harper).

Smith, Jean Edward and Herbert M. Levine (1988), *Civil Liberties and Civil Rights Debated* (Englewood Cliffs, NJ: Prentice Hall).

Varrenti, Mario Giuseppe (2009), 'European Union and Democracy Promotion in Africa: The Case of Kenya', University of Leeds School of Politics and International Studies (POLIS) and the Leeds University Centre for African Studies (LUCAS) 4–5 December 2009.

World Bank, 'Ghana's Concerns'.

World Savvy Monitor, Democracy around the World in 2008, No. 3, 2008.
World Summit 2005 Outcome Document.

Chapter 13

THE MEDIA

Understanding the Mass Media

People often think of mass media as the news, but it also includes entertainment like television shows, books, and films. It may also be educational in nature, as in the instance of public broadcasting stations that provide educational programming to a national audience. Political communications including propaganda are also frequently distributed through the media, as are public service announcements and emergency alerts. Mass media is media that is intended for a large audience. It may take the form of broadcast media, as in the case of television and radio, or print media, like newspapers and magazines. Internet media can also attain mass media status, and many media outlets maintain a Web presence to take advantage of the ready availability of the Internet in many regions of the world. Some people also refer to mass media as the mainstream media, referencing the fact that it tends to stick to prominent stories which will be of interest to a general audience, sometimes ignoring controversial breaking news. Many people around the world, including Ghana, rely on this form of media for news and entertainment, and globally, it is a huge industry.

The Colonial History

In Ghana, historians of the Gold Coast press explained the indigenous enthusiasm for newspapers in terms of an overall strategy by native elites to gain political power. The early Gold Coast weeklies were critical of the colonial government, denouncing specific officials and opposing policies. While the editorial positions of these papers expressed an adversarial stance, the erudite English and ostentatious vocabulary so common to journalism in this period indicates a more complex and attenuated political desire to establish an exclusive class identity as African elites while striking up a gentlemanly conversation with British officials over conditions in the colony. With occasional exceptions, the British adopted a comparatively tolerant approach to the local press in the Gold Coast, as in other non-settler colonies, colonial territories that had no substantial population of European settlers. Author Gunilla Faringer, in her discussion of British policy in non-settler colonies, alluded to the fact that *the colonizers were more concerned with establishing trade bases and making a profit than with exercising political domination.* In contrast, the London Daily Mirror Group, headed by British newspaper magnate Cecil King established *The Daily Graphic* in 1950. The *Graphic* sought to maintain a policy of political neutrality, emphasizing objective reporting by local African reporters. With its Western origin, the *Graphic* sought to position itself as the most professional newspaper in the Gold Coast at the time; it is also true of *The Daily Graphic* today in Ghana.

Through the tactics and approach of these colonial radical presses, Dr Nkrumah's CPP achieved independence in 1957, becoming the first colony in sub-Saharan Africa to gain independence from the British and win political autonomy. As the leader of independent Ghana, Nkrumah became president in 1960 when a new constitution established the nation as a republic. At independence, four newspapers were circulating in Ghana; within a few years Nkrumah had come to dominate them all. Crafting an African form of socialism, Nkrumah saw media as an instrument of state authority, using newspapers as propaganda tools to build national unity and popular support for the ambitious development projects of the new government. Influenced by Lenin, Nkrumah orchestrated a state information apparatus through a hierarchical network of institutions, including the Ministry of Information, Ghana News Agency, Ghana Broadcasting Corporation, and his own press, Guinea Press, Ltd., that published two daily newspapers, one free weekly, and several specialized publications. One of these, Nkrumah's own *Evening News*, became a kind of *Pravda* of the CPP, dominated by party news and adulations of Nkrumah. Unfortunately in 1966, Nkrumah was overthrown by a military coup led by the National Liberation Council (NLC).

In contrast to state control of the media under Nkrumah, the NLC took a more libertarian approach to the news media: releasing independent journalists from prison, closing down the more blatant instruments of state propaganda, and lifting forms of censorship and bans on foreign journalists. Most media at the time were owned by the state and therefore obliged to change their editorial positions overnight, extolling the virtues of Nkrumah and African socialism most of the time and lambasting the violence and corruption of his regime at other times. While the president of the NLC publicly encouraged constructive criticism and the free flow of information, the main newspapers continued to experience indirect forms of state patronage and influence. By the latter parts of 1960s, Ghana had been ruled by a series of military regimes and democratic republics. In the midst of this political oscillation, the media had been subject to alternating policies of libertarian tolerance and revolutionary control. In 1981, Flight Lieutenant Jerry John Rawlings seized power from the democratically elected government of Hilla Limann. Following in the footsteps of Nkrumah, Rawlings summoned the media to actively promote revolutionary ideals of the ruling party, first the AFRC, then the PNDC and later NDC while whipping up popular enthusiasm for the participatory projects of the state. The editorial staff of the state media were reshuffled or dismissed and the editorial policies of the state media were strategically shaped to suit the interests of the new regime. Throughout the 1980s, the state media apparatus applied a variety of techniques of official and unofficial censorship, including repressive laws, public intimidation and harassment, bans on oppositional publications, and arrest and detention of dissident journalists.

The Media Landscape

The media landscape in Ghana is so vibrant that it has and continues to play a key role in politics, particularly in national popular culture and identity. Beginning from the nineteenth century, the media in Ghana has given voice to popular campaigns for independence, maintained calls for national unity and development and the need for the sustenance of democracy. Similarly in the twentieth century, the media in Ghana has distinguished itself as a catalyst for democracy, political activism, civil rights and human rights and continues to play various roles in Ghana political discourse. The first newspaper in Ghana was the *Gold Coast Gazette and Commercial Intelligencer* and was published in 1822–25 by Sir Charles MacCarthy, the then governor of the British Gold Coast settlements. The newspaper located in Cape Coast, was to provide information to European merchants and civil servants in the colony and was instituted as a semi-official organ of the colonial government. The paper also promoted literacy, encouraged rural development, and in most cases quelled the political aspirations of this class of native elites by securing their loyalty and conformity with the colonial system. This behaviour of the newspaper was due to the growing number of mission-educated Africans in the Gold Coast by then.

On the other hand, the appropriation of print media by local African elites began in mid-century with the publication of *The Accra Herald* by Charles Bannerman, son of a British lieutenant governor and a princess from the Asante royal family. Handwritten like McCarthy's former colonial paper, *The Accra Herald* was circulated to some 300 subscribers, two-thirds of them African. Enduring for sixteen years, the success of Bannerman's paper stimulated a proliferation of African-owned newspapers in the late nineteenth century, among them *Gold Coast Times, Western Echo, Gold Coast Assize, Gold Coast News, Gold Coast Aborigines, Gold Coast Chronicle, Gold Coast People, Gold Coast Independent*, and *Gold Coast Express*. Frustrated in their attempts to exercise political power within the colonial order, indigenous elites became increasingly opposed to colonial authority in the early twentieth century. A friendlier dialogue of nineteenth-century newspapers had transformed themselves into full-blown anti-colonial protest in the newspapers of the 1930s. From the 1930s onward, newspapers started demanding that citizens be given political rights, improved living standards, and self-government. As the political agenda of Gold Coast journalism radicalized, newspapers began reaching out beyond the circle of elites, appealing to rural leaders and the urban poor with a more accessible language and fiery oppositional outcry. One of such activism came in 1948, when a political activist by the name Dr Kwame Nkrumah started a newspaper called *The Accra Evening News*, a publication in which Dr Nkrumah stated the views of the Convention People's Party (CPP). Largely written by party officials, this inflammatory newspaper incessantly repeated the popular demand for 'Self-government Now!' while launching angry attacks against the colonial government.

The Resurgence of the Media in Ghana

By 1992, Ghana had returned to democratic rule with the ratification of a new constitution—the 1992 Constitution of Ghana. Rawlings was twice elected president, first in 1992 and then again in 1996. In the democratic dispensation, Rawlings lifted the newspaper licensing law, allowing for the re-emergence of the private press in the early 1990s. Newspapers such as *The Independent*, the *Ghanaian Chronicle*, *The Free Press*, and *The Statesman* gave voice to the angry opposition silenced in years of repression, prompting Rawlings to repeatedly denounce the private media as politically irresponsible and selfishly motivated by profit. Throughout the 1990s, the two state dailies, *Ghanaian Times* and *Daily Graphic*, continued to represent the interests of the ruling-party NDC government. In the 1996 presidential campaign, the premier state paper, the *Daily Graphic*, regularly featured a front-page story celebrating the populist agenda of the state, accompanied by a large colour photograph depicting the stately figure of Rawlings wielding a pickaxe or driving a bulldozer to launch a development project. These flattering portrayals were often countered in the private press by accusations of drug abuse and violent authoritarianism, featuring older photographs of a militant young Rawlings dressed in fatigues and mirrored sunglasses.

The Transition Period

After nineteen years of Rawlings and the NDC, Ghanaians elected John Agyekum Kufuor of the New Patriotic Party (NPP) as their new president in December 2000. While urging the media to be responsible, President Kufuor advocated for free expression, political pluralism, and an independent media as important elements of liberal democracy—a dramatic shift from Rawlings's furious condemnations of the private press. However, President Kufuor's liberal policies were challenged by a national state of emergency in April 2002 involving the assassination of the Dagomba traditional ruler and twenty-eight others in the northern city of Yendi.

Currently about forty newspapers are published in Ghana, the state-funded two daily newspapers and two weekly entertainment papers. *Daily Graphic* and its entertainment weekly, *The Mirror*, are produced in Accra by the state-funded Graphic Corporation. *Ghanaian Times* and its affiliate, *Weekly Spectator*, are produced by the state-funded Times Corporation, also in Accra. *Daily Graphic* boasts a circulation of 500,000 while *Ghanaian Times* reports 200,000. *Graphic* operate offices in all ten regional capitals and both are distributed throughout the ten regions via train, bus, and courier, though travel delays result in lag times of up to a week in more remote areas. In the past (1970s), the government used the air force and Ghana Airways flights to minimize delays in delivery to the regions. *Daily Graphic* is the most common newspaper encountered outside Accra.

Private Press

There are about sixteen independent newspapers that provide national political coverage. The four most influential independent newspapers are *The Ghanaian Chronicle*, *The Independent*, *The Free Press*, and *Public Agency*. Quoted circulation figures for the newspapers are as follows: *Chronicle* at 40,000, *Independent* at 35,000, and *Free Press* at 70,000, though the editors for these newspapers have reported higher numbers. With few exceptions, private newspapers are produced in Accra and circulation is concentrated there as well, though the major independents can regularly be found in Cape Coast, Kumasi, and Tamale. The commonality of English, higher literacy rates, and urban wealth all contribute to a reliable audience for independent papers in the capital. From the standpoint of production, journalists writing political stories in Accra regularly produce new stories of national relevance, while stories from the regions are more occasional and generally less sensational. However, a few independent papers regularly include coverage of regional news, following the example of the state press by maintaining offices and correspondents in the regions. With the privatization of the economy and opening up to global markets, growing interest in economic matters has prompted the emergence of a number of weekly and fortnightly papers devoted to business and finance. Five newspapers have specialized in this area: *The Business Chronicle*, *Business and Financial Concord*, *Business and Financial Times*, *Business Eye*, and *Financial Guardian*.

Media Language

English is the language of state in Ghana and all newspapers are published in English. This has not always been the case. During the colonial period, missionaries published materials in local languages and a few indigenous entrepreneurs published newspapers in the Akan languages of southern Ghana. After independence, local-language newspapers were produced in literacy campaigns by the Bureau of Ghana Languages or by churches for evangelical purposes. These papers have had limited circulation and livelihood. In recent times, while newspapers have neglected local languages, many FM radio stations have introduced very popular local-language programs in Accra and in the regions. Particularly popular are the call-in programs, where disc jockeys and callers alternate between local languages and English in discussions of local, national, and global events.

The major private papers represent distinct ideological perspectives and social groups but all face similar adverse conditions, including high printing costs, lack of equipment, exclusion from state functions, hostile or fearful sources, and difficult access to timely world news. In the early 1990s, economic conditions were so harsh that private newspapers could only afford to publish weekly, though many now appear biweekly and *Ghanaian Chronicle* comes out three or four times a week. Unable to break the daily news, the weekly private papers turned to political commentary and investigative stories in order to compete with the state dailies. A case in point is Abdul Malik Kweku Baako Jnr's *New Crusading Guide*, and Kwesi Pratt's *Insight Newspaper*, which publishes interesting headlines, as well as sensitive news about government and the general public. Mr. Kwesi Pratt and Mr. Abdul Kweku Baako Jnr. Have more or less made their names by leaving polished imprints since the days of former head of state Col. Ignatus.K Acheampong, right through the years of Flt. Lt. Jerry John Rawlings (AFRC/PNDC), and from J.A. Kuffour to the present time. In fact, these two journalists have become lecturers in political science through their submissions on topics ranging from economics to constitutionalism and law. Students, as well as political scientists and members of parliament learn from these two gentlemen daily, when they appear on TV3, Metro news, Joy news or the government owned GBC News. In addition to state competition, the systematic exclusion of private journalists from state sources and assignments, combined with lack of access to wire services, has forced private journalists to design an alternative set of journalistic techniques, incorporating anonymous sources and popular rumour, resulting in a unified challenge to the conservative messages in the state media.

In Ghana, newsprint is purchased through a central government agency, with allocations made according to circulation. Editors of private newspapers have complained that the state media receive a preferential share of available newsprint when supplies are scarce. Since 1993 the price of newsprint has increased over 300 per cent, making it extremely difficult for private papers to turn a profit and stay in business. As a result, the state-funded press endures comfortably, a few private papers with established readership struggle to stay in print, while the vast majority of private papers come and go. In Ghana, the government supplies a substantial amount of advertising to the state press, providing revenue beyond official state provisions. Moreover, in an uncertain political environment, many local businesses are still somewhat wary of public association with the opposition, therefore avoiding the private press and cautiously placing their ads in the state press. Foreign businesses patronize the state press almost exclusively. Advertising in the state press is not merely political, but pragmatic as well, as the state papers are daily and printed on more advanced equipment, giving a more professional appearance.

Press Regulation in Ghana

There is a substantial amount of press freedom in Ghana today compared to thirty years ago. For instance, the 1992 Constitution (Article 12) guarantees the freedom and independence of the media at all times. Article 2 explicitly prohibits censorship, while Article 3 pre-empts any licensing requirements for mass media. Editors and publishers are shielded from government control, interference, or harassment. When the content of mass media stigmatizes any particular individual or group, the media are obliged to publish any rejoinder to remedy the injury caused to the stigmatized party. In short, the 1990s has been hailed by journalists as a new era of free expression in terms of free media in Ghana. Many private newspapers that were prohibited by Rawlings's own 1989 newspaper licensing law have suddenly reappeared, full of anti-government criticism and eager to exercise the new freedoms. Despite the letter of the law, the Rawlings government continued to pressure the state press and intimidate the private press, resorting to more indirect techniques of control. State journalists whose opinions or news stories diverged from the ruling-party line were chastised, demoted, or sent away on 'punitive transfer' to remote offices in the regions, often to places where they did not speak the local language. As the private press investigated corruption among Rawlings's own cabinet, many state officials retaliated with civil and criminal libel suits against private journalists. Since journalists are prohibited from reporting on a story once it has gone to court, such libel cases had the effect of stalling the investigation while channelling the controversy out of the public eye and into the court system, where state officials might expect a more sympathetic audience.

Censorship of the Press in Ghana

In 1979, the government established an independent Press Commission to insulate both state and private media from state control while serving as a buffer between the state and the state media, in particular. With the suspension of the Constitution in the 1981 military coup, the state asserted control over the state media and harassed the private press to near extinction. In 1992 democratization reintroduced the Press Commission, renamed the National Media Commission (NMC) in the new Constitution. The NMC is charged with promoting freedom and independence of media, ensuring the maintenance of professional standards, protecting the state media from government control, appointing members to the boards of directors, or governing bodies of the state media, and regulating the registration of newspapers. The commission is comprised of fifteen members, including representatives of the following: the Ghana Bar Association, private press publishers, the Ghana Association of Writers and the Ghana Library Association, the Christian group (including the National Catholic Secretariat, the Christian Council, and the Ghana Pentecostal Council), the Federation of Muslim Councils and Ahmadiyya Mission, journalism and communications training institutions, the Ghana Advertising Association and the Institute of Public Relations, and the Ghana National Association of Teachers. In addition, two representatives are nominated by the Ghana Journalists Association, another two are appointed by the president, and three are nominated by Parliament. The National Media

Commission's first meeting occurred in 2000, when Parliament and the new president made their nominations to the NMC and the new members were subsequently sworn into office in May 2001. Fulfilling their directive to uphold media standards, the National Media Commission issued statements in April 2002 taking public exception to 'obscene and explicit pornographic pictures' usually published in the *Weekend News and Fun Time* magazine. The Commission advised newspaper editors and publishers to be guided by public morality, decency, and professional ethics.

State-Press Relationships

Since the establishment of the state media, state journalists have enjoyed a privileged relationship to government sources, information, documents, and resources. This privilege is both formal and informal. The government requests the presence of state journalists at daily 'invited assignments' to state events and press conferences. At these events, state journalists are provided with official commentary as well as the printed speeches, facilitating the quick news writing necessary for daily newspapers. The state has media permanent correspondents' posts to cover the president at the Flagstaff House, the seat of the Ghanaian presidency. Many state officials now talk to state journalists and not private ones, who on most occasions are not recognized as official. Through daily involvement with government officials, state journalists develop very cordial and cooperative relationships with them. As journalists rely on these state sources for their daily supply of news stories, state journalists are quite concerned to protect these mutually rewarding relationships and hardly ever publish critical or oppositional stories about the government. Until very recently, private journalists were not welcome at the Castle—the old executive headquarters—or the new Flagstaff house. Not only were they not invited to cover state events, they would be turned away if they showed up to cover the story. It was not until the presidency of President Kufuor, that such behaviour changed dramatically. Today, private news organizations are mostly the first to be invited to post permanent staff to the Flagstaff house, and in most cases, both state and private journalists are now being invited to accompany the president on official visits both nationally and internationally.

The Broadcast Media in Ghana

Radio was introduced into the Gold Coast in 1935 when the colonial governor set up a small wired relay station, ZOY, to transmit BBC programs to some three hundred colonial residents and privileged native elites. Service was subsequently extended to Kumasi, Sekondi, Koforidua, and Cape Coast. British radio not only provided information and entertainment but also a means of countering the anti-colonial campaigns of the nationalist press. In 1954, Gold Coast Broadcasting System was established, later becoming Ghana Broadcast Corporation (GBC) after independence in 1957. GBC provides two domestic radio services, Radio 1 and Radio 2, broadcasting from Accra. Radio 1 is devoted to local-language programs, broadcasting in Akan, Ga, Ewe, Nzema, Dagbani, Hausa, and English. Radio 2 transmits in English. Both stations operate for fifteen and one-fifth hours on weekdays and seventeen and a half hours on weekends. The wireless Radio 3 has been discontinued because of budget cuts. In 1986, GBC began broadcasting in VHF-FM in the Accra-Tema metropolitan area, assisted by the German government. Expanding FM service, GBC opened new FM stations in the regions and districts of Ghana in the late 1980s and early 1990s. Unique Radio operates in Accra, Garden City Radio in Kumasi, Twin City FM in Sekondi-Takoradi, Volta Star Radio in Ho, and Radio Savannah in Tamale, the Northern regional capital city. There are around 2.5 million wireless sets in Ghana, in addition to over 64,000 wired loudspeaker boxes.

Though many thought the 1992 Constitution provided for liberalization of the airwaves, the Rawlings government refused to grant licenses or allocate frequencies to private radio stations until the mid-nineties, maintaining a monopoly on radio with the state-owned GBC. In 1994, opposition politician Dr Charles Wereko-Brobby protested this policy with a series of pirate broadcasts, the infamous *Radio Eye*. Though the government pressed for criminal prosecution of Dr Wereko-Brobby and confiscated his equipment, his provocative action ultimately pressured the government to allow private FM stations. In 1995, the government began allocating licenses and frequencies through the Frequency Registration and Control Board. The first FM license was granted to Radio Universe, the small college station produced at the University of Ghana at Legon. Radio licenses are awarded for seven years, for an initial fee of $5,500. In addition, an annual broadcast fee is collected and distributed to the Copyright Society of Ghana to remunerate artists and musicians. Twelve FM stations currently operate in Ghana, all in Accra or Kumasi. Although most stations focus on musical entertainment, many have news programs and talk shows for discussion of current events in English and Twi. The most popular FM radio stations in Accra are Joy FM, Groove, Vibe, Gold, and Radio Universe.

Ghana's Foreign Media Relationships

Ghana has a high presence of foreign media and also maintains a liberal approach to foreign media and correspondents. In Ghana, there are journalists' representatives of the British Broadcasting Corporation (BBC), Bridge News, Cable News Network (CNN), Union of Radio and Television Network of Africa (URTNA), Canal France International (CFI), Pan-African News Agency (PANA), Agence France-Presse, Associated Press (AP), Reuters, and Voice of America (VOA). Most of these journalists are local Ghanaians with distinguished reputations in Ghanaian journalism and strong global connections. In most cases, these journalists carry out their work without government interference or harassment. In Ghana the outgoing information is not censored and government does not interfere in the reportage that goes on during ceremonies in Ghana. Additionally, incoming information is also free-flowing, though somewhat limited to elite audiences because of cost. Foreign publications such as *Time* and *Newsweek* are sold at the larger news kiosks. In addition, foreign newspapers present in Ghana and most patronized are *The New York Times* and *The Washington Post*, which can mostly be purchased in major hotels.

The Ghana News Agency

Nkrumah set up the Ghana News Agency (GNA) in 1957 to provide more balanced representation of local, national, and continental news. In its historic set-up, Reuters News Agency initially provided guidance and technical assistance but the agency was fully Africanized in 1961. GNA was the first wire service to be established in Africa south of the Sahara and long considered the most efficient news agency in the region. As part of the information apparatus,

GNA was central to Nkrumah's effort to monopolize the production and distribution of news at Ghana while monitoring the flow of information and images from Ghana to the outside world. GNA was originally situated within the Information Services Department but in 1960 became a statutory corporation with a board of directors chosen by the head of state. Since 1992, the National Media Commission selects the members of the board in order to prevent state control of the agency. GNA maintains offices throughout the regions and districts of Ghana, channelling news stories to the head office located in the ministries neighbourhood of Accra. The agency used to have international bureaus in major cities in ten countries, including Lagos, London, Moscow, Nairobi, and New York; however, funding cuts have forced all but the London office to close. Over 140 organizations and diplomatic missions subscribe to the news service, which provides home news, foreign news, African news, features, and advertising. GNA has news exchange agreements with Reuters, Agence France-Presse, TASS, PANA, Xinhua (Chinese news agency), and DPA (German news agency).

Television Broadcast in Ghana

Television was established in Ghana in 1965 by the Nkrumah government in collaboration with Sanyo of Japan. Sanyo wished to promote television in Ghana to support its own television assembly plant in Tema, just outside Accra. Despite Sanyo's commercial impetus, Nkrumah stressed that television should educate citizens for national development rather than merely entertain or generate profit. Radio and television broadcasting were centralized in a single unit, Ghana Broadcasting Corporation, housed in a sprawling compound in Accra. Targeted by coup leaders, GBC has frequently been seized for the public announcement of regime changes in so many dawn broadcasts. Because of this, the GBC compound is surrounded by high walls and barbed wire and guests are obliged to remain in the small reception building outside the compound. Currently, GBC-TV, or simply GTV, broadcasts from its central studios in Accra to transmitters at Ajankote near Accra, Kissi in the Central region, Jamasi in the Ashanti region, and a relay station in Tamale in the Northern region. In 1986, another transmitter was added in Bolgatanga in the Upper East region and since then others have been added in Sunyani in the Brong Ahafo region, Han in Upper West region, Amajofe and Akatsi, both in the Volta Region. Transposers or boosters operate at Ho, Akosombo, Prestea, Sunyani, Oda, Tarkwa, Dunk-wa, and Mpraeso. The Ghana television transmission standard is PAL B-5 with five low power relays. Through these transmitters, 95 per cent of Ghana has access to GTV broadcasts. On weekdays, television programming begins at 5.55 a.m. and concludes at 11.00 p.m. In addition, GTV provides a two-hour education program for schools on weekday mornings. On weekends and public holidays, GTV broadcasts from 6.50 a.m. to 11.50 p.m. After the privatization of the airwaves, the government gave approval to the allocation of frequencies to private television stations as well. Two private channels, TV3 and Metro TV, went on the air in 1997. In the Greater Accra region, Multichoice Satellite System offers subscribers access to BBC World Service Television, CNN, Supersports, and M-Net, a South African commercial network offering mostly Western movies, music videos, and television serials.

Journalism Training in Ghana

In Ghana, there are about three programs that provide journalism training for those aspiring to be journalists. The majority of journalists in Ghana are trained at the Ghana Institute of Journalism (GIJ) in Accra. GIJ was founded in 1958, offering two-year diploma programs in both journalism and public relations / advertising. GIJ also provides a number of short-term courses in advertising, public relations, writing skills, and photojournalism. GIJ has a library with 40,000 volumes for student research and a printing press for instructional purposes. While their first year emphasizes lectures and coursework, GIJ students spend their second year on practical attachments to various media organizations in Accra, learning the application of journalism techniques on the job while making valuable connections for future employment. Established in the Pan-African context of the Nkrumah period, GIJ still emphasizes that students should be trained to become 'truly African in their professional outlook'. GIJ has trained journalists from Nigeria, Liberia, Sierra Leone, Cameroon, Burkina Faso, Swaziland, Namibia, and South Africa. The second training institution, the School of Communication Studies, was founded in 1974 at the University of Ghana at Legon. The school offers a postgraduate training and a master's-level degree in journalism and mass communications. The School of Communications Studies publishes the quarterly journal, *Media Monitor*, dedicated to the discussion of media issues and promoting high professional standards. In addition to formal training, journalists participate in frequent seminars on professional, political, and social issues. The German foundation, Friedrich Ebert Stiftung (FES) is especially committed to educating Ghanaian media to contribute to democracy and development. Working closely with the Ghana Journalists Association and other local media organizations, FES has supported conferences, workshops, seminars, and publications on such topics as electoral coverage, private broadcasting, rural reporting, women in media, environmental reporting, professional ethics, and the state of the media in Ghana.

Conclusion

Since the Gold Coast era, Ghana has had a vigorous press with a distinguished political history. From the 1960s through the late 1990s, journalism has played a crucial role in contemporary processes of democracy in Ghana, providing a common sphere of dialogue among diverse political and economic interests as well as the voices of popular culture. Journalists have enjoyed more freedom, cooperation, and respect in their dealings with the state from President Kufuor (2000–2008) in office to the current dispensation under H.E. John Dramani Manama (2012–). While seriously concerned about the economic viability of the private press, Ghanaian journalists are nonetheless optimistic that the political liberalism of the current administration is laying a foundation for the maintenance of press freedom and professionalism in the future. The media in Ghana is one of the most free in Africa today, but has previously undergone periods of severe restriction. Chapter 12 of the 1992 Constitution of Ghana guarantees freedom of the press and independence of the media, while chapter 2 prohibits censorship. Reporters Without Borders, an international research organization on media freedom around the world, classify the Ghana media environment as being 27th out of 175, with 1st being most free. Following the 6 March 1957 declaration of independence by Ghana from the United Kingdom, there were only around four newspapers. Leader Kwame Nkrumah eventually controlled all the press in Ghana and saw it as an instrument of state authority, providing propaganda which encouraged national unity and creating a hierarchal system of state apparatus to manage the media. The media changed hands from a civilian to a military government, and a series of arrests and imprisonment of political opponents by Nkrumah had a chilling effect on the media. The opposition *Ashanti Pioneer*, which had operated since the 1930s, was shut down by Nkrumah after being subject to censorship. After Nkrumah's overthrow in a coup, many state outlets changed hands, though still under the control of the ruling party. The National Liberation Council imposed stricter controls on domestic private outlets, for example, the Rumors Decree in 1966, which prevented anyone from suing government-owned newspapers.

Key Terms

Mass media censorship Broadcast Journalism Communication Perseverance

Gold Coast Aborigines Gold Coast Exposition   Scepticism   Adhere Forum

Foundation   Journalism   Workshops   Seminars Publications Books Coverage

Organizations Broadcasting Rural reporting Environment Media

Ethics in publication

Works Cited / Further Readings

Ainslie, Rosalynde (1966), *The Press in Africa* (New York).

Ansu-Kyeremeh, Kwasi (1998), *Perspectives on Indigenous Communication in Africa, Volume I: Theory and Applications* (Accra).

Ansu-Kyeremeh, Kwasi and Kwame Karikari (1998) (eds.), *Media Ghana: Ghanaian Media Overview, Practitioners and Institutions* (Accra).

Apter, David (1968), *Ghana in Transition* (New York).

Asante, Clement E. (1996), *The Press in Ghana: Problems and Prospects* (Lanham, Maryland).

Austin, Dennis (1964), *Politics in Ghana: 1946–1960* (London).

Barton, Frank (1979), *The Press of Africa: Persecution and Perseverance* (New York).

Blay-Amihere, Kabral (1994), *Tears for a Continent: An American Diary* (Accra).

Friedrich Ebert Stiftung (1995), 'Activities 1995', Ghana Office. Accra.

Ghana Institute of Journalism (1995), Informational Brochure (Accra).

Graham, Yao (1996), 'Facing Up Against Lawsuits', *Media Monitor*, July–September 1996.

'Kufuor Meets the Press', *Expo Times* (Freetown), May 4, 2001.

Shillington, Kevin (1992), *Ghana and the Rawlings Factor* (London).

Chapter 14

LOCAL GOVERNMENT

Introduction

The Republic of Ghana was established as a unitary state since its creation by the colonial British government. Since its independence in 1957, as the first country in colonial Africa, south of the Sahara, to become independent, successive governments in Ghana have attempted to deepen the processes of the local government system to further the country's developmental agenda. In the then Gold Coast, local governance did not begin with the emergence of the Europeans during colonization of the West African coast. Communities and societies had their own peculiar ways of governing themselves. In Ghana, for example, the head of government in the communities was the chief, supported by his elders. However, following the discovery and settlement of Europeans in Africa, and particularly the Gold Coast, both the leadership and the dynamics of local governance changed dramatically with the chiefs playing less prominent roles to the British resident commissioners.

Colonial Involvement in Local Governance

When the British arrived in the Gold Coast, local government and administration hovered around the chiefs within villages or some local royalty which were in some cases not defined. During the Gold Coast period, the system of local government was referred to as the indirect-rule system (IRS). The units of local government were called native authorities, which were not democratic. The chiefs within the villages were recognized as centres of authority as there were no clearly recognized power wielders. In a bid to control government locally, the colonial government hand-picked some influential people to help them administer law and order. Local government in the Gold Coast can therefore be analyzed along two parallel lines. The first development was that a series of municipal council ordinances regulated local government in the major municipalities while in the other instance, a series of native jurisdiction of ordinances regulated local government in the rest of the country through the state councils and native authorities (Ahwoi, 2010). Following the 1948 disturbances in the major cities in Ghana, and in a bid to address the inadequacies identified by the Coussey Committee in 1949, the first local government ordinance was commissioned in 1951. Unfortunately, there were no marked changes in this ordinance because it did not affect the major councils. As many as 252 local and urban and 26 district councils were created (Ahwoi, ibid.). This further strengthened the undemocratic powers of chiefs, and the result was that the new system was linked with the old system and the chief was announced the president of the new councils, though with limited powers. In just five years of implementing the new system, some inadequacies were identified and F. A. Greenwood headed another commission in 1956 to make propositions to reform the local government system, paying attention to the structure of local government, revenue control systems, expenditure control measures, taxation, and local government financing, among others. Before the report from the Greenwood recommendations could be made public, Ghana gained her independence a year later in 1957.

Local Government from 1957 to 1987

The 1957 Constitution which gave birth to Ghana's independence on 6 March 1957 also provided some reforms in the local government system. The Constitution divided the country into five administrative regions: Eastern, Western, Ashanti, Northern, and the Trans-Volta Togoland regions. Representatives from the Regional Houses of Chiefs headed the regions except the Ashanti, which had been headed by the Asantehene. Every region had an assembly (equivalent of Parliament) and these regional assemblies were responsible for the entire development of the regions. Again, the Constitution retained the local government councils: municipal, district, urban and local councils, as were in existence. Unfortunately, the regional assemblies (Parliaments) did not see their own importance in dispensing local governance, and thus, their activities were marked with grave opposition. This was the situation until the 1960 Republican Constitution was promulgated, which provided for some reforms in the local government system again.

Further Reforms

In the 1960 Republican Constitution regarding local governance, there were further changes that require explanations. Among the changes was the remarkable strengthening of the local government system by the creation of the Central Region, the Upper Regions and the Trans-Volta Togoland, now the Volta region and parts of the Northern region. This brought the number of regions in the country to seven. A year after the promulgation of the Republican Constitution, there was another Local Government Act in 1961, Act 54, which divided the country into cities, municipal, and local area councils (Ahwoi, ibid.: 3). This Act recognized the participation of village, town, and area committees in local government processes but proscribed the representation of traditional authorities. This again was a major reform in Ghana's local government system because it introduced elections to get members of the various committees with a paramount chief chairing the district councils who was appointed by the Minister for Justice to chair and lead the processes leading to electing a substantive chair. The district councils had three-year tenure of office though eligible for re-election. During this period, local government in Ghana was subsumed in the Ministry of Justice and not under Local Government and Rural Development as the case today. The councils had four major functions: environmental management, security which deployed the local authority police, provision of social services and infrastructure. Licenses, permits, fees, land revenues, etc. had been traditional sources of local government financing. Inadequacies in the local government system continued to be catalogued, and by way of reforming, the sector incorporated recommendations from many commissions. There was another Local Administration Act in 1971, Act 359, which conferred the appointive powers of the prime minister to the regional chief executives to head the regional councils. Interestingly, there was an amendment to the 1971 Act in 1974 which created a four-tier structure of local government. The structure had the regional councils, district councils, the area, municipal, urban, and local councils, and then town or village development committees (Ahwoi, ibid). The new system abolished the inadequacies in the old order where there was distinction between the central government and local government and adopted an integrated or fused approach to local government.

The new system created 58 districts and 273 municipal, area, urban and local councils again, basically in charge of organizing and carrying out local development. In 1979, the Constitution that returned the country to civilian rule empowered Parliament to enact a law to create district councils, village, town, and area development committees. This was not a novelty because the 1974 Local Administration Amendment had already provided for these local government units. What was rather a novelty was the reintroduction of the power to appoint some members of the various units. Two-thirds of the membership was elected through universal adult suffrage while the remaining one-third was appointed by traditional authorities. Here again, the appointive power was now conferred on the traditional authorities which sought to reintroduce traditional authorities into local government after they were long excluded by Act 54 of 1961. The functions of these four-tier local government units were basically the same as before. Following the provisions made in chapter 20 of the 1979 Constitution of Ghana, the government in the third republic amended the 1974 Act in 1980 and replaced part 1 of Act 359 of 1971. This amendment redefined the memberships of the various local government units and recreated spaces for traditional authorities as well as reintroduced the appointive powers, now conferred on the president of the Republic of Ghana as well as two representatives from the Regional Houses of Chiefs in the regional councils. This amendment was the last major reform in the local government system of Ghana until the current dispensation of local government, established by the Provisional National Defense Council (PNDC) Law on Decentralization (Law 207 of 1988), informed by the PNDC government guidelines on decentralization in 1982.

Today's Local Government

The latest attempt to employ reforms and further decentralize the local governance system started in 1983, under the flight lieutenant Jerry John Rawlings's military government of the Armed Forces Revolutionary Council (AFRC) and the Provisional National Defense Council (PNDC). The 1992 Constitution marked the end of the rule of the Provisional National Defense Council, and a return to multiparty democracy in Ghana. The country was created as a multiparty democracy as provided by the Constitution of the Republic of Ghana, 1992, which established the fourth republic. However,

Ghana's current program of decentralization was initiated in 1988. The process of decentralization continued and was endorsed by Ghana's first multiparty government that came into power in 1992. At the moment, there is no one coherent policy document defining decentralization policies in Ghana. The latest and overall guiding programming document is that of the National Decentralization Action Plan (NDAP), which was endorsed by the Cabinet in 2004. The government of Ghana and global development partners have from time to time recognized that further real progress of the decentralization reform requires a more comprehensive policy strategy. The government since then has been developing initiatives aimed at achieving the process of decentralization. Indeed, in 2004 and 2012, the government further reviewed the number of assemblies, and thus raised the number of assemblies to 216 metropolitan, municipal, and district assemblies.

Decentralization of the Assemblies

The decentralization reform in Ghana is enshrined in the 1992 Constitution and the subsequent national legislations. Local government is enshrined in the constitution (Article 241/3), as is decentralization (Article 240/2). Article 35(5d) requires the state 'to take appropriate measures to ensure decentralization in administrative and financial machinery of government and to give opportunities to people to participate in decision-making at every level in national life and government'. The constitution also establishes the District Assemblies' Common Fund (DACF) and provides that not less than 5 per cent of the total revenues of Ghana be paid into it for use in district assembly capital works. However, there is a substantial divergence between government intentions for decentralization—including the intentions as stated in the Constitution and the actual practices in the country. The variety of laws that have been over the years enacted to decentralize the governance system result in divergent practices, especially in the choices made by sectors that tend to define decentralization as 'deconcentration'. The divergence can be explained in part by the lack of clarity of the Local Government Act 462 of 1993; it's murky and lacks the way forward. Besides, the chief executives who are duly appointed by the president of the republic are mostly those without the capacity to guide the assemblies in their mandates. Furthermore, Act 462 does not assign functions to different levels of government clearly enough; it also pays very limited attention to sub-district levels, and does not adequately define the extent to which the region level should function as a fully fledged local government unit. The Ghanaian decentralization policy intentions are aimed at devolving for governance structures closer to the people, which can be noted, for example, in the Local Government Act of 1993. The substructures of the assemblies play a vital role in ensuring that people are able to participate in local governance. However, there have been difficulties turning these intentions into practice. The problems stem from two competing concepts of decentralization operating in between.

Which Is Which? Decentralization, Deconcentration, or Devolution?

Decentralization is referred to as the transfer of powers from central government to lower levels in a political-administrative and territorial hierarchy (Crook and Manor 1998, Agrawal and Ribot 1999). This official power transfer can take two main forms. Administrative decentralization, also known as deconcentration, refers to 'a transfer to lower-level central government authorities, or to other local authorities who are upwardly accountable to the central government' (Ribot 2002). In contrast, political, or democratic, decentralization refers to the transfer of authority to representative and downwardly accountable actors, such as elected local governments (Larson). The term *decentralization* is used to cover a broad range of transfers of the locus of decision-making from central governments to regional, municipal, or local governments (Sayer et al.). Decentralization reform refers to 'transforming the local institutional infrastructure, for example, the natural resource management on which local forest management is based' (Ribot). Decentralization is the means to allow for the participation of people and local governments (Morell).

Deconcentration is the process by which the agents of central government control are relocated and geographically dispersed (Sayer et al.). Administrative decentralization is a transfer to lower-level central government authorities, or to other local authorities who are upwardly accountable to the central government (Ribot 2002 in Larson).

Devolution refers to the transfer of natural resource management to local individuals and institutions located within and outside of government

(Edmunds et al. 2003:1), though some people use *devolution* only in reference to direct community transfers (Larson). The transfer of rights and assets is from the centre to local governments or communities. All of these processes occur within the context of national laws that set the limits within which any decentralized or devolved forest management occurs (Sayer et al.)—the transfer of governance responsibility for specified functions to sub national levels, either publicly or privately owned, that are largely outside the direct control of the central government (Ferguson and Chandrasekharan). One form of administrative decentralization transfers specific decision-making powers from one level of government to another (which could be from lower level to higher level of government, in the case of federations, or government transfers decision-making powers to entities of the civil society). Regional or provincial governments, for example, become semi-autonomous and administer forest resources according to their own priorities and within clear geographical boundaries under their control. Most political decentralization is associated with devolution (Gregersen et al.).

Local governance in Ghana has clear elements of the devolution of major political and administrative functions from central government to the local level, but merely described in political circles as decentralization The practices of *deconcentration* and *devolution* contain elements of fuzziness in relation to the Ghanaian legislative framework in general that requires interpretation. The problem of the type of devolution or deconcentration practiced in Ghana is that a legislation from parliament may assign a function to a district assembly, while the same piece of legislation from the same parliament may direct otherwise of other functions with the responsibility of the central government. The confusion stems from the prescriptions of the 1992 Constitution of the Republic of Ghana, which at the time is ambiguous on certain functions of district assemblies. The Constitution seems to aim at decentralization by devolution, but does not clearly prescribe how the laws that are to be enacted to transfer functions from the central government to the local government should define the mode and form of transferring the functions. Thus, the Constitution does not provide a clear guidance for enacting national legislation that is supportive of decentralization by devolution.

Local Government: Position and Structure

The Constitution of the Republic of Ghana provides that a metropolitan, municipal, or district assembly (MMDA) is the highest political authority, and that the MMDA has deliberative, legislative, and executive powers. The MMD assemblies' autonomy is limited by the presidential appointees: 30 per cent of the members of the Assembly and the MMDA chief executive are appointed by the president. The MMDA chief executive heads the executive committee of the Assembly and is the chief representative of the government in the metropolitan, municipal, or district, allowing the central government to exercise considerable control over the affairs of the local government.

The main legislative texts pertaining to local government in Ghana include the following:

- Civil Service Law 1993 (PNDCL 327)
- Local Government Act 462 of 1993
- National Development Planning (System) Act 480 of 1994
- National Development Planning Commission Act 479 of 1994
- District Assemblies' Common Fund Act 455 of 1993
- Local Government (District Tender Boards) Establishment Regulations (which has now been repealed)
- Local Government Service Act 656 of 2003 (and other legislation pertaining to administration of local government and central government personnel at local level)
- Institute of Local Government Studies Act 647 of 2003

There are also a range of finance legislations, such as the MMDA Assemblies Common Fund Act 455 of 1993, and local government fiscal regulations. The local government units in Ghana are called district assemblies. The first district assemblies were established in 1988 after the first district assembly elections.

Organizational Structure of Local Government

The Republic of Ghana is a unitary state divided into ten administrative regions. Each of the regions is headed by a regional minister / deputy regional minister appointed by the president. The principal units of local government are the metropolitan, municipal, or district assemblies (DA), of which there are 216. Between the MMD assemblies and the central government are the regional coordinating councils (RCCs). The RCCs are made up of the representatives from each of the district assemblies in the region and from the regional House of Chiefs. The role of these bodies is to coordinate policy implementation among the district assemblies. The Constitution provides that, for the purposes of local government, Ghana has been divided into districts. The Constitution also provides, among other things, the foundation for determining the composition of the district assemblies, and the basis for their financial resources.

Assembly Composition

Of the total Assembly members within an Assembly, 70 per cent are elected and 30 per cent are appointed by the president of the Republic of Ghana. The assemblies have an executive committee, which is headed by a district chief executive who is also appointed by the president of the Republic of Ghana. The district chief executive has significant authority over the affairs of the Assembly. As already enumerated, assemblies, whether they are metropolises, municipalities, or districts, consist of elected representatives. The composition usually include the chief executive (similar to a mayor) as head and also the head of the district security council (DISEC), the Member of Parliament from the constituency (who has no vote), and other persons who are appointed by the president in consultation with traditional leaders and other interest groups. The number of president-appointed persons cannot exceed the 30 per cent of the total membership of the assembly. Each Assembly has an executive committee, which is responsible for the performance of the executive and administrative functions of the district assembly.

The minister responsible for local government may also establish, with the approval of the Cabinet, sub-metropolitan district councils, urban or zonal councils, town or area councils, and unit committees within the area of authority of the Assembly. The assemblies may delegate some of their functions to these bodies, which comprise elected and appointed members. There are presently a total of 13 sub-metropolitan district councils, 1,300 urban, zonal, town, and area councils, and 16,000 unit committees in Ghana. The internal political structures of all three—the district assemblies, metropolitan assemblies, and the municipal assemblies—are the same. Their functions are a combination of the following adapted from the records of the Institute of Local Government located in Madina, Accra.

Adapted from the CLGF's Local Government System in Ghana:

(x) = discretionary services by the local authority

SERVICE	CENTRAL GOVERNMENT	REGIONS	Assemblies MMDAs (local government)
General admin.			x
Police	x		x
Fire protection			
Civil protection			
Criminal justice	x		
Civil justice	x		
Civil status register			x
Statistical office			x
Electoral register			x
Education			
Preschool			x
Primary school			x
Secondary school			x
Vocational and technical	x		
Higher education	x		
Adult education			
Social welfare			
Kindergarten and nursery			

Family welfare services			x
Welfare homes			x
Social security	x		x
Public health			
Primary care			x
Hospitals	x		
Health protection			x
Housing and Town Planning			
Housing			x
Town planning			x
Regional planning		x	
Transport			
Roads	x	x	x
Transport		x	x
Urban roads			
Urban rail			
Ports	x		
Airports	x		
Environment and public sanitation			
Water and sanitation			x
Refuse collection and disposal			x
Cemeteries and crematoria			x
Slaughterhouses			x
Environmental protection	x	x	x
Consumer protection	x		

Culture, leisure, and sports			
Theatre and concerts			(x)
Museums and libraries	x		(x)
Parks and open spaces			x
Sports and leisure			x
Religious facilities			
Utilities			
Gas services			
District heating			
Electricity	x		
Water supply			x
Economic			
Agriculture, forests, fisheries	x		x
Economic promotion	x	x	x
Trade and industry	x		x
Tourism	x		x

Intermediate Tier Councils and Unit Committees

In addition to the above-discussed local government structures, there are rather complex sub-district level structures. These do not have any legislative or rating powers. They function on the basis of powers delegated by the assemblies. Firstly, because of their size, metropolitan assemblies are subdivided into thirteen sub-metropolitan district councils. Of these, six are in Accra, four in Kumasi, and three in Shama-Ahanta.

Secondly, there are over 1,300 town/area/zonal councils, with the given name dependent on the size and nature of the settlement. These are not elective bodies. Instead, they are composed of five representatives of the assembly, ten representatives of unit committees in the area, and five persons appointed by the government. Essentially, the town/area/zonal councils are implementing agencies of the assemblies.[1] Urban councils represent urban settlements of over 15,000 people, and zonal and town councils represent mostly rural settlements with populations between 5,000 to 15,000 people.

Thirdly, throughout Ghana, there are approximately 16, 000 unit committees, covering settlements of between 500 and 1,000 in the rural areas and roughly 1,500 in the urban areas. Unit committees are partially elected bodies. Their membership consists of ten elected members and five government appointees. They, too, act as implementing agencies for the assemblies. The unit committees are situated below the sub-metropolitan district councils, urban, or zonal councils, and town or area councils in the local government structure, and represent the community level. The assemblies may delegate any of their functions, excluding the power to legislate, levy rates, or borrow money, to sub-metropolitan district councils, town, area, zonal, or urban councils or unit committees.

These sub-district structures are designed to enhance and extend scope for citizens' participation in the democratic process. There have been efforts to hold elections, for example in 2002, but not enough people put themselves forward as candidates. As a result, some unit committees do not have a full complement of elected members. Neither are all of them operative—of the 16,000 unit committees, only about 8,000 are fully operational.

The Constitution provides that an executive committee is established in each Assembly, and that the executive committee is responsible for the performance of the executive and administrative functions of the Assembly. The members of the executive committee are elected by the members of the Assembly from among themselves.

The executive committee has five statutory subcommittees for example for development planning, social services and finance and administration. In addition to these, the Assemblies may establish any other subcommittees.

---

[1] Above information adapted from Crawford (2004: 13).

THE DISTRICTS OF GHANA

Region	No. of Districts
Ashanti	27
Volta	18
Greater Accra	10
Eastern	21
Upper East	9
Upper West	9
Central Region	17
Brong Ahafo	22
Northern	20
Western	17

Local Governance Structure

CENTRAL GOVERNMENT
President
Council of Minister
Council of State
Unicameral Parliament

10 x REGIONS
Regional Coordinating Council, RRC
Regional Ministry

LOCAL GOVERNMENT

METROPOLITAN	MUNICIPAL	DISTRICT
- Metropolitan assembly - over 250 000 inhabitants	- Municipal assembly - over 95 000 inhabitants	- District assembly - Vast geographical areas, consist of both rural and small urban areas - over 70,000 inhabitants
Sub-metropolitan district council **Town council**	**Zonal council**	**Urban/town/area councils**
Unit committees: In urban areas, about 1,500 inhabitants In rural areas, about 500–1,000 inhabitants		

Local Government Elections

As mentioned before, 70 per cent of the Assembly members are elected, and the remaining 30 per cent of the members are appointed by the president. The last elections were held in 2015 after being postponed for lack of legal procedures by the electoral commission.

The assembly elections are conducted by using the first-past-the-post system by adult universal suffrage. The assembly members are elected for a four-year term. The elected Assembly members may stand for re-election for any number of terms. The Constitution and the Local Government Act prescribe that a candidate seeking election to an Assembly or any of the substructures of an Assembly must stand for election as an individual, and not represent any political party. Fifty per cent of the appointed members must be women, and another 30 per cent represent traditional authorities.

Election of Assembly Members

Elections to Assemblies and corresponding sub-district institutions are organized by the Electoral Commission, on the basis of a non-partisan ballot. However, in Ghana, the process has been undermined by open, undisguised promotion of candidates by various political parties, notably the governing parties—the New Patriotic Party (NPP) and the National Democratic Congress (NDC). For an ordinary citizen to be elected, he or she must be a citizen of Ghana, eighteen years old, ordinarily a resident in the district, and paid up on the taxes and rates. By law, individuals willing to participate in these elections must also do so without association with any political party. Through the specialty in the Ghanaian system in which the intermediate-tier councils and the unit committees are in use, efforts are made to enhance and extend citizens' participation in the local political processes. The Assembly elects a presiding member from among its members after the election and the constitution of the first Assembly meeting. The term of office of the presiding member is two years, and he or she is eligible for re-election. The presiding member convenes and presides over the meetings of the Assembly, and performs any other functions prescribed by law. There are also difficulties in maintaining a functioning system of substructures of the assemblies. For assemblies and their substructures of sub-metro to the councils and unit committees, hundreds of thousands of people are to be elected, and several thousand appointed by central government. For unit committees alone, 160,000 people have to be elected, and another 80,000 appointed by the central government. The elections held to constitute this complex set have been disappointing in terms of their outcomes. In the elections held in October 2002, ballots could not be cast in nearly 10,000 units because of insufficient number of candidates. A similar trend occurred in the election of 2006, and the 2015 raising a major dilemma for the suitability and sustainability of this political model.

Local Government Staffing

Local government staff is recruited by the Office of the Head of the Civil Service. However, with the enactment of the Local Government Service Act 2003, appointments, promotions, and disciplining of local government personnel now come under the Local Government Service Council. Unlike in the case of, for example, South Africa, in Ghana, central government staff can be deployed to local government. The assemblies, on their part, are required by law to have a certain number of officers, namely the district coordinating director (the head of the paid service), the finance officer, the development planning officer, and the local government inspector. The town/area/zonal councils must have a secretary, an accounts officer, and a typist. Many of these councils are not, however, fully staffed.

Independent Scrutiny

Generally, in the cases of maladministration, citizens are provided with redress by the Commission on Human Rights and Administrative Justice. However, an unusual feature of the assembly system is the grievance and complaint procedure, which can be used by the local electorate to hold individual Assembly members and officers to account. On the financial side, it is the auditor general who audits the Assembly accounts annually and reports to parliament.

Responsibilities of Assemblies

The assemblies deliver many services at the local level, but with varying degrees of authority and responsibility for the service provision. The sector legislations and legislative instruments establishing the assemblies provide, in many cases, overlapping responsibilities to the assemblies and to the central government. The assemblies deliver many services, such as pre- and primary education, social welfare, health clinics, cemeteries, museums and libraries, water and sanitation, refuse collection, environmental protection, and transport, but with varying degrees of authority and political responsibility for the service provision. The responsibilities of the sub-district local government structures are, to a large extent, unclear and they have virtually no personnel or financial resources to perform functions and duties. Notwithstanding, their duties are complementary in nature.

The Local Government Act of 1993 prescribes broad mandates to the assemblies. However, the Local Government Act is silent on the specific sector functions, and does not specify which ones should fall under the responsibility of the assemblies. In addition, neither the Constitution nor the Local Government Act make distinctions between functions that must be carried out and which functions the assemblies may undertake voluntarily if they choose to do so. In addition, every assembly is established with a legislative instrument which defines its jurisdiction and specifies the functions that it should undertake. The Local Government Act provides that the assemblies may make by-laws for the purpose of a function conferred on it by the Local Government Act or any other enactment. The by-laws have to be submitted to the minister responsible for local government for approval to complement the efforts of central government in the provision to the people at the grass roots.

Revenue

The Constitution provides that each Assembly shall have a sound financial base with adequate and reliable sources of revenue from the central government. Most of the revenues of the assemblies consist of transfers. In 2004, 86 per cent of the district assemblies' total revenues consisted of transfers from the central government known as the common fund (CF) and from international donors. The remaining 16 per cent originated from the assemblies' own source revenues. The high dependency on transfers from the central government and donors indicates that the assemblies have limited authority to set local expenditure priorities. The autonomy of the assemblies is limited by the fact that they have to submit their annual budgets to the Ministry of Finance for approval and be subjected to the central government audit—the Auditor-General Department.

The Local Government Act of 1993 prescribes ten categories of own-source revenues, which in Ghana are called internally generated funds, to the district assemblies. These taxes, rates, levies, fees, and licenses are listed in the Sixth Schedule of the Local Government Act. The minister responsible for local government, in consultation with the minister responsible for finance, may amend the Sixth Schedule with a legislative instrument. The Local Government Act establishes the district authorities as rating authorities in their respective districts. District authorities have three sources of revenue: (a) the assemblies' common fund (ACF), (b) ceded revenue, and (c) assemblies' own revenue raised through local taxation. Ceded revenue refers to revenue received from a number of lesser tax fields that the central government has ceded to the assemblies. Example of ceded revenue sources are timber logging revenue paid by timber contractors to the assemblies. Finally, there is the collection of own revenue through some local taxes such as market tolls from petty traders in the assemblies' markets. This does not, however, amount to much, as the so-called lucrative tax fields (for example the income tax, sales tax, import and export duties) all belong to the central government. The authorities have the power to borrow, but this power is seldom used and such amounts are quite low.

Conclusion

Ghana's decentralization process as enshrined in the Constitution designates district assemblies as the highest political, legislating, budgeting, and planning authority at the local level. The Local Government Act 462 of 1993 reinforces the constitutional provisions. District assemblies are empowered by this Local Government Act of 1993 (Svy 463) to, among other things, exercise political administrative authority in the district, provide guidance, give direction to, and supervise all other administrative authorities in the district. They are also required to exercise deliberative, legislative, and executive functions and are also responsible for the overall development of the district. Additionally, they are enjoined to formulate and execute plans, programs, and strategies for the effective mobilization of the resources necessary for the overall development of the district and promote and support productive activity and social development in the district and remove any obstacles to initiatives and development. District assemblies have been created as the pivot of administrative and developmental decision-making in the district and the basic unit of government administration. The executive committees of the assemblies are presided over by the district chief executives and consist of not more than one-third of the total members of the assembly, excluding the presiding member.

To facilitate a holistic approach to the decentralization process, various structures have been created at the sub national level with the regional coordinating council (RCC) as a coordinating body. Below the RCC are the metropolitan or municipal or district assemblies (MMDAs) and the sub-district structures. Despite the laudable idea behind the decentralization policy, practitioners and decision makers at the local level do not have adequate information and knowledge on the functions and responsibilities of the MMDAs. The various laws pertaining to local governance are not in simple language or in the local languages that the people can read. Again, it is difficult to have access to the various local government laws. In addition to all these problems, there are some stakeholders, such as donor agencies, who do not have enough information to understand the workings of the district assembly in order to effectively participate in the decision-making process.

Key Terms

Non-governmental organizations   Internally generated funds   Indirect Rule System   Sub-district structures   Presiding member Functional and Organizational Assessment Tool District Development Fund   Civil Society Organizations Community-based organizations Decentralization Districts Urban councils Zonal councils   Local government   Municipal government Metropolitan Assembly Parliamentarian   Legislator   Member of Parliament

Works Cited / Further Readings

Beall, Jo (2005), Decentralizing Government and Centralizing Gender in Southern Africa: Lessons from the South African Experience, Occasional Paper 8, United Nations Research Institute for Social Development.

Crawford, Gordon (2004), 'Democratic Decentralisation in Ghana: issues and prospects', POLIS Working Paper No. 9, University of Leeds.

CLGF (Commonwealth Local Government Forum): Local Government System in Ghana.

Constitution of the Republic of Ghana (1992).

Country Gender Profile (2008), Ghana. African Development Bank & African Development Fund, Human Development Department.

Farvacque-Vitkovic, Catherine et al. (2008), 'Development of the Cities of Ghana: Challenges, Priorities, and Tools', Africa Region Working Paper Series No. 110, January 2008 (World Bank).

Federation of Canadian Municipalities (2007), FCM-ICMD Municipal Sector Profile: Republic of Ghana.

Ferrazzi, Gabriele (2006), 'Ghana Local Government Act 1993: A Comparative Analysis in the Context of the Review of the Act', October 2006, Ministry of Local Government, Rural Development, and Environment of Ghana and Deutsche Gesellschaft für Technische Zusammenarbeit.

Human Development Report 2007/2008, UNDP.

Joint Government of Ghana and Development Partner Decentralisation Review. Final Report, 6 February 2007. Nordic Consulting Group Denmark and Dege Consult.

Kuusi, Suvi (2009), 'Aspects of Local Self-Government: Ghana', North–South Local Government Co-operation Programme, Association of Finnish Local and Regional Authorities.

Local Government Act 462 of 1993.

Nkrumah, Stephen A. (2000), 'Decentralisation for Good Governance and Development: The Ghanaian Experience', *Regional Development Dialogue*, 21 (1).

Ofei-Aboagye, Ester (2000), 'Promoting the Participation of Women in Local Governance and Development: The Case of Ghana', a paper prepared for the seminar 'European Support for Democratic Decentralisation and Municipal Development—A Contribution to Local Development and Poverty Reduction', held in Maastricht, 14–15 June 2000.

Ohene-Konadu, Gifty (2001), 'Gender Analysis and Interpretation of Barriers to Women's Participation in Ghana's Decentralised Local Government

System', paper presented at African Gender Institute, University of Cape Town, South Africa.

Peltola, Outi (2008), 'Selvitys Suomen, Namibian, Etelä-Afrikan, Tansanian, Kenian, Ghanan ja Swazimaan paikallisesta ympäristöhallinnosta', North–South Local Government Co-operation Programme, Association of Finnish Local and Regional Authorities.

Simonen, Saara (2009), 'Women in Local Governance Ghana', North–South Local Government Co-operation Programme, Association of Finnish Local and Regional Authorities.

Women's Manifesto for Ghana (2004). The Coalition of Women's Manifesto for Ghana.

Chapter 15

THE POLITICS OF NATIONAL POLICY

Introduction

During the past decade, the role of the Ghanaian government has been steadily changing, with increasing emphasis being placed on setting overall direction through policy and planning, on engaging stakeholders and citizens, and sometimes on empowering stakeholders or partners like the metropolitan/municipal/district assemblies to deliver programs and services. At the same time, the Ghanaian environment for policy and planning has increased in complexity. The ownership of issues is often unclear, especially when more than one department and often more than one level of government is involved in planning of national policy. Communities are also increasingly claiming ownership of policy issues and process across the country. Globalization and fiscal resource limitations from the finances of government contribute to this confusion. In this complex environment, the demand for good public policy development is steadily increasing; such is the capacity of managers, policy analysts, planners, and others involved in the design and delivery of policies and programs. Ghana has gone through stages of policy formulation to make life better for the citizenry. The interventions are in various areas of national development ranging from social programs to economic and agricultural programs.

What Is Public Policy?

There are numerous definitions of public policy. The following are some examples: Public policy is 'whatever governments choose to do or not to do' (Dye 1972, p. 18). Another is 'a proposed course of action of a person, group, or government within a given environment providing obstacles and opportunities which the policy was proposed to utilize and overcome in an effort to reach a goal or realize an objective or purpose' (Frederich 1963, p. 79). Public policy is also defined as 'a broad guide to present and future decisions, selected in light of given conditions from a number of alternatives; the actual decision or set of decisions designed to carry out the chosen course of actions; a projected program consisting of desired objectives (goals) and the means of achieving them' (Daneke and Steiss 1978). Finally, public policy is 'a commitment to a course of plan of action agreed to by a group of people with the power to carry it out' (Dodd et al., nd: 2) and 'a plan of action agreed to by a group of people with the power to carry it out and enforce it' *(et al Capacity Building, p. 1)*. Public policy is the broad framework of ideas and values within which decisions are taken and action, or inaction, is pursued by governments in relation to some issue or problem. Briefly stated, public policy is a choice or decision made by government that guides subsequent actions in similar circumstances. There are three basic areas of public policy schemes used here within the Ghanaian context. Almost any policy can be classified as social, economic, or foreign. Many citizens associate only hot-button issues such as welfare, crime, abortion, education, and healthcare with public policy, but all of these fall under the heading of social policy, and only represent a part of the picture. Public policies are most often established by legislation, but they can also be created by an executive order, a bureaucratic regulation, a city ordinance, or even a court decision. Public policies are generally aimed at one or more of the following:

- Reconciling conflicting claims for scarce resources—e.g. schools, clinics, etc.
- Encouraging or fostering cooperation that would probably not occur without government influence or encouragement—e.g. disaster management, etc.
- Prohibiting morally unacceptable behaviour—rape, criminality, etc.
- Protecting the rights of individuals—civil rights violation, abuse
- Providing direct benefits to citizens—schools, hospitals, protection (police stations), military, etc.

Capturing the nature and scope of public policy in a sentence or two is difficult. Some of the more widely accepted (or at least frequently repeated) descriptions of what government does include:

- 'the authoritative allocation of values for a society'
- 'the process of deciding who gets what, when, where, and how'
- Or more simply, 'what the government chooses to do or not to do about a specific problem'.

These definitions are all useful, but none of them is obviously better than the others. In fact, each captures an important aspect of the public policymaking process, a process that is too complicated to be adequately summarized in just a sentence or two. What can be stated clearly and succinctly about public policy, however, is that it is an integral part of our everyday lives. Public policies of all kinds establish the boundaries of our freedoms and colour the contours of our interactions with other people in our political, social, and economic systems. Making public policy is not a quick or an easy process, although the steps may seem intuitive. Policies tend to fall primarily into one of three overlapping categories: foreign, social, or economic. They typically result from a five-step process. Each step requires a significant amount of time and debate, making what appears to be a quick five-step process into a long struggle, full of vigorous opposing opinions, concessions, and unanticipated complications. The five basic steps are identifying the problem, formulating the policy, adopting the policy, implementing the policy, and evaluating the policy.

Critical Stages in the Policy Process

While the process by which public policies are created and changed is complex and varies significantly from one policy question to the next, there are several general characteristics of the process that are shared. First, a public policy problem must be identified. There are numerous problems that could be addressed by the public policy process but they have yet to be indicated and articulated so they can take their place on the public policy agenda. For example, pollution is a serious problem in Ghana, and has been so for decades. It becomes a public policy problem when, say, policymakers and the public pay attention to it, either through news reportage or when a disaster occurs. A clear example of what can constitute a public policy issue is the collapse of the Melcom Shopping Warehouse building in Achimota, Accra in 2012 and the need then for the reinforcement of building codes in Ghana.

After a problem is identified, potential policy solutions are formulated. Elected officials, interest groups, and citizens participate in discussions and debates. Alternative solutions are compared and critiqued. Where there is consensus (or at least majority support) for one of the policy alternatives, it is adopted, generally through the passage of legislation. Once a policy is enacted into law, it must be implemented. In Ghana, Parliament delegates the implementation (and many of the details associated with it) to executive branch departments and agencies.

Almost the minute a policy is in place, people will begin to evaluate it. Is the policy actually fixing the problem? Is it causing additional unintended problems? Because no policy is ever perfect, policy evaluation invariably leads to new problem identification and the process commences again.

Steps in Public Policy

The first step is to identify a *problem*. Sometimes, the problem is brought to the attention of government officials by individual citizens. Other times, lobbyists or private groups come to speak out on an issue, or the problem may be identified from above, and handed down to Parliament for a resolution. When making public policy, it should be considered whether the problem affects many citizens, and whether the solution will degrade the civil liberties. An example of a policy that followed parliamentary process until it was implemented was the cell phone tax bill of 2009. Once the problem has been identified, government and citizens work together to *formulate* a policy. Government is formed in such a way that, ideally, public opinion should rank among one of the biggest factors in making public policy. Citizens appeal to their parliamentarians and encourage them to vote for or against the policy. However, this sort of lobbying is minimal in Ghanaian parliament. Likewise, supporters or detractors will issue media coverage on the policy and attempt to sway public opinion through these avenues. The policy is critiqued and refined among experts to find the best possible wording and compromises on issues that are important to one side or the other. The next step in making public policy is to *adopt* the policy. Legislators vote on whether or not the formulated policy should be enacted into law. Once it has been enacted, and approved by the president, suggestions for implementation are passed to the executive branch of government for implementation.

Implementation: Governments can implement policy in a number of ways. We refer to these ways as *policy tools* or *policy instruments*. A policy statement describes what is being sought; the tool or instrument is the method by which the desired outcome is pursued. A number of aspects of governance can be described as policy tools. These include legislation, regulation, orders in assemblies' guidelines, standards, procedures, programs, grants, subsidies, and taxes. It has been suggested that something of a nation's character can be seen in the policy instruments that its government chooses to achieve its objectives. To establish an overall context, some political scientists position policy instruments along a continuum. One of the most common characteristics on which to base such a continuum is the degree of choice (or level of coercion) accompanying the policy instrument. When the policy has been in effect for enough time, the legislators *analyze* the effectiveness of the policy. This analysis is based on information gathered from statistics and opinions of the executives (through monitoring of the policy, one of the core functions of parliament) who have worked on implementation. If the policy needs to be altered to account for unforeseen complications, amendments can be added to the policy. Making public policy is never truly finished; it is a revolving process and in reality the process is far from perfect. Issues can always be revisited over time, however, and adjustments, corrections, or improvements can be made.

What Is the Right Amount of Government?

The primary focus of public policymaking is the establishment of an agreeable balance between liberty and order. In other words, the amount of government which is justified as the right amount is the establishment of the right amount of government for the people in terms of service delivery. Public policies are crafted (and frequently adjusted) to embody that balance in terms of demands. One of the most important debates in the public policy process is often whether the government ought to do anything at all in response to a particular problem. The answer to this question has a direct impact on the balance between liberty and order in the Ghanaian political society. At one end of the continuum, a complete absence of public policies would leave individuals free to do whatever they chose. At the other end, a set of public policies that dictated every action an individual took every moment of his or her life would produce a thoroughly ordered society. In either case, the liberty or order that existed could not be fully enjoyed without the presence of the other. At the extremes, the number or reach of a nation's public policies can maximize either liberty or order. From this perspective, an alternative definition of public policy is the process by which a political society—a country like Ghana—balances the freedoms against the need to create a structured environment in which those freedoms can be enjoyed in a meaningful way. This effort is something of a quest to establish just the right amount of government—not too little, not too much, but just the right amount so as to meet the demands of the people.

The Role of the Ghana National Planning Commission in National Policy

Ghana's history in development planning dates back to the colonial period with the first development plan by Gordon Guggisberg, in 1919. Ghana, since then, has had numerous development plans, such as Kwame Nkrumah's seven-year development plan, President Rawlings's Vision 2020, and the Ghana Poverty Reduction Strategy 1 and 2 and currently the Ghana Shared Growth and Development Agenda. Consensus building for national development planning the world over has time and time again been a daunting task, although it is laudable in achieving the best in a democratic dispensation. It is worthwhile to state that when development plans are sometimes clothed in political colours, it makes it difficult for other governments to use them. More often than not, strategies and programs are sometimes abruptly cut short, especially with change in government. This is most probably as a result of the tendency for some politicians to regard particular development strategies as owned by a particular party in government, as such their reluctance to embrace them. It is for this and other reasons that the National Development Planning Commission in Ghana is putting in place a strategic framework for a long-term development plan. Think tanks, parliament, academia, civil society, formal and informal business associations, civil society organizations, faith-based organizations, and youth groups, among others, will make inputs in this long-term development strategy so that it can be nationally owned. It is believed that such a non-partisan, long-term, national development framework, when translated into a long-term national development plan, would serve as yardstick by which programs and manifestos of political parties would be measured. That way, manifestos would come closer and closer to each other, and the differences may be in the pace at which one government wants to develop and how efficiently to apply resources and the capacity to mobilize additional human and material resources.

Mr Seth Terkper, Finance Minister, Dr Henry Wampah, former Governor of Bank of Ghana, and Mr Kwame Pianim

Conclusion

Policymaking involves a combination of processes. Although not always clear-cut or easily distinguishable, political scientists have identified these processes for purposes of analysis. They include the following: *Identifying policy problems*—publicized demands for government action can lead to identification of policy problems. *Formulating policy proposals*—policy proposals can be formulated through political channels by policy planning organizations, interest groups, government bureaucracies, state legislatures, and the president and parliament. *Legitimizing public policy*—policy is legitimized as a result of the public statements or actions of government officials, both elected and appointed in all branches and at all levels. This includes executive orders, budgets, laws and appropriations, rules and regulations, and decisions and interpretations that have the effect of setting policy directions. *Implementing public policy*—policy is implemented through the activities of public bureaucracies and the expenditure of public funds. *Evaluating public policy*—policies are formally and informally evaluated by government agencies, by outside consultants, by interest groups, by the mass media, and by the public. Although this stages, or phases, approach to policymaking has been criticized for being too simplistic, insufficiently explicating that some phases may occur together, and not saying much about why policy turns out as it does, it does provide a way to discuss many of the ways policy is constructed, carried out, evaluated, and made again. All these activities include both attempts at rational problem-solving and political conflict.

Feature Article 15

The Budget

The government's most important policy statement, the budget is the single most important policy statement of any government. The expenditure or outlay side of the budget tells us who gets what in public money, and the revenue side of the budget tells us who pays the cost. The budgetary process provides a mechanism for reviewing government programs, assessing their costs, relating them to financial resources, and making choices among expenditures. The budget lies at the heart of all public policies. In Ghana, the Minister of Finance in conjunction with the Economic Planning department of the Ministry of Finance and Economic Planning rolls out the annual budget. The president follows up in a few months with the State of the Nation address to parliament, where he highlights certain portions of the budget to support his programs.

Key Terms

Budget Implementation Formulation Evaluation Identifying Propensity

National expenditure   Government programs Budget deficit Budget surplus Finance

Implementation Policy statement Assessment of costs Implementing Policy Address

Identifying policy problems Formulating policy Proposal Evaluating Proposals Critics

Budget highlights Legitimizing public policy Implementing policy Evaluation of policy

---

Works Cited / Further Readings

Becker, P. and Raveloson, Jean-Aimé A. (2008), 'What is Democracy Realized by KMF-CNOE & NOVA STELLA' Friedrich Ebert Stiftung (FES) Antananarivo.

Boafo-Arthur, Kwame (2008), 'Democracy and Stability in West Africa: The Ghanaian Experience', Claude Ake Memorial Papers, No. 4, 2008.

Bosin, Yury V. (2009), Measuring Democracy: Approaches and Challenges Associated With Developing Democratic Indices University of New Mexico 2009 by IFES.

Carothers, Thomas and Youngs, Richard (2008), 'Looking for Help: Will Rising Democracies Become International Democracy Supporters?' August 2008.

Economic Commission for Africa (2012), 'Media actors exchange ideas on Africa's potential as new pole of global growth', NEPAD Today Newsletter, 21 March 2012.

Electoral Commission of Ghana (2010), Elections 2008 (Accra, Ghana: Friedrich Ebert Stiftung

Gyimah-Boadi, Emmanuel (2010), Assessing Democracy Assistance: Project Report Ghana. FRIDE May 2010.

Grindle, M. S. (1980), *Politics and Policy Implementation in the Third World* (New Jersey: Princeton University Press).

Lasswell, H. D. (1951), *Psychopathology and Politics* (USA: Free Press) 525 p.

Lee, K. and Mills, A. (1982), *Policy Making and Planning in the Health Sector* (London and Sydney: Croom Helm).

Makinde, T. (2005), 'Problems of Policy Implementation in Developing Nations: The Nigerian Experience', Department of Public Administration, Obafemi Awolowo University, Ile Ife, Nigeria.

Mensah, O. and Schmidt, T. (2009), 'Ghana's national health insurance scheme in the context of the health MDGs: An empirical evaluation using propensity score matching,' Ruhr Economic Papers, No. 157, http://hdl.handle.net/10419/36983

The Carnegie Papers Democracy and Rule of Law July, 2011. Democracy consolidation Strategy paper, Addressing Ghana's democracy gaps, a publication of the IEA / GPPP

Chapter 16

MAKING ECONOMIC POLICIES

Pre-Independence

Present-day Ghana was drawn into long-distance trade as early as the thirteenth century, in large part because of its gold reserves. One of the most wide-ranging trading networks of pre-modern times was the trans-Sahara trade involving an exchange of European, North African, and Saharan commodities southward in exchange for the products of West Africa. The trade included gold, ivory, cola nuts, and primarily, slaves. Present-day Ghana, named the Gold Coast by European traders, was an important source of the gold traded across the Sahara. The Asante kingdom then (now the Ashanti region) included parts of current-day Brong Ahafo and Eastern regions was one of the centralized states at the time, which controlled prices by regulating production and marketing of the above precious commodities. But as the European navigational techniques improved in the fifteenth century, Portuguese and later Dutch and English traders circumvented the Saharan trade by sailing directly to the southernmost parts of the West African coast. Their arrival at the southernmost coast of Ghana led to the building of a fortified trading post at Elmina in 1482 by the Portuguese, who began purchasing gold, ivory, and pepper from African coastal merchants. In the sixteenth century, the introduction of the Atlantic slave trade changed the nature of African export production in fundamental ways. Indeed, the slave trade gathered momentum because an increasing number of Ghanaians, in an effort to enrich themselves, captured fellow Africans in warfare and sold them to slave dealers from North America and South America. The slaves were subsequently transported to the coast and sold through African merchants using the same routes and connections through which gold and ivory had formerly flowed. Africans, in a bid to capture more slaves, received guns as payment in return for their merchandise.

Toward the end of the slave trade and other commodity exchanges, an estimated ten million Africans, at least half a million from the Gold Coast, left the continent as captured and sold slaves to North and South America. Historians like Walter Rodney (1981) have argued that the slave trade robbed Africa of unknown invention, innovation, and production in terms of human brain capacity loss. Rodney further argues that the slave trade fuelled a process of underdevelopment, whereby African societies came to rely on the export of resources crucial to their own economic growth, thereby precluding local development of those resources. Others have argued that the slave trade rather increased the continent's economic resources and did not impede economic development. But most scholars, particularly those of the African American diasporas, still maintain that the subsequent economic history of African continent supports Walter Rodney's interpretation. In recent years, however, prominent scholars and historians have rejected Rodney's interpretation and have themselves advanced their notion that it is the Africans themselves, rather than an array of external forces, that are to blame for Africa's economic plight.

By the nineteenth century, the local economy became the focus of the so-called legitimate trade, which the emerging industrial powers of Europe (like Britain, France, and Germany) encouraged as a source of materials and markets to aid their own production and sales. The British in particular gained increasing control over the sub-Saharan sub region throughout the nineteenth century and promoted the production of palm oil and timber, as well as the continuation of gold production. In return, Africans were inundated with imports of consumer goods that, unlike the luxuries or locally unavailable imports of the trans-Saharan trade, quickly displaced African products, especially textiles. Subsequently, in 1878, cacao trees were introduced from the Americas and it quickly became the colony's major export. By the 1920s, Ghana produced more than half the global yield. From this time onward, African farmers used kinship networks like business corporations to spread cocoa cultivation throughout large areas of West Africa. Even though legitimate trade restored the overall productivity of Ghana's economy, the influx of European goods began to displace indigenous industries, and farmers focused more on cash crops than on essential food crops for local consumption.

Post-Independence

Ghana gained its independence from Britain in 1957, with a very promising economy which appeared stable and prosperous. Thereafter, President Kwame Nkrumah sought to use the apparent stability of the Ghanaian economy as a springboard for economic diversification and expansion. This was occasioned by the fact that Ghana had emerged as the world's leading producer of cocoa and by then boasted a well-developed infrastructure to service trade, and enjoyed a relatively advanced education system. At that point, President Kwame Nkrumah began the process of moving Ghana from a primarily agricultural economy to a mixed agricultural-industrial one. Using cocoa revenues as security, Nkrumah took out loans to establish industries such as the Ghana Industrial Holdings Corporation (GIHOC) that would produce import substitutes as well as process many of Ghana's exports. Nkrumah's plans were ambitious and grounded in the desire to reduce Ghana's vulnerability to world trade. Unfortunately, the price of cocoa collapsed in the mid-1960s, thereby destroying the fundamental stability of the economy and making it nearly impossible for Nkrumah to continue his industrialization plans. Additionally, when pervasive corruption exacerbated these problems in 1966, a group of military officers, led by General Kotoka, overthrew Dr Kwame Nkrumah but inherited a nearly bankrupt country.

Ghana, after the coup d'état, began to experience a cycle of weak commodity demand, coupled with declining supply of particularly cocoa, debt servicing of its past loans, and currency overvaluation. These symptoms resulted in the decay of productive capacities and a high foreign debt. By the mid-1960s, cocoa prices had fallen and Ghana was incapable of generating the needed foreign currency to repay loans, the value of which jumped almost tenfold between 1960 and 1966 because of inflation. To find remedies to the situation, economists recommended that Ghana should devalue its currency—the cedi—to make the price of its main cash crop, cocoa, more attractive on the world market, but devaluation of the cedi further worsened Ghana's loan repayment in United States dollars. Moreover, the call for devaluation further exacerbated the situation, because of increased costs of imports, both for consumers and the emerging and fragile industries in Ghana. From 1966 until the early part of the 1980s, government after government refused to devalue the cedi, until

1971, when the government under the presidency of Dr Kofi A. Busia, devalued the cedi and was overthrown shortly thereafter.

Indeed Ghana's economy during this period and after the overthrow of Dr Busia was in an advanced state of collapse. The Ghanaian Statistical Service reported a per capita gross domestic product (GDP) of negative growth from the mid-1960s, due to a decline in economic activities by 3.2 per cent per year from 1970 to 1981. Most importantly, there was a decline in cocoa production, Ghana's main foreign exchange earner, which recorded a fall by half between the mid-1960s and the late 1970s, thereby drastically reducing Ghana's share of the world market from about one-third in the early 1970s to only one-eighth between the years 1982 and '83. Similarly, mineral production fell by 32 per cent; gold production declined by 47 per cent, diamonds by 67 per cent, manganese by 43 per cent, and bauxite by 46 per cent. Inflation averaged more than 50 per cent a year between 1976 and 1981, hitting 116.5 per cent in 1981. Real minimum wages dropped from an index of 75 in 1975 to one of 15.4 in 1981. Tax revenue fell from 17 per cent of GDP in 1973 to only 5 per cent in 1983, and actual imports by volume in 1982 were only 43 per cent of average 1975–76 levels. In real terms, therefore, productivity, standard of living, and the government's resources had plummeted dramatically (Ghana Statistical Service 1981, 1982, 1983, 1984).

In 1981, a military government under the leadership of Flight Lieutenant Jerry John Rawlings overthrew the Supreme Military Council II of General Akuffo. The Rawlings regime, called the Provisional National Defense Council (PNDC), initially blamed the nation's economic problems on the corruption of previous governments. But within a short time of coming to power, Rawlings soon discovered that Ghana's problems were the result of forces more complicated than economic abuse and corruption. In 1983, following a severe drought that hit the country, the government accepted stringent International Monetary Fund (IMF) and World Bank loan conditions and instituted what came to be known as the Economic Recovery Program (ERP). The IMF-structured ERP fundamentally changed the government's social, political, and economic orientation because this was a major shift in government's planned economic policy. The ERP was structured so as to enable Ghana to repay its foreign debts, as it exemplified the structural adjustment policies formulated by international banking and donor institutions in the 1980s. The program emphasized the promotion of the export sector and an enforced fiscal discipline, which together targeted the eradication of budget deficits. Over a number of years, the PNDC followed the ERP faithfully and gained the support of the international financial community, but the pursuit of such stringent policies led to a lowered standard of living for most Ghanaians.

Trends in Economic History

In accessing Ghana's economic policy, this chapter begins with trends in the 1990s when Ghana's cash crop, cocoa, became an important barometer in estimating the economic performance of the country. By the early 1990s, Ghana's economic recovery still appeared uneven and was primarily oriented toward the exports rather than the Ghanaian market. But there seem to have been gains clocked by Ghana as the GDP had risen by an average of 5 per cent per year since 1984. Inflation had also been reduced to about 20 per cent, and export earnings had reached US$1 billion. Most production came from the export sector, and by the 1992–93 crop years, cocoa production surpassed 300,000 tons, placing Ghana third in the world. By 1990, exports of minerals—primarily gold but also diamonds, manganese, and bauxite—brought in US$234 million, an increase of 23.2 per cent from the year before.

The Ghanaian government's effort to restore the productivity of the economy was at best directed toward boosting the country's exports. The policies had numerous positive consequences on the country's economy. The point here is that, following the initiation of the ERP in 1983 and the devastating drought of 1983, Ghana's GDP had registered steady growth, most of it attributable to the export sector, including cocoa and minerals and, to some extent, timber processing. In current prices, Ghana's GDP rose from ¢511 billion in 1986 to ¢3 trillion in 1992. In constant 1987 prices, these GDP figures amounted to ¢713 billion (US$4.62 billion) in 1986 and ¢934 billion (US$6.06 billion) in 1992. During the 1980s, Ghana's economy registered strong growth of approximately 6 per cent per year because of a reversal in the steadily declining production of the previous decade. Ghana's worst years were 1982 and 1983, when the country was hit with the worst drought in fifty years, occasioned by bush fires that destroyed crops, and the lowest cocoa prices of the post-war period. Growth throughout the remainder of the decade reflected the pace of the economic recovery, but output remained weak in comparison with 1970 production levels. The same was true of consumption, minimum wages, and social services. The ERP policies during the 1980s resulted in increased external debts as well as in relatively high inflation rates for Ghanaians. Projects were funded by foreign loans, notably from the International Monetary Fund (IMF) and the International Bank for Reconstruction and Development (World Bank). At the same time, the government repeatedly devalued the country's currency to raise producer prices for exports and to encourage production, but devaluation led to price rises on all other goods and services. In sum, the World Bank's ERP attempts to promote production in the short term resulted in higher debts and inflation in the country. In addition, growth fell off considerably in 1990 when another drought caused real GDP growth to decline by nearly 2 percentage points. Government estimates claimed at the time that real GDP growth in 1993 was 6.1 per cent, which reflected a recovery in cocoa output and an increase in gold production. At the same time, gross domestic fixed investment rose from 3.5 per cent of the total in 1982 to 12.9 per cent in 1992. The share of public consumption in GDP fell from a peak of 11.1 per cent in 1986 to 9.9 per cent in 1988, but appeared to have risen again to 13.3 per cent in 1992 (Ghana Statistical Service 1984).

Similarly, by the early 1990s, government efforts had resulted in the restoration of many of Ghana's historical trade relationships. Exports were again dominated by cocoa, which earned US$280 million in 1993. Other significant export commodities in 1993 were gold (US$416 million) and timber (US$140 million), followed by electricity, diamonds, and bauxite. Ghana's nontraditional exports, such as furniture, cola nuts, and pineapples, also increased significantly. On the import side, fuel and energy, mainly oil, accounted for 16 per cent of 1990 imports, followed by capital goods (43 per cent), intermediate goods (28 per cent), and consumer goods (10 per cent), according to the World Bank. In addition to supporting traditional export industries such as cocoa and gold, the government also attempted to diversify the content of Ghana's exports. To encourage nontraditional exports in the fishing and agriculture sectors, the government offered to refund 95 per cent of import duties on goods destined for re-export and even to cancel sales taxes on manufactured goods sold abroad. In addition, the government devised a scale of tax rebates ranging from 20 per cent to 50 per cent determined by the volume of total production that was exported. These incentives generated considerable response. By 1988, more than 700 exporters were dealing in 123 export products, the major items being pineapples, marine and fish products (especially tuna), wood products, aluminium products, and salt. By 1990, the last year for which figures were available, the value of nontraditional exports had risen to US$62 million.

During the 1990s, Ghana continued to trade primarily with the European Community, particularly Britain and Germany. Britain continued to be the principal market for Ghanaian cocoa beans, absorbing approximately 50 per cent of all cocoa beans exported. By 1992, Germany was the single most important destination of Ghana's exports, accounting for some 19 per cent of all exports. Britain was next, accounting for about 12 per cent, followed by the United States, 9 per cent, and Japan, 5 per cent. The same year, Britain supplied approximately 20 per cent of Ghana's imports, followed by Nigeria, which provided 11 per cent. The United States and Germany were third and fourth, respectively.

The Rebirth of the Ghanaian Economy

By 1991, significant changes had taken place in the structure of gross domestic product (GDP) of Ghana since the ERP began. Agriculture remained the bedrock of Ghana's economy, accounting for more than 48 per cent of GDP. At the time (from 1988 to 1991), agriculture's long-term importance in the management of the economy had declined in favour of that of industry. The contribution to GDP was more than doubled as it constituted almost 16 per cent of GDP, and in favour of services, the contribution of which was 35.3 per cent in 1991. Notable changes had also occurred within the broader sectors: cocoa's share rose from 5.6 per cent in 1983 to 9.5 per cent in 1991, manufacturing sector contribution increased from 3.9 per cent to 8.7 per cent; and construction output from 1.5 per cent to 3.5 per cent. As for trade since 1983, the promotion of Ghana's foreign trade has been central to all government plans to revive the economy. Under the ERP, export-producing industries received the most direct support. The government also gave indirect support through the improvement of their proximate infrastructure. By promoting exports, the government sought to obtain foreign exchange essential to repay debts and to ease the country's restrictions on imports. Imports, of course, were also necessary to upgrade many of the export industries hamstrung for lack of equipment for production of essential goods.

The prevailing economic conditions at the time conspired to erode the terms of trade to such an extent that Ghanaians had reverted to smuggling goods across the borders as well as to trading on the black market (known as *kalabule*) on a significant scale. Ghanaians who had anything to sell could multiply their earnings by selling their goods in French-speaking countries, especially neighbouring Côte d'Ivoire, and then changing the resultant francs into cedis at *black market* rates. Smuggling cut down the amount of foreign exchange available for official transactions, leading to a reduction in imports, which hit manufacturing enterprises dependent upon imported equipment and raw materials especially hard. As a result, many consumer goods were no longer available in Ghana, which further boosted smuggling across borders of those countries where such goods could be obtained. By 1982, the World Bank estimated that transactions on the parallel, or black, market constituted 32.4 per cent of all domestic trade.

By 1992, the government's Ghana Export Promotion Council announced a plan to raise nontraditional exports to US$335 million by 1997 through increased market research, trade missions, trade fairs and exhibitions, and training. Among its most ambitious specific targets were increases in tuna and shrimp sales to US$45 million and US$32 million, respectively, by 1995, and increases in pineapple sales to US$12.5 million. In the manufacturing sector, wood products, aluminium goods, and processed rubber were targeted to yield US$44 million, US$42 million, and US$23 million respectively. Earnings from salt were projected to rise to US$20 million.

Sub regional Economic Alliances

Earlier in 1975, Ghana had signed a protocol to be a member of the sixteen-member Economic Community of West African States (ECOWAS), founded in 1975 with headquarters in Abuja, Nigeria. ECOWAS so established is designed to promote the cultural, economic, and social development of its component states. To achieve these ends, ECOWAS seeks to foster regional cooperation in several areas, including removal of barriers to the movement of peoples and trade, harmonization of agricultural policies, improvements in infrastructure, and as of 1991, renewed commitment to democratic political processes and non-aggression against member states. Because of numerous economic issues in relation to sub regional currency convergence, ECOWAS is not able to make significant progress, comically.

Ghana also has a number of barter trade agreements with several East European countries, China, and Cuba. Under the agreements, imports of goods and services are paid for mainly by cocoa from Ghana. A major change occurred in 1991 when the German Democratic Republic (GDR, or East Germany) abrogated its barter trade agreement with Ghana following the union of the two Germanys. In spite of this, agreement was reached between the two countries to honour existing commitments. In late 1991, the Ghanaian government showed renewed interest in trade with the countries of Eastern Europe following the adoption of free-market systems in the wake of political upheavals in those countries. Ghanaian trade officials expect that the barter trade system will give way to open market operations.

The Economic Recovery Program (ERP)

In 1983, the Ghanaian government launched the Economic Recovery Program (ERP) under the guidance of the World Bank and the IMF. The purpose of the ERP was to scale down Ghana's external and internal debts and to improve its trading position in the world. The policies that government at the end of the day wanted to achieve included restoring production incentives to industry; rehabilitating infrastructure to improve conditions for the production and export for goods and services; lowering inflation through stringent fiscal, monetary, and trade policies; increasing the flow of foreign exchange into Ghana and directing it to priority sectors; and increasing the availability of essential consumer goods in the country. The target was to restore economic productivity at minimum cost to the government so as to generate capital for the country.

In 1986, the government began to rebuild infrastructure through a US$4.2 billion program, more than half of which was provided by external sources.

This amount was divided roughly (but equally) among infrastructure repair, energy imports (oil for machinery), and export industries. Increased imports financed by the IMF, the World Bank, and other sources made possible the rehabilitation and repair of some key parts of the infrastructure through the supply of spare parts and inputs for industry, mining, utilities, and agriculture. Although the ERP was geared primarily toward restoring the country's international economic standing, it came under popular criticism inside Ghana for ignoring the plight of those not involved in the export sector. The overwhelming shift in resources was toward cocoa rehabilitation and other export sectors, not toward food production. Government employees, especially those in state enterprises, were actively targeted, and many lost their jobs. Farmers suffered as the percentage of the total budget devoted to agriculture fell from 10 per cent in 1983 to 4.2 per cent in 1986 and to 3.5 percent in 1988, excluding foreign aid projects. Although cocoa contributed less to Ghana's GDP than food crops, cocoa nonetheless received 9 per cent of capital expenditures in the late 1980s; at the same time it received roughly 67 per cent of recurrent agricultural expenditures because of its export value.

The government in 1983 initiated a US$85 million program called the Action to Mitigate the Social Costs of Adjustment (PAMSCAD). From 1988, the program created over 40,000 jobs within two years, aimed at the poorest of the poor in terms of individuals and small-scale miners and artisans. As part of PAMSCAD, GHC10 billion was slated in the 1993 budget for the rehabilitation and development of rural and urban social infrastructure. The new program, initiated by and run by PAMSCAD and municipal/metropolitan and district assemblies, was designed to focus on improving water supply, sanitation, primary education, and healthcare. Additionally an amount of GHC 51 billion was set aside for redeployment and end-of- service benefits for those who had lost their jobs within the civil service and government-led reorganizations.

The government of Ghana by the end of 1991 improved the country's international financial standing because the government was able to make loan repayments (not wipe out foreign debt) and also made its first entry onto the international capital market. Critics maintained, however, that the ERP had failed to bring about a fundamental transformation of the economy, which still relied on income earned from cocoa and other agricultural commodities. Critics also contended that many Ghanaians had seen few, if any, benefits from the program. In addition to its focus on stabilizing the country's financial structure, the ERP was also aimed at promoting production, especially in the export sectors.

What is PAMSCAD? Program of Action to Mitigate the Social Cost of Adjustment

In 1983 the government of Ghana adopted a Structural Adjustment Program (SAP) locally dubbed the Economic Recovery Program (ERP) under the guidance of the World Bank and the IMF. The overriding purpose of the ERP was to reduce Ghana's debts and to improve its trading position in the global economy. The stated objectives of the program focused on restoring economic productivity at minimum cost to the government and included the following policies: lowering inflation through stringent fiscal, monetary, and trade policies; increasing the flow of foreign exchange into Ghana and directing it to priority sectors; restructuring the country's economic institutions; restoring production incentives; rehabilitating infrastructure to enhance conditions for the production and export of goods.

The Banking System

The introduction of dynamic monetary policies occurred in 1989 involving a phase-in of indirect controls and market-based policy instruments. A further series of measures were introduced in 1990 to strengthen the responsiveness of interest rates to changes in liquidity conditions. Also introduced were phased increases in the Bank of Ghana's rediscount rate from 26 per cent to 35 per cent by mid-1991, the introduction of three- and five-year instruments later that year, and a widening of access to Bank of Ghana financial instruments in favour of the nonbank financial sector. Indeed, these policies were quite effective. Similarly, money supply growth was brought convincingly under control in 1990 and 1991; however, a decline in interest rates and in monetary control, compounded by salary increases in the public sector, prompted monetary growth in 1992. But in January 1994, the Bank of Ghana relaxed its monetary policy. As a result, the government's 91-day Treasury bill discount rate was lowered 5 percentage points to 27 per cent. The interest rate equivalent of the discount rate fell from 34.78 per cent to 28.95 per cent. Similarly, savings deposit rates also fell in December 1993 from 17.5–22 per cent to 15–22 percent. The wider range suggests competition for funds in the banking market. The range for longer-term money (two-year) declined, 22–32 per cent to 25.2–28.0 per cent.

In terms of the banking industry, Ghana has a well-developed banking system that had been used extensively by previous governments to finance and to develop the local economy. By the late 1980s, the banks had suffered substantial losses from a number of bad loans in their portfolios. In addition, cedi depreciation had raised the banks' external liabilities. In order to strengthen the banking sector, the government initiated comprehensive reforms in 1988. In particular, the government amended the banking law of August 1989, which required banks to maintain a minimum capital base equivalent to 6 per cent of net assets adjusted for risk and to establish uniform accounting and auditing standards. The law also introduced limits on risk exposure to single borrowers and sectors. These measures strengthened the Bank of Ghana supervision, improved the regulatory framework, and gradually improved resource mobilization and credit allocation. Other efforts were made to ease the accumulated burden of bad loans on the banks in the late 1980s. In 1989, the Bank of Ghana issued temporary promissory notes to replace non-performing loans and other government-guaranteed obligations to state-owned enterprises as of the end of 1988 and on private-sector loans in 1989. The latter were then replaced by interest-bearing bonds from the Bank of Ghana or were offset against debts to the bank. Effectively, the government stepped in and repaid the loans. By late 1989, some ¢62 billion worth of non-performing assets was offset or replaced by central bank bonds totalling about ¢47 billion (Bank of Ghana data, Bulletin 1990, 1992).

In the 1990s, Ghana's banking system included the central bank (i.e. the Bank of Ghana), three large commercial banks, (i.e. Ghana Commercial Bank now GCB Bank Limited, Barclays Bank of Ghana, and Standard Chartered Bank of Ghana), and seven other secondary banks. Three merchant banks specialized in corporate finance, advisory services, and money and capital market activities: Merchant Bank, Ecobank Ghana, and Continental Acceptances; the latter two were both established in 1990. These and the commercial banks placed short-term deposits with two discount houses set up to enhance the development of Ghana's domestic money market: Consolidated Discount House and Securities Discount House, established in November 1987 and June 1991 respectively. At the bottom of the tier were 100 rural banks, which accounted for only 5 per cent of the banking system's total assets. By the end of 1990, banks were able to meet the new capital adequacy requirements. Similarly, the government announced the establishment of the First Finance Company in 1991 to help distressed but potentially viable companies to recapitalize. The company was established as part of the financial sector adjustment program in response to requests for easier access to credit for companies hit by ERP policies. The company was a joint venture between the Bank of Ghana and the Social Security and National Insurance Trust (SSNIT).

Ghana's banking and currency system was now functioning accordingly, offering some of the highest lending rates in West Africa, and enjoying increased business in the early 1990s because of high deposit rates. Indeed, the Bank of Ghana raised its rediscount rate in stages to around 35 per cent by mid-1991, driving money market and commercial bank interest rates well above the rate of inflation, thus making real interest rates substantially positive. And as inflation decelerated over the year, the rediscount rate was lowered in stages to 20 per cent, bringing lending rates down accordingly. There was clear evidence that more money had moved into the banking system in 1991 than in 1990; time and savings deposits grew by 45 per cent to ¢94.6 billion and demand deposits rose to ¢118.7 billion. Similarly, loans also rose, with banks' claims on the private sector going up by 24.1 per cent, to ¢117.4 billion. In that vein, Ghanaian banks' claims on the central government continued to shrink in 1991, falling to a mere ¢860 million from ¢2.95 billion in 1990, a reflection of continued budget surpluses. Similarly, claims on non-financial public enterprises rose by 12.6 per cent to ¢27.1 billion. In a move to increase local supplies of foreign exchange, foreign bank accounts, which were frozen shortly after the PNDC came to power, were permitted by mid-1985. It was mandated that foreign currency accounts could be held in any of seven authorized banks, with interest exempt from Ghanaian tax and with transfers abroad free from foreign exchange control restrictions. Foreign exchange earnings from exports were specifically excluded from these arrangements.

Similarly, the Ghana Stock Exchange began operations in November 1990, with twelve companies considered to be the best performers in the country. Although there were stringent minimum investment criteria for registration on the exchange, the government hoped that share ownership would encourage the formation of new companies and would increase savings and investment. After only one month in operation, however, the exchange lost a major French affiliate, which reduced the starting market capitalization to about US$92.5 million (Bank of Ghana Bulletin, 1986).

By the end of 1990, the aggregate effect of price and volume movements had resulted in a further 10.8 per cent decrease in market capitalization. Trading steadily increased, and by mid-July 1992, 2.8 million shares were being traded with a value of ¢233 million, up from 1.7 million shares with a value of ¢145 million in November 1991. The market continued to be small, listing only thirteen companies, more than half in retailing and brewing. In June 1993, Bank of Ghana removed exchange control restrictions and gave permission to non-resident Ghanaians and foreigners to invest on the exchange without prior approval from the Bank of Ghana. In April 1994, the exchange rate received a considerable boost after the government sold part of its holdings in Ashanti Goldfields Corporation. Control of money-supply growth and liquidity management has been among the ERP's most difficult tasks, and expansion has generally exceeded targets for most of the 1980s. The initial phase of monetary policy (1983–86) focused on reducing government borrowing from the domestic banking system and on using quantitative controls via credit ceilings. Although these succeeded in reducing domestic credit growth, larger-than-expected foreign earnings and the money market's inability to process them efficiently contributed to a rapid expansion in the broad money supply until the late 1980s.

Ghana's Currency System

Ghana's unit of currency is the cedi, which is divided into 100 pesewas. Ghana broke away from the British pound sterling and pegged the value of the cedi to the US dollar in 1961. But soon after that, Ghana's terms of trade worsened and the real value of the cedi fell. However, successive governments, for fear of inflation, did not want to float the cedi or to adjust its value, thereby causing the rise of imports and consumer prices. This fear is borne out of the overthrow of the Dr Busia regime in 1971, following the introduction of a devaluation package, which reinforced the unpopularity of such a move. However, the Colonel Acheampong government reversed course and revalued the cedi, increased the money supply to pay Ghana's debts, which led to a sharp divergence between the official and the real rates of exchange. In so doing, the overvalued cedi on the one hand and low regulated prices for commodities on the other led to a robust smuggling industry and to an extensive black market in currency referred to earlier as *kalabule*. It became common practice for Ghanaians, especially those living along the country's border, to smuggle Ghanaian produce such as cocoa, coffee, and minerals (gold, diamond, etc,) into neighbouring francophone countries for higher returns. After selling on the local market, Ghanaians would then return home and exchange their hard currency, Central African francs (CFA) for cedi on the black market, thereby making handsome profits. Smuggling and illegal currency operations became so extensive by 1981 that the black market rate for cedi was 9.6 times higher than the official rate, up from 1.3 in 1972. At the same time, reliable estimates placed transactions in the parallel economy at fully one-third of Ghana's GDP. In April 1983, fifteen months after the PNDC came to power, government began efforts to devalue the cedi. The chairman of the PNDC, Flight Lieutenant J. J. Rawlings, introduced a system of surcharges on imports and bonuses on exports that effectively devalued the currency, because the surcharges on imports amounted to 750 per cent of the amount being spent, and the discounts on exports amounted to 990 per cent. Further, an official devaluation began in October 1983 in which the exchange rate reached ¢90 to US$1 by March 1986. By 1993 ¢720 equalled US$1, and by late 1994, ¢1,023 equalled US$1 (Bank of Ghana indices 1993).

In September 1986, the government sought alternative methods for establishing the value of the cedi. At that time, the government relinquished its direct role in determining the exchange rate. The rate was instead determined at regular currency auctions under the pressure of market forces on the basis of a two-tier exchange-rate system, with one rate for essentials and another for non-essentials. In April 1987, the two auctions were unified. In subsequent reforms also designed to diminish smuggling and illegal currency dealings, private foreign-exchange bureaus were permitted to trade in foreign currencies beginning at the end of March 1988. By July 1989, there were 148 such bureaus operating—ninety-nine in Accra and thirty in Ashanti region, with the remainder in other urban centres. In 1987, US$207 million was allocated through the auction, and in 1988, US$267 million. By comparison, the foreign-exchange bureaus in the first year of operation, ending in March 1989, traded US$77 million worth of foreign currency, or about one-fourth the amount of foreign exchange allocated through the auction. Initially, prices at the auction and those at the foreign-exchange bureaus differed greatly. Efforts to reduce the difference, however, brought the gap from 29 per cent in March 1988 to approximately 6 per cent by February 1991. In early 1992, the auction was closed, although no official announcement was given. Purchasers were referred to the Bank of Ghana, which used an exchange rate determined largely on the basis of market forces. The government also successfully slowed growth in the money supply. In the late 1980s, the average annual growth rate reached 61 per cent; by 1990 it had dropped to 13.3 per cent but accelerated slightly to 16.7 per cent, standing at ¢317 million the following year. In 1991 the Bank of Ghana introduced a ¢1,000 note, the highest denomination issued since independence in 1957. Previously, the highest denomination had been ¢500. A total of ¢50 billion of the new notes was printed. But Ghana's currency notes were replaced and redenominated in 2006 under President J. A.Kufour. The redenomination was done by removing several zeros from each currency note. A one-thousand cedi note was now equivalent to one cedi note; a ten-thousand note became ten cedis, and so on.

Ghana's State Enterprises

State-owned enterprises (SOEs) in Ghana date back to the colonial period and especially to the post-World War II era. Public utilities, such as water, electricity, postal and telegraph services, rail and road networks and bus services were organized by the British government. And to foster exports of coffee, palm kernels, and cocoa, the Agricultural Produce Marketing Board was founded in 1949. Other establishments by the British government included the Industrial Development Corporation and the Agricultural Development Corporation to promote industries and agriculture. In the mid 1970s, the National Redemption Council, under Colonel I. K. Acheampong, emphasized the need for state enterprises. The Acheampong government established a number of new enterprises and partly or wholly nationalized a number of foreign-owned companies, including the Ashanti Goldfields Corporation and Consolidated African Selection Trust. Intermittent efforts to improve performance and efficiency often led to the transfer of duties and functions to alternative state bodies but not to the wholesale privatization of ownership rights and assets. By the 1980s, state enterprises were suffering along with most businesses in Ghana, but they were also held to blame for the economy's general condition. In particular, many were heavily subsidized and were draining much of the country's domestic loan capital. Under pressure from the World Bank and in accordance with the principles of the ERP, in 1984 the government began to sell state enterprises to private investors, and it initiated the State Owned Enterprise Reform Program in 1988.

In 1984, there were 235 state enterprises in Ghana. The government announced that twenty-two sensitive enterprises would not be sold, including major utilities as well as transport, cocoa, and mining enterprises. In 1988, thirty-two were put up for sale, followed by a further forty-four in 1990 under what was termed the Divestiture Implementation Committee. By December 1990, thirty-four enterprises had been either partially or totally divested. Four were sold outright, a further eight were partially sold through share issues, and twenty-two were liquidated. Divestiture of fifteen additional enterprises was also underway, and by 1992 plans were afoot to privatize some of the nation's banks (DIC Bulletin 1995). In their stead, joint ventures were set up for four enterprises, including two state mining companies—the Prestea Goldfields and the Ghana Consolidated Diamonds. By 1992, the Divestiture Implementation Committee introduced resource-pooling programs to enable smaller domestic investors to buy up state enterprises. This pooling was to accelerate the program, but more importantly, it was to enable the Provisional National Defence Council (PNDC) to deflect charges that it was auctioning off the nation's assets to foreigners, to either themselves or to their cronies without due diligence. At the end of 1989, fifteen enterprises had responded positively, turning a combined pre-tax loss of ¢418 million from the previous year into pre-tax profits of ¢19 billion, following a 9 per cent cut in costs and a 30 per cent increase in sales. In early 1992, the executive chairman of the State Enterprises Commission announced that the government would pass legislation requiring state-owned enterprises to register as limited liability companies by 1993, to stimulate competition and to improve their performances. Therefore, between 1987 and 1999, Ghana's privatization program generated revenues for the government equivalent to about 14 per cent of GDP from a moribund public sector which had previously been dependent on state subventions, and thus succeeded in fulfilling a key role in easing the fiscal crisis and in fostering the Structural Adjustment Program. But since that time, big questions have remained: whether the privatization process would help the growth of Ghanas economy and help maximize political gain, or the government would have to create another avenue for state-owned-enterprises.

Income and Wages

From the late 1960s, a lot of efforts have been made by successive governments to address wages and salaries coupled with poor conditions of service that exist in the public service, and to manage the government wage bill efficiently. This effort has culminated in the formation of many commissions to address the issue. Among the many efforts were the formations of the following commissions: the Mills Odoi commission (1967), Issifu Ali committee (1973), Azu Crabbe commission (1979), the National Committee for Wage and Salary Rationalization (1983), and the Gyampoh salary commission (1992); but most of these commissions have been short and their existence ad hoc. The challenge therefore of the Ghanaian government has been to find a sustainable mechanism to reform the public services in terms of improving the pay and conditions of service of public service workers. Because of the non-implementation of the recommendations of the above ad hoc commissions, the Ghana Universal Salary Structure (GUSS) was introduced in 1977 with the objective of arresting the inequities in pay within and across the public sector of the country. The end result was that the objective to place all public sector workers on pay levels was regrettably not successful, including the absence of a legal backing; sadly, the disparities in pay and grading continued to exist in the public sector.

Similarly, in 2006, the government of Ghana began another comprehensive grading and pay reform to address the following: low level of public service pay, inequalities in public service pay within and across service classifications, multiplicity of allowances in the public service, lack of government control over the public service wage bill. However, following the recommendations of CoEn consulting in 2006, the government of Ghana finally decided to adopt the Single Spine Pay Policy (SSPP) as the most appropriate pay policy for the public service to promote equity and fairness in salary administration in Ghana. In furtherance of the above, the government of Ghana on 26 November 2009, issued a White Paper adopting the Single Spine Pay Policy (SSPP) as the new pay policy for public sector employees, effective January 2010, allowing the first six months to be used as a period to handle technical issues. In 2009, the road map for the implementation of the SSPP was adopted by all stakeholders, giving the commission the green light to start with the implementation of the SSPP.

In the whole of Africa, Botswana pays its top public servants about US$40,235 per annum and Uganda pays its top public servants about US$12,908 per annum while Ghana pays about US$3,373 per annum. Moreover, data from Ghana Living Standard Survey (GLSS) 5 (2005/2006) shows that wages from employment constitute a major source of income for 28.6 per cent of Ghanaians. Incidentally, those whose major source of income is from wage employment constitute 39.5 per cent among those in the highest quintile. GLSS5 survey (2005/2006) further revealed that out of the 18.2 per cent of Ghanaians who live below the poverty line of GHC3, 373 per annum, 8.3 per cent of them are public service workers. Although increases in the minimum daily wage under the PNDC appeared spectacular, they were linked to the steady devaluation of the cedi and had not overcome a constant erosion of worker purchasing power. Beginning in April 1984, the government increased the minimum daily wage to ¢35, then to ¢70 in January 1985, ¢90 in January 1986, and ¢122 in 1987. In March 1990, the minimum wage was raised to ¢218, and by August 1991, it had risen to ¢460, an increase of 111 per cent as agreed to by the government, the Trade Union Congress, and the Ghana Employers Association. In the face of popular elections and increasing strikes, the government agreed to massive pay raises at the end of 1992, including a 70 per cent increase for nurses. Overall, civil service pay increases added more than ¢50 billion to the wage bill, reaching ¢175 billion in 1992, or 50 per cent of government revenue. At the same time, the government moved in to contain the wage bill by freezing staff recruitment in public-sector organizations as well as state salaries that exceeded those in the civil service.

Single Spine Salary Structure

The single spine salary structure (SSSS) came as a result of the following issues within government. In 1997, the government of Ghana decided to address disparities that had emerged between the pay of civil servants and those in the wider public sector. A nationwide job evaluation exercise was undertaken and a new grading and salary structure was developed to create equity. Despite these efforts, the Ghana Universal Salary Structure was only marginally successful as most public sector institutions did not convert to the new system. Between 1999 and 2006, the few institutions that did so were considered consistently disadvantaged as a result of re-established pay and grade disparities. In 2006, the Kufuor administration addressed these problems, hence the single spine salary policy. But the aim to merge and rationalize the different public sector salary structures into one has thrown government's prudent spending policy out of gear, hence a program instituted in 2014 by the International Monetary Fund (IMF) to correct the imbalances in the Ghanaian economy.

Agriculture

Of all the sectors mentioned, Ghana's most important economic sector is agriculture, which employs more than half the population on a formal and informal basis and accounts for almost half of GDP and export earnings. The country produces a variety of crops in various climatic zones which range from dry savannah to wet forest and runs in east-west bands across the country. Agricultural crops such as yams, grains, cocoa, oil palms, cola nuts, and timber form the base of Ghana's economy. Ghanaian agricultural output had consistently fallen since the 1960s. Beginning with the drop in commodity prices in the late 1960s, farmers have had to face fewer incentives to produce, as well as a general deterioration of the necessary infrastructure and services required to commercialize agriculture. Farmers in Ghana have had to deal with increasingly expensive inputs, such as fertilizer, because of overvaluation of the cedi on a yearly basis. Food production has fallen as well, with a decline in the food self-sufficiency ratio from 83 per cent in 1961–66 to 71 per cent in 1978–80, coupled with a fourfold increase in food imports in the decade prior to 1982. By 1983, when drought hit the sub-Saharan sub region, food shortages were widespread, and export crop production reached an all-time low. Going back to the economic policies of the 1980s, the Rawlings government identified agriculture as the economic sector that could rescue Ghana from its financial ruin. Accordingly, the government invested significant funds in the rehabilitation of agriculture. Primarily through the use of loans and grants, the government directed capital toward repairing and improving the transportation and distribution infrastructure serving export crops. In addition, specific projects were aimed at increasing cocoa yields and at developing the timber industry. Except for specific development programs, the government tried to allow the free market to promote higher producer prices and to increase efficiency.

Even though the government was criticized for focusing on exports rather than on food crops under the ERP during the early 1990s, the PNDC government under Flight Lieutenant J. J. Rawlings had begun to address the need to increase local production of food. In that direction and in early 1991, the government announced that one goal of the Medium-Term Agricultural Development Program 1991–2000 was to attain food self-sufficiency and food security by the year 2000. To that end, extension services for farmers were improved including crop-disease research. Despite the statements concerning the importance of food crops, the plan was still heavily oriented toward market production, improvement of Ghana's balance-of-payments position, and provision of materials for local industrial production. Furthermore, following World Bank guidelines, the government relied more heavily on the private sector for needed services to reduce the role of the public sector, and to provide a clear disadvantage for subsistence producers. In particular, industrial tree crops such as cocoa, coffee, and oil palm seedlings were singled out for assistance. Clearly, agricultural sectors that could not produce foreign exchange earnings were assigned a lower priority under the ERP. Additionally, government reduced its role in marketing and assistance to farmers in several ways. Of particular importance was government's role in the Cocoa Marketing Board. Government steadily relinquished its powers over the pricing and marketing of cocoa in the country. Furthermore, the government established a new farmers' organization known as the Ghana National Association of Farmers and Fishermen in 1991 to replace the Ghana Federation of Agricultural Cooperatives. The new organization was funded by the farmers themselves to operate as a cooperative venture at the district, regional, and national levels. Although the government argued that it did not want to be accused of manipulating farmers, the lack of government financial support again put these subsistence producers at a disadvantage. The situation from that time until now is not any better for Ghanaian farmers.

Ghana's agriculture accounts for about 40 per cent of GDP and more than half the workforce; out of all the cash crops exported, cocoa is the only commercial crop of economic significance. While other industrial crops, including cotton, rubber, and tobacco are grown, they are small potatoes compared to cocoa and other exports. (The major exports are timber, gold, diamond, bauxite, and manganese.) Cocoa is the only one with a specific framework for facilitating trade. All cocoa grown for export must be sold to the Ghana Cocoa Board (Cocobod), which aggregates the crop for sale in the international market. The main food crops grown in Ghana are maize, yams, cassava, and to a lesser extent, sorghum and millet. International demand and the presence of a single buyer to coordinate trade means the market for cocoa is guaranteed. Cocobod has experimented over the last thirty years with various market liberalization tactics in order to make the industry more competitive, including privatizing more companies and investing in the development of the market.

The Cocoa Economy

In Ghana, cocoa plays a major role in the economy and Ghana can be referred to as an economy dominated by cocoa. Ghana has been supported from independence until today by cocoa, without which the country wouldn't have been considered a developing one. Ghana is the world's biggest producer of cocoa after Ivory Coast, and reports that it will exceed this season's (2014/2015) target, because of good weather and an increase in plantings, according to the country's industry regulator. Cocoa production occurs in the forested areas of the country—the Ashanti region, Brong-Ahafo region, Central region, Eastern region, Western region, and Volta region—where rainfall is 1,000–1,500 millimetres per year. The crop year begins in October, when purchases of the main crop begin, while the smaller midcrop cycle starts in July. All cocoa, except that which is smuggled out of the country, is sold at fixed prices to the Ghana Cocoa Board. Although most cocoa production is carried out by peasant farmers on plots of less than three hectares, a small number of farmers appear to dominate the trade. Indeed, some studies show that about one-fourth of all cocoa farmers received just over half of total cocoa income.

Ghana's Cocoa History

The history of cocoa, one of Ghana's economic engines, started in 1937, when farmers in the then Gold Coast, a colony of the British Empire, refused to continue selling cocoa at the low prices set by European merchants and decided to withhold cocoa from the market. The strike went on for eight months, until the British government acted by setting up the Nowell Commission of Enquiry to investigate the issue. The Nowell commission report advised the government to assist cocoa farmers by establishing a marketing board. Soon after that, in 1940, the government established the West African Produce Control Board to purchase cocoa under guaranteed prices for all farmers from all West African countries. The WAPCB operated successfully until 1946 when it was dissolved. Ghana Marketing Board was established by ordinance in 1947 with the sum of 27 million Ghanaian cedi as its initial working capital. In 1979, this board was dissolved and reconstituted as the Ghana Cocoa Board. Consequently in 1984, Cocobod underwent institutional reforms to instil prudent market forces into the cocoa sector. In the ensuing years, Cocobod's role was reduced, and 40 per cent of its staff, or at least 35,000 employees, were dismissed. In addition, a new payment system known as the Akuafo Check System was introduced in 1982 at the point of purchase of dried beans. The reforms were, among others, to initiate programs aimed at controlling pest and diseases of cocoa, coffee, and shea nut in the country and to undertake, promote, and encourage scientific research aimed at improving the quality of cocoa, coffee, shea nut, and other tropical crops. Cocobod was also regulated to purchase, market, and export cocoa and cocoa products produced in Ghana which are graded under the Cocoa Industry (Regulations) Consolidation Decree, 1968 NLCD 278, or any other enactment as suitable for export and to assist in the development of the cocoa, coffee, and shea nut industries of Ghana. In short, Ghana emerged as the second leading producer of cocoa after Ivory Coast but experienced a major decline in production in the 1960s–70s, with a near collapse of the sector in the early 1980s. However, production steadily recovered in the mid 1980s after the introduction of economy-wide reforms, whereas the 1990s marked the beginning of a revival with production nearly doubling between 2001 and 2003.

Ghana is highly competitive in one key cash crop, cocoa, for which it controls 21 per cent of the world market—and involved in the exportation of several others. While agriculture accounts for 37 per cent of GDP, this percentage is spread across hundreds of thousands of 1–2-hectare, smallholder farms. The big export industries—timber, gold and other mining activities, and oil—are the key drivers of economic growth. But there are still a lot of opportunities for import substitution and raising food output for consumption, even if export is out of the question in some cases (i.e. maize, rice, poultry, etc.). Despite an increase in cocoa production levels in 2011, the overall agricultural sector grew 0.7 per cent and in 2012, the sector saw no growth. This is an unpleasant development since the sector has been on decline for some time. Moreover, the sector still remains a large employer of the rural population and it is critical to both Ghana's food security and mitigating rural urban migration.

From the analysis made so far, Ghana's economy is still based on commodity production and is dependent on revenues from cocoa, gold, and to a lesser extent, timber. Other exports include: tuna, aluminium, manganese ore, gold, diamonds, and horticulture. With its newly acquired status as an oil-producing nation, expected revenues from crude oil are projected to be the most important growth factor in the economy. In late 2010, Ghana became a lower middle-income country when a new calculation basis for the country's national accounts was used. For 2011 when oil production started in earnest, the estimated growth was 14.4 per cent. Inflation was in single digits, registering 9.5 per cent for July 2012. Gross International Reserves of the Bank of Ghana declined to US$4.3 billion as at 8 June 2012, equivalent to 2.5 months' imports cover of goods and services. Ghana's economic goal for the medium to long term is to ensure sustained economic growth and development. Real GDP growth over the medium term is expected to be around 8 per cent on the average, reflecting strong expansion in both the non-oil and oil sectors of the economy. The growth forecast assumes a favourable investment climate and expanded social and economic infrastructure. Monetary policy will be geared at maintaining single-digit inflation over the medium term, and the Bank of Ghana will continue to maintain a flexible exchange rate regime designed to support Ghana's inflation target.

Ghana's Fiscal Deficit

Ghana as of 2015 recorded its lowest deficit since 2011, according to Bank of Ghana statistics on the Ghanaian economy. The fiscal deficit for the eleven months of the year, measured on cash basis, was 5.7 per cent of gross domestic product (GDP). This figure was significantly lower than the 6.8 per cent target for the period which a year ago was widely regarded as overly ambitious in the wake of the 9.4 per cent cash deficit recorded for the whole of 2014. Accordingly, the deficit for the whole of 2015 was 7.0 per cent, lower than the target of 8.0 per cent, despite the lump sum payment of arrears made to the various statutory funds at the end of the year. In 2014 total revenue accruing to government for the first eleven months of the year amounted to 21.0 per cent of GDP on the back of a sharp upsurge in tax revenue in October and November, which brought cumulative tax revenue to 16.1 per cent of GDP. Ghana in 2015 initiated steps to restore macroeconomic stability through fiscal consolidation by ruthlessly tightening its monetary policy. It witnessed the monetary policy rate (MPR) rise to 26 per cent by the end of the year, its highest levels since it was introduced nearly a decade ago. In February the first week of 2016, the Bank of Ghana Monetary Policy Committee elected not to raise it further for now, opting to see out the effects of the two consecutive 100 basis point hikes implemented in the last quarter of 2015.

The tight monetary posture of the central bank has been criticized by industry and many economic commentators as being a policy that is strangulating Ghana's economic growth potential. This has witnessed a substantial slow growth in money supply for 2015. For instance, broad money (M2) grew by 24.8 per cent in the twelve months up to November of 2015, down from year on year growth of 33.0 per cent in 2014. Total liquidity growth (M2+) has slowed even faster to 26.1 per cent year on year as at November 2015, down from 36.8 per cent in 2014. But interest, tighter monetary controls have not translated into higher interest rates as was widely feared by critics of the central bank's monetary policy stance.

Structural Changes within the Ghanaian Economy

1. Interest Rates

The average lending rates in Ghana fell from 29.0 per cent in September 2015 to 27.5 per cent by November even as the MPR was raised by 200 basis points during that period. In Ghana, falling lending rates have been in line with declining interest rates on government short-term debt securities which large-scale depositors use as a guide to negotiate rates from banks on fixed deposits. Similarly, the rate on 91-day treasury bills fell from 25.3 per cent to 23.1 per cent during the last quarter of 2015, while 182-day treasury bill rates declined from 25.9 per cent to 24.4 per cent; although the yield on one-year treasury notes rose marginally from 22.5 per cent to 22.8 per cent as the central bank seeks to correct the inverted yield curve to encourage pricing efficiency of financial assets by the money market.

2. Inflation

The downward side of the measures taken to narrow the fiscal deficit in Ghana, in terms of tight monetary controls, has not cut inflation as targeted consumer price inflation rose to 17.7 per cent by the end of 2015, up from 17.0 per cent in 2014. Ghana's economy is credit driven; it generates cost-push inflation rather than curbs demand-pull inflation. However, the impact of monetary tightening on the cedi exchange rate, the single biggest determinant of inflation in Ghana, illustrates its effectiveness. In 2016, the Finance Minister announced that the government has taken measures to reverse election year trends characterized by large expenditures resulting in high fiscal deficit, high inflation, high interest rate, and unstable exchange rate. The government of Ghana has targeted a fiscal deficit of 5.3 per cent of gross domestic product (GDP) for 2016.

3. Depreciation of the Cedi

The cedi; the official Ghanaian currency depreciated by 15.7 per cent in 2015, compared with 31.3 per cent recorded in 2014 against the US dollar. This occurred despite a widening of the trade deficit last year to 4.3 per cent of

GDP, up from 1.7 per cent a year earlier. Most instructively, the cedi's much-improved stability has extended so far into the two months of 2016—January and February; it depreciated by just 0.5 per cent against the US dollar in January this year; it was stable against the euro and actually appreciated by 4.1 per cent against the pound sterling. In total, government's fiscal position is expected to improve further during the first half of 2016 as a plethora of new taxes and levies have been introduced and public utility tariffs have been hiked by nearly 60 per cent. But there are widespread doubts and hesitations as to whether the government can maintain its restored fiscal discipline during the second half of the year as a general election slated for November may force government spending as well as borrowing by and from the Bank of Ghana.

Ghana Economic Statistics

GDP (purchasing power parity)	$90.41 billion (2013 est.) $83.79 billion (2012 est.) $77.64 billion (2011 est.) **note:** data are in 2013 US dollars
GDP (official exchange rate)	$45.55 billion (2013 est.)
GDP—real growth rate	7.9% (2013 est.) 7.9% (2012 est.) 15% (2011 est.)
GDP—per capita (PPP)	$3,500 (2013 est.) $3,400 (2012 est.) $3,200 (2011 est.) **note:** data are in 2013 US dollars
Gross national saving	21.1% of GDP (2013 est.) 17.9% of GDP (2012 est.) 17.5% of GDP (2011 est.)
GDP—composition, by end use	**Household consumption:** 64.2% **government consumption:** 14.2% **investment in fixed capital:** 31.7% **investment in inventories:** 0.7% **exports of goods and services:** 50.2% **imports of goods and services:** -61% (2013 est.)

GDP—composition by sector	**agriculture:** 21.5% **industry:** 28.7% **services:** 49.8% (2013 est.)
Population below poverty line	**28.5% (2007 est.)**
Labour force	**12.07 million (2013 est.)**
Labour force—by occupation	**agriculture: 56%** **industry: 15%** **services: 29% (2005 est.)**
Unemployment rate	**11% (2000 est.)**
Unemployment, youth ages 15–24	**total: 16.6%** **male: 16.4%** **female: 16.7% (2000)**
Household income or consumption by percentage share	**lowest 10%: 2%** **highest 10%: 32.8% (2006)**
Distribution of family income—Gini index	**39.4 (2005–06)** **40.7 (1999)**
Budget	**revenues: $10.56 billion** **expenditures: $14.87 billion (2013 est.)**
Taxes and other revenues	**23.2% of GDP (2013 est.)**
Budget surplus (+) or deficit (-)	**-9.5% of GDP (2013 est.)**
Public debt	**53.1% of GDP (2013 est.)** **50% of GDP (2012 est.)**
Inflation rate (consumer prices)	**11% (2013 est.)** **9.2% (2012 est.)**
Central bank discount rate	**18% (31 December 2009)** **17% (31 December 2008)**
Commercial bank prime lending rate	**27% (31 December 2013 est.)** **22.8% (31 December 2012 est.)**
Stock of narrow money	**$6.256 billion (31 December 2013 est.)** **$6.153 billion (31 December 2012 est.)**

Stock of broad money	$12.59 billion (31 December 2013 est.) $12.17 billion (31 December 2012 est.)
Stock of domestic credit	$13.31 billion (31 December 2013 est.) $12.56 billion (31 December 2012 est.)
Market value of publicly traded shares	$3.465 billion (31 December 2012 est.) $3.097 billion (31 December 2011) $3.531 billion (31 December 2010 est.)
Agriculture—products	cocoa, rice, cassava (manioc, tapioca), peanuts, corn, shea nuts, bananas, timber
Industries	mining, lumbering, light manufacturing, aluminium smelting, food processing, cement, small commercial shipbuilding, petroleum
Industrial production growth rate	10.5% (2013 est.)
Current account balance	-$5.149 billion (2013 est.) -$4.778 billion (2012 est.)
Exports	$13.37 billion (2013 est.) $13.54 billion (2012 est.)
Exports—commodities	oil, gold, cocoa, timber, tuna, bauxite, aluminium, manganese ore, diamonds, horticultural products
Exports—partners	France 13.6%, Italy 12.4%, Netherlands 8.9%, China 7.4%, Germany 4.3% (2012)
Imports	$18.49 billion (2013 est.) $17.76 billion (2012 est.)
Imports—commodities	capital equipment, refined petroleum, foodstuffs
Imports—partners	China 25.6%, Nigeria 11%, US 7%, Netherlands 6.2%, Singapore 4.5%, UK 4.1%, India 4% (2012)

Reserves of foreign exchange and gold	$6.016 billion (31 December 2013 est.) $5.705 billion (31 December 2012 est.)
Debt—external	$14.68 billion (31 December 2013 est.) $12.64 billion (31 December 2012 est.)
Stock of direct foreign investment—at home	$NA
Stock of direct foreign investment—abroad	$NA
Exchange rates	cedis (GHC) per US dollar 2.018 (2013 est.) 1.796 (2012 est.) 1.431 (2010 est.) 1.409 (2009) 1.1 (2008)
Fiscal year	calendar year

4. The Export Sector

Ghana's export sector has evolved significantly over the years. In line with Ghana's economic and industrialization ambitions, exports have gradually included non-traditional products to the largely indigenous export products. Although there is an impressive development in the export sector, the perceived idea of transforming Ghana's economy into an export-led economy has made it necessary to adopt a policy to drive this laudable idea. In that regard, the government, in the 2015 budget statement before Ghana's parliament, announced its intention to establish an export-import bank to spearhead the strategic positioning of the country as an export-led economy. In 2016 budget reading from the Finance Minister to parliament, a seed capital of $250 million dollars had been lodged with the UBA bank in Accra for the commencement of the bank. The proposed bank, which is still being debated in parliament as of February 2016, is envisaged to promote the acceleration of the country's drive toward achieving a more diversified economy to make it resilient to external shocks, alongside an improved capacity to produce goods and services in the competitive global marketplace.

5. The Impact of the Oil Sector

According to the Standard Chartered Research, crude oil is now Ghana's second main export, increasing moderately in the past two years from $2.7 billion in 2011 to $3.0 billion in 2012. Oil, gold, and cocoa account for 85 per cent of Ghana's total exports of goods, and the value of gold and cocoa exports alone has risen by more than 90 per cent since 2009. Ghana oil production in 2011 and 2012 averaged 90,000 barrels per day, missing production targets, because of technical factors stemming from the absence of gas infrastructure (the prohibition on flaring means that gas must be re-injected into the Jubilee field for the time being, leaving Ghana vulnerable to output volatility). The discovery of new sites adjacent to the Jubilee field development, which targets 500 million barrels in estimated oil reserves, should enable the country to increase production to about 250,000 barrels per day of oil equivalent by 2021. Current production is estimated to be around 110,000 barrels per day. But Ghana, an emerging (but small) player oil country, needs to brace up for further cost efficiency, as worldwide oil prices are coming down. The latest report by the World Bank lowered its 2016 forecast for crude oil prices to $37 per barrel from $51 per barrel in its earlier projections. Brent crude hovered around $29.50 in the second week of February, while OPEC's daily basket price fell to $25.58 a barrel. According to the commodity outlook report a number of supply and demand factors, including resumption of exports by the Islamic Republic of Iran, greater resilience in US production (due to cost cuts and efficiency gains), a mild winter in the Northern Hemisphere, and weak growth projects in major emerging market economies, play major roles in the cheap-oil era. However, from their current lows in oil prices, a gradual recovery in oil profits is expected over the course of the year, for several reasons, according to the World Bank. Among the reasons are first, the sharp oil price drop in early 2016 does not appear fully warranted by fundamental drivers of oil demand and supply, and is likely to partly reverse. Second, high-cost oil producers are expected to sustain persistent losses and increasingly make production cuts that are likely to outweigh any additional capacity coming to the market. Third, demand is expected to strengthen somewhat with a modest pickup in global growth, the report concluded. Therefore, it appears Ghana's oil returns will not for now, and in the immediate future, be a factor in contributing significantly to the economy.

The Way Forward for Ghana's Government—Creativity

Ghana's economy has been strengthened by a quarter century of relatively sound management, a competitive business environment, and sustained reductions in poverty levels. In late 2010, Ghana was re-categorized as a lower middle-income country. Ghana is well endowed with natural resources, and agriculture accounts for roughly one-quarter of GDP and employs more than half of the workforce, mainly small landholders. The services sector accounts for 50 per cent of GDP. Gold and cocoa production and individual remittances are major sources of foreign exchange. Oil production at Ghana's offshore Jubilee field began in mid-December 2010, and is producing close to target levels. Additional oil projects are being developed and are expected to come online in a few years. Estimated oil reserves have jumped to about 700 million barrels and Ghana's growing oil industry is expected to boost economic growth as the country faces the consequences of two years of loose fiscal policy, high budget and current account deficits, and a depreciating currency. Bank of Ghana faces challenges in managing an economy in which the people are unhappy with living standards and that they are not reaping the benefits of oil production because of perceived political corruption. Looking at the current structure of the economy, it is imperative for the Ghana government to be more creative and look for other policy options that can spruce up the economy; that is, re-engineer the manufacturing sector and create more jobs. Government over-reliance on the oil sector could be counterproductive and unhealthy for the overall economic development. It is necessary to invest in the agriculture sector and make it healthier than it is now, and as the largest employing sector in the economy, it has the potential to stir growth. Government's creativity must also stretch to plug the holes in the system that allow for wastage of national funds.

Conclusion

Ghana's economy went through a transformation in the 1980s and has been considered a test case for structural adjustment prescriptions advocated by international banking institutions in Africa. Africa was faced with enormous growing impoverishment as well as in much of the so-called developing world. So the World Bank and the International Monetary Fund proposed radical programs to revive troubled economies and to restore their productivity. In

1983, Ghana's government under Flight Lieutenant Jerry John Rawlings turned to the World Bank and the International Monetary Fund (IMF) and accepted their recommendations in exchange for assistance packages to ease Ghana's economic and social transformation. Foremost among the changes enacted in Ghana were the disengagement of the government from an active role in the economy and the encouragement of free-market forces to promote the efficient and productive development of local resources. The reforms cut government budgets, privatized state-owned enterprises (SOEs), devalued the currency (the cedi), and rebuilt industrial infrastructure by means of assistance programs. As in other countries of Africa in the 1980s, government was identified as the problem, and free-market forces were seen as the solution to the socio-economic uplifting of their economies.

By the 1990s, the effects of structural adjustment in Ghana were beginning to be assessed. According to the World Bank and other Western financial institutions, the economy had become much more stable, and production was on a more solid footing than it had been a decade earlier. Exports were up, government deficits had been reduced, and inflation was down. Many Ghanaians, however, questioned whether the structural adjustment benefited all Ghanaians or just a few sectors of the economy. Critics of the World Bank charged, moreover, that it concentrated on infrastructure such as airports, roads, and other macroeconomic projects that did little to improve the lives of the average Ghanaian.

Under the sway of free-market forces, production had increased in Ghana's traditionally strong sectors, cocoa and gold, thereby reverting to the pre-independence economic structure; still, a more broadly based economy had not developed. In addition, substantial loans had been incurred by the government to promote those sectors—at the expense of recurrent budget expenditures such as health and education—without a compensatory increase in government revenues. Ironically, the tax breaks prescribed to encourage these sectors worked against increased government revenues, so that by 1992, tax revenues began to drop. In addition, jobs not only had been cut from the once-bloated public sector but also had not expanded in the more successful export sectors. Although the government claimed its finances were much healthier in the 1990s than in the 1980s, the long-term economic and social impact of structural adjustment was uncertain.

Relying heavily on the exploitation of some non-renewable and even endangered resources, Ghana's economic recovery still had to be expanded to create a broader and better balanced economy. In addition to cocoa, Ghana's leading export commodities are gold, a non-renewable resource, and timber, the harvesting of which has included more than eighteen endangered species of trees and has led to alarming deforestation. Furthermore, it is imperative for the Ghana government to be more creative and look for other policy options that can spruce up the economy—re-engineer the manufacturing sector and create more jobs. Government over-reliance on the oil sector could be counterproductive and unhealthy for the overall economic development. It is necessary to invest in the agriculture sector and make it healthier than it is now, and as the largest employing sector in the economy, it has the potential to stir growth. Government's creativity must also stretch to plug the holes in the system that allow for wastage of national funds.

Key Terms

Fiscal policy   Flat tax   Monetary policy   Progressive tax   Regressive tax

Regulating the economy   Promoting the economy   Economic policies

International Monetary Fund   World Bank   Liquefied petroleum gas

Monetarism   Keynesian   Single-digit inflation   European concessionaires

Monetary fund policy   World Labor Organization   European Union

Potential growth economy   Static growth economy   Inflation   Hyperinflation

Works Cited / Further Readings

Constitution of the Republic of Ghana (1992), Chapter 6, Article 40

Daily graphic Newspaper. 'What will save Ghana's textile industry?'

'Ghana: The World's Fastest Growing Economy in 2011, Press Centre, The presidency, Republic of Ghana. 1 January 2011. Retrieved 13 June 2011.

International Institute for Democracy and Electoral Assistance (2005), Electoral System Design: New International IDEA Handbook.

International Monetary Fund, 'Ghana', retrieved 22 January 2014.

Internet World Stats, 'Ghana: Internet Usage and Telecommunications Report', http://www.internetworldstats.com/af/gh.htm access date 24 April 2014.

Keukeleire, Stephan and Schunz, S. (2008) 'Foreign policy, globalization and global governance: The European Union's structural foreign policy', paper prepared for the ECPR Standing Group on the European Union Fourth Pan-European Conference on EU Politics, Riga), 25–27 September 2008.

McFaul, M., Magen, A., and Stoner-Weiss, K., 'Evaluating International Influences on Democratic Transition', a concept paper for Freeman Spogli Institute for International Studies, Stanford, California.

Millennium Development Authority. Ghana Fact Sheet, Kotoka International Airport Perishable Cargo Center, 2007–2013.

_____, Ghana Fact Sheet, Volta Lake Transport Services Ltd, 2007-2013.

Rakner, L., Menocal, A. R., and Fritz, V. (2007), 'Democratization's Third Wave and the Challenges of Democratic Deepening: Assessing International Democracy Assistance and Lessons Learned', a research project of the Advisory Board for Irish Aid.

Schedler, Andreas (1997), 'Concepts of Democratic Consolidation', paper prepared for delivery at the 1997 meeting of the Latin American Studies Association (LASA), Continental Plaza Hotel, Guadalajara, Mexico, 17–19 April 1997.

Schumpeter, Joseph (1974), *Capitalism, Socialism, and Democracy*, 2nd ed. (New York: Harper).

Rodney, Walter (1981), *How Europe Underdeveloped Africa* (Washington, D.C.: Howard University Press) revised edn.

Struthers, J. (1981), 'Inflation in Ghana (1966–78): A Perspective on the Monetarist v Structuralist Debate'.

World Bank, 'Data: GDP, PPP (current International $)', http://data.worldbank.org/indicator/NY.GDP.MKTP.PP.CD retrieved 2014-07-15.

Chapter 17

MAKING SOCIAL POLICY

What Is Social Policy?

When most Ghanaians hear the term 'social policy', they may probably think first about social policy emanating from laws, programs, and rules that address issues such as welfare, healthcare, crime, environmental problems, abortion, and education. Social policy debates tend to be complex and contentious because people often hold sharply contrasting views about the best course of action that benefits the people. Social policy is, to a large extent, dominated by economic policy, because economic policy determines the amount that government is prepared to spend. There are two main views of public spending: monetarist and Keynesian.

- *Monetarism* is based on a view of the economy as self-stabilizing. The economy requires actions intended to assist reduce hardship; for example, in times of economic stringency, such as inflation or depression, it is necessary for government to reduce spending, to allow for increased saving that will eventually lead to increased growth in the coming years. Furthermore, the monetarists believe that should the government fail to balance its budget, such will lead to inflationary pressures in the economy, reducing the value of that country's currency, and ultimately reducing the resources available to the private sector for the economy to expand productively.
- *Keynesianism* on the other hand sees government's intervention in the economy as necessary for the stability of the economy. Public spending is an important regulator, which can be used to stimulate the economy at a time of a slump or to damp down growth if it happens too quickly. Unemployment is unnecessarily wasteful. In the long run, Keynes

argued, the economy may correct itself; but in the long run, we are all dead.

In recent years, both views have been supplanted by a new financial orthodoxy, which combines government regulation with market-based provision, targeted expenditure, and balanced budgets.

Social Policy and Administration

Social policy and administration is an academic subject concerned with the study of social services and the welfare state. It developed in the early part of the twentieth century as a complement to social work studies, aimed at people who would be professionally involved in the administration of welfare. In the course of the last forty years, the range and breadth of the subject has developed. The principal areas relate to

- policy and administrative practice in social services, including health administration, social security, education, employment services, community care, and housing management;
- social problems, including crime, disability, unemployment, mental health, learning disability, and old age;
- issues relating to social disadvantage, including race, gender, and poverty; and
- the range of collective social responses to these conditions.

Social policy is a subject area, not a discipline; it borrows from other social science disciplines in order to develop study in the area. The contributory disciplines include sociology, social work, psychology, economics, political science, management, history, philosophy, and law.

Generally speaking, social policy debates are waged at two levels—at the big-picture, philosophical level and at the practical, implementation level. Philosophically, people may differ in their support for government action or inaction, the emphasis they place on liberty or order, republicanism or democracy. These opposing views are often deeply held and have significant implications for the ways citizens and politicians approach policy problems.

As an academic subject, social policy gained prominence in British universities after the Second World War, when the rapid expansion of key public services prompted interest in the emerging welfare state. In its early days, the subject was primarily concerned with what William Beveridge, the chief architect of the British welfare state, had termed the five giants. In modern terms, these giants were *poverty, ill health, poor housing, insufficient education,* and *unemployment*. For Beveridge, tackling these social ills was an essential part of post-war reconstruction. The roll-out of services to address these social ills marked a distinct shift in social citizenship and it was only natural that a new body of scholars would turn their attention to this important aspect of government policy.

However, over the course of the post-war period, social policy analysts began to identify gaps in the Beveridgean welfare state. Some highlighted the persistence of poverty amidst plenty. Others pointed to hidden giants of sexism and racism that the welfare state had failed to address. These criticisms reflected not only a concern with the weaknesses of government policy but a broadening of the focus of the academic subject of social policy, which began to draw much more widely on ideas from sociology and political science and adopted a more critical perspective on the welfare state. Moreover, the subject had become more international in scope too, recognizing that different countries adopted very different solutions to common problems.

In recent years, the subject has broadened its focus still further. The growing recognition that government needs to work with other groups in order to deliver effective social policies has meant that discussion of the role that charities, businesses, communities, and families can play features prominently in debate. The subject has become more international in scope, too, recognizing that different countries adopt very different solutions to common problems, making a focus on Britain alone unnecessarily restrictive. Indeed, the subject now recognizes that the global nature of key social problems—and the role of globalization in shaping the modern world—demand a global perspective. Added to this, social policy has drawn ideas from an even broader range of subjects—such as geography, demography, economics, management, and environmental science—as it looks for answers to the question of how best to maximize the well-being of people by a government such as Ghana's.

These philosophical differences also manifest themselves at the practical level. Assuming a societal value can be agreed upon, what is the best policy or set of policies to foster that value? For example, while Social Democrats in the National Democratic Congress (NDC) or the socialist Convention People's Party (CPP), the People's Progressive Party (PPP), and property-owning conservatives in the National Patriotic Party (NPP) generally agree that abortions should be rare and that poverty should be eliminated, they disagree sharply about the way to achieve these outcomes. Despite a broad support for quality education, there seems to be a difference of opinion in how many years, for example, high schools need to obtain a diploma in this country, but liberals, for instance, generally favour more national governmental involvement while conservatives support local independence and control. Bridging these practical gaps is not easy because of the philosophical foundations from which they arise.

The General Welfare versus Individual Interests

By definition, social policies are aimed at promoting the good of society at all times. The good of society, however, is not easily agreed upon. Virtually every public policy is aimed at making particular individuals better off. At the same time, other individuals might actually be made less well-off (at least in the short term) by the policy. For example, if a billionaire is required to pay hundreds of millions of dollars in taxes to support programs that provide food and shelter for the poor, the billionaire is financially worse off. Society (including the billionaire), however, is arguably better off because of the broader societal benefits of these programs, such as the curbing of armed robbery. Not everyone, though, agrees with this definition of societal good. Some people believe that the good of society is best promoted by giving individuals the tools (such as education and job training) to compete in a free market economy, not by redistributing wealth from the rich to the poor. That is why the livelihood and empowerment program (LEAP), currently being promoted by the Ministry of Women, Children and Social protection is not a good response to redistributing wealth in the country.

As the foregoing example illustrates, more often than not, differences in social policy debates often come down to different priorities in balancing liberty and order. People who emphasize liberty tend to believe that the government should play only a minimal role in the lives of the people, intervening only to protect their lives, liberty, and property. In contrast, those who emphasize order are more willing to sacrifice some measure of individual liberty to allow the government to provide more order and equality in society. For example, a policy that provides all individuals with an equality of start (the same educational opportunities and the same chances to compete fairly in the marketplace) emphasizes individual liberty and freedom. Alternatively, a policy that provides equality of finish, or roughly the same socio-economic outcomes for all individuals emphasizes order and equality.

In the United States, most social policies represent a carefully crafted balance between liberty and order. In many instances, dual policies address the same problem from both directions. For example, the economic well-being of individuals and families is promoted by the provision of public education and financial assistance for university education. It is also promoted through social welfare programs, such as free housing, health insurance benefits, and unemployment benefit payments. In the one case, individuals are given the tools to compete, while in the other they are provided with a safety net when they don't fare well in the economic marketplace.

Welfare Reform

In 2006, the New Patriotic Party (NPP) government dramatically shifted the balance between liberty and order in the delivery of welfare benefits to low-income individuals. Instead of guaranteeing welfare benefits to anyone who falls below a particular income level, the government allows assemblies to offer payments to old people and to people who are physically challenged. The change in policy guarantees less order and stability and while emphasizing individual liberty and responsibility. After a few years under the new program, the results are generally positive but some observers worry that many people, and especially young university graduates, are not finding satisfactory employment to take care of themselves.

Welfare policy debates in Ghana continue to be focused on balancing our freedom and justice against order, and equality against personal economic freedom. Significant problems loom large on the horizon—there are persistently high levels of individuals and families without health insurance and current projections suggest that the Social Security trust fund will not cover benefits ever, since what is paid out has become negligible. These and other issues will require citizens and their elected representatives to address and readdress societal priorities and the ways they are pursued.

The Welfare Application

There are ways of applying welfare to its recipients. The two methods are universality and selectivity. Universal benefits and services are benefits available to everyone as a right, or at least to whole categories of people (like old people, or children). Selective benefits and services are reserved for people in need. The arguments refer to the same issues as institutional and residual welfare, but there is an important difference. Institutional and residual welfare are principles; universality and selectivity are methods. A residual system might use a universal service where appropriate (e.g. a residual system of healthcare might be associated with universal public health); an institutional system needs some selective benefits to ensure that needs are met.

Universal services can reach everyone on the same terms. This is the argument for public services, like roads and sewers; it was extended in the 1940s to education and health services. The main objection to universal services is their cost. Selectivity is often presented as being more efficient: less money is spent to better effect. There are problems with selective services, however: because recipients have to be identified, the services can be administratively complex and expensive to run, and there are often boundary problems caused by trying to include some people while excluding others. Selective services sometimes fail to reach people in need.

The Politics of Welfare

Edmund Burke wrote that government is a contrivance of human wisdom to provide for human wants. Governments have a wide range of possible actions.

- *Governments establish rules.* Governments set the rules by which they and other organizations (like companies or charities) operate.

- *Governments coerce.* Governments can prohibit action (such as child abuse), or require some forms of action (such as sending children to school).
- *Governments provide or purchase services.* Provision means that states provide services themselves. Public housing, national health services, or state education are examples. Purchasing services implies that the state accepts responsibility for ensuring provision, but that the service can be obtained from another agency.
- *Governments subsidize.* Subsidy consists of a financial inducement to act in a particular way, which may be a reward for doing things (e.g. increasing employment), a form of compensation, or an incentive to do things. Tax can be used in the opposite direction, as a negative subsidy, e.g. to deter people from smoking.
- *Governments persuade.* Examples are propaganda, exhortation, and directed education.
- *Governments plan.* Governments steer a society by watching and adjusting policy.
- *Governments produce.* Like independent organizations, governments may offer services to customers, e.g. insurance, banking, or commercial production. There is no rule which says that government activity has to be tax-based or financed.

What Is Social Protection?

In the literature on social policies, there are many different definitions of social protection a country extends to its citizens. The International Labour Organization (ILO) defines social protection as having to do with a country instituting measures intended to 'put in place security measures in the face of vulnerabilities and contingencies; such as having access to health care and working in safety'. Social protection is an important strategy to protect people from chronic poverty and from risks and shocks. Other definitions explain the term 'social protection' as a broader meaning than the term 'social security'. There are two main dimensions of social security: income security and availability of medical care. The term 'social protection' includes the different measures and programs which are introduced to achieve the aims of social security. The measures are supposed to provide a healthy life and a secure retirement through, for example, health insurances and pension schemes. A social protection scheme has to support the people who cannot afford, for example, a short or extended hospital stay. It is based on financial support of the state and on contributions by the members of the schemes. A national social protection program is supposed to promote income security through a basic set of guarantees. Social protection scheme also provides:

- a nationwide access to healthcare services
- income security for children by cash transfers or transfers in kind to ensure the access to nutrition, education, and care
- financial support of disabled and diseased people and people who are not able to work for a limited duration because of maternity or illness
- income security for residents in old age and with disabilities.

Social Protection in Ghana

a. *Program / Strategy / Law and Date Subject Matter (Social Security Act 1965)*—provident fund scheme, lump sum payment for old age, invalidity and survivor's benefits
b. *Social Security Law 1991*—conversion of the provident fund scheme to a Pension scheme (SSNIT)
c. *Ghana Growth and Poverty Reduction Strategy (GPRS I) 2002–2005*—established in order to achieve the Millennium Development Goals of the United Nations
d. *National Health Insurance Scheme (NHIS) 2003*—introduced a contribution scheme for the Health Insurance under the National Health Insurance Authority (NHIA)
e. *Ghana School Feeding Program (GSFP) 2005*—government offers one hot meal a day for every schoolchild in Ghana
f. Ghana Growth and Poverty Reduction Strategy II (GPRS II) 2006–2009—government initiative to make Ghana a middle-income country by 2015

Social Protection in Ghana

At Ghana's independence in 1957, the government provided free healthcare services to its population which was solely financed from tax revenues. However, it was not sustainable because the government of Ghana redirected its resources on other sectors of the economy. From that time on, different nominal fees were introduced to social programs that the government started to introduce to Ghanaians. After a while the cash and carry system was established which provided medical treatment solely by direct payment of citizens. Besides the governmental system, there had always been traditional systems of social protection which were based on the help and support of the extended family. Culturally in Ghana, families were responsible for taking care of their old and invalid members of the family (rural extended family care). The elderly people took care of the children and they expected the younger ones to take care of them when they retired. Adults were responsible for financing the material needs of the children and the elderly members of the family.

But with the rise of modern society and the expanding globalization and urbanization, the extended family system was weakened. Because of the migration of the younger family members into the cities, there was now a lack of support in the traditional social protection scheme. The family was no more capable of supporting the diseased and old members of the family on their own. Informal and traditional forms of social protection which were based on the above-mentioned extended family system or religious networks therefore came to an end, hence the introduction of many of the programs that we see today in Ghana. Despite the fact that there had been ambitions to cover all the needy people, there are still many people excluded from the benefits of being socially protected. Most of all, the problem that is confronting government today is how to cover the workers in the informal sector of the economy. In addition there is the problem of how to integrate women and youth into the scheme, because if they are excluded there is a high risk for them of sliding into a lifelong poverty with all its negative aspects.

In 1991 a provident fund scheme became a pension scheme through the implementation of the Social Security Law. The pension scheme named Social Security and National Insurance Trust (SSNIT) mandated that there ought to be a contribution of 17.5 per cent in total of the monthly workers' salaries. The law stipulated that, for every pay cheque that a worker gets, 5 per cent of the earnings should be paid by the employee and 12.5 per cent by the employer. The self-employed were expected to contribute the total amount of 17.5 per cent by themselves. The three basic benefits were (1) old age pension, (2) invalidity pension, and (3) death-survivors payment. When the National Social Protection Strategy started in 2007/2008, as will be described in the following section, several new measures arose with it. Because of the implementation of the New Pensions Act / National Pension Regulatory Authority (NPRA) in 2010, the SSNIT contributions were raised in total from 17.5 per cent to 18.5 per cent of the monthly workers' salaries. Furthermore, the structure of the pension scheme was enlarged by the introduction of a third tier. The newly established three-tier scheme was constructed as the following elaborations show: (1) a mandatory basic national security system (SSNIT) → defined benefit scheme, (2) a mandatory fully funded and privately managed occupational pension scheme → defined contribution scheme, (3) a voluntary fully funded and privately managed provident fund and personal pension scheme → defined contribution scheme. Out of the 18.5 per cent of the monthly workers' salaries, 13.5 per cent goes to the first-tier mandatory, the SSNIT, and 5 per cent goes to the private mandatory second-tier. From the SSNIT money, 2.5 per cent goes to the National Health Insurance Scheme Levy for Health Care, which is going to be explained in the following section of this chapter, and 11 per cent goes to the pensions. The minimum age to enter the SSNIT is fifteen years and the maximum age is forty-five years. The third tier was newly established in 2010. People can join it voluntarily in addition to the mandatory first and second-tier. First of all this is a benefit for the people working in the informal sector because they were not covered by the SSNIT and by the private mandatory second-tier. The introduction of the third tier is highly important for the Ghanaian Social Protection System because over 80 per cent of the workers are working in the informal sector. The workers who want to be covered from the third tier have to contribute 16.5 per cent of their monthly salaries. The informal workers have two different accounts: (1) the retirement account, (2) the personal savings account. Because of the second account, informal workers are able to receive benefits before their retirement. Currently the SSNIT has an active membership of over one million people; amongst them are over 100,000 pensioners and 90,000 contributors from the informal sector. Since January 2011, pensioners who were already on the SSNIT receive a financial amount of 52.14 GHS per month whereas new pensioners get 45.06 GHS since the implementation of the Social Security Act. A provident fund scheme was created, which provided money for lump sum payments for old age, invalidity, and survivor's benefits.

The implementation of the NPRA Act 766 in 2010 affected the contributions to SSNIT in a negative way. Contributions to SSNIT dropped by 27 per cent. This is because the annuity for lump sums payments extended from seventy-two to seventy-five years, and at the same time, the minimum monthly contribution needed for retirement had dropped from 240 to 180 GHS per month. This led to an effect which was not intended.

Highly Indebted Poor Country (HIPC) Fund

In 2003 the government decided to establish the Highly Indebted Poor Country (HIPC) Fund; this was an instrument intended to reduce poverty and the debt burden of the country. At the time Ghana spent almost half of its gross domestic product to service external debts. Because of this situation that Ghana found itself in during the time, there was only little money left for investments in the social sector, and poverty started affecting the way the country was developing along the United Nations development index. Ghana therefore took advantage of a request to join what was then known as highly indebted categories of countries. By joining the HIPC Initiative, Ghana's main creditors agreed to erase, over time, all old debts that Ghana owed, so the intended interest and debt payments could be reinvested in the social sector to reduce poverty. Hence the country had to develop a poverty-reduction strategy and used the money from the HIPC fund to finance the programs out of this strategy.

National Social Protection Strategy and Ghana

By recognizing that growth and mainstream development interventions are not sufficient to reduce the huge number of people living in poverty and to protect the people from natural or economic shocks, the Ghanaian government further decided on two strategies to ameliorate the situation of the vulnerable groups:

government introduced the National Social Protection Strategy (NSPS) and the Ghana Growth and Poverty Reduction Strategy (GPRS), which actually was a build-up of the Strategies I and II programs. Furthermore, in 2007/2008 the NSPS started, which contained several different measures intended to reduce poverty and lead to achieving the first Millennium Development Goal of the UN. It included three main strategies to tackle extreme poverty. The first was to establish a new social grant scheme to provide a basic and secure income for the most vulnerable households. The second was a better poverty strategy targeting existing social protection programs. The third was a package of complementary inputs. The first GPRS (2002–2005) found its major topic in establishing special programs for the excluded and vulnerable. By this time the Poverty and Social Impact Assessment (PSIA) pointed out that just the economic growth would not be sufficient to counteract exclusion and extreme poverty. Hence the GPRS II (2006–2009) focus was on growth and Ghana becoming a middle-income country by the year 2015. The aims of the NSPS and the GPRS I and II were also intended to achieve a poverty reduction by implementing measures such as the Livelihood Empowerment Against Poverty (LEAP) social grants scheme and the National Health Insurance Scheme (NHIS), which will be explained in the following section. Among other things, the GPRS I intended to end gender discrimination as a consequence of poverty and that it has to be removed by poverty reduction strategies.

National Health Insurance Scheme (NHIS)

The Government of Ghana established the National Health Insurance Scheme (NHIS) under Act 650 in 2003. The scheme was launched in order to provide basic healthcare services to persons resident in the country through mutual and private health insurance schemes. It was launched to replace the former cash-and-carry system which forced people to pay money in cash when they needed to see a doctor or to go to a hospital. There are three types of schemes available under the law: (1) the district-wide mutual health insurance scheme (they operate across a district where all residents can become members), (2) the private mutual health insurance scheme (these private schemes are not restricted to a specific region or district, all Ghanaians can become members), (3) the private commercial health insurance scheme—these provide health insurance services for particular groups of people like church members, who build their own mutual health insurance schemes. Within the establishment of this scheme, the districts of Ghana are divided into health insurance communities to give all the Ghanaians the opportunity to participate in the scheme. By the implementation of the National Health Insurance Scheme (NHIS), the people who are benefiting from the scheme get a card which enables them to go to the hospital without making immediate cash payments. The hospital will then send the bills to one's scheme provider which then pays for the delivered services by the health clinic or hospital. The NHIS is financed by (a) the premiums of subscribers (one has to register and then pay a premium depending on one's income) (b) 2.5 per cent National Health Insurance Levy (c) 2.5 per cent SSNIT, deductions from the formal sector (d) funds from the government of Ghana to be allocated by Parliament and (e) returns from investment. In 2008 there were almost 12.3 million registered members representing 54 per cent of the Ghanaian population. Because of the fact that there was still a lack in covering the most vulnerable groups, the president of Ghana decided in May 2008 that all children under eighteen would receive a free membership to the health insurance scheme; besides, all pregnant women during their pregnancy will be offered free medical services under the program.

School Feeding Program (SFP)

The Ghana School Feeding Program (GSFP) was launched in 2005 in order to achieve the Millennium Development Goal concerning the reduction of hunger. It is an initiative of the Comprehensive Africa Agricultural Development Program (CAADP) pillar 3 assisted by the New Partnership for Africa's Development (NEPAD). The cost of the GSFP is shared between the government of Ghana and its international development partners and donors. One of the most important donors is the government of the Netherlands, who commits about twenty-five million US dollars for the program every year. The main overriding objectives of the GSFP are three: (1) to aid in increasing school enrolment, attendance, and retention; (2) reduce hunger and malnutrition; (3) boost domestic food production. Moreover, children in deprived public primary schools and kindergartens receive at least one hot nutritious meal a day. The meal should be prepared from locally grown foodstuffs; however, the program's objectives are being abused because the children are fed from imported rice rather than locally grown rice, which is nutritious. The program started with 10 pilot schools out of each Ghanaian region. Currently the GSFP covers about 1,698 public schools, and by doing this, it provides one hot meal a day to 656,624 children in the 170 districts of Ghana. In the years from 2006 to 2010, the program has covered 1,500,000 pupils spread throughout the districts of Ghana. The GSFP was supposed to end in 2010 but President John Mahama's administration agreed to extend the program for another year.

Livelihood Empowerment against Poverty (LEAP)

The Livelihood Empowerment against Poverty (LEAP) social grant scheme is a program that is coordinated from the offices of the Ministry of Manpower, Youth, and Employment (MMYE). The objective of the programs is to decrease poverty levels in Ghana and to provide a better life for the Ghanaian population. It started as a five-year pilot program from 2008 to 2012 and it offers financial support to orphan/vulnerable children, people over sixty-five years, and people with disabilities. It had been implemented since mid-2009 and in 2010 it covered 81 of 170 districts with 45,000 households. Until this program, there had never been a program like this before that provided the most vulnerable groups in Ghana livelihood of any sort. The needy households are selected on a base which contains the combination of poverty status and presence of any one of the three categories of vulnerable groups. Around 28.5 per cent of Ghana's population is poor, whereof 18.2 per cent can be described as extremely poor and are targeted by the LEAP authorities. LEAP supports selected households with monthly cash transfer between GHS 8 and GHS 15, which depends on the number of needy people living in the household. The cash transfers to the people with disabilities or the old people above sixty-five are unconditional. To get the cash transfer for orphan/vulnerable children households, they have to follow conditions as listed below: (1) promise to send children to school, (2) not allowing child labour whether at home or in farm work, (3) enrolment of family members onto the National Health Insurance Scheme (NHIS), (4) registering the childbirth of all children. The cash transfers are funded by the government of Ghana and the money comes from the consolidated fund of the government. The total cost of LEAP is between 0.1 per cent and 0.2 per cent of total government expenditure (something in the figure of, say, 4.2 million US dollars). Because of the increase of food and fuel prices in 2008, the World Bank decided to support the government of Ghana by providing cash transfers to additional 28,000 households to protect them from the negative impact of the price hikes. There are other donors who invested in the MMYE, like UNICEF, ILO, and the government of Brazil. Besides the cash transfers, all the people who are covered by the LEAP have access to a free health insurance. They have to go to the responsible office in their district to register.

Other Social Protection Programs in Ghana

In addition to the above programs, there are other programs which are supposed to reduce poverty and to build up an effective and sufficient social protection scheme. Other social programs, not specifically mentioned and narrated are the (a) social welfare programs, (b) the Supplementary Feeding Program, (c) capitation grant, (d) the National Youth Employment Program, (e) the Integrated Agricultural Support Program, (f) the microfinance schemes operated by MASLOC, and the emergency management schemes.

Challenges and Prospects of Social Protection in Ghana

There have been attempts by the government of Ghana to establish an efficient social protection scheme that are comparable and good in contrast to many ones by other African governments to reduce poverty. But the programs so established in Ghana have a lot of problems stemming from the very moment most of them were established in Ghana, hence the fact that many are facing several challenges. The following parts are some selected challenges and solutions proffered to help overcome some of the challenges. Furthermore, this section offers suggestions on some possible prospects of the social protection scheme in Ghana.

Conclusion

In most welfare states like Ghana, substantial efforts are also made to mitigate socio-economic inequalities in primary income distribution through secondary redistribution, that is, government spending on social programs funded by progressive income taxation together with tax expenditures (tax deductions for social insurance or charity contributions, as well as negative income taxation for the working poor). Historically, such reductions in socio-economic inequality have been pursued to achieve four objectives: (1) to reduce the costs of production for employers, especially through unemployment, health, and pension schemes; (2) to maintain social peace, that is, to forestall both radical unionism within the factory, primarily via accident insurance, as well as threats to private property from leftist or rightist political radicalism in society as a whole, particularly, that of ethnicism; (3) to secure equality of economic opportunity, seen as conducive both to social peace and to economic growth; and (4) to enrich the status of citizenship beyond civil and political equality by including a social dimension, as articulated by T. H. Marshall in 1950. In Ghana, the Ministry of Gender, Children, and Social Protection, have instituted a set of government programs aimed at ensuring citizens' welfare in the face of contingencies of life. All welfare states provide direct state assistance to the poor in cash (e.g. social assistance) and in kind (e.g. housing and social services), as well as social insurance against the financial consequences of certain biological risks (illness, incapacity to work, childbirth, child-rearing, old age) and occupational risks (unemployment, accident, or injury). Whereas social assistance—in the United States popularly termed *welfare*—entails redistribution from the non-poor to the poor, social insurance rarely does so and instead can be understood primarily as redistribution across the individual life course, from periods of employment to periods of inability to work. In Ghana, legislation for the provision of a modern national social security system went into effect in 1965. Further legislation was passed in 1970 to convert the system into a pension plan to provide for sickness, maternity, and work-related injury benefits. Government welfare programs at the time were the responsibility of the Department of Social Welfare under the Ministry of Labour and Social Welfare (now the Ministry of Gender and Social Protection). As the national economy was reformed, the Workers' Compensation Act of 1986 was passed to guarantee wages to workers in the private sector while they were undergoing treatment for work-related injuries.

Social security is a human right as it is stated in the Declaration of Human Rights from 1949. However, there is still much space for improvements in existing social security schemes, especially in Africa. The already implemented National Social Protection Strategy (NSPS) in Ghana contains different measures which all intend one goal: building a social protection system which is affordable to everyone and further protects them from risks and shocks. The Millennium Development Goals, signed by the United Nations (UN) and expected to be achieved by the year 2015, was missed. Addressing many different aspects of extreme poverty, the first goal was to halve proportion of people living in extreme poverty during the years from 1990 to 2015. Hence, Ghana started to introduce different measures in order to achieve those goals. The persistence was a key dimension in the debate about poverty, which ought be overcome by implementing social protection strategies, for the short but also for the long term. In doing so, Ghana took examples of different measures in several developing or emerging countries which have worked out efficiently. Such a program on social security in Ghana is geared to this program as will be shown later in this chapter. The first part of this chapter is going to give a short introduction into the topic of social protection. Further it is going to give a brief overview of some of the programs currently taking place in Ghana with the objective of solidifying Ghana's social policies. Some of the social interventions that Ghana is taking to showcase its social policies are the following: the Social Security and National Insurance Trust (SSNIT), the National Health Insurance Scheme (NHIS), the Ghana School Feeding Programs (GSFP), and the Livelihood Empowerment Against Poverty (LEAP). These programs are just some examples out of the number of programs from the Ministry of Manpower, Youth, and Employment (MMYE), which the government is piloting. The brief overview of the strategies and programs is given in order to assist as a background for the second part of the chapter which is going to deal with the prospects and challenges of the social protection scheme and its measures in Ghana. It is going to figure out under what conditions government and political elites have to implement them and sustain social protection policies and also how the short to the long term would look, for the social protection scheme in Ghana.

Key Terms

Policy feedback   Unionism   Social democracy   Fascism   Legitimating

Neoliberal   Social policy   Political change   Social welfare

Keynesian economics   Feedback   Liberal individualism   Liberty

Equality   Fraternity   Social doctrine   Compensation

Government welfare programs   National Economic Reforms

Compensation Act   Workers' compensation   Social security Legislation

Redistribution Equality   Social insurance   Prudence   Articulation
Reforms   Social net   Multiculturalism

Works Cited / Further Readings

Adu-Gyamfi, O. (2011), 'SSNIT increases pension payment'.

Agyepong, I. A. and Adjei, S. (2007), 'Public social policy development and implementation: a case study of the Ghana National Health Insurance scheme'.

Aidukaite, Jolanta (2004), 'The Emergence of the Post-Socialist Welfare States—The Case of the Baltic States: Estonia, Latvia, and Lithuania', Ph.D. diss., Stockholm University.

Alesina, Alberto, and Glaeser, Edward L. (2004), *Fighting Poverty in the US and Europe* (Oxford: Oxford University Press).

Baidoo, R. (2009), 'Toward a Comprehensive Healthcare System in Ghana', retrieved 14 September 2011.

Banting, Keith G. and Kymlicka, Will (2004), 'Do Multiculturalism Policies Erode the Welfare State? in Philippe van Parijs (ed.), *Cultural Diversity versus Economic Solidarity*, 227–284 (Brussels: Deboeck Université Press).

Bommes, Michael and Geddes, Andrew (2000) (eds.), *Immigration and Welfare: Challenging the Borders of the Welfare State* (London and New York: Routledge).

Bonoli, Giuliano (1997), 'Classifying Welfare States: A Two-Dimensional Approach'

, *Journal of Social Policy*, 26 (3): 351–372.

Brooks, Clem and Jeff Manza (2006), 'Social Policy Responsiveness in Developed Democracies', *American Sociological Review* 71 (3): 474–494.

Castles, Francis G. (1985), *The Working Class and Welfare: Reflections on the Political Development of the Welfare State in Australia and New Zealand, 1890–1980* (Wellington, New Zealand: Allen and Unwin).

——— and Deborah Mitchell (1993), 'Worlds of Welfare and Families of Nations', in Francis G. Castles (ed.), *Families of Nations: Patterns of Public Policy in Western Democracies*, 93–128 (Aldershot, U and Brookfield, VT: Dartmouth).

Cichon, M., C. Behrendt, and V. Wodsak (2011), 'The UN Social Protection Floor Initiative: Moving forward with the Extension of Social Security', retrieved September, 20, 2011

Dei, H. (2001), 'Public Pension Fund Management in Ghana', retrieved 16 August 2011.

Ghana Ministry of Finance and Economic Planning (2011), http://mofep.gov.gh/budget.cfm, http://mofep.gov.gh/hipc.pdf

Ghana School Feeding Program (2011), Ghana School Feeding Program Initiative and the Farmers Dream, retrieved 23 August 2011.

Garcia, A. B. and Gruat, J. V. (2003), 'Social Protection / Social Justice—A life cycle continuum investment', retrieved 25 August 2011 from

Hippler, Arthur (2005), *Citizens of the Heavenly City: A Catechism of Catholic Social Teaching* (Catholic Answers).

The Peerage, 'William Henry Beveridge, 1st and last Baron Beveridge http://www.thepeerage.com/p14225.htm#i142249 retrieved 29 March 2013.

Pierson, Paul (1993 'When Effect Becomes Cause: Policy Feedback and Political Change', *World Politics* 45 (4): 595–628.

Vatican, *Compendium of the Social Doctrine of the Church*, available online from http://www.vatican.va/roman_curia/pontifical_councils/justpeace/documents/rc_pc_justpeace_doc_20060526_compendio-dott-soc_en.html

Yeates, Nicola (2002), 'Globalization and Social Policy: From Global Neoliberal Hegemony to Global Political Pluralism', *Global Social Policy* 2 (1): 69–91.

Chapter 18

MAKING FOREIGN AND DEFENCE POLICY

Understanding Foreign Policy

Foreign policy dictates how a country will act with respect to other countries politically, socially, economically, and militarily, and to a somewhat lesser extent, how it behaves towards non-state actors. Foreign policy can also be known as international relations policy or simply diplomacy. In the African context, foreign policy has been around from time immemorial when large tribes would presumably interact from time to time without engaging in an all-out war. However, these relations today are handled by governments through ministers of state, ambassadors, and other envoys selected by their countries to perform these responsibilities.

In broad terms, Ghana's foreign policies are aimed at maintaining and promoting the favourable position and security of the Republic of Ghana in the international arena. The goals of Ghanaian foreign policy, however, are not always clear. How involved should Ghana be in the affairs of other nations? Should it only use its military to defend and intimidate others at its borders or should it be involved in peacekeeping efforts around the world? Should Ghana attempt to trade freely with other nations, or should it enact restrictive tariffs to protect Ghanaian companies and manufacturers? As Ghana faces the new millennium, there are familiar calls to become more isolated from the rest of the world, while others argue that the nation must remain an active participant in the world community, even as the world becomes a more uncertain and dangerous place.

Ghana's foreign policy since independence has been characterized by a commitment to the principles and ideals of non-alignment and pan-Africanism as first enunciated by Kwame Nkrumah in the early 1960s. Non-alignment meant complete independence from the policies and alliances of both East (then USSR) and West (America and Europe) and support for a worldwide union of so-called non-aligned nations as a counter to both East and West power blocs. Pan-Africanism, by contrast, was a specifically African policy that envisioned the liberation of African peoples from Western colonialism and the eventual economic and political unity of the African continent. Another important principle of Ghana's foreign policy involves the closest possible cooperation with neighbouring countries with which the people of Ghana share cultural history, ties of blood, and economics. The results have included various bilateral trade and economic agreements and permanent joint commissions involving Ghana and its immediate neighbours, sometimes in the face of latent ideological and political differences and mutual suspicion, as well as numerous reciprocal state visits by high-ranking officials. These measures have contributed significantly to sub regional cooperation, development, and the reduction of tension.

Who Makes Foreign Policy?

The Constitution of Ghana gives the president the clear upper hand in the conduct of foreign policy. The president is the commander-in-chief of the nation's armed forces. As the single officer of Ghana charged with receiving the leaders of other nations and with negotiating treaties, the president is also the nation's chief diplomat. The president, however, does not have the authority to make foreign policy independently. The Constitution gives the Parliament the power to check the president's foreign policy powers in important ways. While the president can order Ghana's military into action to respond to emergencies and threats to the security of the nation, Parliament must authorize him to officially declare war. In treaty making, the president must also work together with the Parliament. While the president is free to negotiate treaties between Ghana and other nations, treaties must be ratified by the Parliament before they are officially binding on Ghana.

Ghana's Foreign Policy

Foreign relations of Ghana are controlled by the Ministry of Foreign Affairs of Ghana. In Ghana, the Ministry of Foreign Affairs is the sector body responsible for the conduct of Ghana's external relations as spelt out in articles 40, 41, 73, and 84 of the 1992 fourth republican Constitution. Its mission and statement of purpose is to promote and protect the interest of Ghana and its citizens abroad and safeguard Ghana's security and prosperity through the promotion of friendly and productive relations with all countries, to enhance Ghana's image abroad. The ministry is also to promote economic cooperation between Ghana and other countries through increased Ghana exports, foreign investments, expanding tourism, and seeking scientific, technology, and cultural links. Its functions also include the provision of economic, political, and security information and advice to government, as well as the provision of prompt and reliable information to Ghanaian nationals abroad to encourage them to participate in Ghana's economic development. In addition to the above, the ministry is also to advise government on the formulation of policies on international development likely to affect the enhancement of Ghana's security and to implement Ghana's foreign policy objectives; to play an active role as a member of the UN, AU, ECOWAS, NAM, ACP, the Commonwealth, and other international organizations of which Ghana is a member. The ministry is also to promote healthy political and economic relations with all countries, and to provide efficient consular services within and outside Ghana. Finally, the ministry is to upgrade the ministry's human and institutional capacity for the efficient execution of Ghana's foreign policy objectives and others.

Ghana is active in the United Nations and many of its specialized agencies, the World Trade Organization, the Non-Aligned Movement, the Organization of African Unity (OAU), the African Union (AU), and the Economic Community of West African States. The broad objectives of Ghana's foreign policy thus include maintaining friendly relations and cooperation with all countries that desire such cooperation, irrespective of ideological considerations, on the basis of mutual respect and non-interference in each other's internal affairs. Africa and its liberation and unity are naturally the cornerstones of Ghana's foreign policy. As a founding member of the Organization of African Unity (OAU), Ghana's foreign policy is to adhere faithfully to the OAU (now AU) charter.

Besides close commitment to the African Union (AU), Ghana's foreign policy is based on good neighbourliness, with its centrepiece being the West African region and the Economic Community of West African States (ECOWAS), consisting of fifteen countries. Apart from the relationship to the nearest French-speaking neighbours, Côte d'Ivoire, Burkina Faso, and Togo, relations with Nigeria are of particular importance to Ghana. Ghana is mindful of threats from terrorism, organized crime, drug trafficking, and maritime criminality—threats which are best handled through a regional approach. African unity has been central to Ghanaian foreign policy ever since its independence in 1957. Ghana was, thus, the founder of the Organization of African Unity (OAU), the predecessor of the AU. Therefore, Ghanaian governments always side closely with the AU on international issues. Ghana also founded the Non-Aligned Movement and entered the G77 group, and other South–South collaborations that continue to play a major role in the Ghanaian foreign policy. For both political and economic reasons, the relations to the BRIC countries have been strengthened. Ghana is also a major contributor to UN peacekeeping operations, and currently Ghanaian troops (military, police, and civilian) are involved in a number of UN missions in Africa. Another important principle of Ghana's foreign policy involves the closest possible cooperation with neighbouring countries with which the people of Ghana share cultural history, ties of blood, and economics. The results have included various bilateral trade and economic agreements and permanent joint commissions involving Ghana and its immediate neighbours, sometimes in the face of latent ideological and political differences and mutual suspicion, as well as numerous reciprocal state visits by high-ranking officials. These measures have contributed significantly to sub regional cooperation, development, and the reduction of tension.

From March of 2015, President John Mahama has headed ECOWAS as chairman of the regional organization, and Ghana has hosted several high-level meetings to handle threats through a regional approach. The pressing issues on the agenda of the ECOWAS chairman were the fight against terrorism, and being carried out by Boko Haram in Nigeria, critical issues regarding the ECOWAS Early Warning System, and how ECOWAS could provide military and economic support in the fight against Ebola. The Ebola virus has as at March 2015 claimed over 8,000 lives in Guinea, Sierra Leone, Liberia, Senegal, and other countries around the West African sub region. Liberia in March opened its borders for the first time in six months since the start of the Ebola virus and the resultant deaths in the sub region.

Ghana's Defence Policy

The origins of the Ghana Army stemmed from the command structure of the British Army—the then West Africa Command. The last command of this structure was dissolved on 1 July 1956 when Lt. Gen. Sir Otway Herbert left the West Africa Command in 1955 as the last commander. When Ghana obtained its independence in 1957, the Ghana Army consisted of its headquarters, support services, three battalions of infantry, and a reconnaissance squadron with armoured cars. At the time, the total strength of the Ghana Army was approximately 5,700 men. There was an oversupply of British officers after the end of the Second World War. There was only 12 per cent of the officer corps in Ghana; 29 officers out a total of 209 in all were Ghanaians at independence. Under the command of Major General Alexander Paley, there were about 200 British officers and 230 warrant officers and senior commissioned officers posted throughout the Ghanaian Army.

To immediately Africanize the Ghana army, Ghana's Prime Minister Kwame Nkrumah quickly established the following: in 1961, 4th and 5th Battalions were established, and in 1964 6th Battalion was established, from a parachute unit originally raised in 1963. Additionally, the second infantry brigade group was established in 1961 to command the two battalions inaugurated that year. However, 3rd Battalion was disbanded in February 1961 after an August 1960 mutiny while on *Operation des Nations Unies au Congo* service at Tshikapa in the Democratic Republic of the Congo. But the changeover from British to Ghanaian officers meant a sudden lowering of experience levels since most of the senior British officers had either retired or were sent back to England. Initial British planning by Paley before his departure in 1959 had provided for all British officers to be withdrawn by 1970; however, under pressure from Nkrumah, Paley's successor Major General Henry Alexander revised the plans, by ensuring that all British personnel departed before 1962. Determined to indigenize his armed forces fully, Dr Nkrumah by September 1961 abruptly dismissed his British officers, including Major General Henry Alexander after some years of accelerated promotion of Ghanaian personnel.

The Ministry of Defence

The Ministry of Defence (MOD) exists to proactively promote national defence interests through effective formulation, coordination, monitoring and evaluation of defence policies and programs. The army is also established to maintain the Ghana Armed Forces (GAF) in a high state of preparedness for national and international engagements, and be always active in the promotion of peace and stability in the country and the sub region.

Aims and Objectives

In pursuit of the above vision and mission, the ministry is guided by the following objectives: to enhance defence policy and control and to improve the state of combat readiness of the military. The army is also established to improve the national effort aimed at transforming the nature of the economy to achieve growth and accelerate poverty reduction especially among the vulnerable and excluded. The army is to improve logistics and infrastructure facilities in the country and, most importantly, improve civil-military relations.

Functions

In keeping with its mission, the ministry exercises supervisory role and ministerial responsibility over the following institutions: (a) the Ghana Armed Forces, consisting of the Army, Navy, and Air Force, and the following specified training institutions with the GAF: (b) Veterans Association of Ghana (VAG), (c) Offices of the Defence Advisers attached to Ghana's mission in London, Washington DC, New Delhi, Abuja, and Cairo. The military works in close collaboration with the National Security Council and the Ghana Armed Forces Council in the formulation of national defence policies relating to internal security and external peacekeeping operations. The ministry also prepares and executes Defence Annual Estimates. It also defends other interests of the GAF and VAG before Cabinet and Parliament and provides political leadership, guidance, and sound interpretation of government policies.

The Office of Defence, Military, Naval, and Air Attaché (DMNAA) of Ghana's embassy worldwide serves the interests of Ghana's government by promoting national defence issues between Ghana and the rest of the world. The main objective of the department is to uphold the mission and vision of the Ministry of Defence in Ghana through effective harmonization, monitoring, and assessment of defence policies and programs as well as supporting and justifying Ghana's defence policies around the world. The department also provides the Ministry of Defence in Ghana with information on various countries' military and political issues, fosters and strengthens continues relationship between Ghana and the rest of the world and also serves as the Ghana's ambassadors' adviser on defence issues, among others. Ghana's army has since its inception contributed forces to numerous UN and ECOWAS operations, including the Balkans, Afghanistan, Democratic Republic of the Congo, Lebanon, and Liberia (ECOMOG and UNMIL). Ghana contributed UN peacekeeping in UNAMIR during the Rwandan genocide.

Conclusion

Foreign policy constitutes a critical component of a country's conduct of public policy as it relates to other actors (both state and non-state) in the larger international system or the external environment. In this regard, consideration must be given to all the important actors on the international scene that affect the policymaking and implementation processes of the country concerned. The policy decisions include relations with other nations, international and non-governmental organizations, institutions, and agencies, as well as individuals, in so far as they impact on the system of inputs and outputs. The dynamics of policy choice that entail the processes of formulation and implementation, sometimes conflicting, other times cordial, determine the character, content, direction, and the possible impact of the country's foreign policy. Foreign policy has attracted different meanings and definitions from both scholars and practitioners. It is viewed by some as 'the sum total of official external relations conducted by an independent actor (usually a state) in international relations'. Increasingly, however, different categories of actors and their relations, not exclusively states but encompassing international actors such as agencies, companies, and organizations, have entered the matrix of foreign relations. In this regard, multinational corporations, religious organizations and movements, intergovernmental institutions and non-governmental organizations (NGOs), development agencies and charities like Oxfam, CARE, etc. have become critical components in the foreign policy calculus and determination.

Key Terms

Bureaucracy   Policy option   Open borders   Cooperation   Regionalism

Borderless   Terrorism   South–South collaborations

Permanent joint commissions   Non-interference   Non-Aligned Movement

Restrictive tariffs   Latent ideological   French-speaking neighbours

Agenda   Mutual respect   Early warning system

Non-alignment   Bilateral trade   Immemorial   Organized crime

Works Cited / Further Readings

Asante, K. B. (2006), 'Are we developing a complex of inferiority?' *Daily Graphic*, 19 June 2006, p. 7.

Dougherty, James and Robert Pfaltzgraff (2001), *Contending Theories of International Relations* (New York: Longman), pp. 553–554.

Ikenberry, G. John (2002), American Foreign Policy—Theoretical Essays, fourth edition (New York: Addison-Wesley Educational Publishers Inc.), pp. 4–5.

Morgenthau, Hans (1993), *Politics among Nations: The Struggle for Power and Peace*, brief edition (New York: McGraw-Hill Inc.), pp. 124–179.

Nkrumah, Kwame (1963), *Africa Must Unite*, p. 136–137

Waltz, *Theory of International Politics*, p. 126.

Chapter 19

REGIONALISM AND REGIONALIZATION IN AFRICA

Regional Integration

The interest by many countries in regional integration and cooperation around the world became a phenomenon because of the success of the European experience. The idea of regional integration reflected a growing appreciation of the benefits to be derived from regional unity and cooperation in meeting the challenges posed by increasing competitiveness in world markets. Scholars have written and spoken severally of the benefits of coming together as one condition, among many of achieving economic integration. They have also written about how unity deriving from small countries can serve as a way of collectively arresting those countries' political, economic, and social problems. For such 'want to develop' countries, a comprehensive document intended to arrest the various levels of poverty, by De Melo and Panagariya in 1992, CEC 1992, called 'New Regionalism', spoke about the benefits of globalization. Globalization, they stressed, is the process of integration of cultures—a new phenomenon that was sweeping across the world. Globalization comes about from the interaction of people from different cultures and societies. Globalization is driven by the process of international trade and investment that has opened the way for greater and easier communication among people globally. The era of globalization is said to be present with us, but probably began thousands of years ago with the beginning of commercial trade, which exposed societies to new ideas and concepts. The process of globalization gained impetus as means of communication and transport improved. Faster and better means of transport meant more goods could be traded and at better prices, making them accessible to more people. In Africa, therefore, the attempt by countries to form cooperative agreements or unite regionally was a means by them to arrest the aggregate decline in their competitiveness against their trading partners. Most of them have come to the realization that regional integration is a possible solution to the continent's deep and prolonged economic and social crisis. As this chapter will reveal, however, there have been numerous false starts, by way of *policy failures* and *teething problems*, which have limited these bold attempts in the eyes of both students and scholars of regional economic integration on the African continent. In Africa, therefore, the objectives by countries to respond to the global phenomenon and to follow examples like the European integration, among others, have been mostly regional aspirations and not attempts at regional integration. Because regional integration, as shared by scholars, statesmen, intellectuals, and citizens alike, reflects a general desire to break the confines of the nation state, and a denial of all that divides regions and sub regions, including the multiple barriers to the free movement of goods and services, people, and capital among the countries attempting to integrate. The desire for coming together can also be described as the awareness by West Africans that the kingdoms and cultures of West Africa were relatively well integrated in pre-colonial times, as accounts by scholars amply attest (Oliver and Atmore 1981a, b), and the quest for regional unity is, in many respects, a search for those roots. More to the point is that regional aspirations also constituted a response to the incapacity of the many of these states to generate development on their own without handouts from the developed world. With all these reasons, African nation states in the early 1980s extended beyond this capability of providing, to seek for a better regional infrastructure and a better management of the region's resources and freedoms, set out for regional integration attempts.

Regionalism's Mixed Record

Regionalism in Africa has a mixed and an uncertain record. This is because there are fourteen kinds of regional economic groupings at various stages of development in Africa. Of these, there are five of them that stemmed from the OAU's decision in March 1976 to outline five regions of the OAU, namely the north, south, east, west, and central regions. These OAU-designated regions were represented, in the main, by the Arab Maghreb Union (UMA) in the north, the Southern African Development Community (SADC) in the south, the East African Community (EAC) in the east, the Economic Community of

West African States (ECOWAS) in the west, and the Economic Community of Central African States (ECCAS) in central Africa. The emerging African architecture at the time collectively called for the streamlining of the regional organizations, although not necessarily under these five jurisdictions. Of Africa's fourteen regional and sub regional organizations, at least four of them (ECOWAS, SADC, EAC, ECCAS/CEEAC), included peace and security components and embraced democracy in their establishing treaties. In addition these four entities possessed protocols dealing outright with these matters. The remaining were therefore left without any direct pronouncements on democracy and its defence and advancement in those regions. This begs the question that if democracy was not deemed a worthwhile pursuit at such a localized level, what would its pursuit deem any more worthwhile at a continental level? This was a question to be answered later on by the AU in its attempts to interact meaningfully with the RECs. But while norm sharing may have existed at the regional or sub regional level, the conclusion cannot be prematurely drawn that this could be transposed to the continental level. In a nutshell therefore, the development of regionalism on the continent and its resultant impediments rests solely on the relationship between the AU and the RECs. But before we interrogate the dynamics of such a relationship, however, we need to take a look, from the point of view of New Partnership for Africa's Development (NEPAD), at the impediments to regional integration in Africa.

Impediments to African Regionalism

From the mid- to the late 1970s, regionalism was touted as a possible solution to Africa's economic, social, and even its political problems. Displaying a mix of both Western and African solutions to problems on the continent, its appeal to African states emanated from many sources. Not least of these attractions were the prospects of larger markets, greater solidarity in international negotiating forums, and the possibility of sharing knowledge and expertise. In the emerging global political economy, however, it has been suggested that the West has far less to gain from African solidarity and, as such, has done (or had been doing) all in its (often overwhelming) power to impede it. But over time, Africa has cultivated a few obstacles of its own, as will be discussed in this section. Special emphasis is accorded to NEPAD because it is the AU-sanctioned continental socio-economic program.

Non-inclusive integration efforts are recognized by the NEPAD secretariat as one of the most fundamental of impediments to regional integration. In the typology of five regionalist categories outlined by Andrew Hurrell (1995), regional cohesion is one of the requirements for a movement toward full regional integration. Clearly, NEPAD was established for the conception of regional cohesion that will bring about a cohesive and consolidated regional unit, with the African continent acting concertedly to improve its current conditions. It is unabashedly a plan for Africa's reinsertion into the thick of world affairs as a credible and respected actor, a plan that must be underwritten by continental unity to ensure success. But it is unclear to what extent NEPAD envisages the conception of regional cohesion, which includes the notion of a region forming the organizing basis for policy within the region, across a range of issues. As we all agree, such a policy will be treacherous to tread on; that will be an attempt to venture into the terrain of national sovereignty. It is this very lack of evidence that the region is an organizing basis for region-wide policy (as opposed to each given national state pursuing, if not expressly its own interests, then at least greater benefits than costs to itself from given policies) that hampers the progress of regional integration in Africa. This is not without good reason. African regional organizations need to contend with their members' preoccupations with problems related to domestic development and often even their very political survival. It is probable that governments are loath to actively recruit the support of extra-governmental actors involved in regional decision-making, because they are of the view that the region is an untested terrain where national sovereignty is (or should best remain) indivisible. This inclination may be stronger where it concerns states with authoritarian tendencies. They may have less of an interest in inviting the participation of non-state actors that do not directly add to their position of strength domestically. NEPAD should thus create a space for non-government actors, but simultaneously put in place provisions that will safeguard the rights to freedom of speech and association of such actors.

Although NEPAD, as one of the pillars of the African Renaissance, engenders much pan-African sentiment, it is worth remembering that states remain at the forefront of such plans. These states have foreign policies unique to each and operate in a hostile global environment. It is not only disparate politics, but also vastly different economic situations from one African country to the next that have proven hindrances to regional integration in the past. These economic disparities are most evident in the official record of formal cross-border flows. It is these records that, advertently or not, hide less formal flows—both those from the continent and those from international governmental organizations. This problem is part of the wider problem of a lack of reliable information. Astonishingly, according to NEPAD's Regional Integration Initiative, officially recorded intra-regional trade accounts for just one-third of cross-border flows among African countries. This may be linked in no small part to the restrictive, arguably outdated, immigration policies of most African countries. It may thus be inevitable that the focus is on officially recorded information, given that those other, unofficial cross-border flows, whether of people, or of goods, are often associated with criminality and illegality. Another serious problem is posed by the different levels of economic and financial advancement experienced by each member state of a regional body. While limitations on government spending and tax cuts may endear the South African finance ministry to the international financial institutions, these policies may be followed at greater cost in countries of lesser economic advancement, where governments are under pressure to take the lead in providing basic services and better standards of living for their people. The more uneven regional partnerships are (in terms of the economic development of the contracting states), the more disproportionate the gains and losses from regional integration. Adequate compensation for losses is yet to be resolved, resulting in less commitment to regional projects. Furthermore, the issue of overlapping integration groupings is a symptom of a larger problem, namely, that membership in regional intergovernmental organizations has not borne the benefits for African states that it has promised, while exacting costs those weak economies may not be able to bear. The departure of Seychelles from SADC, reportedly because the $500,000 annual membership fee did not provide value for money provides a sobering insight into the costs, monetary and other, of membership in regional organizations for small, poor countries. Hard hit by the post-September global tourism slump, Seychelles could not rely upon SADC for assistance, but had instead to relinquish its membership and funnel its meagre resources elsewhere. Several countries find themselves in similar positions with regard to the AU.

The general poverty of the African continent and the mixed results of regional integration appear to render intergovernmental organizations something of a luxury, especially among the poorest states. It is clear that many of the regionalist projects, if not all, have not reached their stated goals. Time may be a factor, given that many bodies were established only in the 1970s and beyond, and have to grapple not only with the complexities of economic integration, but also with those of political integration, limited domestic interest and support for integration projects, and domestic development problems. Supply rigidities have led to an inadequate supply of high-quality and competitively priced goods. African governments and architects of regional integration are not aware that ameliorating inelastic supply issues and eradicating poverty may entail extensive partnerships with external governmental actors.

Other Minor Groupings

Among the states of the Horn of Africa, the Intergovernmental Authority on Development grew out of the desire among Eritrea, Ethiopia, Uganda, and Djibouti to combat and to better prevent the effects of drought in their region. The Mano River Union has just three members, namely Liberia, Sierra Leone, and Guinea. They came together in 1973, predating the larger West African grouping of ECOWAS by two years, to constitute a customs and economic union in order to improve the living standards of their respective populations. Lastly, as is well documented, SADCC resulted from the efforts of southern African states to resist the South African apartheid state and relax their economic dependence on it, among other factors. NEPAD does not cut to the quick of the problems with regional integration on the continent. The underlying problems of regionalization for development persist in the face of regionalist projects that attempt to emulate projects in more developed parts of the world. Some ways of ameliorating the problems with regional integration to date include improving the stock of information that governments have access to. Also, all-inclusive regional organizations should have mechanisms that provide for different levels of integration. Some commentators have isolated procedural shortcomings within regional organizations themselves, such as the requirement for unanimous decision-making and the peripheral involvement of bureaucrats employed in secretariats. States like Ghana have (in the past) shown their commitment to regional integration by appointing a ministry (during President Agyekum Kufuor government), to deal with matters of regional integration and NEPAD. This should be the level of commitment of every African state, or continental projects will not progress from the vapid inertia that characterized the OAU. The NEPAD document, although promoting the fortification of regional intergovernmental organizations, does not go far enough in spelling out the modalities of interaction between the existing regional bodies and the AU. One has to look to the AU and the memorandum of the CSSDCA for such guidelines.

Conclusion

In Africa, and for that matter, West Africa, political instability is the most visible of the political problems with which regional organizations must contend. Nevertheless, interstate politics plays a primary role in regional integration. While most regional integration projects were initiated with economic motives in mind, it has become increasingly difficult to separate political motives from economic motives in African politics. Besides, external interference has long been cited as an impediment to regionalism in Africa. In West Africa for example, France's continuing influence in its former colonies in has been blamed for a lack of coherence in ECOWAS. Moreover, certain divisions within SADC have been attributed to South Africa's 1999 trade agreement with the European Union. It is true, however, that external factors, while sometimes responsible for undermining efforts at regional integration, can also work to solidify such efforts. The formation of SADCC preceded by the front-line states (FLS) in response to South African aggression in the 1970s and '80s is a case in point. The pervasiveness of external influence in regional affairs, however, is bound to replicate itself in continental politics. This was never demonstrated more clearly than in the dilemma faced by Angola, Cameroon, and Guinea in the lead-up to the ill-fated Security Council vote on war in Iraq in early March 2003, in spite of the stated anti-war stance of the AU. African continental projects also run the risk of being overshadowed, and even threatened, by events in the world at large, such as the 'war on terror'. In spite of these shortcomings, however, the success of NEPAD depends heavily on the effectual operation of RECs. RECs must be strengthened in order for the outcomes envisioned by NEPAD to take shape. Regional bodies, even lacking in capacity and institutional leadership as they are, are mostly organic outgrowths brought into being as solutions to particular problems. As such, each regional organization has evolved its own particular character and is geared, at least in theory, toward addressing the most pressing questions in its neighbourhood.

Works Cited / Further Readings

Asante, S. K. B. (1986), *The Political Economy of Regionalism in Africa: A Decade of the Economic Community of West African States* (New York: Praeger).

—— (1996), *Regionalism and Africa's Development* (London: Macmillan).

'ECOWAS Turns Down Sani Abacha's Request for Use of Force against Sierra Leone', *Economist,* 6 September 1997, 46.

Ejime, Paul (1997), 'ECOWAS New Chief Outlines Priorities', Dakar, Senegal: PanAfrican News Agency.

International Monetary Fund (1997), 'Fund for Co-operation, Compensation, and Development' (Washington: International Monetary Fund).

John(1992), 'Science, Technology, and Development in ECOWAS', *Journal of Asian and African Studies,* January–April 1992, 114–23.

Okolo, Julius (1990), *West African Regional Cooperation and Development* (Boulder, CO: Westview Press).

World Bank (1994), pp. 62–76, 230–231.

What Are the Realities for Africa's Regionalism?

The treaty establishing the African Economic Community (AEC) was signed in Abuja, Nigeria in 1991. The AEC offers a *framework* for continental integration. Regional economic communities within Africa (RECs) were established to serve as building blocks toward the full realization of the AEC's agenda of a United States of Africa. The AEC treaty has a set of no less than *six* stages to be fully operational. Starting from 1994, it has allowed *thirty-four* years for full political and economic integration. That makes 2018 or 2019 a vigil year for Africa's economic and political emancipation—an important year. So, if we're lucky, by 2020, the African Economic Community should be fully operational, with the eight AU-recognized RECs (AU-RECs) possibly *subsumed* under regions of North, Central, East, South, and West African economic communities. These are very ambitious dreams, but from the various pieces of articles assembled, these dreams cannot be realized by 2020. The analysis stipulates that the African Union has tried but failed to maintain its pan-African mandate as espoused by its founders while dealing with the inevitable dynamism of growing African economies greatly influenced by globalization. The conclusion to be drawn here is that the AU needs to reinvent itself if it is going to prove relevant to Africa's and indeed the world's current issues.

We use the term 'regional unity', or regionalism, to refer to and include both economic integration and political association. As we take a look at the second generation of regionalism on the African community, it is opportune to stand back from the dominant debates on forms of integration—common market, monetary union, fast-tracking or snail-walking of the African Union project, etc.—and ask certain core questions: What exactly is the vision, the lodestar, so to speak, of the regional or the continental projects? What are the historical geneses? What are the driving forces of the project, in whose interest, and for what purpose? How does the project relate to the larger global forces and, in particular, to the changing world hegemonies? It is only by asking these bigger questions that we can critically assess where we are going and chart the possible way forward. It is not my intention to enter into a debate on the merits or demerits of the forms of economic integration or the speed of political association. That aspect has been covered in my book on policy implications of regional integration in West Africa. Rather, I wish to pose the question as to whether we are asking the right questions.

Reader no. 1 is on the broad strokes of the historical pan-Africanist project as a progenitor of African nationalism leading to the independence movement. The central argument of this section is that the discourse and contentions on the African Federation (AF) among the first-generation nationalists was located in pan-Africanism. The second section is broadly divided into two parts. The first part addresses the contentions surrounding the first-generation regionalism located in the first twenty-five years of postcolonial, territorial nationalism. Reader no. 2 touches on the defeat of the national project, the rise of neo-liberalism and locates the second-generation regionalism—or regional integration, as it is called in the dominant AEC-speak—within the neo-liberal project. Reader no. 3 suggests that new pan-Africanism is back on the historical agenda with even greater relevance than it was fifty years ago. I conclude with the question 'What are the social and political forces that will drive the new pan-Africanism and chart a way forward for continental unity with suggestions?'

The Political and Economic Mythology of Africa's Regionalism

Reader 1

Abstract

Research on some key determinants of Africa's regionalism has implicated the pan-African agenda for continental unity by 2025 or thereafter. To forge harmonization of the regional integration schemes in Africa, some fundamentals need to be handled first before progressing to other parts of the pan-African cooperation. While the attention of several scholars has always targeted the internal problems and consequences of regional integration in Africa, this paper examines the political and economic myths that surround the processes of the African Economic Community agenda. It argues that while such myths once placed an important role in fostering identification and support for the process, they no longer serve that function. Instead, these myths have become a focal point for contestations and concern. This is because regional integration, conceptualized as the construction of international economy and polity within negotiated regions, should target economic development.

Introduction

The Abuja Treaty for establishing the African Economic Community (AEC) embodies Africa's will to transform itself from a continent of individual least developed and developing economies to a strong, united bloc of nations. The treaty calls for forming the African Economic Community in six phases over thirty-four years. The first phase rightly focuses on strengthening the regional economic communities to become effective building blocks for the African Economic Community. The communities are expected to evolve into free-trade areas, customs unions, and eventually, a common market spanning the continent. Coordinating and harmonizing the activities of the regional economic communities have been among the key concerns of the African integration agenda. The African Economic Community Treaty devotes an entire chapter to the need for the communities to march in unison. The recent Constitutive Act of the African Union reiterates the importance of a harmonious approach to realizing the union. But forging this unity of purpose and action requires a solid political consensus. With coordination and harmonization imperative for successful regional integration in Africa, bringing the regional economic communities together has become a key challenge. Toward a united Africa, the various regional integration schemes are consulting regularly among themselves at the various fora enumerated here:

- In West Africa growing rapport between ECOWAS and UEMOA has borne fruit in a common program of action on trade liberalization and macroeconomic policy convergence. ECOWAS and UEMOA have now agreed on common rules of origin to enhance trade, and ECOWAS has agreed to adopt UEMOA's customs declaration forms and compensation mechanisms. It enables experts from STC, commissioners as well as presidents of the commissions of ECOWAS and UEMOA to discuss issues of convergence and coordination of the various programs sector driven by two subregional organizations. UEMOA's headquarters is in Ouagadougou, Burkina Faso and UEMOA is composed of eight countries which are part of the fifteen

member states of ECOWAS (Benin, Burkina Faso, Ivory Coast, Guinea-Bissau, Mali, Niger, Senegal, and Togo).[2]
- In Central Africa, ECCAS is adopting a trade regime that takes into account the dispensations in CEMAC.[3]
- In East and Southern Africa, IGAD and IOC are applying most of the integration instruments adopted by COMESA, while the EAC and COMESA have concluded a memorandum of understanding to foster harmonization of their policies and programs. In addition, COMESA and SADC have set up task forces to deal with common issues and to invite each other to policy and technical meetings.[4]
- At the continental level, the protocol on the relationship between regional economic communities and the EAC provides for a coordination committee that meets at the level of chief executives.

These initiatives are improving the prospects of narrowing discrepancies among the regional economic communities, overcoming the problems of overlapping membership, and accelerating progress toward the African Union. But these self-driven efforts by the various regional economic communities require the support of a strong continental coordinating mechanism not yet in place. At the moment, coordination appears ineffective. The African Economic Community also has numerous ancillary protocols not yet ratified; those that have been ratified are not playing out as planned. With the exception of the protocol governing the relationship between the African Economic Community and the regional economic communities, most protocols have not yet been finalized.[5]

---

[2] Economic Commission for Africa (2003), 'Assessment of Regional Integration in Africa (ARIA)'. See more at http://www.ecdpm.org/Web_ECDPM/Web/Content/Content.nsf/0/0AFF1EE6DDE15146C12579CE004774B2?OpenDocument#sthash.kwavZsAv.dpuf

[3] Dinka, T. and Kennes, W.1 (2007), 'Africa's Regional Integration Arrangements: History and Challenges', ECDPM Discussion Paper 74 (Maastricht). See more at http://www.ecdpm.org/Web_ECDPM/Web/Content/Content.nsf/0/0AFF1EE6DDE15146C12579CE004774B2?OpenDocument#sthash.kwavZsAv.dpuf

[4] See Regional integration strategy paper on East African integration (2011-2015), World Bank, October, 2010.

[5] Stevens, Christopher (2006), 'The EU, Africa and Economic Partnership Agreements: unintended policy consequences of policy leverage', *Journal of Modern African Studies* 44 (3): 441–458.

Myths and Arguments of Africa's Regionalism

Africa's integration is surrounded by political and economic myths. The Lagos Treaty of 1975 and that of the Abuja Treaty of 1991 both explain how the process started and what drives it forward; they suggest where it is headed, how to measure its success, and what may be the cause(s) of its drawbacks or failure. But not all of these myths are consistent with each other, even though each plays a useful narrative role.[6] More important is perhaps the fact that the ensemble of political and economic myths lies at the heart of African Union's (AU) sense of self. Africa has become more complicated and supporters of Africa's political and economic integration have become more critical of these myths, as a result. Nevertheless, simply embracing this new complexity is not the issue, but that a new set of myths must be created about the process of integration if they want this more complicated incarnation of Africa to succeed. This paper begins by taking a look at the role of political and economic myths in the process of Africa's integration. The second part of the paper provides a literature review of Africa's regionalism. The following section explains why these myths no longer play a constructive role in the integration process. The last part concludes by stating how difficult it will be to move from AU's current predicament to the African Economic Treaty agenda of continental unity. The African Union can no longer rely on mere political and economic wishes (myths) for sustenance; the challenge is to come up with something new for that collective surge toward Africa's emancipation and development.

A Review of Africa's Situation (Myths)

The implication of the word 'myth' in this context is obvious; although the term has a number of negative connotations suggesting either falsehood or doubtfulness, at least in its colloquial use. The word 'myth' here is to cast my analysis and, more importantly for the arguments that I am about to make, so that myth-making then plays a central role in putting forward the explanations and models that are vital in our understanding of, in the functional sense, attitudes toward the identification of the political and economic institutions

---

[6] Oyejide, Ademola, Ibrahim Elbadawi and Paul Collier (eds.), (1997), *Regional Integration and Trade Liberalisation in Sub-Saharan Africa, Volume 1: Framework, Issues and Methodological Perspectives* (London: Macmillan Press, London).

under discussion. The theoretical basis for this claim builds on works from the constructivist works of Benedict Anderson (1991, 1983) and John R. Searle (1995), Roland Barthes (1972, 1975), and Peter Berger and Thomas Luckmann (1996). These taken together will forge a link from the simplifications used to understand causal patterns in the real world to the self-sustaining patters of interaction that structure our political and economic life. Having said that, the goal here is limited to showing how such a link could operate to bring about the social construction of the African integration project which this article is all about.

Barthes (1972) develops the notion of myths around four features that analytical arguments share—at least as sketched in the first chapter of King et al. (1994). Myths build on existing speech in the same way that arguments build on the existing literature. Myths do not hide the truth and yet they do simplify and so distort our view of the empirical world. Myths tend toward (or to evolve into) regularities or generalizations. And myths lay claim to a 'depoliticized' objectivity that is not free from the constraints of the subjective observer but that nevertheless promises to reveal something enduring about the world as we perceive it. Most important for Barthes (1972), myths reveal the intentions of the myth-maker. Myths do not just come with an agenda, they are the agenda—and that is what sets them apart from normal speech: 'Myth is not defined by the object of its message, but by the way in which it utters this message: there are formal limits to myth, there are no "substantial" ones. Everything, then, can be a myth. Exactly, I believe this' (Barthes 1972). Arguments work that way as well; at least if they lay claim to be scientific, since the content of science is primarily the methods and rules, not the subject matter, which is used to study virtually anything' (King et al. 1994).

This is where the argument moves from Barthes to Berger and Luckmann (1966). It is also where the implications for Africa begin to become more apparent. Berger and Luckmann (1966) offer a short chapter on legitimation in their longer analysis of the institutionalization of social relations and cultural norms. In their argument, 'legitimation is the process of explaining and justifying' (Berger and Luckmann, 1966) and so depends as much upon knowledge as upon values. In turn, legitimacy depends upon a positive as well as a normative assessment of the state of the world. People have to accept that this is how the world actually works before they are going to be willing to accept that this is how they as a collective should respond. For instance, a formal interest in the unfolding events in the realm of Africa's regionalism bring to the immediate fore two overlapping, if not mutually inclusive, tendencies: On the one hand, there is an increasing drive toward a robust revitalization and a steady proliferation of regional integration efforts; on the other—particularly within the historical framework of post-Cold War era—there is the erratic and sometimes violent fracturing of national entities into irredentist sub national claims, variably shaped by the potential for internecine conflicts.

In more general terms, Benedict Anderson (1991) shows the significance of this difference in perspective through his analysis of political nationalism. Anderson's (1991) self-declared ambition is to contrast a creative view of nation-building as an act of collective imagination with the more austere imposition of an invented nationalism by powerful ruling elites. His ostensible foil is Ernest Gellner, who makes a structuralist argument linking nationalism to modernization and to the organization requirements of the modern economy. Anderson accepts the structuralist logic, but he insists that there is more to nation-building than competition and self-interest. The problem that Anderson's nationalists confronted was the contradiction between the reality of linguistic diversity, on the one hand, and the desire for political community, on the other. This problem was made surmountable by changes in technology—which greatly increased the scope and speed of communication. It was only by *creating* and transmitting the symbols of the nation, however, that elites could begin to foster a sense of national identification. There is also a postmodern dimension to Anderson's argument as well. Like the Barthes myths, Anderson's 'imagined communities' face the danger of becoming disconnected from the empirical (and social) world. The challenge is to understand what this disconnection might mean in practical terms. If the African Economic Community agenda for a United States of Africa does not have nationalism, it nevertheless does have a collective intentionality. And while this collective intentionality is narrated through myths that originate as models and arguments about the real world, its success lies in the wider propaganda of such myths across different actors in the African community (Jabko 2006). In turn, these myths offer Africa some legitimation. Milward's (1992) rescue of the nation-state is one example but there are countless others. Following the logic of those arguments, both policymakers and everyday citizens can generate expectations as to what this African Economic Community agenda has to offer. They can set benchmarks and targets to assess its performance as well (Scharpf 1999). Hence while it is easy to admit that Africa lacks the institutional strength of the nation-state, it is important to note that it is also stronger than any conventional international organization (Menon 2008).

Whatever the strengths, Africa's performance will have to live up, at least in spirit, to the expectations set by the arguments, models, or myths that abound. So long as performance is in line and any inconsistencies can be ignored, Africa should benefit from narrative legitimation in Berger and Luckmann's (1966) sense of the term. Most contemporary analysts of Africa's democratic deficit have ignored this implication. For them, it is enough to assert that the African Union lacks democratic legitimacy, full stop. This analysis of myths pushes that concern for the breakdown of legitimacy somewhat farther along. However, most analysts would like to avoid that fate. Indeed, we study Africa both in order to better understand the nature of its construction and to suggest how it could benefit from improvement targeted at enhancing the welfare of its people. The directions of change and the thrust of the recommendations we sometimes offer to politicians are not always consistent. But the motive of having a persuasive influence on the literature (and perhaps even on policy) remains the same. Moreover, while we may pretend to offer objective insight in depoliticized language, there is no guaranteeing that our arguments will not assume significance beyond our control. Indeed, if we are successful in attaining influence, then they will find wide circulation. Once cut from the context of their original research and publication, and placed in the hands of other myth-makers, they become free-floating symbols of what Africa is or can become. It is uncomfortable to view scientific research, social inquiry, or academic discourse in this manner, and yet it is inevitable that this should happen.

From this perspective, there are as many potential political and economic myths surrounding the process of African quest for integration as there are economic arguments about Africa. Consider Bela Balassa's definition of the different degrees of economic integration from free trade area to customs union to common market (Balassa 1961). As a set of conceptual markets, it provides a useful framework, as a description (or interpretation) of how integration has actually taken place elsewhere, and where there are very many exceptions to the rule. Nevertheless, it is often regarded as 'natural' for countries to progress from one stage of Balassa's definition of integration to the next. Further economic myths have taken on more sinister dimensions: What exactly is the vision, the lodestar, so to speak, of Africa's regional integration project? What is its historical genesis? What are the driving forces of the project, in whose interest, and for what purpose? How does the project relate to the larger global forces and, in particular, to the changing world hegemonies? It is only by asking these bigger questions that we can critically assess where we are going and chart the possible way forward. It is not my intention to enter into a debate on the merits or demerits of the forms of economic integration or the speed of political association. Rather I wish to pose the question as to whether we are asking the right questions. My plan is to take the middle road and to illustrate some of those myths that I believe reside at Africa's core. In doing so, I draw upon the whole spectrum of possibilities suggested by Berger and Luckmann (1960), from the easy asides of national diplomats and African Union Commission officials to the strongest or most prominent arguments made in recent literature on Africa's regionalism. My intention is to show how even the most important contributions to our understanding of African integration can assume a mythical form in the language of Barthes (1972).

The Myth of Inevitability

No serious historian of Africa believes that economic integration was inevitable. On the contrary, most are acutely aware of the many false starts that took place along the way. More to the point, contemporary writers like S. K. B. Asante,[7] Hurrell, Rodrik, and de Melo, Panagariya[8] et al. went to great pains to show how regional integration in Africa exhibited processes of overlapping, inward-looking, and conflicting integration against the backdrop of common market among countries in Africa. Nevertheless, every story needs to have a beginning and for Africa that is either the Economic Commission for Africa's

---

[7] See *Africa's Development: Adebayo Adedeji's Alternative Strategies* by S. K. B. Asante, hardcover (Hans Zell Publications).

[8] 'The New Regionalism: Country Perspective' by de Melo, Panagariya, and Rodrik. World Bank Policy Research Working Papers, 1994.

intention to propose the development agenda for African unity or the signing of the various agreements to fit into the Lagos Plan of Action. Whatever the motive, though, the myth of inevitability has become a standard justification to explain the start of Africa's integration. African regionalism began as an economic organization—because it was always meant to start that way. Yet if Africa's regionalism started as economic organizations, then there must be some deeper logic behind it and the two most obvious candidates are institutional rationality or economic self-interest. The debate between neo-functionalists and neo-realists reflects the different weights that can be given to these two explanatory factors. Neo-functionalists emphasize institutional rationality (spill over) and suggest that this gives rationality to institutions (through lower transactions costs and binding commitments). Taken to its extreme, the who trajectory of African integration can be reduced either to a process of institutionalization (Stone Sweet et al. 2001) or intergovernmental bargaining between nation states acting on behalf of domestic economic interest groups (Moravcsik 1998). Either way, the point is the same: the evolution of Africa's regionalism is a function of politics and economics.

The Myths of Instability

Not all economic arguments imply visions of peace and stability. Some—like Abdelwahab El-Alfendi's (2009) work on the perils of regionalism: regional integration as a source of instability in the Horn of Africa?[9]—suggest that some parts of Africa's regionalism have a potential for violence. Invariably, these claims centre on the problem of managing distributive conflict. The African Economic Community Treaty creates both losers and winner through the construction of institutions at the African Union Commission and other levels and through the policies that these institutions pursue. Hence many economists worry that should Africa lack the instruments for managing the unintended consequences of this redistribution, there will be nothing to prevent groups (both governmental and civil society) from organizing to combat African Union policies or to tear African continental agenda down. This argument derives in no small measure from the fact that in spite of all the harmonization problems, the rationalization problems, the African Union

---

[9] See the *Journal of Intervention and Statebuilding*, 3 (1): 1–19, ISSN 1750-2977.

still proposes a theory of optimum areas which is conducive for the intellectual bulwark for Africa's economic development (Herbst 2007). The basic premise is that the stability of regional integration arrangement is somehow a function of its economic rationality across the different groups, regions, or countries that make up the proposed union of African states as a whole. Hence there is a need to shore up the sense of political community—transferring resources from winners to losers first, until the bad economic situation goes away or until a new consensus in support of the African continental agenda can be found. The thrust of this argument is that Africa is in a situation of temporary instability or, perhaps better, political disequilibrium. The cost of going backward is prohibitive and yet it cannot stay where it is right now because of globalization factors.[10] The conclusion is that Africans are in a dilemma: a choice between moving forward with the process of integration or accepting a costly and debilitating reverse. This condition would not only make everyone (countries in that respect) worse off, it might also incite them into pointing fingers at some particular countries, as well as invoke issues of their colonialization backgrounds—leading to conflict(s) across the continent.

Myths of Interdependence: Perpetual Peace

There are other myths or arguments that bind countries together in the form envisaged by the pan-African ideology aimed at concretely establishing a union government of Africa. Probably the strongest among these is the belief that economic interdependence is a wellspring for continuing African peace and proposed unity. This argument has a pedigree going back at least to the period between the 1950s and 1960s, the birth of the Organization of African Unity, which marked a revolution in African politics—it was pan-Africanism brought home from the diaspora. The organization of African Unity (OAU), now the African Union (AU), saw the light of day in May 1963. It was the fruition of the dream of African unity echoed toward the end of the nineteenth century by African nationalists and championed largely by Marcus Garvey and W. E. B. Du Bois. These nineteenth-century pan-Africanists decried the torture, racism, and all forms of discrimination directed at the black race. It was thanks

---

[10] See Manboah-Rockson, Joseph K. in 'Regionalism and Integration in Sub-Sahara Africa: A Review of Experiences, Issues and Realities at the Close of the Twentieth Century', Innovation, 2000, University of Calgary.

to them that pan-Africanism became a worldwide movement and was brought to Africa in the twentieth century. The aims and objectives of the organization were spelt out in its charter. It sought to promote international cooperation, improve the lives and living conditions of Africans, defend the solidarity, independence, and territorial integrity and independence of all states, and eradicate colonialism and racism. How the AU succeeds in realizing these noble objectives is a reflection of its level of success or failure. The biggest challenge that confronted the OAU and derailed its pursuit of a continental unity plan in the 1960s—the Cold War—has now been taken over by the effects of globalization. The effect of the Cold War rendered the organization completely powerless, if not useless, as member states looked either to the United States or Russia for support and protection. The OAU stood helpless as proxy wars and coups erupted in Africa one after the other. Unable to provide solutions to recurrent conflicts, illiteracy, migration, chronic poverty, and diseases, many Africans saw the OAU as being good only in name.

But how does this earlier African history of the past resonate with the late Muammar al-Qaddafi? The late Libyan leader Colonel Qaddafi had used recent AU meetings to drum for a united Africa (a USA of some sort) embodying the want for territorial union. His memories so far begat scepticism in good measure, mostly arising from the difficulty to even dream of a beginning point to unity, given the incompatible nature of African states, chiefly political. My intention here is not to denigrate that history and neither is it to deny the importance of the various regional integration arrangements. Rather, my focus is on the particular problem that the notion of interdependence represents. Thinking along the lines of Richard N. Cooper (1968), an economist, he describes a situation where any country's ability to achieve its policy objectives depends upon prior knowledge of how other countries will respond. In that context, Cooper (1968) argues, institutionalized cooperation is necessary to ensure policy effectiveness for which the African economic and political situation is in distress. More cooperation begins in one area; however, it also shapes the possibilities for cooperation elsewhere. The dynamic is not the same as neo-functionalist spillover and it is not strictly the result of the intergovernmental intermediation of economic self-interest either. Instead it is an expression of the convergence of expectations and the promulgation of norms in the context of international regimes (Krasner 1983).

Putting It All Together

Bringing together, in a common and single space, a continent characterized by diversity and extraordinary asymmetries, is not an easy task.[11] The African continent is composed of different spaces, countries, cultures, and societies not yet sharing a common sense of destiny. But if there is to be a single United States of Africa, then a new regionalism has to emerge and represent a road map to a new governance framework implying the deepening of liberal economic and institutional reforms. Resistance and obstacles for this continent-wide agenda remain numerous and perhaps the biggest challenge is to address the complex issues related to harmonization of the various regional integration schemes and the hegemonic position of world powers such as France in particular and the rest of Europe at large. If the process of building the US of Africa can be depicted as an attempt to define governance in an era of market-led integration, the paradox is that its eventual success depends on the capacity to transcend the immediate commercial and trade orientations and create a true community of democracies. In other words, building a united Africa must now go beyond market-led integration, beyond France's hegemonic governance, and foremost, recognize the diversity of cultures, its people, values, and identities on the African continent.[12]

The illustrations are all compatible if not exactly consistent. It was inevitable that Africa would start with economics both for economic reasons and for other reasons as well. Great leaders like Dr Kwame Nkrumah, Julius Nyerere, General Eyadema, and others put forward grand ideals and pulled increasing numbers of followers behind them. They built institutions from the Organization of Africa Unity (1963) and other regional agencies that offered great benefits but asked for significant commitments. More than that, they inaugurated a new African economic treaty, and invigorated the OUA into the African Union (AU), marked by greater cooperation, tolerance, respect for the rule of law, and abhorrence of violence. The problem is that their project is unfinished and their progeny are not clear where to take it. Worse, this unfinished creation is unstable as well. The time has come for new leaders with new vision to lead

---

[11] Introduction to this subject includes comments taken from de la Torre and Kelly (1992), de Melo et al. (1993), and Pangariya (1995: 15).
[12] See Panagariya (1994) and Jaggi (1995).

the call to action. The fate of Africa is at stake and the possibility of failure is too awful to contemplate.

Africa's Complicated Reality

As mythical narratives go, the African one is compelling—even if it does emerge from the dismal science. Nevertheless, it leaves a series of questions unanswered, not least about the nature of popular support. It is one thing to show how economic arguments can develop into myths; it is quite another to anticipate which of these myths will resonate with the people. Scholars of regional integration schemes and particularly civil society groups are now curious to know about the numerous regional integration schemes in Africa. A while back, this was not a problem so long as African integration schemes were primarily an economic enterprise and the economy was doing well. But it is presently a major dilemma, particularly after the end of the Cold War, and the emergence of the new wave of regionalism across the world. It is a bit late in this article to open a new line of analysis on the various types of regionalism we experience in Africa, or the determinants of public opinion on this[13] and I have also covered the subject of the impact of globalization on Africa's regionalism elsewhere, in *Innovations Journal* (Manboah-Rockson 2000). For the moment, my goal is to show how the economic myths sketched in the previous section have become difficult to sustain as the questions they leave unanswered have become more pressing. The analysis is every bit as gloomy as the previous section was uplifting. This should not be misinterpreted. My point is not to decry the end of Africa's regional integration programs, but rather to show how the economic myths at the heart of the process can also be turned around. In fact, there are strong analytic claims to be made about the need for rational

---

[13] See a full coverage of the four types of partnerships in Africa's regionalism by Seatini (2005). The four are divided into two broad categories: those that fit into the Lagos Plan of Action and those that were either in existence or came about outside the LPA. The first one is the Lagos Plan, which was promoted by the ECA and launched in a special initiative by the OAU. A second group of integration arrangements has grown up outside the LPA. Two important RTAs are associated with the former CFA zone. There is the West African Economic and Monetary Union (WAEMU) within the ambit of ECOWAS and the Economic and Monetary Union of Central Africa (CEMAC) within the proposed ECCAS region.

reform. Unmoored from their proper context, these arguments become a new sort of economic myth about how Africa's regional integration arrangements are running aground.

The question about completion of Africa's regional integration arrangements is where the story about economic instability left off—with the asymmetric constitution of the African Union Commission. According to MarCarthy (1995), intra-regional trade in Africa as a share of total foreign trade has traditionally been low compared to other regions. Figures in the early 1990s suggest that the proportion was only 8.4 per cent in 1993 compared with Western Europe (69.9 per cent), Asia (49.7 per cent), North America (33 per cent), and Latin America (19.4 per cent) (WTO source, quoted in McCarthy 1995: 21). Moreover, the dependence of many African countries on their former colonial powers works against viable regional groupings. The importance of North–South linkages (Franco-African and Commonwealth links and various Lomé Conventions), have distracted commitment from intra-African groupings.[14] Furthermore, given the disparities in economic weight that exist between members of some groupings, new policy instruments to deal with the fears of economic polarization are not in place, for example, multispeed arrangements (allowing weaker members more time to liberalize), compensation schemes, regional investment banks, or structural solidarity funds such as the Food Security Financial Instrument and many others.[15]

Furthermore, Africa's proposed single market suffers from a similar sort of dilemma, but rather than entering on one big institutional deficit, it operates through myriad jurisdictional conflicts, implementation failures, and what Fritz Scharpf (1991) refers to as joint-decision traps. As a result, the proposed internal market is littered with inefficiencies and inequalities that work against both its effective functioning and its perceived legitimacy. In this vein I turn to agree with several scholars that the only resolution to this dilemma is to accept that the African Union is not going to become the United States of Africa, but rather a confederation of states or a confederation of regional integration schemes. This would entail making the whole process more transparent

---

[14] See Summers, Lawrence (1991), 'Regionalism and the World Trading System'.
[15] Robert McCleery (1993) makes a compelling analysis in respect of how developing countries are modeling NAFTA.

(including the finality) and making explicit delegations to independent agencies rather than relying so heavily on the African Union Commission. The question I ask is whether any of the principal African community agencies—such as the Council of Ministers, the Social and Economic Council, and many others—of the various subregional groupings and member states themselves would ever agree to go down this road. In particular, the heads of state and governments seem comfortable maintaining two different conversations, one African and the other national, that allow them to shunt much of the blame for unpopular but necessary measures onto the shoulders of the African Union Commission.

Conclusion

The main thrust of this paper is that the economic mythology of Africa's integration did not emerge fully formed. On the contrary, it came together in a piecemeal fashion and with a number of fits and starts. The paper sketched the economic as well as political myths inherent in the objectives and ambitions of the African Economic Community agenda calling for the implementation of Africa's regional integration in stages. The analysis is every bit as gloomy and mostly not uplifting in its current form. This should, however, not be misinterpreted. The points made are not to decry the end of Africa's regional integration methodology but rather to show how the economic myths at the heart of the process can be turned around.

Moving forward on integration requires stronger and unwavering political commitment, more visionary leadership, and more intense effort than have been demonstrated so far. The African Union should provide an impetus for relaunching the integration agenda and positioning Africa in the global economic and political mainstream. It should be the vehicle to help transform Africa and bring hope and prosperity to its people. For the African Union to accelerate integration, several fundamental questions must be answered immediately. To ensure that the African Union is well anchored, member states must reinforce their institutional foundation and political will and address some of the immediate sectoral challenges. The institutional architecture of the regional economic communities lacks the authority, power, and resources to enforce decisions and see the implementation of programs through to their logical conclusions. Successful integration requires secretariats with the staffing, financial resources, and authority to act for member states. And regional economic communities must be able to sanction indifferent performance or failures to fulfil commitments to protocols and treaty obligations. The African Union cannot simply depend on loose non-enforceable protocols whose implementation depends on best-endeavour efforts of member states. Decisions by the African Union and regional economic communities should not be implemented only when a member state is ready and willing to abide by them—they should be implemented as a single legally binding undertaking. The African Union structures, especially the regional economic communities, the African Parliament, and the Court of Justice, need supranational clout to enforce African Union interests over parochial national interests. Finally, once expected to serve as the building blocks of the African Economic Community, the regional economic communities must gear up to form the basis of the African Union. The communities must mute their independence and rein in their interdependence, and adopt policies in their entirety, particularly the Abuja Treaty's path to a continental unity. Until hard and fast rules bind integration agendas to the continental framework, and a supranational authority provides oversight, the African Union Commission's dream of a continental unity will remain a mirage.

Works Cited / Further Readings

Anderson, B. (1991), *Imagined Communities* (London: Verso).

Balassa, Belay (1961), *Theory of Economic Integration* (Irwin).

Barthes, R. (1972), *Mythologies*, trans. A. Lavers (London: Granada).

Berger, P. and Luckmann, T. (1966), *The Social Construction of Reality: A Treatise in the Sociology of Knowledge* (London: Penguin).

Cooper, R. N. (1968), *The Economics of Interdependence: Economic Policy in the Atlantic Community* (New York: McGraw-Hill for the Council on Foreign Relations).

Faroutan, Faizeh (1993), 'Regional Integration in Sub-Saharan Africa: Past Experience and Future Prospects', in Jaime de Melo and Arvind

Panagariya (eds.), *New Dimensions in Regional Integration* (Cambridge University Press).

Herbst, Jeffrey (2007), 'Crafting regional cooperation in Africa', in Amitav Acharya and Alastair Johnston (eds.), *Crafting Cooperation: Regional International Institutions in Comparative Perspective* (London: Oxford University Press), p. 144.

Hix, S. (2008), *What's Wrong with the European Union and How to Fix It* (Cambridge: Polity).

Jabko, N. (2006), *Playing the Market: A Political Strategy for Uniting Europe, 1985–2005* (Ithaca, NY: Cornell University Press).

King, G., Keohane, R. O., and Verba, S. (1994), *Designing Social Inquiry: Scientific Inference in Qualitative Research* (Princeton, NJ: Princeton University Press).

Krasner, S. (1983) (ed.), *International Regimes* (Ithaca, NY: Cornell University Press).

McCleery, Robert (1993) makes a compelling analysis in respect of how developing countries are modelling NAFTA.

Menon, A. (2008), *Europe: The State of the Union* (London: Atlantic Books).

Milward, A. S. (1992), 'The Social Bases of Monetary Union?', in Gowan, P. and Anderson, P. (eds.), *The Question of Europe* (London: Verso).

Moravcsik, A. (1998), *The Choice for Europe: Social Purpose and State Power from Messina to Maastricht* (Ithaca, NY: Cornell University Press).

Scharpf, F. (1999), *Governing in Europe: Effective and Democratic?* (Oxford: Oxford University Press).

Searle, J. R. (1995), The Construction of Social Reality (London: Penguin).

Stone Sweet, A., Sandholtz, W., and Fligstein, N. (2001) (eds.), *The Institutionalization of Europe* (Oxford: Oxford University Press).

Summers, Lawrence (1991) 'Regionalism and the World Trading System'.

Reader 2

Policy Implications of Africa's Experience with Regionalism: Charting a New Course for Continental Unity

Introduction

Africa's vision for continental economic and political integration continues to fascinate nations around the world and inspire countries within the continent. Mansfield and Milner briefly discuss the many different ways that regionalism can be defined. In this paper, it is defined as their description of Fishlow and Haggard's explanation of it, 'a political process characterized by economic policy co-operation and co-ordination among countries' (Mansfield and Milner 1999: 592). By engaging in the respective regional economic integration efforts, peace and progress (with the exception of Darfur, Somalia, Guinea Bissau, and Mali) has suddenly brought calm to a continent that had been marred by continual warfare and divisions during the Cold War era. After the Cold War period, visionary beginning for regionalism in Africa would surely have been best, but the historical window of opportunity for such visionary beginnings, in terms of development and growth, was missed. This is because the concrete foundations of Africa's regionalism were poured without a plan. Regionalism on the African continent since then has also undergone an interruption: the old regionalism and the new regionalism.[16] In view of these, Africa's regional economic integration schemes are confronted by two policy implications: a false-start development coupled with a breakneck speed without any vision or plan, and management of proliferating bilateralism and the multilateralism it

---

[16] The first wave (old regionalism) faltered and gradually fizzled out in the 1960s and early 1970s, especially in the wake of the 1965 European Community crisis and the challenge to supranationalism**Supranationalism** is a method of decision-making in political communities, wherein power is held by independent appointed officials or by representatives elected by the legislatures or people of the member states.
.....**Click the link for more information.** posed by Charles de Gaulle's high politics. The second wave of regionalism and a concurrent revival in its study came about as a result of a series of momentous structural and policy changes in the late 1980s and early 1990s, all of which are said to have greatly increased the significance of the intrinsic dynamics of regional forces, in particular those in Africa at the expense of global factors.

implies. In other words, Africa's idea of coming together in blocs is a collective action problem which the African Union Commission (AUC) must realize and begin to deal with.

This article is organized as follows: the next section provides a background and the political economy framework of trade liberalization in general and preferential trade liberalization in particular. Section 3 presents the current state of play on the continent. Section 4 uses the political-economy narrative framework in section 2 to organize thinking about the causes of Africa's regionalism, with a discussion of African version of the 'domino effect' theory developed by Baldwin (1993, 1997), taking the central stage. The section also employs the framework to trace out the likely evolution of Africa's regionalism in the just past. Section 5 discusses options for taking the continent toward an integrated Africa. This includes a more detailed discussion of suggested management priorities. Drawing on the lessons from the European Union—the best known regional integration arrangement of our time—this paper discusses short and long-term institutional options for Africa's regionalism. The final section concludes the paper.

The Politico-economy of Africa's Regionalism

Regional economic integration involves preferential reductions in protection. The determinants of the scope of regionalism are therefore intrinsically tied to the political economy of protection. Although this logic can be extremely simple in most cases, it can be quite involved in complex situations like the overlapping prevalent in Africa. It is therefore fruitful to review the basic political economy logic of protection before turning its application to Africa's regionalism. From a political economy perspective, exports are good and imports are bad for any country in the world economy. This is why trade negotiators refer to tariff cutting as a 'concession' when their own nation does it, but 'improved market access' when their trade partners do it. Governments, in other words, are driven by mercantilist motives when it comes to trade policy. People are afraid of liberalization because of a number of factors, including the possibility of unwanted competition in the local market, the outsourcing of work to other countries, and the loss of control over the market by the government. In short, it allows countries to conduct trade negotiations based on an exchange of market access, known as reciprocity in World Trade Organization (WTO) jargon.

The next argument is the suggestion that regional trade agreements (RTAs) erode vested opposition to multilateral liberalization and reduce the value of preference, reducing their discriminatory impact over time (Best and Christiansen 2008: 437). Sandholtz and Stone Sweet describe the neo-functionalist theory of regionalism (2010). Although this theory is used to describe how to effectively integrate regionally, it can also be applied through the processes of the positive spillover effect, to the increased number of transactions, and the transfer of domestic allegiances predicted by the theory that increased integration should lead to greater allegiance to a regional market. The question is then whether this action could be recreated on a multilateral level. It is possible to argue that it could, because of the fact that larger companies and those acclimatized to existing in a regional market are more likely to survive in a multilateral free trade situation, and therefore are more likely to push for it. In tandem they are more likely to gradually squeeze out or change those industries that would oppose it. In another development, Mansfield and Milner's paper demonstrates how Oye purports this view (1999: 603), though they also include a quote from Krueger that suggests that exporters' desire for multilateral liberalization may be stunted by regionalism due to vested interests profiting from trade diversion increasing in size (p. 603–604).

In consideration of how RTAs help developing countries learn how to trade and test out liberalization in an environment protected from global competition, Lamy illustrates how RTAs can be used as a tool of development. With emphasis by Best and Christiansen (2008: 437), it is possible to provide 'closer and more stable economic relationships with immediate neighbouring countries to underpin and lock in political reform' and to support a country's economy through non-reciprocal trade agreements (Lamy 2002: 1405). In buttressing this point, Baldwin states that one of the reasons that the US entered NAFTA was its desire to divert foreign investment to Mexico (because of its privileged access to US markets) that would have otherwise gone to third world countries, therefore using it as a development tool (Baldwin 1993: 2). Though indeed useful, the World Bank notes in its 2005 report that this could be creating future problems, with poorer countries being reluctant to let go of their comparative advantages (World Bank 2005: 134). This is a glaring weakness in the advocacy of the use of non-reciprocal trade agreements as instruments of development. Ethier, on the other hand, uses the example of the former Soviet countries and their entrance into high numbers of regional agreements to show how a country can use these agreements in order to highlight a commitment to reform and market openness, to attract investment and capital. Furthermore, the creation of dispute settlement mechanisms and procedures offer those committing the investment and capital some assurance that they can take action in the case of a backslide from commitments (Ethier 1998: 1155). The trust built and experience earned from these agreements will provide solid ground upon which to build closer and more stable trade relationships.

The final point is in relation to the unwieldiness of the GATT/WTO in trade issues. Baldwin, although not a proponent of the idea himself, notes that the GATT/WTO is 'outmoded and too cumbersome to deal with the complexities of contemporary trade issues' (Baldwin 1993: 2). The idea behind this argument is that regions can advance liberalization in ways that the GATT/WTO cannot. As Ethier notes, 'fewer participants presumably mean fewer conflicts of interest and fewer areas of disagreement' (Ethier 1998: 1153). However, looking at RTAs in a different way, one may consider them to be a mechanism for larger and more powerful countries to hold on to their power. Mansfield and Reinhardt (2003) note that as WTO membership expands, larger membership reduces the ability of individual countries to influence the content and pace of most favourite nation (MFN) liberalization, and makes it more difficult to formulate coordinated positions. As we can see from this section, there are strong arguments for the use of RTAs as means to act on needs that have less to do with trade than with development, politics, and efficiency. It must be accepted, however, that there are legitimate concerns arising from some of these agreements, especially in the areas of non-reciprocal trade agreements, large countries using RTAs to protect their interests, and trade diversion.

Preferential Trade Liberalization

The next point we will look at purports the view that RTAs generally are not actually about trade within a region, but are used for other reasons. On

NAFTA, Baldwin comments, 'The entire Mexican economy is smaller than that of the Los Angeles basin . . . It is highly unlikely that the US views this . . . as substituting in any way for global trade liberalization' (Baldwin 1993: 2). Baldwin attributes it instead to geopolitical reasons. We can see many examples of countries using RTAs as part of strategic or political alliances, such as the pooling of steel and coal production in the European Coal and Steel Community (ECSC), as a way of avoiding future conflicts leading to wars (Lamy 2002: 1405). This assumption believes such relationship strengthens ties between states and builds trust. Where these kinds of agreements are not beneficial to trade liberalization, they generally do not harm it either. RTAs are also used to reinforce established trading links between countries, as Summers notes, *"Most seriously contemplated efforts at regional integration involving industrialized countries cement what are already large and disproportionately strong trading relationships. To this extent they are likely to be trade creating rather than trade diverting"* (Summers 1991: 298). It is possible, however, that over time these relationships may become trade diverting as industries within the region strive to protect their interests. This is a potential weakness and will be examined more closely later in the case of Africa's regional integration schemes. Finally, states use regional agreements to attract foreign capital, whether through commitment to reform, reduction of duties, or other methods, so that they have a better chance of success in the multilateral trading system (Ethier 1998: 1157). In this situation, RTAs encourage enthusiasm for the multilateral trading system, and the development and stabilization of the economy of a country using these means will lead to their further participation in liberalization and the global economy.

Other scholars in this area have abandoned their attempts to make this argument, instead claiming that this is in fact irrelevant. Lamy states that in theory, multilateral liberalization is best because it avoids the risks of trade diversion, but goes on to make the point that if one removes the assumption that there is an environment of perfect competition, then we begin to see a different picture regarding the benefits of competition and scale effects of RTAs on the participating economies (Lamy 2002: 1401–1402). Looking at the situation through Lamy's lens, we can see the other effects of RTAs in the areas of investment, growth, and the removal of non-tariff barriers; arguably, the strength of these factors in trade creation outweighs any possible trade diversion. Moreover, Ethier states that there is a big difference between what he calls 'new regionalism' and 'old regionalism', and blames the preoccupation with the trade diversion / trade creation argument in this area on a hangover from the discussion of old regionalism (Ethier 1998: 1150). There are other kinds of diversions to worry about in the context of regionalism and its effect on multilateral trade liberalization: 'Proliferating regional agreements absorb scarce negotiating resources (in the case of Africa's regional trading blocs) and crowd out policymakers' attention' (World Bank 2005: 133). Attention diversion is a major concern. Panagariya discusses how options made available through regional agreements might distract countries from multilateral liberalization processes (Panagariya 2000). This concern could be challenged, because the current trend since the proliferation of new regionalism since the 1980s suggests that we have little to worry about, given the steadily rising membership of WTO/GATT (WTO 2012). However, it is very difficult to accurately measure the concept of attention, with other arguments easily promoted by using other methods of measurement, such as the number and frequency of bilateral and regional trade agreements versus WTO/GATT multilateral agreements. Here a possible negative effect of RTAs on multilateral liberalization must be conceded.

The final argument is that the formation of RTAs may lead to the emergence of a trade block mentality. 'As [a] country accedes to the bloc, the potential economic benefits of entry for the next country on the outside margin rises and may offset the higher noneconomic costs of entry it faces' (Panagariya 2000: 318). This suggests a snowball effect, and the eventual existence of major competing trading blocs. This, it must be accepted, is a legitimate concern. The only way to battle the threat of a trade bloc situation arising is to continue momentum in the area of multilateral trade liberalization, to keep it relevant and to continue to monitor and control the possible negative effects of RTAs on the mentalities of the states involved. Arguably, the findings levelled to paint RTAs as negative in the drive for multilateral trade liberalization can, for the most part, be undermined or, at the very least, considered questionable. It is in the areas of trade bloc formation and attention diversion, especially among developing countries, that concern may be directed. However, these concerns are not reason to abandon RTAs.

Current State of Play on the African Continental

In Africa's case, the context in which regionalization takes place is markedly different for several reasons. The rules have changed and it seems that what is now called the 'new regionalism' is a very different creature from the 'old regionalism' of the post-war years. Increasingly, regionalism is viewed by many states as a solution to many of the ills engendered by a new international economic order. For most states, the pressing question now is not whether regionalism is desirable, but rather how its potential may best be harnessed. One of the central elements in Nkrumah's seminal work *Neocolonialism: The Last Stage of Imperialism* is the concept of an integrated African economy. He argued that there could be no sustainable development in Africa in the interest of the African people unless there was a continent-wide integration of the production system as a whole, in particular the use of resources—oil, forest products, minerals, etc.—to build an integrated industrial complex (Nkrumah 1965: 234). In the same vein, he emphasized that the initial capital for constructing such a complex was being lost through siphoning off of surplus from Africa by the multinationals (ibid.: 238). He further underlined the importance of common markets within and of Africa. Nkrumah was a great believer in economic synergies and economies of scale on the African level. Two decades later, Nkrumah's vision was concretised in the Lagos Plan of Action, 1980, drawn up by the Economic Commission for Africa. But as Adebayo Adedeji puts it, 'These [plans] were opposed, undermined and jettisoned by the Bretton Woods institutions and Africans were thus impeded from exercising the basic and fundamental right to make decisions about their future' (Adedeji 2002: 35–36). The argument is that both regional and continental unity—whether economic or political—had to be cast in a pan-African vision which by definition was anti-imperialist and still remains so.

For African countries in the wake of liberation from colonial powers, the need to regionalize seemed obvious. Given their weak economies and overwhelming dependence on the export of low-cost primary commodities for trade, it was argued that only through integration and cooperation could Africa hope to achieve the benefits of larger markets, economies of scale, and functional spillovers from cooperation. Countries could pool benefits arising from a greater exploitation of comparative advantage, and Africa's highly mobile labour forces would be freed from the artificial barriers to movement imposed by colonialism. Also, solidarity would allow for cooperation on the international stage, and give Africa a much stronger voice in bargaining with powerful developed economies. The economic and political rationale for regionalism was further reinforced by the apparent success of European integration and, at home, given impetus by the popular ideology of pan-Africanism—the prospect of reuniting and knitting together all African peoples artificially separated by cultural and geographical borders imposed during colonial rule.

Despite a proliferation of well-intentioned regional initiatives by African leaders proclaiming the need for regional integration, the historical track record reveals an overwhelming preponderance of failed or ineffective organizations. The blame can be attributed to two critical factors: the structural characteristics of post-liberation African economies, which have extremely low levels of industrialization and technological capability, and the failure of the pan-Africanist unification project started in the 1960s. This means that opportunities to create technological spillover effect and economies of scale by integrating common productive processes were scarce and hence the spillover of political cooperation from technical cooperation predicted by functionalist and neo-functionalist theories failed to materialize. Another major factor in the failure of early African schemes is their continuous reliance on inward-looking regionalism. Elements of this approach, justified by popular dependency theories, suggested that African countries could liberate themselves from the exploitation to which they had been subjected during colonialism by closing themselves off to outside countries and relying on the expansion of a large internal market to generate growth and development. But individual African countries remain so small in economic terms that even when taken as a whole, entire regions are still relative lightweights compared to developed countries. In addition, the reliance of African countries on North–South trade remains too great to allow for isolation. Finally, there is still what some have called the central problem of regionalism. Quite simply, regionalism requires member countries to cede some level of authority and sovereignty to the regional level and the regional levels to the fulfilment of the African Economic Community agenda. In Africa, attempts at integration continue, even as at now to intensify rather than reduce differences between countries. This is because in noncore countries, socio-economic conditions are quite different from those in Europe. The decision to engage in areas of low politics, as described by neo-functionalism, is highly politically charged, as national governments are required to concede certain degrees of autonomy over domestic matters, even if they are primarily technical (Axline 1979: 5).

In the modern era, Europe provides the most successful example of regionalism at work. Early theories of regionalism were almost entirely Eurocentric, and many of the ideas which first emerged in response to the European experience are still influential today. In particular, Haas's (1958 and 1964) concept of functional spillover represents a watershed in the development of the literature and, as we argue later, is still of central importance to the case of African regionalization. Haas is generally regarded as the father of a theory called neo-functionalism. His theory (and its theoretical antecedent, functionalism) arose out of the European integration experiences in the early post-war years. The idea of a united Europe has historical roots that predate the twentieth century, but in its modern form, it began as the European Coal and Steel Community (ECSC) in 1951, which expanded to become the European Economic Community (EEC). The original intent of the ECSC was to stabilize the production of steel across Europe in order to prevent ruinous competition during the 1950s, and its importance was twofold. First, by creating solidarity between governments, the possibility of war would become extremely improbable. Second, the joint regulation, and the ending of tariffs and border controls, laid out a model for the rest of Europe where national interests could still be met by giving up regulation to a supranational authority (Jones 1996: 9–10).While functionalism was limited to the formation of non-political institutions, neo-functionalism built on it to eliminate the artificial separation of politics from economics, by including the notion of functional spillovers. Haas (1958 and 1964), using the framework of functionalism and building on the theories of Deutsch, Sidney, and Kahn (1958), suggested that increased trans-border exchanges and cooperation in technical areas (such as the production of coal and steel) would lead to increased transnational interdependence and in turn create functional spillovers into other realms, essentially allowing the integration process to be driven under its own steam.

Haas (1964: 38) noted, 'Certain kinds of organizational tasks most intimately related to group and national aspirations can be expected to result in integration *even though* the actors responsible for this development may not deliberately work towards such an end.' According to the theory, initial cooperation on the creation of common institutions in non-political (and hence non-controversial) policy areas is, over time, not only deepened, but also widened to include the realm of other connected policy areas. The deliberate design of institutions is seen as the most effective means for solving common problems, and these, in turn, are instrumental to 'the creation of functional as well as political spillover and ultimately to a redefinition of group identity around the regional unit' (Fawcett and Hurrell 1995: 59). Importantly, governments of member states are locked into the integration process and have little room to manoeuvre. The structural and functional implications of trans-border exchanges inevitably coerce national governments into greater degrees of cooperation, coordination, and integration.

Early attempts at South–South cooperation produced organizations such as the G-77, the Non-Aligned Movement, the United Nations Conference on Trade and Development (UNCTAD), and the Organization of African Unity (OAU), all operating under the similar notion that organizing regionally was one way to improve their economic lot in the global order. Significantly, these organizations were grounded in the preferred method of state industrialization at the time, namely import-substitution strategies. Accepted wisdom suggests that the optimal route to economic development lay in the imposition of strong regional tariff barriers which would, over time, allow industries to grow strong enough to compete internationally. For developing countries, regionalization seemed to offer protection from the 'cold winds of intensifying world-market competition' (Arrighi, Silver, and Brewer 2003: 23), while allowing infant industries to take advantage of expanded regional markets behind high protectionist barriers. A case in point is early attempts at regional integration by Africa.

Taking the Developmental Regionalism Model

As mentioned in the introduction, it would have been optimal for Africa's regionalism to have developed from visionary beginning, but this was not to be. The African Economic Community agenda, for example, envisioned the continent moving from subregional trading blocs to a bona fide regional community of nations where collective efforts are made for peace, prosperity, and progress. This, they suggested, could be catalyzed by the progressive integration of the African economy, ultimately leading to the African economic and monetary community. Vision, unfortunately, takes time—a lot of time—to come to fruition. Europeans discussed the future shape of regional integration on and off for about ten years from the late 1940s to the late 1950s. Although various visionaries in Africa have proposed many schemes since the independence movements of the 1960s, the leaders of the region's main powers have yet to hold an extended discussion on visions for regional integration. At this state it is not useful to highlight scary, low-probability events for Africa's regionalism, but it is crucial to point out that regional trade flows are the key to each African nation's competitiveness in the world economy. If something happened to disrupt intra-regional trade for example, Nigerian firms would find it extremely hard to be competitive in other African countries when it comes to timelines, quality, and price; the same can be said of other sub regional integration scheme members. To paraphrase an old saying, if Africa's sub regional economic schemes don't hang together on trade, they will be hanged separately on trade in the world marketplace. All of Africa has a stake in ensuring that regional trade is well managed. But as the situation stands today, nothing and no one takes responsibility for this 'collective action' problem. This is why I believe that what the sub regions need today is management, not vision. One name for this could be the *New African Inter-regional Management Commission*, the NAIMAC for short. This is because the several efforts initiated by the African Union Commission to date is only summitry in nature and will not lead to any ultimate integration of the regional trading blocs.[17]

Charting a New Course for Africa's Regionalism

The developmental integration model derives from the notion of the developmental state and encapsulates the idea of state intervention in

---

[17] There are currently more than forty-two organizations and institutions on the continent that would need to be integrated into the AU's structure. This task is compounded by the fact that despite the similarities, there exist distinct differences in institutional structures, financial patrons, as well as ideologies and strategies between these organizations and the AU, from which only the former benefits.

markets to promote national development agendas (Leftwich 1996). Like open regionalism,[18] it is based on the idea that market expansion can create opportunities for firms to become internationally competitive; but looking at many of the Africa's regional economic integration projects, they are falling apart because most have problems that are not associated with openness. Africa's integration project needs a new proposal as a corrective measure to the static character of the market approach and its sole focus on trade creation and trade diversion, and the continent's open regionalism's one-sided goal of market liberalization and tendency to widen economic differences between less developed and more developed areas. In what the African Economic Community (AEC) agenda aims to do, their intentions have much to do with the European kind of integration based on market-based theories of integration. But the conclusions drawn here are that the AEC must still acknowledge that social and political forces matter, and that the state is still seen as the driving force behind regional projects. The behaviour of states in Africa must be coerced to snap out of their still-embedded colonial mentality of tying their economic and social development to the fortunes of their colonial masters. Africa requires a developmental approach to regional integration, phasing in the four most prominent regional economic blocs for the gradual pulling of their efforts toward a community per the Abuja Treaty.

The developmental integration approach is characterized by a number of central propositions. First, the objective of the integration process is economic and social development—a major departure from other economic models of integration, with their emphasis on efficiency maximization (Lee 2002). For countries with low levels of industrialization and little productive capacity, increased efficiency through regional market expansion is often meaningless. Instead, integration is more likely to further exacerbate underdevelopment by removing the few remaining barriers protecting domestic industries. Unable to compete on a level playing field with other regional and international industries, what little productive capacity a country has is either absorbed by firms with headquarters in other countries, or migrates elsewhere in the region. While this might result in the enhancement of total regional efficiency and

---

[18] See Edward Mansfield and Helen Milner (1999), 'The New Wave of Regionalism', *International Organization* 53 (3): 590.

expansion in production, the reality is that most of the benefits accruing to those areas of the region which are already the most developed may not reach other areas in need of development.

In order for domestic industries to take advantage of expanded markets, productive capacity must first be enhanced through such measures as improved infrastructure, policy coordination, state loans, and subsidy incentives. Since regionalization often results in a polarizing effect between member states with differing levels of industrial capability, developmental integration includes the implementation of compensatory and corrective measures to redress the balance (Lee 2002: 24–27). Such compensatory measures include financial transfer and tax transfer mechanisms, while corrective measures include planned regional industrial development, priority loans, improved conditions for development, and differing reductions on tariffs and common fiscal incentives to invest. This requires an approach to integration with greater state involvement in economic and social matters, in order to allocate industry and development funds within a liberalizing regional economy. The need for the redistribution of gains and the enhancement of productive capacity suggests a further departure of developmental integration from traditional economic models, namely the role played by explicit political commitment and state involvement in the regionalization process. In contrast to open regionalism, developmental integration views these factors as the backbone of the process (Mittelman 1999: 48).

Managing Africa's Regional Integration Schemes

As it stands now, the functionality of Africa's inter-regionalism architecture is heavily dependent on an efficient and credible African Union Commission as an embodiment of a renewed pan-Africanist body and a catalyst for continental integration. Indeed, the African Economic Community agenda must include in its plans to fully engage regional blocs into both intra- and intergovernmental cooperation to establish adequate redistributive mechanisms and coordinate policies that will deepen their relationships.[19] For example, a major feature of

---

[19] However, as an organization with a huge and diverse membership representing a poor and conflict-ridden continent, the AU is bound to face a number of challenges to its unifying efforts, such as managing the impending implementation crisis from within or fulfilling the world's high expectations despite its meagre funding.

developmental integration is to plan regional industrial development projects, often in the form of economic 'zones of development', 'regional bloc corridors', or 'regional growth triangles' which may transcend state borders and rely on a combination of public and private capital, and intergovernmental partnerships to succeed. Industries should be allocated to specific areas of the sub regions on the basis of comparative advantage, not only to supply the needs of the regions on a more efficient basis, but in the process to result in employment creation, technology transfer, and infrastructure development. Such industries according to Nesedurai (2003), within the ambit of developmental regionalism are neither a complete resistance to globalization, nor complete acquiescence to global market forces. Instead, it encompasses a period of temporary and limited resistance to aspects of globalization during which capacity is enhanced to ensure that domestic businesses can eventually participate in global market activities (Nesedurai 2003: 214).

Second, the need for the 'New Inter-Regional Management Commission' (NAIMAC) by the AU Commission is pressing, to enable major reforms within the African Economic Community agenda and to rationalize the existing institutional arrangements. Since the regional integration arrangements in Africa already have foundations (secretariats), what is needed is just some firming up of the various protocols and the linkages required to pull out four major regional integration arrangements together as the first batch toward an overall continental unity. This new arrangement (NAIMAC) will act as the new African WTO in terms of managing the various trade flows, both in terms of intra- and inter-regional integration on the continent.

Management Priorities for Growth

The priority of this new inter-regional management effort (commission) should be to ensure that the four blocs of RIAs do not become a source of friction; neither would they remain stumbling blocks, other than building blocks for the achievement of continental unity. Consequently, there is very little institutional or legal resistance to raising tariffs back up. As a first step in the new African management effort, attention should be paid to reduce the fragility of the system by bringing the legal constraints of the four major regional integration arrangements in Africa in line with the political constraints (the fact that all would lose from a tariff war). The first priority is to convince the African nations to bundle their applied rates within the WTO. The invigorated RIAs should, as blocs, insist that nations doing this get full credit in the Doha Round market access talks. Indeed, this move would encourage other developing nations to do the same with their applied rates, and such would contribute positively to unblocking progress in the ongoing WTO round. These actions would give the new organization (NAIMAC) a high and strongly positive international profile, demonstrating to the world that the new groupings are WTO-friendly.

The third priority for the New African Regional Management Effort would be to improve transparency within the RIAs. There are several obvious deliverables here. The first would be to set up an African information clearing house for preferences, rules of origin, and the like. Indeed, as part of the new management effort, the participating nations could commit themselves to notifying the African Union Commission of any and all trade policies or legal changes that affect trade within the inter-regional blocs. The new regional management effort could also agree on minimum standards for the four selected RIAs in Africa to accept trade agreements that meet the NAIMAC conditions. Of course, the point of departure may be to set conditions that would be mild enough to fit all the existing RIAs (just like what GATT had to legalize existing preferences in 1947 with the British Commonwealth). These measures would be an improvement over the current lack of discipline faced by the RIAs that are not notified under Article 24 of WTO/GATT rules. The value of such standards would become apparent if nations fail to fulfil the liberalization promises made within the RIAs. Given the vast differences around the world, the WTO has found it impossible to improve the discipline of RIAS, especially those notified under the enabling clause. In a sense, the RIAs compliant status would provide a level of discipline intermediate to Article 24 and the enabling clause. Such a thing might prove attractive to other South–South RIAs. Third, as it stands, there is no systematic surveillance and enforcement mechanism covering all the African RIAs. Given the diverse political situation of nations in the sub regional blocs, such surveillance and enforcement would have to be of the fair-broker or technocratic type. There is no way those RIAs members could agree to give such a body any sort of teeth like those that the European Union's commission has, but the very existence of an unbiased observer and reporter of facts can often go a long way to resolve dispute or avoid them in the first place. Just to give one example—nations have often been known to implement subtle measures that nullify and impair the effect of tariff reductions they have committed to. If the tariff cutting was done in the context of the WTO, an aggrieved party could always ask a WTO panel to make a determination on the matter. In Africa, there is no single body for investigating such claims. Actually, the old GATT panels are a better analogy than the current system of WTO panels. Before the Uruguay Round, the findings of GATT panels could be locked in, and occasionally they were, but the very existence of such a fair-broker body reduced trade tensions around the world.

Long-term Management Effort

Turning now to longer-run issues is the fact that most regional integration efforts in the world have two main goals: to foster political harmony among their members and to instil an economic efficiency in the economies of member states for growth and development. A very broad range of organizational and institutional arrangements are needed to achieve such goals, which in themselves are not easy. Regional integration schemes lie on a continuum of supranationality—at least, in the history that we have studied of successful ones. At the supranational end of the spectrum is the EU with its legal system, supremacy of EU Court, and decision-making by majority voting. At the other end of the spectrum is the purely intergovernmental arrangement like the North Atlantic Free Trade Area (NAFTA). In between are regional trade arrangements such as the European Free Trade Association (EFTA) that are intergovernmental in terms of decision-making but which have institutions and organizations that induce and lock in cooperation. The crucial dividing line between intergovernmental and supranational lies in decision-making. If the regional organization can make decisions that bind all the members, yet need not be approved by each member, then we can say that the organization is supranational. For example, the EU decides its common external tariff—including anti-dumping duties—on the basis of majority voting. Consequently, EU members frequently find themselves having to adopt trade policies that they do not want; in intergovernmental organizations such as NAFTA and EFTA, all nations must agree to everything.

The NAIMAC: Could That Function Like EFTA?

The challenge of regionalism therefore is the lack of common values based on the trend among African states who want to forge regional ties without any serious attempts to create building blocks for a shared inter-regional or subregional identity. In terms of Africa's desire for continental unity, the EU model is a non-starter for Africa's regional integration effort.[20] Imagine how ridiculous it would be to propose an African regional economic integration in which South Africa would have to adopt a trade policy it disagrees with because Nigeria and Egypt voted for it. The nations in the continent are perfectly uninterested in transferring national sovereignty over trade policy to a supranational trade body. And this fact is completely independent of the question of existing conflicts among potential members of any such arrangement. Whether we are talking about Egypt and Libya in North Africa, South Africa and Mozambique in the south, Nigeria and Cameroon in the west of Africa, Kenya and Tanzania in the east, and the Central African Republic and DRC—these countries within the bloc of ECOWAS, COMESA, SADC, the Economic Community of Central African States (ECCAS), and the like cannot accept the pooling of sovereignty that the African Union intends to do or the European Union would imply. The barrier is not nature or membership of an African Continental version of the EU; it is the necessity of sacrificing national sovereignty to such a body. Supranationality, even limited to trade policy, is not for Africa, not now and not for the foreseeable future.

The North Atlantic Free Trade Area (NAFTA) provides an alternation template, but it too is wrong for Africa's regionalism. NAFTA is one of the few regional arrangements outside of Europe that has really worked in the sense of liberalizing trade that would not otherwise have been liberalized and thus significantly shifting trade patterns (Holmes 2005). However, NAFTA's success has nothing to do with its institutional arrangements. It works for reasons akin to the reason the international trade system worked before WWI when Pax Britannica held sway. It is dominated commercially by a single nation and that nation really wants it to work. The United States market (as measured by GDP) is eighteen times that of Mexico's and twelve times that of Canada. Since market size equates with

---

[20] See excerpts from the African Association for Public Administration and Management 1969, in *Problems and Prospects of Regional Cooperation in Africa* (Nairobi: English Press).

negotiating power in trade arrangements, it is easy to see why NAFTA works. A single nation, the United States of America, has 90 per cent of the negotiating power and yet really cares about the organization's success for political, geo-strategic and commercial reasons. NAFTA's institutions are not notably more developed than those of African Union Commission (each of the three NAFTAns maintains a national section that sits in its own capital, coming together only periodically). If NAFTA institutions were applied to the free trade areas among three roughly equal nations, it would have failed just as the vast majority of over two hundred RTAs in the world have failed or have been non-performing.

In the case of Africa's regionalism, the European Free Trade Association (EFTA) provides the best model for the long-run shape of the African Economic Community agenda of continental integration since EFTA is purely intergovernmental but has an efficient secretariat and enough institutional structure to deal with new challenges, new members, and the expansion of the integration regime. In its early days, EFTA included advanced industrial nations like the United Kingdom and Switzerland, but also had developing nations like Portugal and was able to produce special rules for such developing countries. Therefore, given the great disparities in Africa regional integration programs, the African Economic Community agenda currently managed by the African Union should include (General Scheme of Preferences) GSP-like policies and a 'structural funds' set-up as in the European Union.[21] This arrangement would mitigate the overlapping prevalent in Africa and avoid the regional incompatibilities by bringing coherence to preferences and the rules of origin problems. The above will also allow for a conditionally open regionalism in Africa, which would result in many of the efficiency aspects of regional integration schemes and still harness the critical political forces that are generated by reciprocal trade liberalization. Since South Africa is a more developed country in Africa, attempts must be made to link such similar countries within Africa in the likes of Egypt, Kenya, Nigeria, Ghana,

---

[21] The *structural funds* and the *cohesion fund* are financial tools set up to implement the regional policy of the European Union. They aim to reduce regional disparities in terms of income, wealth, and opportunities. Europe's poorer regions receive most of the support, but all European regions are eligible for funding under the policy's various funds and programs. The current regional policy framework is set for a period of seven years, from 2007 to 2013.

Zimbabwe, Botswana, Ivory Coast, Cameroon, Libya, DRC, and a few others who may be willing to begin the nucleus of the new inter-regional management effort (NAIMAC) pilot project towards a continent-wide integration of their various subregional integration blocs.

Conclusion

In this article, I have attempted to apply the lessons of European Community's integration to the African situation stemming from the pan-African vision of continental unity of Africans. While the situation in the European Union in the 1950s shares some features of the pan-African continental agenda of unity in the 1960s, the nature of the African vision is remarkably different. The difference lies in the fact that, while the European model based its vision on an economic premise and tying that to key minerals coal and steel that were important to their economies at the time, Africa's vision of regional integration schemes were hurriedly conceived out of the freedom from colonialism and were targeted at imperialist measures that were impeding their development into full-fledged counties with sovereignty. While the European model relies more on markets that are large and well developed, Africa's markets are still developing and require much more interactions to match those of the EU. Moreover, the African vision of unity was not initially to come together but to end neo-colonialism. Besides, most of the countries in the African setting lack manufacturing industries required for growth. In effect, when drawing lessons from Europe's experience, African leaders, especially those managing the African Union Commission at Addis Ababa should critically observe the pan-African vision and how radical such thinking was by today's standards. Nowadays, almost all political leaders in Africa, apart from the late Libyan leader, Muammar al-Qaddafi, view a loss of national sovereignty as a negative, in fact a cost that might be worth paying to enjoy the economic and political benefits of tighter economic integration with one's brothers (neighbours). Putting the above statements in another way, today's African leaders view the loss of sovereignty as the cost and the economic integration as the benefit. In the 1950s, Europeans' leaders saw the loss of national sovereignty as the goal; economic integration was the means to achieve that goal. Can our leaders relegate their respective national sovereignties for the lone goal of Africa's unity? And that is the million-dollar question.

Works Cited / Further Readings

Adedeji, Adebayo (1984), 'The economic evolution of developing Africa', in Crowder, Michael (ed.), *The Cambridge History of Africa—Vol. 8* (Cambridge: Cambridge University Press), 231.

Arrighi, G., B. Silver, and B. Brewer (2003) 'Industrial convergence, globalization, and the persistence of the north–south divide', *Studies in Comparative International Development* 38(1). Axline, W. A. (1994) (ed.), *The political economy of regional integration* (London: Frances Pinter).

Baldwin, R. (1993), 'A Domino Theory of Regionalism', *Nber Working Paper Series*, No. 4465 (Cambridge, MA: National Bureau of Economic Research).

——— (1997), 'The Causes of Regionalism', *The World Economy*, 20(7): 865–888.

——— and C. Wyplosz (2006), *The Economics of European Integration*, 2nd edition (McGraw Hill) 1st edition, 2003.

Best, E. and Christiansen, T. (2008), 'Regionalism in International Affairs', in Baylis, J., Smith, S., and Owens, P. (eds.), *The Globalization of World Politics*, 4th ed. (New York: Oxford University Press), pp. 436–439.

Bergsten, F. (1997), 'Open Regionalism', *The World Economy*, 20(5): 545–565.

Deutsch, K., B. Sidney, and R. Kahn (1958), *Political community in the North Atlantic area* (Princeton: Princeton University Press).

Ethier, W. J. (1998), 'The New Regionalism', *The Economic Journal*, 108(449): 1149–1161.

Fawcett, L. and Hurrell, A.(1995) (eds.), *Regionalism in world politics. Regional organization and international order* (Oxford: Oxford University Press).

Fishlow and Haggard,

Frieden, J. A. (2007), *Global Capitalism: Its Fall and Rise in the Twentieth Century* (New York: Norton).

Haas, E. B. (1964), *Beyond the Nation State: Functionalism and International Organization* (Stanford: Stanford University Press).

—— (1968), *The Uniting of Europe: Politics, Social and Economic Forces, 1950–1957*, 2nd edition. (Stanford: Stanford University Press).

Hanrahan, C. and Johnson, R. (2010), *The US-EU Beef Hormone Dispute* (Washington DC: Congressional Research Service).

Holmes, T. (2005), 'What Drives Regional Trade Agreements that Work?' HEI master's thesis, Geneva.

Jones, Robert A. (1996), *The Politics and Economics of the European Union: An Introductory Text* (Cheltenham, UK: Edward Elgar).

Lamy, P. (2002), 'Stepping Stones or Stumbling Blocks? The EU's Approach Towards the Problem of Multilateralism vs Regionalism in Trade Policy', *The World Economy*, 25(10): 1399–1413.

Lee, M. (2002), 'Regionalisms in Africa: part of the problem or part of the solution', *Polis/R.C.S.P/C.P.S.R.9*, Numéro Spécial.

Leftwich, A. (1996) (ed.), *Democracy and Development* (Cambridge: Polity Press).

Manger, M. S. (2010), 'Vertical Trade Specialization and PTA Formation', workshop, The Politics of Trade Agreements: Theory, Measurement, and Empirical Analysis, Niehaus Center for Globalization and Governance, Princeton University, 29–30 April 2010.

Mansfield, E. and Milner, H. (1999), 'The New Wave of Regionalism', *International Organization*, 53(3): 589–627.

—— and Reinhardt, E. (2003), 'Multilateral Determinants of Regionalism: The Effects of GATT/WTO on the Formation of Preferential Trading Arrangements', *International Organization*, 57(3): 829–862.

Mittelman, J. (1999), 'Regionalisation in response to polarizing globalization', in B. Hettne, A. Inotai, and O. Sunkel (eds.), *Globalism and the New Regionalism*, 48 (New York: St. Martin's Press).

Nesadurai, H. (2003), *Globalisation, domestic politics and regionalism: the ASEAN Free Trade Area* (London: Routledge).

Nkrumah, Kwame (1965), *Neo-Colonialism: The Last Stage of Imperialism* (London: Thomas Nelson & Sons, Ltd.).

Panagariya, A. (2000), 'Preferential Trade Liberalization: The Traditional Theory and New Developments', *Journal of Economic Literature*, 38(6): 287–331.

Summers, L. H. (1991), 'Regionalism and the World Trading System', in *Federal Reserve Bank of Kansas City Proceedings, 1991* (Kansas: Kansas City Federal Reserve), pp. 295–301.

Winham, G. R. (1999), 'Regionalism and the Evolving Global Trade System', in Barry, D. and Keith, R. C. (eds.), *Regionalism, Multilateralism, and the Politics of Global Trade* (Vancouver: UBC Press), pp. 54–70.

World Bank (2005), *Global Economic Prospects: Trade, Regionalism, and Development.* (Washington DC: World Bank).

WTO (2012), 'Understanding the WTO: Members and Observers', World Trade Organization website http://www.wto.org/english/thewto_e/whatis_e/tif_e/org6_e.htm accessed 19 November 2012

Reader 3

The Difficulty to Reconcile the Rhetoric: Pan-Africanism and Africa's Regionalism

Abstract

Majority of academics and policy analysts are overly idealistic about the potential of state-led regional cooperation. This line of thought is particularly strong in the debate about African regional integration organizations. Indeed, African regionalism is often seen as beneficial and an instrument for achieving socio-economic development and, more recently, also for security provision and good governance. This paper is of the view that deep regional integration should not be seen as an end, but rather a means to an end of greater economic growth. While the EU model promises the growth that African states seek, there are a number of reasons to question whether evolving into intergovernmental and supranational structures is the right model for the African Union.

Introduction

Beginning from the mid-1950s, Kwame Nkrumah of Ghana argued for African unity. At a rally in Accra in 1960, Nkrumah argued that all independent states in Africa should work together to create a union of African states. On 6 March 1960, he gave further support to his vision when he declared in a radio broadcast that so deep was Ghana's 'faith in African unity that we have declared our preparedness to surrender the sovereignty of Ghana, in whole or in part, in the interest of a union of African states and territories as soon as ever such a union becomes practicable'. In his book *I Speak of Freedom*, published in 1961, he reminded all Africans that imperialism had so thoroughly distorted and disarticulated African social formations that only continental unity could save the region from further deterioration. In *Africa Must Unite*, published in 1963, he articulated a clear agenda for the establishment of an African common market to complement the union of African states. As far as Nkrumah was concerned, the unity of Africa and the strength it would gather from continental integration of its economic and industrial development, supported by a united policy of non-alignment, could have a most powerful effect for world peace. This position was supported by Nnamdi Azikiwe (see 'The Future of Pan-Africanism', 1962); Modibo Keita (see 'The Foreign Policy of Mali', 1961); and Sekou Toure (see 'Africa's Future and the World'). In today's terms, Nkrumah was talking about the impacts of globalization on African economies because of their export nature of mainly primary and unprocessed goods as against the developed economies. This commitment to regionalism was part and parcel of the broader aspiration of continental integration, a vision that led to the creation of the Organization of African Unity (OAU) in 1963. The recent transformation of the OAU into the African Union (AU) has significantly strengthened the movement towards the goal of pan-African political and economic union. However, the new set-up at the continental level leads to the question of how the regional and sub regional initiatives and the AU can become mutually reinforcing.

In addition to the regional initiatives within Africa, there have been proposals and actual negotiations aimed at establishing North–South integration arrangements between Africa and developed countries or regions. These include the Economic Partnership Agreements (EPAs) presently being negotiated between four groups of African countries and the European Union (EU). At the global level, almost all African countries have become members of the World Trade Organization (WTO) or have applied for membership. Apart from the tariff reductions negotiated through the General Agreement on Tariffs and Trade (GATT) and, since 1995, under the World Trade Organization (WTO), the movement toward economic integration in Western Europe, Latin America, Africa, North America, and Asia has been the most important development affecting the level and structure of international trade in the post–World War II era. Many believe that integration of the economic (and ultimately political) systems of nation states is a way of bringing about not only rapid economic growth but also lasting peace through increased trade (ADB 2005). As a result, regional initiatives in Africa must adhere to the rules of the multilateral trading system, which, among other things, are important for the North–South trade arrangements. Another relevant point is the extent to which regional initiatives could help the African countries participate more effectively and take fuller advantage of the global economy.

This paper, which aims to shed some light on these issues, is structured as follows. First, a brief summary of the history of regional integration in Africa is provided. This sets a comparative stage for a thematic review of the constraints at country and regional levels in determination of the progress (or lack thereof) of regional integration. The final part will deal with the linkages between the regions and the global economy in respect of what Africa must do to chart a way forward.

The European Affair

In the history of the world, no other regional association has come as close to representing the ideals and effects (both positive and negative) of regionalism like the European Union. The history takes us back to around 1951, with the formation of European Coal and Steel Community (ECSC) between France, West Germany, Belgium, Luxembourg, and the Netherlands to pool the steel and coal resources of its member states. This treaty was signed in Paris. This was a fulfilment of a plan developed by a French economist, Jean Monnet, and publicized by the French foreign minister Robert Schuman, which was also strongly supported by the United States. The Treaty of Paris entered in force by 1952 and was time limited to fifty years. This coalition was very important because steel had played an important part in arms production in World War II and was a fundamental resource of the Western European states. The goal was a common program of post-war production and consumption of steel and coal that would unite in cooperation and reconciliation between the two countries, France and Germany, by controlling steel and coal, which were fundamental to war industries.

Indeed, the Treaty of Rome in 1957 witnessed the first organization to be based formally on principles of unity and certain aspects of supranational thought, which eventually spurred into existence the concepts of common markets and the like. In short, the first instances of the concept of a united European front have for its impetus *the First World War and the inadequacies of the peace settlement which induced the first sustained efforts to find an alternative to the fragmentation of Europe* (Heater 1992). The ECSC was the promoter for the later development of the European Community, who became later the European Union. Encouraged by the United States, an attempt was made to create a European Defense Community (EDC) and a European Political Community (EPC) to allow troops to be raised from Germany to face the Soviet threat but these attempts proved overambitious. Further, despite the retreat into an isolationist policy, the United States as the superpower of the time prompted the coal and steel concept to become *the linchpin of European economic and, arguably, political stability* (Kent 1989: 15).

The European Union will have a European Commission that is formally the Commission of the European Communities as the executive body, and alongside it, the European Parliament and the Council of the European Union, where the three main institutions govern the union. The Treaty of Maastricht identified five goals designed to unify Europe in more ways than just economically. The goals are:

> To strengthen the democratic governing of participating nations
> To improve the efficiency of the nations within the community
> To establish an economic and financial unification of the community
> To develop the community social dimension, and
> To establish a security policy for involved nations.

In order to reach these goals, the Treaty of Maastricht had various policies dealing with issues as industry, education, and youth. In addition, the treaty put a single European currency, the euro, in the works to establish fiscal unification in 1999. Within a four-year span, from 2004 to 2007, the European Community of countries expanded, bringing the number to twenty-seven (Lipgens 1982). To this end, therefore, the early years of European regionalism and their accompanying history are *directly linked to the post-war processes of international liberalization and international interdependence* (Tsoukalis 1997: 223). The need to unify, to present a strengthened front and to rebuild the continent are therefore the sources of rationale behind the early European regionalist principles which shaped the modern aspects of Europe's regional identity. Increasingly, the states of the continent began to see the possibilities afforded by cooperation and amicable relations, which are tenets of what is today considered the liberal school of thought in international relations.

The African Affair

In relation to Africa's arrangements, much has changed, but not enough in the continent's pursuit toward regionalism. Across the continent, Africa's leaders and citizens have taken dramatic steps to open and transform centralized economies, to invigorate the African private sector, and to build the institutions that can sustain political stability and economic development. Regional economic communities now operate in West, East, Central, and Southern Africa, and the treaty establishing the African Economic Community sets forth a vision of a continental community by 2025. The OAU Charter and the Constitutive Act establishing the African Union have placed emphasis on regional integration as one of the foundations of African unity. In addition, the Lagos Plan of Action in 1975 and the Abuja Treaty of 1991 elaborate the specific economic, political, and institutional mechanisms for attaining this idea. The adoption of the New Partnership for Africa's Development (NEPAD) also provides an overall development framework for the continent which assumes regional integration as one of its core objectives. In 1994, when the Abuja document became operational, it suggested where things were headed, how issues were going to be measured and handled in a step-by-step mode, and how the policy outcomes were finally going to unify Africa into a political community of states. Indeed, the establishment of the Commission of the African Union, and agreement on its priorities, makes it clear that Africa's leadership is committed to move the regional integration process forward, effectively and efficiently. Furthermore, the creation of the Commission of the African Union and the resounding commitment of Africa's leadership to regional integration means that Africa is now poised to move from the drawing board to implementation. But sadly to report, Africa's regionalism is surrounded by economic myths. However, not all of these myths have been consistent with each other, as each has played a useful narrative role in the process of integration. More important, perhaps, is that Africa's RIAs are an ensemble of economic myths that lies at the heart of African Union's sense of self.

Africa's Symbolic Regionalism

It is commonly understood that the Organization of African Unity (OAU) from 1963, when it was inaugurated, was merely talking shop (Farrell, Hettne, and van Langenhove). Rhetorical and symbolic diplomacy can of course be relevant, and the positive effects of the OAU, for instance, in the fight against colonialism and apartheid should not be ignored. Interestingly, the OAU's primary characteristic had never been implementation of agreed policies, and a similar discursive logic has been institutionalized in many regional organizations on the African continent. Indeed, most political leaders in Africa frequently engage in symbolic and discursive activities, whereby they praise the goals of regionalism and regional organization, sign cooperation treaties and agreements, but with only sporadic implementation of the protocols. Ever since the formation of most regional integration schemes across Africa, summitry has become part of such discursive and symbolic regionalism. The summits of heads of states of the main intergovernmental regional organizations, such as the African Union (AU), the Common Market for Eastern and Southern Africa (COMESA), the Economic Community of West African States (ECOWAS), and the Southern African Development Community (SADC), are gigantic events where the political leaders show to the world and their citizenry that they are promoting the cause of African regional cooperation and at the same time show that their state is important (or at least visible) on the international diplomatic stage. These summits and conferences are crucial elements in a discursive and even imaginary construction of regional organizations, and this social practice is then repeated and institutionalized at a large number of ministerial and other meetings, which in reality involves little debate and no wider consultation within or between member states.

The argument raised here is that symbolic regionalism has become chronic African and that it is used as image-boosting instrument whereby leaders can show support and loyalty for each other, which enables them to raise the profile, status, formal sovereignty, and image of their (often authoritarian) regimes, but without ensuring implementation of agreed policies. As Jeffrey Herbst correctly points out, 'African leaders are extremely enthusiastic about particular types of regional cooperation, especially those that highlight sovereignty, help secure national leaders, and ask little in return' (Herbst 2007: 1–2). Importantly, this logic should not necessarily be understood as a failure of regional cooperation. From the point of view of the political leaders, such discursive practices can be a rational and well-calculated strategy of non-implementation. Those who idealistically (even naively) believe that regional institutions are designed in order to implement agreed goals and solve collective action dilemmas will fail to understand the underlying logic of such. The overlapping membership of regional organizations on the African continent has been debated for several decades. The seemingly ineffective overlap is often taken as an indicator of a poor political commitment to regional cooperation. However, considering that the overlap is such a distinctive feature of African regional organizations, surprisingly few scholars try to answer for what purpose and in whose interest the overlap actually prevails. Part of the answer may be that the maintenance of a large number of competing and overlapping intergovernmental regional organizations is deliberate in order to increase the possibilities for rhetorical and discursive regionalism. One related hypothesis in need of further actualization is that weak political regimes are particularly prone to such behaviour and may search for as many arenas as possible to satisfy their quest for formal status and recognition. One such posture may well be that eventually it will not be the African Union but the most advanced and deep sub regional groupings—the building blocks of an African Economic Community that may become Africa's equivalent of the European Union. That means the African Union may continue to serve the prime objective of promoting African unity as a matter of identity and the external projection of African claims. Or yet still, the African Union may continue to represent the symbolic dimension of African unity, where some of the building blocks may evolve into strong representatives of deep regional arrangements.

What Kind of Political Union?

Indeed, the goal of regional organizations throughout the world is generally twofold: to foster political harmony among members and to foster economic efficiency of the member economies, all without actively causing harm to non-members. A very broad range of organizational and institutional arrangements have been used to attain these goals. The history of regional integration schemes rests on a continuum of supranationality. At the supranational end of the spectrum is the EU with its legal system, supremacy of the EU Court, and decision-making by majority voting. At the other end of the spectrum are the many purely intergovernmental arrangements such as NAFTA. In between are regional trade arrangements, such as the European Free Trade Association (EFTA), that are intergovernmental in terms of decision-making but which have institutions and organizations that induce and lock in cooperation. The crucial dividing line between intergovernmental and supranational lies in decision-making. If the regional organizations can make decisions that bind all the members, yet need not be approved by each member, then we can say that the organization is supranational. For example, the EU decides its common external tariff—including anti-dumping duties—on the basis of majority voting. Consequently, EU members frequently find themselves having to adopt trade policies that they do not want to adopt in their respective countries. But pertaining to intergovernmental organizations such as NAFTA and EFTA, all nations must agree to everything. In the case of Africa's regional integration agreements, they are importantly rooted in their respective colonial history, which differs markedly from Europe's history. This raises the fundamental question of whether deep regional integration toward a political union of states, and along the lines of the EU model, is the best way to achieve development goals for Africa.

Which Way for Africa?

The Union of African States was an early confederation established by Kwame Nkrumah in 1958 in the context of decolonization. The pan-Africanist Congress of Azania is a political party of South Africa established in 1959. Like many others on the African continent, it advocated African nationalism, socialism, and continental unity. Its body of ideas was drawn largely from the teachings of Anton Lembede, George Padmore, Marcus Garvey, Kwame Nkrumah, and W. E. B. Du Bois. In 1963, at the formation of the OAU, Ghanaian president Kwame Nkrumah proposed African political unification but was outmanoeuvred by the Nigerian-led Monrovian Group, which favoured a gradualist process to integration, starting with economic cooperation and leading eventually to a political union. At the July 2007 AU summit in Accra, Ghana, the creation of a union government of Africa was proposed and eventually became a precursor to the main topic of discussion. But apart from the absurdities in this proposal, the late Qaddafi was at least in good company, as far as the basic idea was concerned. Perhaps he received some inspiration from Winston Churchill, who, shortly after the Second World War, proposed the formation of a United States of Europe as the best way forward for the then war-prone continent. (See the 'Origin 1945–1957—The History of European Union and Citizenship' speech at Zurich University on 19 September 1946 by Winston Churchill.)

Europe, of course, did not opt for Churchill's model. It chose the incremental path, starting with the supranational European Coal and Steel Community

(ECSC), progressing from there to the relative success story it has had today after fifty years. Of course, because of unique conditions, the European Union (EU) model cannot be replicated in Africa, but its implementation strategy echoes the Monrovian incremental approach, which seems the optimal course for Africa. Unfortunately, unlike Europe, Africa has not succeeded in moving beyond the most rudimentary stages of the process, something equivalent to the European Coal and Steel Community (representing supranationalism). Such does not even exist in the case of any of the sub regional schemes in Africa unless something is invented. The biggest stumbling block facing Africa's regionalism is unquestionably is the sovereignty issue. For the moment, no African president wants to be made a governor, or become subservient to another in terms of the power to lead. While the EU has found and works with a more or less hybrid model based on intergovernmentalism and supranationalism (the community method), African countries, in spite of the notions of African unity and pan-Africanism, are stacked rigidly and evangelically to the Westphalian model of absolute national sovereignty for each country. For African governments, the sharing of sovereignty in the essence of regional integration is strictly not on the agenda of African heads of state and governments any time they meet in a summit. What they prefer is intergovernmental cooperation, which is not regional integration as meant by the term; at best Africa's regionalism is a work in progress. This applies to the AU itself, as well as the host of sub regional economic communities (RECs) on the continent. To a varying extent, of course, these RECs have facilitated and promoted regional economic cooperation or integrative cooperation, one could call it. But they all play second fiddle to the whims of member states and one cannot talk about integration in any serious way. This is the problem that pan-Africanism and African unity fail to address and this is also the reason why regionalization remains in the realm of utopian ideas in Africa. Looking for successful solutions is a perennial pursuit among those who care about Africa.

Since decolonization, grand plans to save the continent have indeed proliferated at a pace. Such plans began with the United Nations' development decades for Africa, the World Bank's Berg Plan, the Lagos Plan of Action (1975) and the Full Act of Lagos (1980), the Abuja Treaty (1991), the 2001 New Partnership for Africa's Development, Tony Blair's Africa commission, and the various proposals of the Group of Eight industrialized nations. Even though, the late Qaddafi's US of Africa plan may be far too ridiculous to warrant a place on this list, the fact is that it was entertained at an occasion as austere as an AU summit, which highlights the barren nature of the integration debate and process in Africa. What must be debated is why the preferred gradualist Monrovian model doesn't show results or experts are not invited to present other viable models for Africa's regionalism. Perhaps Qaddafi was at least right in his assessment at the July 2007 summit in Accra that a new order of things is required if integration is going to work in Africa.

The alternative to Qaddafi's immediate unification of Africa is perhaps the step-by-step approach toward a union government. Often referred to as the gradualist school, this position was advanced by former South African president, Mbeki and Uganda's president Yoweri Museveni, among others. They preferred the integration of regional economic communities (RECs) into the building blocks of the union government. While this sounds more practical, sceptics argue that RECs have produced limited socio-political experiences of solidarity and that the proponents of this thinking have not demonstrated at what point RECs will ultimately be harmonized into a union government.

Overall, if pan-Africanism is a socio-political world view / movement that encourages the solidarity and economic progress of Africans, it remains difficult to reconcile the rhetoric about pan-Africanism with the ambivalence with which African leaders seem to regard building genuine African unity. A basic tenet that is often ignored in pan-Africanism debates is the need to create a union of African people. This means that the pan-Africanist project must focus on African people, rather than African states. The unity of Africans must be rooted in the mobilization of the African masses through civil society groups across the continent's artificial borders. More to the point here, the power of African citizenship can be harnessed through the free movement of people, goods, and services, obviously within agreed-upon rules. Unfortunately, today the majority of African countries have put in place impediments to uniting African people with expensive visas and strict immigration rules. Sometimes there is genuine fear that the free movement of people, goods, and services might result in opportunity cost in respect of job losses and increased pressure on housing and infrastructure, among others, in recipient countries. However, if the right rules are put in place, the benefits of free movement can outweigh the losses. Based on the experiences of the East African Community and the Economic Community of West African States, it is apparent that the free movement of people, goods, and services has concrete economic benefits. Those opposed to it, however, seem motivated by its perceived threat to national cohesion, something that pan-Africanism seeks to transcend.

Alternative Ventures for Africa?

The North Atlantic Free Trade Area (NAFTA) is another example which provides an alternate template for African regionalism. NAFTA is one of the few regional arrangements outside of Europe that has really worked in the sense of liberalizing trade that would not otherwise have been liberalized and thus significantly shifting trade patterns (Holms 2005: 16). However, NAFTA's success has nothing to do with its institutional arrangements. It works for reasons akin to the reason the international trade system worked before World War I when PaxBritannica held sway—it is dominated commercially by a single nation and that nation really wants it to work. The United States market (as measured by GDP) is eighteen times that of Mexico's and twelve times that of Canada. Since market size equates with negotiating power in trade arrangements, it is easy to see why NAFTA works. The United States of America as a single nation has 90 per cent of the negotiating power and yet really cares about the organization's success for political, geo-strategic, and commercial reasons. Comparatively, NAFTA's institutions are not notably more developed than those of ECOWAS, SACU, NAFTA, or the African Commission; indeed in many ways these African institutions are more highly structured since at least they have a permanent secretariat. But in terms of each of the three NAFTAns, they maintain a national section that sits in its own capital, coming together only periodically when there is the need to do so.

As enumerated above, if NAFTA institutions were applied to a free trade area (FTA) among three roughly equal nations, it would have failed just as the vast majority of the numerous regional trade areas (RTAs) in Africa are failing to fly. In this sense, one would be tempted to conclude that the European Free Trade Association (EFTA) provides the best model for the long-run shape of Africa's regionalism since EFTA is purely intergovernmental and has an efficient secretariat and enough institutional structure to deal with challenges of new members and expansion of the integration regime. In this case, the African Union Commission must identify at least genuine and committed African Community of countries reminiscent of the European Coal and Steel Community (ECSC) to join forces, say, in a commodity that they believe can unite them toward that continental objective. Examples of success stories abound, one being that in its early days, EFTA included advanced industrial nations like the United Kingdom and Switzerland but also developing nations like Portugal and produced special rules for Portugal, which was the least developed amongst them.

Conclusions

Regionalism is the pursuit of a common identity, common aims and goals, as well as shared values and structures existing within a specific geographical region. Africa has never been short of solutions to its numerous crises and contradictions. These solutions are usually advanced by politicians and bureaucrats with only a cursory understanding of African realities. From import substitution, growth-pole development, bottom-up development, basic needs, joint ventures and indigenization, nationalization and partnerships, and most recently, structural adjustment, African leaders have gone through their entire gamut of socio-economic and political prescriptions and we can all see what they have to show for their efforts today. The implication here is that colonial brutalization, domination, manipulation, exploitation, and marginalization did better for Africans than three decades of summits and conferences since 1960 in the name of economic models for growth and development.

What Africa needs as part of its new agenda is not multiparty elections but the total *democratization* of the political, social, and economic landscape of Africa. From universities to research institutions, and through households to governments, there must be a renewed spirit of and enthusiasm for democracy, empowerment, accountability, social justice, equality, respect for human rights, popular participation, and the guarantee of freedoms and liberties. This must be done in the context of a revitalized pan-African ideology aimed concretely at establishing a union government of Africa. We cannot remain oblivious to developments in North America, the Pacific Rim, and Europe. What the

African Union's intentions are for regionalism in the present is well known. The union is a valid hallmark of regionalism itself, for the concrete example of pursuing goals and aims beyond any state. However, what the African Union ultimately wants to achieve with regionalism on the African continent in the future will depend on what it undertakes today. In its history, it has moved beyond the rhetoric of an intended common economic progress; AU now has a large say in other aspects of statecraft through the commission, the heads of state and governments, the Pan-African Parliament, as well as international initiatives and partnerships with other regional and global associations. In conclusion, the African Union must stop talking shop on how Africa is going to be united, but be an institution to serve as the custodian and guardian of all the regional associations on the African continent. It is a view of the possible future, a state in many respects though also subservient to member initiatives, a world economic powerhouse and a home to policies commonly instituted. The African Union is no longer just an external body, but a concrete expression of African unity and is at least a partial fulfilment of the African ideals expressed after the Abuja Treaty of 1991. Indeed, the African Union is an African establishment unlike any other, and as it has been in the earliest stages of its history until the present, is the changing face of regionalism on the African continent.

Works Cited / Further Readings

Anderson, B. (1991), Imagined Communities (London: Verso).

Bach, Daniel (1998), 'Regionalism versus regional integration: the emergence of a new paradigm in Africa', in Jean Grugel and Wil Hout (eds.), *Regionalism Across the North-South Divide: State Strategies and Globalization* (London: Routledge), p. 162.

—— (ed.) (1999), *Regionalization in Africa: Integration and Disintegration* (Oxford: James Currey.

Balassa, Bela (1961), *The Theory of Economic Integration* (Irwin).

Bilal, Sanoussi (2002), 'The Future of ACP-EU Trade Relations: An Overview of the Forthcoming', in Andrew L. Stoler (ed.), *Managing the Challenges of WTO Participation: 45 Case Studies* (World Trade Organization, Cambridge University Press) chapter 27, pp. 374–393.

Baldwin, Richard E. and Wyplosz, Charles (2006), *The Economics of European Integration* (McGraw-Hill Higher Education).

Brenton, Paul and Mombert Hoppe (2006), *The African Growth and Opportunity Act*, WPS 3996 (World Bank).

Commission of the European Communities (1985), 'Completing the internal market', COM (85) 310 final, 14 June.

Cooper, R. N. (1968), *The Economics of Interdependence: Economic Policy in the Atlantic Community* (New York: McGraw-Hill for the Council on Foreign Relations).

Crawford, Jo-Ann and Roberto Fiorentino (2005), *The Changing Landscape of Regional Trade Agreements*, WTO Discussion Paper No. 8.

Dinka, Tesfaye (2007), 'Regional Integration in Africa: Constraints and Potential', in Tijan M. Sallah (ed.), *Africa's Governance and Development: Visions, Re-Visions, and Reflections: Essays in Memory of Dunstan Wai.*

Economic Commission for Africa (2003), Assessment of Regional Integration in Africa (ARIA).

Faroutan, Faizeh (1993), 'Regional Integration in Sub-Saharan Africa: Past Experience and Future Prospects', in Jaime de Melo and Arvind Panagariya (eds.), *New Dimensions in Regional Integration* (Cambridge University Press).

Farrell, Mary, Bjorn Hettne, and Luk Van Langenhove (2005) (eds.), Global Polictics of Regionalism (London).

Fink, C. (1984), *The Genoa Conference* (Chapel Hill: Univ. of North Carolina Press) pp. 18–19.

Global Coalition for Africa (2005), 'Rationalization of Integration Institutions: Proposed Measures', mimeo.

Hantos, E. (1926) 'The European Customs Union', *Weltwirtschaftliches Archiv* 23: 229–30, 235–38.

Heater, D. (1992), *The Idea of European Unity* (Leicester: Leicester University Press).

Herbst, Jeffrey (2007), 'Crafting regional cooperation in Africa', in Amitav Acharya and Alastair Johnston (eds.), *Crafting Cooperation: Regional International Institutions in Comparative Perspective* (London: Oxford University Press), p. 144.

Kent, B. (1989), *The Spoils of War: The Politics, Economics and Diplomacy of Reparations* (Oxford: Oxford University Press).

Lipgens, Walter (1982), *A History of European Integration* (Oxford: Clarendon Press).

Milward, Alan (2005), *Politics and Economics in the History of the European Union* (Routledge).

Page, Sheila (2000) (ed.), *Regions and Development: Politics, Security and Economics* (Frank Cass Publishers).

SAPSN, 'Making Southern African Development Cooperation and Integration a People-centered and People-driven Regional Challenge to Globalization', Declaration to the Governmental Summit of SADC, Windhoek, 1–7 August 2000, p. 1.

Tsoukalis, L. (1997), *The New European Economy Revisited* (Oxford: Oxford University Press).

Chapter 20

THE AFRICAN UNION (AU)

The Formation of the AU

The African Union is an African formation and one of the world's most important intergovernmental organizations. It is composed of fifty-four countries in Africa and is loosely based on the European Union concept. The African countries who have signed to be part of the African Union work diplomatically with each other—despite differences in geography, history, race, language, and religion—to try to improve the political, economic, and social situations for the approximately one billion people that live on the African continent. The African Union promises to protect Africa's rich cultures, some of which have existed for thousands of years. The historical foundations of the African Union originated in the Union of African States, an early confederation that was established by Dr Kwame Nkrumah of blessed memory in the 1960s, as well as subsequent attempts to unite Africa, including the Organization of African Unity (OAU), which was established on 25 May 1963, and the African Economic Community in 1981. Scholars of African politics and critics alike argue that the OAU in particular did little to protect the rights and liberties of African citizens from their own political leaders, often dubbing it the Dictators' Club. In the view of a more prosperous continental unity, there was the need to form a more dynamic one, hence the African Union. The African Union was officially formed when notable leaders like Colonel Muammar al-Qaddafi of Libya saw that some OAU objectives were contrary to many African countries' visions and objectives. Therefore, the African Union was formed after the dissolution of the Organization of African Unity (OAU) in 2002. The OAU was formed when many African leaders wanted to accelerate the process of European decolonization and gain independence for a number of new nations on the continent of Africa.

The OAU, indeed, wanted to promote peaceful solutions to numerous conflicts that were afflicting Africa at the time, ensure sovereignty forever, and raise living standards of Africans. But the OAU was largely criticized from the beginning for being particularly lukewarm to the ideals and aspiration of unity on the African continent, particularly so because of the role and low commitment of the Francophone countries to the unity item on the agenda of the OAU. This situation was because of the still-deep economic, political, and social ties that these Francophone countries had with their colonial masters. It was not only the Francophone countries alone, but most African countries within the OAU associated themselves with the ideologies and ideals of either the United States or the Soviet Union during the height of the Cold War. The African Union was launched in Durban by its first chairperson, South African Thabo Mbeki, at the first session of the Assembly of the African Union. The second session of the Assembly was in Maputo in 2003, and the third session in Addis Ababa on 6 July 2004.

The headquarters of the African Union is in Addis Ababa, Ethiopia. Its official languages are English, French, Arabic, and Portuguese, but many documents are also printed in Swahili and other African local languages. The aspirations of the African Union are to promote health, education, peace, democracy, human rights, and economic success. The African Union, or AU, includes every independent African country except Morocco (as of 2002). Additionally, the African Union recognizes the Sahrawi Arab Democratic Republic, which is a portion of Western Sahara; this recognition by the AU caused Morocco to resign. South Sudan is the newest member of the African Union, joining on 28 July 2011, less than three weeks after it became an independent country. The Constitutive Act of the AU declares that it shall 'invite and encourage the full participation of the African Diaspora as an important part of our Continent, in the building of the African Union'. The African Union government has defined the African Diaspora as 'consisting of people of African origin living outside the continent, irrespective of their citizenship and nationality and who are willing to contribute to the development of the continent and the building of the African Union'.

Symbols

The emblem of the African Union consists of a gold ribbon bearing small interlocking red rings, from which palm leaves shoot up around an outer gold circle and an inner green circle, within which is a gold representation of Africa. The red interlinked rings stand for African solidarity and the bloodshed for the liberation of Africa; the palm leaves for peace; the gold, for Africa's wealth and bright future; the green, for African hopes and aspirations. To symbolize African unity, the silhouette of Africa is drawn without internal borders. The African Union adopted its new flag at its 14th Ordinary Session of the Assembly of Heads of State and Government taking place in Addis Ababa 2010. During the 8th African Union Summit, which took place in Addis Ababa on 29 and 30 January 2007, the heads of state and government decided to launch a competition for the selection of a new flag for the union. They prescribed a green background for the flag symbolizing hope of Africa and stars to represent member states.

Pursuant to this decision, the African Union Commission (AUC) organized a competition for the selection of a new flag for the African Union. The AUC received a total of 106 entries proposed by citizens of nineteen African countries and two from the diaspora. The proposals were then examined by a panel of experts put in place by the African Union Commission and selected from the five African regions for shortlisting, according to the main directions given by the heads of state and government. At the 13th Ordinary Session of the Assembly, the heads of state and government examined the report of the panel and selected one among all the proposals. The flag is now part of the paraphernalia of the African Union and replaces the old one. The old flag of the African Union bears a broad green horizontal stripe, a narrow band of gold, the emblem of the African Union at the centre of a broad white stripe, another narrow gold band, and a final broad green stripe. Again, the green and gold symbolize Africa's hopes and aspirations as well as its wealth and bright future, and the white represents the purity of Africa's desire for friends throughout the world. The flag has led to the creation of the 'national colours' of Africa of gold and green (sometimes together with white). These colours are visible in one way or another in the flags of many African nations. Together the colours green, gold, and red constitute the pan-African colours.

The Vision, Mission, and Objectives of the AU

The vision of the African Union is that of *'an integrated, prosperous, and peaceful Africa, driven by its own citizens and representing a dynamic force in global arena'*. This vision of a new, forward-looking, dynamic, and integrated Africa will be fully realized through relentless struggle on several fronts and as a long-term endeavour. The African Union has shifted focus from supporting liberation movements in the erstwhile African territories under colonialism and apartheid, as envisaged by the OAU since 1963 and the Constitutive Act, to an organization spearheading Africa's development and integration. The mission of the commission is to become *'an efficient and value-adding institution driving the African integration and development process in close collaboration with African Union Member States, the Regional Economic Communities, and African citizens'*. The values to guide and govern the functioning and operations of the Commission are respect for diversity and teamwork, Think Africa above all, transparency and accountability, integrity and impartiality, efficiency and professionalism, and information and knowledge sharing. The objectives of the AU are:

1. To achieve greater unity and solidarity between the African countries and the people of Africa;
2. To defend the sovereignty, territorial integrity, and independence of its Member States;
3. To accelerate the political and socio-economic integration of the continent;
4. To promote and defend African common positions on issues of interest to the continent and its peoples;
5. To encourage international cooperation, taking due account of the Charter of the United Nations and the Universal Declaration of Human Rights;
6. To promote peace, security, and stability on the continent;
7. To promote democratic principles and institutions, popular participation, and good governance;
8. To promote and protect human and peoples' rights in accordance with the African Charter on Human and Peoples' Rights and other relevant human rights instruments;

9. To establish the necessary conditions which enable the continent to play its rightful role in the global economy and in international negotiations;
10. To promote sustainable development at the economic, social, and cultural levels, as well as the integration of African economies;
11. To promote co-operation in all fields of human activity to raise the living standards of African peoples;
12. To coordinate and harmonize the policies between the existing and future Regional Economic Communities for the gradual attainment of the objectives of the Union;
13. To advance the development of the continent by promoting research in all fields and particularly in science and technology;
14. To work with relevant international partners in the eradication of preventable diseases and the promotion of good health on the continent.

Structure of the African Union

In its structure, the AU somewhat resembles the European Union, but it also reflects the tradition of the OAU. The AU comprises the following decision-making and administrative organs:

1. *The Assembly of the Union*: The AU Assembly is the primary decision-making body of the AU and will be made up of the heads of state of each of the fifty-three member countries. The Assembly of the AU will meet at least once a year. The Assembly will be the supreme decision-making body for the union. The chairman of the Assembly will rotate each year between the presidents of the member states. The Assembly in structure and function is almost exactly the same as the OAU Heads of State Summit, which also met once a year and which was the supreme decision-making body of the OAU.

2. *The Executive Council of the Union* are the foreign ministers (same as Secretary of State in the US) and meet twice a year in regularly scheduled meetings. The Executive Council will be responsible for making decisions and developing policies in areas of common interest to the member states, including foreign trade, energy development, food/agriculture, water resources, environmental

protection, transport and communications, education and human resource development, health, science and technology, immigration, and social security. Foreign ministers had similar responsibilities in the OAU.

3. *The Pan-African Parliament*: The Pan-African Parliament was established in order to ensure the full participation of African peoples in the development and economic integration of the continent. The first Parliament was inaugurated on 18 March 2004 in Addis Ababa, Ethiopia and its headquarters is in *Midrand, South Africa*. The ultimate aim of the Pan-African Parliament shall be to evolve into an institution with full legislative powers, whose members are elected by universal adult suffrage. However, until such a time as the member states decide otherwise by amending the protocol, the Pan-African Parliament shall have consultative and advisory powers. The protocol is currently under review. The objectives of the Pan-African Parliament are to:

- Facilitate the effective implementation of the policies and objectives of the OAU/AEC and ultimately the African Union
- Promote the principle of human rights and democracy in Africa
- Encourage good governance, transparency, and accountability in member states
- Familiarize the peoples of Africa with the objectives and policies aimed at integrating the African Continent within the framework of the establishment of the African Union
- Promote peace, security, and stability.
- Contribute to a more prosperous future for the peoples of Africa by promoting collective self-reliance and economic recovery.
- Facilitate cooperation and development in Africa.
- Strengthen continental solidarity and build a sense of common destiny among the peoples of Africa
- Facilitate cooperation among Regional Economic Communities and their respective Parliaments; among others.

Member states are represented in the Pan-African Parliament by five parliamentarians, at least one of whom must be a woman. The representation of each member state must reflect the diversity of political opinions in each National Parliament or other deliberative organ.

4. *African Court of Justice*: This is a new institution. The OAU did not have an inter-African court. The African Court on Human and Peoples' Rights (the Court) is a continental court established by African countries to ensure protection of human and peoples' rights in Africa. It complements and reinforces the functions of the African Commission on Human and Peoples' Rights. The Court was established by virtue of Article 1 of the Protocol to the African Charter on Human and Peoples' Rights on the Establishment of an African Court on Human and Peoples' Rights, the protocol which was adopted by member states of the then Organization of African Unity (OAU) in Ouagadougou, Burkina Faso, in June 1998. The protocol came into force on 25 January 2004 after it was ratified by more than fifteen countries. To date, only the following twenty-six states have ratified the protocol: Algeria, Burkina Faso, Burundi, Côte d'Ivoire, Comoros, Congo, Gabon, Gambia, Ghana, Kenya, Libya, Lesotho, Mali, Malawi, Mozambique, Mauritania, Mauritius, Nigeria, Niger, Rwanda, South Africa, Senegal, Tanzania, Togo, Tunisia and Uganda.

The Constitutive Act provides for a Court of Justice to rule on disputes over interpretation of AU treaties. A protocol to set up the Court of Justice was adopted in 2003 and entered into force in 2009. It is likely to be superseded by a protocol creating a Court of Justice and Human Rights, which will incorporate the already established African Court of Justice and Human and Peoples' Rights (see below) and have two chambers—one for general legal matters and one for rulings on the human rights treaties. The African Court on Human and Peoples' Rights (the Court) is a continental court established by African countries to ensure protection of human and peoples' rights in Africa. It complements and reinforces the functions of the African Commission on human and peoples' rights.

The Court has jurisdiction over all cases and disputes submitted to it concerning the interpretation and application of the African Charter on Human and Peoples' Rights, the (the Charter), the Protocol, and any other relevant human rights instrument ratified by the States concerned. According to the Protocol (Article 5) and the Rules (Rule 33), the Court may receive complaints and/or applications submitted to it either by the African Commission of Human and Peoples' Rights or state parties to the Protocol or African intergovernmental organizations. Non-governmental organizations with observer status before the African Commission on Human and Peoples' Rights and individuals from states that have made a declaration accepting the jurisdiction of the Court can also institute cases directly before the Court. As of October 2012, only five countries had made such a declaration. Those countries are Ghana, Burkina Faso, Malawi, Tanzania, and Mali.

The Court

The Court is composed of eleven judges, nationals of member states of the African Union. The first judges of the Court were elected in January 2006, in Khartoum, Sudan. They were sworn in before the Assembly of heads of state and government of the African Union on 2 July 2006, in Banjul, the Gambia. The judges of the Court are elected, after nomination by their respective states, in their individual capacities from among African jurists of proven integrity and of recognized practical, judicial, or academic competence and experience in the field of human rights. The judges are elected for a six-year or four-year term renewable once. The judges of the Court elect a president and vice president of the Court among themselves, who serves a two-year term. They can be re-elected only once. The president of the Court resides and works on a full-time basis at the seat of the Court, while the other ten judges work on a part-time basis. In the accomplishment of his duties, the president is assisted by a registrar who performs registry, managerial, and administrative functions of the Court. The Court officially started its operations in Addis Ababa, Ethiopia in November 2006, but in August 2007 it moved to its seat in Arusha, the United Republic of Tanzania, where the government of the republic has provided it with temporary premises pending the construction of a permanent structure. Between 2006 and 2008, the Court dealt principally with operational and administrative issues, including the development of the structure of the Court's registry, preparation of its budget, and drafting of its Interim Rules of Procedure. In 2008, during the Court's Ninth Ordinary Session, judges of the Court provisionally adopted the Interim Rules of the Court, pending consultation with the African Commission on Human and Peoples' Rights, based in Banjul, the Gambia, in order to harmonize their rules to achieve the purpose of the provisions of the Protocol establishing the Court, which requires that the two institutions must harmonize their respective rules so as to achieve the intended complementary roles of the African Court on Human and Peoples' Rights and the African Commission on Human and Peoples' Rights. This harmonization process was completed in April 2010, and in June 2010, the Court adopted its final Rules of Court.

5. *The Commission of the Union* serves as the secretariat of the union. As is the case of the EU, the AU secretariat is responsible for administering the projects of the AU and carrying out the decisions made by the Assembly and Executive Council of the union. The Commission (like the OAU) will have its headquarters in Addis Ababa, Ethiopia and it will be headed by the secretary general of the African Union. The secretariat will be comprised of AU civil servants who be recruited from and will serve in all of the member states. The AU Commission is chaired by Nkosazana Dlamini-Zuma of South Africa. On 15 July 2012, Ms Dlamini-Zuma won a tightly contested vote to become the first female head of the African Union Commission, replacing Jean Ping of Gabon. The African Union's new headquarters complex is in Addis Ababa. The main administrative capital of the African Union is in Addis Ababa, Ethiopia, where the African Union Commission is headquartered. A new headquarters complex, the AU Conference Centre and Office Complex (AUCC), was inaugurated on 28 January 2012, during the 18th AU summit. The complex was built by China State Construction Engineering Corporation as a gift from the Chinese government, and accommodates, among other facilities, a 2,500-seat plenary hall and a twenty-storey office tower. The tower is 99.9 metres high to signify the date 9 September 1999, when the Organization of African Unity voted to become the African Union.

6. *The Permanent Representatives Committee*: Just as there are ambassadors to the United Nations from each of the UN member states, so too there are ambassadors from the AU member states who will be specifically assigned to the AU and who will reside in Addis Ababa. These representatives will meet regularly in the Permanent Representatives Committee.

7. *Financial Institutions of the AU*: The African Union has created three financial institutions in a bid to facilitate trade within the continent. They are the African Investment Bank (AIB), the African Monetary Fund (AMF), and the African Central Bank (ACB).

a. *African Investment Bank (AIB)*

The African Investment Bank is one of the three financial institutions planned for in the Constitutive Act of the African Union. The mandate of the African Investment Bank was envisioned to aid in fostering economic growth and accelerating economic integration in Africa in line with the broad objective of the African Union. To achieve these objectives, the bank will carry out the following tasks: (i) promote investment activities of the public and private sector intended to advance regional integration of the member states of the African Union, (ii) utilize available resources for the implementation of projects contributing to the strengthening of private sector and the modernization of rural sector activities, (iii) mobilize resources from capital markets inside and outside Africa countries, and (iv) provide technical assistance as may be needed in African countries for the study, preparation, financing, and execution of investment projects. The headquarters of the African Investment Bank is in Tripoli, the capital of Libyan Arab Jamahiriya.

A formal agreement with the host country to establish a steering committee in order to commence technical studies on the institutional and organization aspects of the bank was signed. The mission of the technical steering committee is to spearhead studies leading to the setting up of the bank, including working out the fine-print details of its sources of funding, management, and institutional framework.

b. *African Monetary Fund (AMF)*

The African Monetary Fund is stipulated in the Abuja Treaty in the Constitutive Act of the African Union, Article 19, in a bid to facilitate the integration of African economies, through the elimination of trade restrictions and enhance greater monetary integration. The main objective of the African Monetary Fund is to (i) provide financial assistance to AU member states, (ii) act as a clearing house as well as undertake macroeconomic purveyance within the continent, (iii) coordinate the monetary policies of member states and promote cooperation between the monetary authorities in these states, and (iv) encourage capital movements between and amongst member states. The headquarters of the African Monetary Fund is in Yaoundé, Republic of Cameroon.

A memorandum of understanding to set up a technical steering committee to undertake the implementation for the hosting of the African Monetary Fund was signed on 30 June 2008, between the African Union Commission and the Cameroon government, at the margins of the 11th Ordinary Session of the African Union Summit of Heads of States and Government that took place in Sharm El Sheikh, Arab Republic of Egypt.

c. *African Central Bank (ACB)*

The African Central Bank was created following the 1991 Abuja Treaty and reiterated by the 1999 Sirte Declaration that called for the speeding up of the implementation process.

The ACB, just like the other African financial institutions, is aimed at building a common monetary policy and creating the African currency as a way for accelerating economic integration in Africa. The objective of the African Central Bank would be to (i) promote international monetary cooperation through a permanent institution, (ii) promote exchange stability and avoid competitive exchange rates depreciation, (iii) assist in the establishment of a multilateral system of payments in respect of current transactions between members and eliminate foreign exchange restrictions which hamper the growth of world trade. The headquarters of the African Central Bank is Abuja, Republic of Nigeria.

Differences/Similarities

In its composition, the AU does have some similarities with the OAU, but there are also important differences. For example, the AU will have a Parliament with representatives for each member country. The Pan-African Parliament will be more representative and allow for a much greater diversity of voices to be heard than was the case in the OAU.

The African Court of Justice will provide a place where disputes between nations can be heard in an unbiased venue. Just as importantly, the AU will be able to hold those guilty of gross human-rights abuses accountable for their actions. The African Central Bank, the African Monetary Fund, and African

Investment Bank will provide strong institutional support for economic cooperation and coordination throughout the continent. Perhaps in the not-too-distant future, the AU will institute a common African currency similar to the euro in the EU.

Supporters of the AU point out that in addition to the structural differences from the OAU, the AU Charter commits the union to be more actively engaged in the affairs of the member states than was allowed by the OAU charter. Given the OAU's strong commitment to the complete sovereignty of each state, the OAU was not permitted to intervene in the internal affairs of a member state. Consequently, in its forty-year existence, the OAU never directly intervened to stop a civil war or human rights violations, not even in 1994 in Rwanda during the genocide that killed more than 500,000 people in the space of a few months. The AU Charter specifically commits the AU to intervene in civil wars within member states and when there are clear indications of human right abuses. Moreover, the AU promises to promote democracy and good governance in its member states. This is a great change from the OAU charter that clearly prohibited the OAU (or any member states) from intervening or interfering in the internal political affairs of any member country. Will the African Union be as successful as the European Union in realizing its goals and agenda? Of course, it is much too early to answer this question. Africans from across the continent have many different perspectives on this question. Some people are quite optimistic that the AU will play a positive role in promoting cooperation, democracy, and economic development. Others are more pessimistic, believing that Africa's political and economic problems are too complex to be effectively addressed by any organization. The pessimists also think that in spite of its charter, some of the African presidents who make up the AU Assembly will not permit the AU to develop the powers necessary to effectively engage Africa's political problems, particularly if this means intervening in the internal affairs of African countries.

Functions of the Specialized Technical Committees

There are specialized and technical committees which assist the various constitutive departments of the AU. Among the prominent ones are (a) committees who prepare projects and programs of the union and submit it to the Executive Council; (b) a committee which ensures the supervision, follow-up, and evaluation of the implementation of decisions taken by the organs of the union; (c) a committee which ensures the coordination and harmonization of projects and programs of the union; (d) a committee which submits to the Executive Council, either on its own initiative or at the request of the Executive Council, reports and recommendations on the implementation of the provisions of this Act; and (e) a committee which carries out any other functions assigned to it for the purpose of ensuring the implementation of the provisions of this Act. Both the Abuja Treaty and the Constitutive Act provide for specialized technical committees to be established, made up of African ministers to advise the Assembly. In practice, they have never been set up. The ten proposed themes are Rural Economy and Agricultural Matters; Monetary and Financial Affairs; Trade, Customs, and Immigration; Industry, Science, and Technology; Energy, Natural Resources, and Environment; Transport, Communications, and Tourism; Health; Labour and Social Affairs; and Education, Culture, and Human Resources.

Economy of the African Union

The combined states of the African Union constitute a nominal GDP of US$1.627 trillion. By measuring GDP by PPP, the African Union's economy totals $2.849 trillion, ranking it sixth after Germany. The AU's future goals include the creation of a free trade area, a customs union, a single market, a central bank, and a common currency (see African Monetary Union), thereby establishing economic and monetary union. The current plan is to establish an African Economic Community with a single currency by 2023.

Languages of the African Union

Founded in 2001 under the auspices of the AU, the African Academy of Languages promotes the usage and perpetuation of African languages among African people. The AU declared 2006 the Year of African Languages. According to the Constitutive Act of the African Union, its working languages are Arabic, English, French, and Portuguese, and African languages 'if possible'. A protocol amending the Constitutive Act, adopted in 2003 but as of 2007 not yet in force, added Spanish, Swahili, and 'any other African language' and termed all six 'official' (rather than 'working') languages of the African Union. In practice, translation of documents of the AU into the four current working languages, which used to cause significant delays and difficulties to the conduct of business, has known a great leap forward since late 2007, when modern translation tools and working methods were introduced.

Geography of the African Union

The member states of the African Union cover almost the entirety of continental Africa and several offshore islands on the continent. Consequently, the geography of the African Union is wildly diverse, including the world's largest hot desert (the Sahara), huge jungles and savannahs, and the world's longest river (the Nile). The AU covers an area of 29,922,059 km^2 (18,592,705 mi.^{2}), with 24,165 km (15,015 mi.) of coastline. The vast majority of this area is on continental Africa, while the only significant territory off the mainland is the island of Madagascar (the world's fourth largest), accounting for slightly less than 2 per cent of the total.

Foreign Relations of the African Union

The individual member states of the African Union coordinate foreign policy through this agency, in addition to conducting their own international relations on a state-by-state basis. The AU represents the interests of African peoples at large in intergovernmental organizations (IGOs); for instance, it is a permanent observer at the United Nations General Assembly. Both the African Union and the United Nations work in tandem to address issues of common concerns in various areas. The African Union Mission in the United Nations aspires to serve as a bridge between the two organizations. Membership of the AU overlaps with other IGOs and occasionally these third-party organizations and the AU will coordinate matters of public policy. The African Union maintains special diplomatic representation with the United States and the European Union.

The African Union works closely with diplomats from the United States, European Union, and United Nations. It receives aid from countries around the world to deliver on its promises of peace and health for all Africans. The

African Union realizes that its member nations must unite and cooperate to compete in the world's increasingly globalized economy and foreign relations. It hopes to have a single currency, like the euro, by 2023. An African Union passport may exist one day. In the future, the African Union hopes to benefit people of African origin living throughout the world.

A major goal of the African Union is to encourage the collective defence, security, and stability of its members. The African Union's democratic principles have gradually reduced corruption and unfair elections. It tries to prevent conflicts between member nations and solve any disputes that do arise quickly and peacefully. The African Union can impose sanctions on disobedient states and withhold economic and social benefits. It does not tolerate inhumane acts such as genocide, war crimes, and terrorism. The African Union has intervened militarily in conflicts across the continent and has since its inception sent peacekeeping troops to alleviate political and social disorder in places like Darfur (Sudan), Somalia, Burundi, and Comoros. However, some of these missions have been criticized as being too underfunded, undermanned, and untrained. A few nations, like Niger, Mauritania, and Madagascar, have been suspended from the organization after political events like coup d'états.

Challenges of the AU

The AU faces many challenges, including health issues such as combating malaria and the AIDS/HIV epidemic; political issues such as confronting undemocratic regimes and mediating in the many civil wars; economic issues such as improving the standard of living of millions of impoverished, uneducated Africans; ecological issues such as dealing with recurring famines, desertification, and lack of ecological sustainability; as well as the legal issues regarding Western Sahara. The African Union has improved stability and welfare, but it does have its challenges. Poverty is still a tremendous problem. The organization is deeply in debt and many consider some of its leaders to still be corrupt. Morocco's tension with Western Sahara continues to strain the entire organization. However, several smaller multistate organizations exist in Africa, like the East African Community and the Economic Community of West African States, so the African Union can study how successful these smaller regional organizations have been in combating poverty and political strife.

The African Union and Pan-African Cooperation

Cooperation between African nations did not begin in July 2002 with the formation of the African Union. African countries have a rich tradition of collaboration that dates back for decades to the formation of the *Organization of African States (OAU)* in 1963. From the start of political independence of many African countries more than fifty years ago, relationships between the countries have been very important. Although there is great diversity in Africa, the many societies and peoples of Africa have shared an experience that brings a sense of unity and solidarity among African peoples and nation states. The most relevant of these shared experiences has been colonialism. Colonial oppression and exploitation within colonies prior to the 1960s has helped unite different ethnic and religious groups in a struggle against colonialism. Not surprisingly, such feelings of solidarity have for many years been carried across the national country boundaries established by colonialism. In addition to colonialism, leaders such as Dr Kwame Nkrumah of Ghana, Nyerere of Tanzania, Kaunda of Zambia, just to mention a few, and citizens of countries who gained their independence early showed great support for the nationalist struggles in countries that were not yet independent. Many Africans agreed with the statement that was very popular in the 1960s and 1970s: *No African is free until all Africans are free!* Apart from leaders and citizens alike, official government support for those struggling for freedom, particularly in the southern African settler colonies of Angola, Mozambique, Rhodesia (now Zimbabwe), Namibia, and South Africa, was a central foreign policy focus of most African countries, most often led by Ghana and Nigeria, until these countries gained their independence.

In other words, support for freedom and independence for all African countries was not the only uniting theme in post-independence inter-African policy, but that most of the nationalist leaders who helped lead their countries to independence were influenced by the ideas associated with pan-Africanism. Pan-Africanism, like most ideas, has undergone different translations and versions. But at the heart of pan-Africanism has been the idea that all Africans have shared experiences that could help unite them or comfort them in search of their development goals. The shared experiences have been the exploitation of Africa and Africans in the past, beginning with the slave trade and culminating in colonialism and what is described today as modern economic exploitation—neocolonialism. Additionally, pan-Africanists (promoters of pan-Africanism), argue that these factors unite not just the people living on the continent of Africa, but Africans in the diaspora—most of whom had been forced out of Africa by slave trade and more recently by the lack of economic opportunity in a number of African countries. The pan-African movement, which began in the early twentieth century with a series of pan-African congresses in Europe, from its very beginnings asserted that Africa and its grand diversity of peoples and societies could only prosper economically and become free and powerfully, politically if Africa was politically united in a pan-African country—*a United States of Africa.*

Pan-Africanists are well aware of the fact that colonialism has worked in Africa in part because European powers were able to separate societies and peoples through a policy of 'divide and rule' in the past. Pan-Africanists have further argued that Africa can only be strong and take its place among the world's economic and political powers if it were united. An Africa divided into more than fifty countries, some of which are smaller than a mid-size American state, is destined to be politically and economically weak. Early in the postcolonial era, the ideal of pan-Africanism came into direct conflict with the imperative of national sovereignty. Even among African presidents, like Kwame Nkrumah (first president of independent Ghana), who were strong advocates of African unity, there was a realization that unity would take a long time to achieve. In the meantime, African governments had to institute policies that would defend their country's sovereignty. Not surprisingly, those policies and practices that were instituted and aimed at protecting national sovereignty have been the same policies that continue today to make unity between African nations more difficult.

The Question of a Union Government

The principal topic for debate at the July 2007 AU summit held in Accra, Ghana, was the creation of a union government, with the aim of moving towards a United States of Africa. A study on the union government was adopted in late 2006, and proposes various options for completing the African Union project. There are divisions among African states on the proposals, with some (notably Libya) following a maximalist view leading to a common government with an AU army, and others (especially the southern African states) supporting instead a strengthening of the existing structures, with some reforms to deal with administrative and political challenges in making the AU Commission and other bodies truly effective. Following a heated debate in Accra, the Assembly of Heads of State and Government agreed in the form of a declaration to review the state of affairs of the AU with a view to determining its readiness towards a union government. In particular, the Assembly agreed to accelerate the economic and political integration of the African continent, including the formation of a union government of Africa; conduct an audit of the institutions and organs of the AU; review the relationship between the AU and the RECs; find ways to strengthen the AU and elaborate a time frame to establish a union government of Africa. The declaration lastly noted the importance of involving the African peoples, including Africans in the diaspora, in the processes leading to the formation of the union government. Following this decision, a panel of eminent persons was set up to conduct the audit review. The review team began its work on 1 September 2007. The review was presented to the Assembly of Heads of State and Government at the January 2008 summit in Addis Ababa. No final decision was taken on the recommendations, however, and a committee of ten heads of state was appointed to consider the review and report back to the July 2008 summit to be held in Egypt. At the July 2008 summit, a decision was once again deferred, for a 'final' debate at the January 2009 summit to be held in Addis Ababa.

Conclusion

The large-scale economic liberalization that followed the demise of the Soviet Union and the end of the Cold War brought about an adjustment of the OAU's operational focus. Several factors, such as the growth of regional economic communities and more sensitivity to dispute resolution, required states to redefine the terms of interaction within the OAU. The constructs of the organization seemed too narrow to capture the broader ambitions of an economically evolving Africa. On the 9th of September 1999 (a date acknowledged by the height of the African Union's headquarters: 99.9 meters), the OAU agreed to the Sirte Declaration, a move pushed in particular by Libyan leader Muammar al-Qaddafi, which heralded the formation of the

African Union (AU). This new incarnation sought to implement the principles of the Abuja Treaty, signed earlier in the decade, in establishing an African Economic Community, an African Central Bank, an African Monetary Union, an African Court of Justice, and a Pan-African Parliament. Whereas the OAU was a political administration that discussed matters of economic and social concern, the AU is an organization aimed at economic integration and social development which would foster political unity.

Works Cited / Further Readings

African Development Bank (2005), 'Regionalism: Trade and Development in Africa', African Development Bank Economic Research Series.

African Union (2007), 'Accra Declaration', Assembly of the Union at its 9th Ordinary Session in Accra, Ghana, 1–3 July 2007.

——— 'Decision on the Report of the 9th extraordinary session of the executive council on the proposals for the Union Government', DOC. Assembly/AU/10 (VIII), Assembly/AU/Dec. 156 (VIII).

Farrell, Mary, Bjorn Hettne, and Luk Van Langenhove (2005) (eds.), *Global Politics of Regionalism: An Introduction*.

Gordimer, Nadine (1990), 'Censorship and Its Aftermath', in *Contemporary Authors* (Detroit: Gale Research Co.).

Hooker, Richard (1996), 'World Civilizations: An Internet Classroom and Anthology' n. page. Online. Washington State University. Available http://www.wsu.edu:8000/~dee/WORLD.HTM last accessed Jan. 2000.

Julien, Eileen (1995), 'African Literature', in Phyllis M. Martin and Patrick O'Meara (eds.), *Africa*, 3rd ed. (Bloomington: Indiana UP), 295–312.

Lipgens, Walter (1982), *A History of European Integration* (Oxford: Clarendon Press).

Malone, Barry (2011). 'AU won't recognize Libyan rebel council: diplomats' *The Daily Star*, retrieved 26 August 2011.

Moyers, Bill (1989), Chinua Achebe on *A World of Ideas* [Public Broadcasting Service television series, The Moyers Collection] Distr. PBS Video, Public Affairs Television, WNET/New York and WTTW/Chicago, Alexandria, VA, 1989; Films for the Humanities, 1994.

Pambazuka News (2006), 'An African Union Government: Towards a United States of Africa', published online 6 Jun. 2006 http://www.pambazuka.org/governance/african-union-government-towards-united-states-africa See also Decision on the Union Government, Doc. Assembly/AU/2(VII) for further discussion of this proposal.

Thabo Mbeki (2002), ABSA Stadium, Durban, South Africa: africa-union.org retrieved 8 February 2009.

Tsoukalis (1997) p. 223.

Soyinka, Wole (1978), *Myth, Literature and the African World*, Canto ed. 1990 (Cambridge and New York: Cambridge University Press).

Printed in Great Britain
by Amazon